PERSONAL PSYCHOLOGY
FOR LIFE & WORK
5TH EDITION

RITA K. BALTUS PH.D.
NORTHCENTRAL TECHNICAL COLLEGE
WAUSAU, WISCONSIN

Glencoe
McGraw-Hill

New York, New York   Columbus, Ohio   Woodland Hills, California   Peoria, Illinois

Photo Credits List
Cover Illustration by Silver Moon Graphics; **2** D. Carroll/The Image Bank; **9** Cartoon Features Syndicate; **11** Frank Cezus; **12** ©Harley L. Schwadron; **14** Doug Martin; **21** D. Carroll/The Image Bank; **22** Telegraph Colour Library/FPG; **25** PEANUTS reprinted by permission of United Feature Syndicate, Inc.; **26** Wilder Photo Files; **33** Bushnell-Soifer/Tony Stone Images; **39** Used with permission of Bob Thaves; **45** Telegraph Colour Library/FPG; **46** David Brownell; **57** Doug Martin; **59** Universal Press Syndicate, Inc.; **60** North Central Technical College, Wausau WI, **61** Universal Press Syndicate, Inc.; **69** David Brownell; **70** Robert Brenner/ PhotoEdit; **72** William Weber; **74** James Westwater; **75** Used with permission of Bob Thaves; **78** Spencer Grant/PhotoEdit; **81** Elaine Shay; **89** Reprinted from The Saturday Evening Post; **93** Robert Brenner/PhotoEdit; **94** Laurence Monneret/Tony Stone Images; **97** John Manciani, Wisconsin Rapids Daily Tribune, Wisconsin Rapids WI; **101** ©Baloo/Rothco; **104** Reprinted from The Saturday Evening Post; **113** Wausau Daily Herald; **117** Laurence Monneret/Tony Stone Images; **118** Michael Newman/PhotoEdit; **121** Steve Davis, Wisconsin Rapids Daily Tribune, Wisconsin Rapids WI; **129** Universal Press Syndicate, Inc.; **131** Bob Mullenix; **135** ©Tribune Media Services, Inc. All Rights Reserved. Reprinted with permission; **142** Doug Martin; **150** Cobalt Productions; **151** Cartoon Feature Syndicate; **156** Wausau Daily Herald; **162** ©1979 Good Houskeeping. Reprinted by permission of Orlando Busino.; **163** Joseph DiChello Jr.; **168** David Harry Stewart/Tony Stone Images; **172** Doug Martin; **173** Jon Feingersh/ The Stock Market; **174** Wausau Daily Herald; **177** Cartoon Feature Syndicate; **178** Glencoe photo; **180** Crown Studios; **188** Cartoon Feature Syndicate; **192** Bob Mullenix; **197** Tony Freeman/PhotoEdit; **200** Used with permission of Bob Thaves; **201** Myrleen Ferguson/ PhotoEdit; **208** Matt Meadows; **215** ©Patrick Hardin; **221** Bob Mullenix; **222** Richard Price/FPG; **225** Susa Photo Files; **226** PEANUTS reprinted by permission of UFS, Inc.; **244** Wilder Photo File; **246** Jeff Greenberg/PhotoEdit; **247** ©Lynn Johnston Productions Inc./Dist. by United Feature Syndicate, Inc.; **250** Richard Hackett; **254** ©1992 by North American Syndicate, Inc. World rights reserved; **255** StudiOhio; **258** Robert Ginn/PhotoEdit; **268** Reprinted from The Saturday Evening Post; **269** Doug Martin; **284** Jim Pickerell/Tony Stone Images; **291** DUOMO/Chris Trotman; **295** Reprinted from The Saturday Evening Post; **296** Northcentral Technical College, Wausau WI; **301** Wausau Daily Herald; **303** Cartoon Features Syndicate; **311** Jim Pickerell/Tony Stone Images; **312** Tom Sherman/Tony Stone Images; **314** McKay Photo Files; **316 317** Susa Photo File; **318** The American Legion Magazine; **324** MAK-1; **325** McKay Photo Files; **336** Used with permission of Bob Thaves; **345** Tom Sherman/Tony Stone Images; **346** F. Martinez/PhotoEdit; **349** PEANUTS reprinted by permission of United Feature Syndicate, Inc.; **355** Midstate Technical College, Wisconsin Rapids WI; **365** Doug Martin; **366** Universal Press Syndicate, Inc.

Library of Congress Cataloging-in-Publication Data
Baltus, Rita K.
 Personal psychology for life and work / Rita K. Baltus. — 5th ed. p. cm.
  ISBN 0-02-804294-8 (softcover)
 1. Self-actualization (Psychology) 2. Success. I. Title.
BF637.S4B35 1998   98-27342

Psychology for Life and Work, Fifth Edition   CIP

Printed in the United States of America

Send all inquiries to:
Glencoe/McGraw Hill
936 Eastwind Drive
Westerville, Ohio 43081

ISBN: 0-02-804294-8

1 2 3 4 5 6 7 8 9 0 024 05 04 03 02 01 00 99 98

Contents

PREFACE   XI

1   Psychology in Our Changing World   2

Why Study Psychology?   4
Why Look to the Future?   5
Threats, Challenges, and Promises   6
Life in a Global Community   7
The Workplace—Today and Tomorrow   9
Lifelong Learning   13
Workplace Skills for the Twenty-First Century   15
The Quality of Life   16
Maintaining Balances   17
Chapter 1 Review   18

2   Self-Concept and Personality   22

Self-Concept   23
Self-Esteem   25
Personality   27
Difficult or Different?   32
How Did You Get to Be You?   32
Sexuality   35
Integrate: Self and Personality   36
One Is Three?   37
Personality Change   38
Personality and Job Success   40
Chapter 2 Review   42

3   Motives and Values   46

Behavior Is Complex   47
Human Behavior Theories   50
Needs and Wants   53
Self-Actualizing People   56
Motivating Others and Yourself   57
Values   61
Chapter 3 Review   66

4 **Senses and Perception**   **70**
Factors That Affect Perception   72
Exterior Senses   77
Principles of Perception   84
Learning Styles   86
Learning Disabilities   87
Other Senses   87
Illusions   88
Parapsychology   88
Widen Your World   89
Chapter 4 Review   90

5 **Emotions**   **94**
Development of Emotions   96
Classifications of Emotions   97
Physiological Effects of Emotion   98
Fear   100
Anger   104
Love   106
Hate   107
Other Emotions   108
Emotions in the Workplace   110
Emotional Intelligence   111
Emotions Can Enrich Living   112
Chapter 5 Review   114

6 **Attitudes**   **116**
Influences on Attitudes   120
Attitudes and Behavior   122
Positive and Negative Attitudes   123
Prejudice   125
Discrimination   127
Work-Related Attitudes   128
Changing Attitudes   133
What's Your Attitude?   136
Chapter 6 Review   138

7 **Thinking and Problem Solving**   **142**
Your Incredible Brain   144
Stages of Cognitive Development   147
Intelligence or Intelligences?   148
Learning and Memory   149
Contributors to Learning and Memory   151
Experience and Common Sense   153
Guidelines to Problem Solving   154
Creative Thinking   157
Group Problem Solving   160

Intuition and Insight   162
Life and Problem Solving   163
Chapter 7 Review   164

(8) Communicating Effectively   168

Components of Communication   170
Listening   173
Nonverbal Communication   177
Communicating to Get That Job   179
Group Participation   182
Interpersonal Communication   183
Barriers to Communication   188
Chapter 8 Review   190

9 Human Relations at Work   192

Motivation to Work   194
Job Enrichment   196
Emotions in the Workplace   197
Employer-Employee Relations   199
Coworker Relations   203
Customer or Client Relations   204
Ethical Standards and Relations   205
Conflict, Competition, or Cooperation   206
Teams at Work   208
Communication at Work   213
Sexual Harassment at Work   215
Friendships at Work   216
Chapter 9 Review   218

10 Coping With Stress   222

What Is Stress?   224
Major Adjustments in Life   224
Job-Related Adjustments   228
Death and Dying   232
Coping Mechanisms   235
Effects of Coping Mechanisms   239
Neurosis   239
Inability to Cope   241
Ways to Reduce Stress   241
Chapter 10 Review   248

11 Wellness   250

Nutrition   252
Physical Fitness   257
Threats to Wellness   261
Proper Treatment   268

Mental Health   270
Psychological Disorders   270
Treatment of Psychological Disorders   273
Your Job and Wellness   275
Employee Assistance Programs   276
Habits   277
Balances   279
Chapter 11 Review   280

12   **Valuing Diversity**   **284**

Why Value Diversity?   285
Dimensions of Diversity   288
A Personal Approach   297
What Communities Are Doing   299
What Education Is Doing   300
Diversity in the Workplace   302
Guidelines for Valuing Diversity   306
Progress Continues   307
Chapter 12 Review   308

13   **Life-Span Development**   **312**

Your Lifetime and Life Span   314
Life-Span Stages   314
Early Childhood   315
Childhood   318
Adolescence   318
Young Adulthood   321
Dependence or Interdependence?   322
Middle Adulthood   324
Later Adulthood   326
Stages of Psychosocial Development   326
Moral Development   329
Mature Behavior   331
Signs of Immaturity   341
Chapter 13 Review   342

14   **Goal Achievement**   **346**

What Are Your Goals?   348
Factors That Contribute to Goal Achievement   350
When You Fail   356
Procrastination   360
Career Goals and Advancement   361
Who Becomes a Leader?   363
Putting It All Together   365
Chapter 14 Review   368

GLOSSARY   **370**
INDEX   **380**
LEARNING ACTIVITIES   **LA-1**

Preface

The fifth edition of *Personal Psychology for Life and Work* prepares students to successfully meet the many challenges they will face in their personal and career lives. Meeting these challenges and achieving one's goals begins with an understanding of oneself and others. This text helps students understand basic psychological principles and how they can be applied in a variety of situations. Many students find immediate use for what they are learning. This information also prepares them for future experiences and events.

LEARNING A LIVING: A Blueprint for High Performance, also called *A SCANS Report for America 2000,* was used as a guide to chapter content and activities related to Workplace Know-How: Workplace Competencies and Foundation Skills. These skills and competencies are specifically identified in Chapter 1 and applications can be found throughout the text and related activities.

As technology becomes an inseparable part of our daily lives and work, we must not lose sight of the importance of human relationships. *Personal Psychology for Life and Work* emphasizes the need for developing self-esteem and positive attitudes, managing emotions and stress, developing communication, thinking, and problem solving skills, and maintaining overall wellness. These are just some of the topics that are the focus of this edition.

Society in general and the workplace in particular are experiencing changes at a rapid rate. Change in itself, whether considered desirable or undesirable, creates stress as individuals strive to adjust and use change to their advantage. Clearly, we live in a global society, where we need to live and work with different dimensions of diversity. We must learn not only to tolerate but to value this diversity.

Though the content of this edition has been expanded and updated, we've kept the text-workbook format that has proven so effective in past editions. In-text questions and quizzes provide a way for students to self-check applications of the material to their beliefs and experiences. Each chapter begins with Learning Objectives that give the student a preview of how the chapter can be most meaningful to them. Chapter summaries are also correlated to these objectives.

Psychology in Practice activities, found at the end of each chapter, give students opportunities to make further application of related learning to their lives. An icon identifies small-group activities. Learning Activities for each chapter reinforce chapter content and give students opportunities to make practical applications of what they are studying. Enrichment Activities provide further opportunities for students to do research, visit community organizations, and expand their knowledge and understanding of the field of psychology in a variety of ways. A comprehensive glossary provides definitions for key terms used in the text.

NEW IN THE FIFTH EDITION

Two new chapters are included in this edition. Chapter 8, "Communicating Effectively" recognizes the importance of communication on all levels and provides guidelines and experience in improving one's communication skills. Chapter 12, "Valuing Diversity" discusses why we should value diversity, dimensions of diversity, a personal examination of one's attitudes and behavior, and guidelines for valuing diversity.

INSTRUCTOR SUPPORT

The Instructor's Manual contains comprehensive teaching suggestions based on the author's extensive experience, answers to the learning activities, selected teaching resources, and transparency masters. A new microcomputer test bank is available.

ACKNOWLEDGMENTS

My sincere appreciation is extended to the following people for their contributions and assistance with *Personal Psychology for Life and Work,* Fifth Edition: Dan Dougherty, Linda Layton, Kathy Kanz and MaryAnn Van Slyke, educators at the Northcentral Technical College; Mary Susa and Lee Susa, educators at Midstate Technical College, Audrey Kast for her contributions on wellness, Therese Wilder and Joe Baltus for their assistance with various aspects of manuscript development; the library staff of the Northcentral College, the staff of Marathon County Public Library; and to Ashish Patel of Northcentral Technical College for technical assistance. Special appreciation goes to Maggie McKay for her assistance with many aspects of this edition and especially with her extensive input on Chapter 8, "Communicating Effectively."

We would like to thank the following reviewers whose comments and suggestions helped to make this fifth edition what we believe to be the best ever.

Jessica Campaz
Crown College

Michael Wheeler
Clover Park Technical College

Ralph Soney
Western Piedmont Community College

Esther Tremblay
Duffs Business Institute

Terrence LaBorde
Dubois Business College

About the Author

Rita K. Baltus taught psychology and oral communication classes at the Northcentral Technical College for thirty years. Early in those years, she developed a practical psychology course for students in vocational programs. The objectives of this course were to help students gain an understanding of themselves and others and to apply psychology to their lives and the world of work. The material she developed for this course over a number of years evolved into *Personal Psychology for Life and Work.*

Dr. Baltus received her B.A. from the University of Michigan and her M.A. and Ph.D. from the University of Wisconsin. During her career, she has been involved in numerous aspects of vocational, technical, and adult education on local, state, and national levels. She has been an active member in numerous educational associations, including the American Vocational Association, American Association of Community and Junior Colleges, National Council for Occupational Education, American Society for Training and Development, American Association for Adult and Continuing Education, and Phi Delta Kappa, an honorary education society. Her experience has also included conducting workshops for business and industry and making presentations at conventions and conferences. In 1995 she was selected as Wisconsin Vocational Teacher of the Year.

FOR **Jon, Kyle, Charlie, Matt, Courtney, Joey, Kristen, and Caitlin**

Psychology in Our Changing World

1

I am prepared this day to declare myself a citizen of the world, and to invite everyone everywhere to embrace the broader vision of our interdependent world, our common quest for justice, and ultimately for Peace on Earth.

Theodore Hesburgh

LEARNING OBJECTIVES

After completing this chapter, you should able to do the following:

1. Explain why we study psychology.

2. Explain why it is important to be concerned about the future.

3. Explain why it is important to recognize that you are a member of the global community.

4. Discuss how technological advances have changed the workplace environment.

5. Explain why it is important to be aware of and value diversity in the workplace.

6. Discuss why it is important to anticipate the future and prepare for it.

7. Discuss two methods of continuing your training while on the job.

8. Explain why it is important that you adopt a commitment to lifelong learning.

9. Describe the five workplace competencies listed in the SCANS guidelines as keys to workplace success.

10. Discuss the various factors you should try to balance in your life.

The world in which we live influences who we are and what we do probably more than we realize. It is also important for us to remember that we, individually and collectively, can influence our world and the conditions of our lives.

> You are one of over 5 billion people in the world.
> You are a unique individual in a changing world.
> You, an individual, can affect tomorrow's world.

The world in which you live is different from what it was in your grandparents' youth, in your parents' youth, and even from the world in which you were a child. It is even different in some ways from what it was a year ago—or perhaps yesterday.

The rate of change has increased so much that today's young people are involved in more radical discoveries and changes than have ever before occurred in one generation. It is an exciting time to live, but change also requires the ability to make choices and adapt.

WHY STUDY PSYCHOLOGY?

Psychology
the scientific study of human behavior.

Would you like to lead a more satisfying, productive life, with less conflict and hassle? Responses might range from, "I seem to be doing all right so far," to "There is no way to remove problems, frustration, and disappointment from life." Regardless of what your particular response would be, there are few people who could not improve the quality of their lives if they were willing to gain a better understanding of themselves and others and put related, proven principles into practice.

Psychology is defined as the scientific study of human behavior. Although you already know a great deal about human behavior simply from having lived and associated with others for many years, you may not have studied behavior from a scientific perspective before. As with most things that you have learned from casual observation and experience in life, some of what you think you know is probably incomplete, or even inaccurate. And even if you have had a previous psychology course, your current learning can give you opportunities for personal, practical application to your activities at this time as well as achievement of goals in the future.

Interest in the functioning of the mind and causes of behavior can be traced back at least to Aristotle, who lived from 384–323 B.C. However, the first psychological laboratory was established by Wilhelm Wundt at Leipzig, Germany, in 1879. Since that time a more orderly, objective study of human behavior has developed. Since psychology is a social science, pertaining to human beings, it cannot be as exact as other sciences, such as physics, for example. Although psychologists have not yet reached complete agreement on theories of behavior, it can be a challenge to each of us to examine their work and develop our positions on how we believe our own lives and the world in which we live can be improved.

Comparative methodology
a method used to compare observations of behavior to identify similarities and differences.

Correlational methodology
a method that looks for a pattern of relationships in a set of observations.

Experimental Methods
methods that involve studying two groups of individuals—an experimental group and a control group.

The aims of psychology are usually identified as to *describe,* to *understand,* to *predict,* and to *control* or *influence* behavior. Different methods of studying human behavior attempt to achieve these aims. For example, a **comparative methodology** is used to compare observations of behavior to identify similarities and differences. A **correlational methodology** looks for a pattern of relationships in a set of observations. A study may be done to determine the correlation between students using tutoring assistance and their grades, for example. It is important to note that when two things are happening at the same time, it doesn't necessarily mean that one *causes* the other. **Experimental methods** involve studying two groups of individuals: an experimental group and a control group. The experimental group receives a change in what they are experiencing to determine possible effects. The control group does not receive this change so that the effects of the change to the experimental group can be determined.

Validity
the degree to which a measuring device actually measures what it intends to measure.

Reliability
the accuracy or consistency of results.

Those who conduct psychological studies must be concerned about validity and reliability of their methods of measuring or recording behavior. **Validity** refers to the degree to which a measuring device actually measures what it is intended to measure. A study to measure the effects of bonuses on the quality of work, for example, would have validity if that is what the study actually measured. **Reliability** refers to the accuracy or consistency of results. Two similar tests could be given to the same group, for example, to compare results. Consistency in results would determine reliability.

Theory
a belief based on present
knowledge and thinking
about the behavior of an
individual or group.

Principle
incorporates a generally
accepted theory into a
statement that applies to
most cases and
situations.

It might also be helpful to distinguish between the terms *theory* and *principle* as they pertain to the science of psychology. A psychological **theory** is a belief based on present knowledge and thinking concerning the behavior of an individual or group. A **principle** incorporates a generally accepted theory into a statement that applies to most cases and situations. In upcoming chapters we will study *theories* of motivation, for example, and *principles* of perception. We must remember, however, that social sciences, those sciences involving people, are not as exact as sciences such as physics. There can be exceptions in examples of human behavior. The exceptions in behavior in any given situation can cause problems, but they also make life much more interesting.

Numerous other factors must be considered in conducting psychological studies. Only a basic consideration of methods is presented here. It isn't likely that you will be conducting psychological studies, but some understanding of how studies are done can give you confidence in the results. The scientific study of human behavior has contributed to our understanding of ourselves and others in ways that will enrich our lives. The entire spectrum of psychology has many specialized areas of study. Some of these are *clinical, counseling, industrial, education,* and *sports.* In this course we are interested primarily in understanding principles of human behavior and their applications to our lives and work.

WHY LOOK TO THE FUTURE?

What will your future be like? One reason for interest in the answer to this question may be simple curiosity. We are usually curious about where we are going and what is likely to happen when we get there. But there are additional reasons for interest in the future. If we have some idea what to expect, we can prepare for our roles in the future. This knowledge is particularly important as it pertains to preparing for work, updating job skills, and retraining for new jobs. We can benefit from knowing what will be available in health care, housing, transportation, communication, educational opportunities, and other important aspects of our lives so that we can prepare for them to the extent that it is possible or practical. We are in a better position to take advantage of opportunities if we are prepared.

Another reason for "future awareness" is to use our best efforts to control or influence what is happening to us and the world in which we live and work. Although we may feel somewhat ineffective as individuals in many situations, what we do can make a difference. When we join forces with others who have similar interests and concerns, we can have an even greater impact. We can influence the outcome of what is happening in our schools, neighborhood, community, state or nation, and thus even in the world. Take the responsibility to understand yourself, those around you, and the world in which you live. The amount of influence you can have, individually or working with others with similar interests, can make remarkable differences. You will find many chapters in this book that will help you do this. Chapters 2 and 3 will give you a solid foundation.

In other instances we may foresee a change that we, individually or as a society, may want to prevent. If we are unable to prevent undesirable events, we may at least be able to delay or minimize them. There are orderly, constructive ways to do this, especially if we are sure of what we want and know our options.

It is easier to identify and oppose undesired changes in the planning stage than to counteract them after they are realities. Some of the things we might be able to prevent are discussed as threats in the next section of this chapter.

Still another reason for paying attention to the future is to promote desired change. We can bring about some changes that would not occur without our efforts. If we want to live in a safer world with more advantages and opportunities, we cannot simply rely on luck, the natural course of events, or the efforts of others. The discussion of challenges that follows relates to such opportunities.

Since everyone in a society does not have the same needs or values, others do not always want what you want. In fact, some may want the opposite. These contradictions complicate the process of change and reaction to it. All persons cannot have what they want, but in a democracy voices are heard and everyone has responsibilities. Upcoming chapters on self-concept and personality, motives and values, and attitudes will give you a foundation for satisfying your own needs, living and working with others, and making the world a better place in which to work and live.

THREATS, CHALLENGES, AND PROMISES

A look at today's world and into the future reveals threats but also challenges and exciting promises. Many challenges are related to overcoming today's threats. Also, promises are often the result of challenges that have been resolved successfully. It will help to keep these relationships in mind as you consider threats, challenges, and promises.

THREATS

Today's world is extremely complex. It is also obvious that we do not live in a perfect world. Therefore, we must be aware of the many threats to our well-being, the well-being of others, the environment, and other values in our lives and in society. For example, diseases such as AIDS and cancer, for which we still do not have reliable preventions or cures, pose serious threats. Environmental pollutants; weather hazards resulting from global warming; terrorism and the taking of hostages; illegal drug use; crime and violence; job insecurity caused by downsizing, relocation of companies, and technology; possible misuses of genetic research and biotechnology; unethical or incompetent leadership at all government levels; breakdown of public and private ethics; and loss of security and privacy due to computer and other technological capabilities are some of the major threats we face today. Most of these threats affect all of us, directly or indirectly. We simply cannot ignore them. Problem-solving strategies presented throughout this book can be helpful in responding to these threats as well as in solving personal problems and challenges.

CHALLENGES

We are challenged to solve problems related to the threats mentioned above or to avoid future situations and events that will pose these or similar threats. No doubt, we will also be confronted with some threats that we cannot foresee. For example, the possibility of cloning human life through biotechnology is considered a threat by some, but this type of research is also considered a challenge by others. Genetic researchers are also working to prevent or correct birth defects and hereditary diseases. To continue such research in responsible ways and to use the knowledge gained to improve human life is a momentous challenge. Other challenges pertain to the use of robotics in both the workplace and in our personal lives, the protection of natural resources and environment, gender equality in the workplace, correcting entitlement abuses, realistic use of credit, reducing the national debt, negotiating fair trade agreements, promoting peace in the world, and protecting human rights.

We are also challenged to solve additional problems that are accidentally or unavoidably created in the process of solving problems. One example of such a problem is the undesirable side effects of using chemotherapy for cancer treatment. Some of these effects have been lessened but it is still not known how to avoid them completely. Although this challenge is part of scientific research and medicine, we should be aware of undesirable outcomes in attempting to solve some social problems. We need prisons, for example, for the protection of society, but many of our prisons are becoming overcrowded, which is a new problem to be solved. There are also side effects in our own jobs and lives that we may be effective in eliminating or at least reducing. We might find that our promotion within a company will lessen the amount of time we can spend with our families. We can then take up the challenge of making the time we do spend with members of our families more meaningful. When undesirable results are unavoidable, we have to decide whether the consequences of our choices are worth accepting or whether we should work out solutions to additional problems that may arise. These decisions are sometimes based on our personal preferences or values, but they should be given careful consideration nonetheless.

PROMISES

A promise pertaining to our future can be thought of as a desirable result of years of effort by groups or dedicated individuals in the past. One of these promises is less discrimination in the workplace and in society as a whole. Although progress has been slow and often discouraging, globalization and experience with diversity have contributed to our understanding and acceptance of others. Advances in medicine and maintaining health include cures for more diseases and hope for those who have experienced disabling spinal injuries, laser technology with amazing accuracy, improvement in home health monitors, and lifelike artificial replacement parts. According to a 1997 issue of *Newsweek,* "Bioengineers are discovering that almost any human tissue can be coaxed from a culture dish and what can't be grown will someday be manufactured" (1). There are also promises related to the use of robotics in our homes and workplaces and exciting opportunities in space exploration and travel. The world of telecommunications also promises advances that will change our lives.

LIFE IN A GLOBAL COMMUNITY

We live in a global community—a term that appears almost to be a contradiction. We often think of a community as a relatively small town or city. *Global,* on the other hand, refers to encompassing the whole earth or globe. Yet the term *global community,* is appropriate because our lives have become interrelated in a number of ways with people in all parts of the world.

Cultural diversity or multiculturalism differences identified by culture within a group.

Cultural diversity, also called **multiculturalism,** refers to differences identified by culture within a group. When we speak of a *culture,* we refer to the values, beliefs, customs, and lifestyles that characterize members of a group of people with a common ancestry or national background. Some of the primary cultural characteristics pertain to dress, language, religious beliefs, family structure, values, and work ethics. What holidays are celebrated and how they are celebrated are also part of a culture. Taboo behaviors that are objectionable or offensive to one culture may be common and acceptable in another. Culture affects one's values and perception of others and of the world. These ideas will be amplified in Chapters 3 and 4.

It may be interesting to be a temporary guest or observer within a culture, but it can be much more challenging to understand and respect cultural differences. It is important to remember that everyone, including you and me, is a member of a culture or a combination of cultures. Cultural diversity will be discussed further in Chapter 12.

The more we can enlarge our experiences in life, the more we can appreciate life itself. We must open our minds, however, and let go of any prejudices or misconceptions about others. Chapter 6 will help you examine unfounded beliefs and gain an understanding of how they affect our lives and our relationships with others.

We begin early in this book, with Chapter 2, to gain a better understanding of ourselves, which is truly the basis for leading a meaningful life and understanding others. The study of the whole spectrum of human relations can be a valuable foundation to living in a global community.

How are goals met and problems solved in a global community? The answer is complex, but there must be unified efforts and cooperation among countries. The United Nations and numerous international organizations, for example, recognize both responsibilities and opportunities in the global community. The United Nations, organized in 1945 after World War II, states in the preamble of its charter:

We the peoples of the United Nations determined

to save succeeding generations from the scourge of war which twice in our lifetime has brought untold sorrow to mankind, and
to reaffirm faith in fundamental human rights, in the dignity and worth of the human person, in the equal rights of men and women and of nations large and small, and
to establish conditions under which justice and respect for the obligations arising from treaties and other sources of international law can be maintained, and
to promote social progress and better standards of life in larger freedom,

and for these ends

to practice tolerance and live together in peace with one another as good neighbors, and
to unite our strength to maintain international peace and security, and
to ensure, by the acceptance of principles and the institution of methods, that armed force shall not be used, save in the common interest, and
to employ international machinery for the promotion of the economic and social advancement of all peoples,

have resolved to combine our efforts to accomplish these aims.

The United Nations has been criticized for not being more effective in accomplishing these aims in its fifty or so years, but its very existence sends a message

What Do You Think? *How does the preamble of the United Nations charter emphasize the need for practicing psychology?*

to the world. Also, the United Nations has accomplished more than the average person probably realizes. There is evidence of its force and effectiveness.

It is no longer a matter of deciding whether we want to be involved. We are already living in a globalized society. How does responsibility to this society affect the decisions we make and the opportunities we have? What is the importance of a global society to the individual?

One of the most important issues for countries throughout the world is how to provide for national security and still be a positive force in promoting peace in the world. The North Atlantic Treaty Organization (NATO) continues to direct its members toward peace. We cannot leave the quest for peace and protection of human rights to national and international forces, however. Peace in the world should begin with peace within ourselves and with other human beings.

THE WORKPLACE—TODAY AND TOMORROW

The workplace you will be entering or reentering will be different in many ways than it was a few years ago and will continue to change during your years in the workforce. If you have returned to college to retrain or upgrade your work skills, you may have firsthand experience with some of these changes. Work no longer offers the job security that was taken for granted a generation ago. Your parents or grandparents, for example, may have retired from a company that employed them all their working years. Downsizing, or reducing the number of employees to lower costs, has become a reality for many who thought they were relatively secure in their jobs and is an ongoing threat to many others. The relocation of plants and businesses has also become more common, causing employees to find themselves without a job or with difficult choices regarding moving, returning to college for retraining, or, for some, retiring.

The number of people employed is growing faster in some types of businesses than in others. For example, the number of employees in goods-producing industries has declined in recent years, whereas the number working in services has increased steadily. Services related to technology, health care, food, and business will continue to create most of these jobs. Almost everyone entering the world of work will be expected to know about related technology, including the use of computers.

Employers are demanding more of their employees. In "The Future of Work," Rich Feller states, " . . . continuous improvement, international quality standards, self-management, teamwork and high skill expectations

"I didn't quit! The company relocated and didn't tell me."

Reprinted by permission of the Wall Street Journal.

now are the norm for the majority of workers. Time-compressed distribution, product development and process innovation have literally transformed jobs. There is no room for the low-skilled, high-wage jobs in a fast-paced, competitive, technological environment" (2). Today's rapidly changing world demands that workers have skills related to technology, critical thinking, problem solving, team functioning, communications, human relations, and continued learning.

The workplace, with the rest of society, has become increasingly diversified in the last decade, and this trend will continue. Cultural diversity has become an outstanding characteristic of the workplace as well as of the global community discussed earlier. The term *workplace diversity* in use today refers to cultural differences as well as differences in gender, age, abilities and disabilities, and so on. These factors will be discussed in depth in Chapter 12.

The composition of the workforce is changing in other ways. A few years ago it was estimated that at the beginning of the twenty-first century, the majority of people entering the U.S. market for the first time will be women and minorities. There are still more males than females in the workforce, but the margin is narrowing. The 1996–97 edition of the *Occupational Outlook Handbook* projected that by 2005, women would comprise 48 percent of the labor force, compared to 46 percent in 1994 (3). Consequently there are more two-income families today also.

Although the number of women and minorities in the workforce is increasing, advancement opportunities and pay equity are still issues that have not been resolved completely. As the number of two-income families has increased, so have child-care needs. Many businesses and organizations have responded with child-care facilities for their employees. This benefit has not only helped families but resulted in employees that can perform better on the job.

Changes in where and when people work will also increase in the years ahead. Millions of people are now working at least part-time in their home. Some are self-employed, but growing numbers contract their work for businesses. There are many advantages to working at home, including no travel time, traffic congestion, parking expenses and problems, having less expense for lunches and clothing, and caring for one's children and working at the same time. People can also arrange their schedules to attend outside activities and health care appointments.

Increased neighborhood contact and fewer burglaries of empty houses have also been noted as advantages. There are also disadvantages, however, which include less direct accessibility to coworkers for consultation about problems. One also misses the social interaction of the workplace. Many who work at home or have tried it say that there can also be many more distractions at home. Working at home requires more self-discipine and personal scheduling than does working in an office.

Nontraditional careers have become more common today. It has taken a long time for societal attitudes to change about what was considered "man's" work and "woman's" work. But members of both sexes who earlier were willing to be looked upon with some disfavor or distrust to follow their true choice of careers have paved the way for others. For example, it is more common today than even a decade ago for males to choose a career in nursing and for females to choose a career in law enforcement. In fact, we are moving away from the use of the terms *traditional careers* and *nontraditional careers*. Both males and females are choosing any career for which they have the desire and potential.

Despite educational and occupational opportunities, young people can be under numerous pressures related to their life's work. The more career opportunities and choices they have, the more responsibility they have for making decisions and fulfilling related requirements. They must be more willing to change, adapt, and continue to learn. These are the characteristics of stimulating, challenging years in the workforce. Work today need not be boring. It is likely that you will not be doing the same job all your working life. In fact, you may change jobs many times in your lifetime. This will not mean that you "can't keep a job" or that you "won't stay put." It is representative of the changing world of work.

Unless both companies and individuals can foresee some changes in the world of work, they may experience surprising and unfavorable consequences. These changes are brought about by the economy, competition and trade, wages, composition of the workforce, restructuring of companies, new technology, variations in the demand for products and services, as well as other factors. These same factors provide opportunities and challenges for those who know how to look to the future and prepare for it. You can see how many of the threats, challenges, and promises discussed earlier pertain to the workplace.

This young woman is training to enter the construction trade. Twenty years ago, it would have been difficult for a woman to break into this profession. Today it is much more common.

Flextime
somewhat flexible work schedule developed to fit the needs of employees.

There have been many changes in work schedules and hours spent on the job. One of these is **flextime,** which allows flexibility in one's workday schedule. Some people, because of either other responsibilities or personal preferences, want to start work later in the morning but are willing to work later in the day. Others prefer to start earlier and finish earlier. Still others may need a longer lunch hour but can start earlier or work longer. Although an employee usually has a fixed schedule, he or she has some say in what that schedule will be. This has worked well for both companies and employees in most cases.

Another change in the world of work pertains to a type of part-time work known as **job sharing.** As the term suggests, this involves sharing a full-time job with another person. Some people do not want to work full-time or may not want to work during the summer. The sharing can be done in various ways. Naturally, any arrangement must have the approval of the employer; however, many employers like the idea.

Part-time workers are changing the workforce in another way. Growing numbers of part-time workers who seek work through temporary employment agencies work nearly the equivalent of full-time at different part-time jobs. The variety of jobs and the flexibility appeals to many of these workers. Another factor that has made this type of work more popular is that some of these employment agencies are offering benefits such as health insurance.

Robotics will become more common in the workplace of the future as well as in other areas of our lives. When we hear the term *robotics,* we often think of robots. Today **robotics** is used to describe any computer-controlled machine capable of doing work. According to the Robotics Institute of Carnegie Mellon University in Pittsburgh,

> Robotics is one of the most exciting new disciplines to emerge in modern science. Robots and other automated devices have the potential to improve our economy, our health, our standard of living, and our knowledge of the world we live in. The applications of robotics are as varied as inspecting chickens, conducting laboratory experiments, assisting surgeons, making automobiles, and exploring seas, volcanoes, glaciers, and outer space.

Job sharing
working part-time by sharing a job with another person.

Robotics
any computer-controlled machine capable of doing work.

© Harley L. Schwadron.

Even when robotics technologies were relatively primitively, their potentially key role in boosting the productivity and competitiveness of the United States was foreseen as an important trend in the global marketplace. Robotics encompasses all areas of science and technology needed to develop a new generation of robots, smart autonomous systems that can plan their own actions, perceive and analyze their environment, and interact at a high level of abstraction with human controllers (4).

Robotics will replace some jobs, but some of these jobs will involve repetitive procedures or will be hazardous to humans. Job loss in some industries will be inevitable, particularly by those who have been in the workplace for a long time and are not interested in learning new job skills. Those who prepare adequately for the world of work and who are willing to change and continue to learn need not be threatened by robotics.

In recent years more attention has been given to the capabilities and well-being of workers. Designing machines and the working environment to accommodate the worker is known as **human factor engineering** or **ergonomics.** In the past it was taken for granted that the worker would have to do his or her best to adjust to the job, equipment, and working conditions. Ergonomics was first practiced in aerospace, but now it is evident in most businesses and industries. Business equipment and the work environment are designed, for example, to avoid eye strain, back fatigue, and general stress.

The difference between the work of management and their employees is lessening. All typing used to be done by secretaries, for example; now many managers use computers to produce most of their messages and records. Secretaries and other personnel are now likely to be part of the team and may make contributions to management decisions. The same type of team functioning is becoming a major characteristic of numerous businesses and industries. Therefore, those doing the hiring will attempt to identify candidates who can function effectively as a member of a team in addition to possessing the required job skills.

A growing respect for the abilities of workers has been an outstanding characteristic of work in the 1990s and this respect is expected to increase into the next century. In an article entitled "Moving Labor into the 21st Century," Stephanie Overman writes, "When management, when ownership, when entrepreneurship, talk about capital assets, they must remember that the most valuable assets that any company has are the people who work there. That's not a cost; that's a capital asset, and it must be maintained. It must be improved" (5). The significance of the workforce factors discussed here will be considered in more depth in Chapter 9.

Human factor engineering or **ergonomics** the design of machines and the working environment to accommodate the worker.

LIFELONG LEARNING

The expression *getting an education* is misleading in the context of today's workplace. You can attend a school or college for several years and even receive a diploma, but you must recognize and embrace the idea that learning is a lifelong process. The primary mission of most technical and community colleges today is to prepare individuals for entry or reentry into the world of work. As we have already noted in the previous section on the workforce, the world of work is rapidly and continuously changing, however. Edward Cornish states in "The Cyber Future," "Skills and knowledge will become obsolete faster than ever.

Employers look for workers with leading-edge skills, but the leading edge can soon become the laggard edge. . . . Constant retraining is essential to keep people from becoming increasingly less qualified for their jobs" (6).

The best approach is to *continue* to learn on the job and in any way you can that is related to the service, business, or industry in which you are employed. These businesses and industries recommend or even require that their employees update their skills and develop new skills. According to an article in *Nation's Business*, "A new study by the American Association of Junior Colleges finds that nearly 80 percent of employers say that new training is needed by at least one-fourth of their workers; some employers say it's needed by everyone on their payroll" (7). Some companies pay the expenses of continued learning for their employees. Others offer their own training programs. Motorola, for example, trains or retrains a large proportion of its employees each year. DuPont is another company that has an extensive employee training program. There are many others. In addition to businesses and industries conducting their own training programs, many allow their employees to take advantage of customized training and educational courses offered by colleges. The Center for Business and Industry at the Northcentral Technical College in Wisconsin, in defining its services, states, "As organizations seek to survive and flourish in today's increasingly competitive global economy, many are finding that an investment in training can improve employee performance, business productivity, product quality and company profitability" (8). Training of this type takes place in the business or industry facility itself or at the college training center.

Today, people can make more choices about their life work. Adults of many ages choose to enter trade school or college to advance their careers. These adults, once called "nontraditional students," are now becoming so common they are considered "traditional" in some settings.

Learning occurs in many places other than classrooms, and it takes many forms. Distance-learning through interactive television, videotapes, video conferencing, and the Internet, for example, is available to many who cannot otherwise attend classes. Colleges offer classes at times and places that are convenient for people who are employed or cannot attend traditional classes for other reasons. Some earn their initial degree by taking part-time classes, and others take classes or seminars to upgrade their knowledge and skills. The School of Criminal Justice at Michigan State University and the School of Criminal Justice at West Virginia University are just two examples of many educational institutions that offer a wide range of choices in how, when, and where one learns.

Communication technology will continue to offer multiple choices in ways to remain a lifelong learner.

It is imperative that individuals not only take advantage of learning opportunities but that they also take personal initiative to learn about their area of work and how it is changing. According to the *Vocational Education Journal,* "The workplace has little patience with employees who do not know how to take responsibility for their own learning and who think that the need to learn ends when they begin working. Since learning creates human capital and expands worker potential to solve value-added problems, self-directed learners are more of an investment than a cost to employers" (9).

WORKPLACE SKILLS FOR THE TWENTY-FIRST CENTURY

Preparing oneself for the world of work requires a broad base of knowledge and skills. According to *Learning a Living*: *A Blueprint for High Performance* also known as *A SCANS Report for America 2000,*

> [A] high performance workplace requires workers who have a solid foundation in the basic literacy and computational skills, in the thinking skills necessary to put knowledge to work, and in the personal qualities that make workers dedicated and trustworthy. . . . But a solid foundation is not enough. High-performance workplaces also require competencies: the ability to manage resources, to work amicably and productively with others, to acquire and use information, to master complex systems, and to work with a variety of technologies. The know-how identified by *SCANS* is made up of five competencies and a three-part foundation of skills and personal qualities that are needed for solid job performance. To be prepared for the workplace, you need to develop the following skills:
>
> - **Resources**—Know how to allocate time, money, materials, space, and staff.
> - **Interpersonal skills**—Work on teams, teach others, serve customers, lead, negotiate, and work well with people from culturally diverse backgrounds.
> - **Information**—Acquire and evaluate data, organize and maintain files, interpret and communicate, and use computers to process information.
> - **Systems**—Understand social, organizational, and technological systems; monitor and correct performance; and design or improve systems.
> - **Technology**—Select equipment and tools, apply technology to specific tasks, and maintain and troubleshoot equipment.
>
> Foundation Skills—Competent workers in the high-performance workplace need:
>
> - **Basic skills**—Reading, writing, arithmetic and mathematics, speaking, and listening.
> - **Thinking skills**—The ability to learn, to reason, to think creatively, to make decisions, and to solve problems.
> - **Personal qualities**—Individual responsibility, self-esteem and self-management, sociability, and integrity (10).

Of the five workplace competencies defined above, developing your interpersonal skills is the focus of this course. All three of the foundation skills are included in the various chapters of this text and related activities, and specifically in Chapters 2, 6, 7, 8, and 9.

**What Would
You Do?**   *What is one thing you can do to improve the quality of your
life? What has been keeping you from doing this?*

One of the most valuable skills a person can have today is knowing *how* he or she learns because there isn't one best way; it depends to some extent how *you* learn best. Some people learn best by listening, others by seeing, and still others by doing. Learning also depends on how we perceive and process information and experiences. We all learn in many ways, of course, but gaining some understanding about how you learn best can be helpful in your present and future learning experiences. There is still much for all of us to learn about learning, however. Sophfronia Scott Gregory discusses this challenge in *Time*:

> The greatest mystery for the next century is whether scientists will discover fundamental ways to affect how the mind learns. The human brain has evolved over millions of years to process information in a certain way—the very act of perceiving the world is an integral part of the way it is understood. Can learning speed and capacity be "souped up"? While scientists have found ways to improve the learning ability of people with damaged and dysfuntional brains, nothing as yet emerged that could radically improve a normal brain's ability. No secret pill or process is on the horizon, just a steady enhancement of abilities people already have. And the most powerful ingredient will be motivation, since the working world will become even more knowledge driven and information intensive. In the 21st century, nothing will be more fashionable—and essential—than doing one's homework (11).

THE QUALITY OF LIFE

Quantity, or the number of years one lives, does not guarantee quality, or the degree to which one's life is satisfying and meaningful. Life expectancy is increasing, however, and most people consider a longer life desirable. A person born in 1800 could expect to live only thirty-five years. Life expectancy is now more than double that figure. **Life expectancy** is defined as the average number of years a person of a given population can expect to live beyond his or her present age. Life expectancy is also related to cultural and socioeconomic background. Control of disease and the aging process, organ transplants, synthetic organs, new surgical techniques, and improved environmental conditions contribute to longer life.

Life expectancy
average number of years a person of a given population can expect to live beyond his or her present age.

Concern for the quality of life is a characteristic of today's workforce. Everyone wants to be comfortable and happy and wants life to be satisfying and meaningful. The characteristics of quality living are largely a matter of personal values, of course. A better life is not guaranteed by more conveniences, more material possessions, or more free time. To a great extent it is the responsibility of the individual to make life meaningful and satisfying, but the society in which we live can make it easier. Many severely disabled individuals would tell you that the quality of their lives is high. We will have a better world if we can agree to some extent on the kind of world we want and are willing to work together to attain it. This need not interfere with individual rights and values.

MAINTAINING BALANCES

The world in which we live will continue to change. Although this process of change is inevitable, it can be either disturbing or desirable. Any kind of change, momentarily at least, disturbs the status quo. Even with change that is welcome, adjustments are required.

We need balances to avoid extremes. We need balances between:

Old and new in social institutions

Work and recreation

Rest and exercise

Nourishment and overeating

Dependence and independence

Individuality and conformity

Rights and responsibilities

Care for others and care of ourselves

We also need balance between what we would like to do and what we can do as individuals and as a nation. We must constantly seek a balance in all of these respects.

Summary

Psychology, the scientific study of human behavior, can improve our lives and the world in which we live. The purposes of psychology are to describe, to understand, to predict, and to control or influence.

Not only is the world in which we live constantly changing, but the rate of change is constantly increasing. We cannot help but be affected, but we can also affect the change that is taking place. If we can foresee some change, we can decide whether or not we want it to happen. Depending on our evaluations and decisions, we then can either support or attempt to counteract the trend. Even a small group or an individual can influence change in society. If we cannot immediately affect a condition to the degree we would like, we can prepare to cope with it while we initiate further action. We can also promote change we desire.

We must recognize that we live in a global community. Companies from all parts of the world are doing business with one another. The company you might be working for will have a much more diverse workforce than in the past. We must learn to understand one another and to work together for everyone's benefit.

The world we live in holds a number of threats, presents challenges, and offers some promises. Some of the major threats pertain to health hazards, the environment, social problems, job insecurity, and unethical or incompetent leadership. Challenges pertain to removing or reducing threats, and also to finding positive ways to improve ourselves and the world in which we live and work. There are also promises to be expected in the future. Some of these are in the fields of medicine, technology, and cultural diversity, for example.

The workplace has seen numerous changes in recent years, with more to come in the 21st Century. The numbers of part-time workers and those who perform their job in their homes have increased. Robotics will become a more familiar part of the workplace and our homes. Numerous other technological advances

PSYCHOLOGY IN PRACTICE

1. Talk to several part-time workers. Ask them what they believe are the advantages and disadvantages of part-time employment.

2. We are continuously seeking—and often finding—solutions to problems in today's world. These solutions often have undesirable side effects or aftereffects. Some products, for example, cause pollution. Identify another problem that has resulted from the solution to a different problem. Discuss with two other students how the side effects or aftereffects might have been prevented.

3. Investigate how a company or business in your area provides for training and retraining of their employees. Find out who provides the training, where it takes place, and the joint commitment between the employer and the employees. Compare the training program to what is recommended in SCANS WorkPlace Know-How. Report your findings to the class.

in the workplace make preparation for jobs more demanding but will also make work more challenging.

Lifelong learning has become a reality and a necessity. We must keep up with technology and meet other demands of the workplace. Multiple learning opportunities are everywhere. Business and industry support the learning of their employees in a number of ways but continued learning must also be an individual responsibility. Some of the ways one can continue to learn while working are through customized job training, video conferencing, seminars, and use of the Internet.

The *SCANS Report for America 2000* has identified skills needed for today's and tomorrow's workforce. These include basic skills, technical, interpersonal, and thinking skills, as well as personal qualities.

The quality of life should not be overlooked in the rapidly changing world in which we live. We should also strive to maintain balance in numerous respects in our personal lives and in our relationships with others.

Reacting to change is closely related to the way we see that change as affecting our immediate needs and wants or long-range goals. What we want for ourselves and others can begin with a better understanding of self-concept and personality, the subject of Chapter 2.

Key Terms

Psychology
Comparative methodology
Correlational methodology
Experimental methods
Validity
Reliability
Theory
Principle
Cultural diversity or multiculturalism
Flextime
Job sharing
Robotics
Human factor engineering or ergonomics
Life expectancy

Learning Activities

Turn to page LA-1 to complete the Learning Activities and Enrichment Activities for this chapter.

Endnotes

1. Goeffrey Cowley, "Replacement Parts," *Newsweek,* January 27, 1997, p. 66.
2. Rich Feller, "The Future of Work," *Vocational Education Journal,* April 1, 1996, p. 25.
3. *Occupational Outlook Handbook,* 1996–97 Edition, U.S. Dept. of Labor, Bureau of Labor Statistics, Bulletin 2470, p. 5.
4. Takeo Kanade and Sandy Rocco, "Welcome to the Robotics Institute," The Robotics Institute, Carnegie Mellon University, Pittsburgh (http://www.ri.cmu.edu/ri-home/ri -welcome.html), May 4, 1997.
5. Stephanie Overman, "Moving Labor into the 21st Century," *HRMagazine,* December 1991, p. 39.
6. Edward Cornish, "The Cyber Future," *The Futurist,* January–February 1996, p. 7.
7. James Worsham et al., "Challenges We Face," *Nation's Business,* February 1997, p. 26.
8. "Working Solutions for a Technical Advantage," brochure, Center for Business and Industry, Northcentral Technical College, Wausau, WI, Spring 1997, no page number.
9. Rich Feller, "Preparation for the Changing Workplace," *Vocational Education Journal,* April 1, 1996, p. 27.
10. "Workplace Know-How," *Learning a Living: A Blueprint for High Performance, A SCANS Report for America 2000,* The Secretary's Commission on Achieving Necessary Skills, U.S. Dept. of Labor, April 1992, pp. xiii–xiv.
11. Sophfronia Scott Gregory, "The Future Is Here," *Time,* Fall 1992, p. 60.

Self-Concept and Personality

2

No one can make you feel inferior without your permission.

Eleanor Roosevelt

LEARNING OBJECTIVES

After completing this chapter, you should be able to do the following:

1. Define the terms *self-concept* and *self-esteem*.

2. Describe three theories of personality development.

3. Identify characteristics of each of the Big Five personality factors.

4. Explain why some people might consider a person to be difficult when he or she is only different.

5. Describe possible influences of heredity and environment on personality development.

6. Explain how sexuality affects an individual's identity.

7. Identify and define the three forces that, according to Freud, influence behavior.

8. Describe how personality changes through experience and opportunity.

9. Identify personality characteristics important to job success.

Self-concept
how individuals perceive themselves and how they feel toward themselves.

Personality
person's total habitual social behavior or social self; personal identity as perceived by others.

You are a unique individual. There is nobody, anywhere, exactly like you. But are you entirely and absolutely different from every other person? You have only to look at the person beside you or the next person you see to verify that you have much in common with others. To understand yourself and others you must understand both similarities and differences. You should remember that not only are you unique, but every other human being is also unique. We are who we are, and we act toward others as we do because of numerous factors. This chapter will give you a better understanding of yourself and others in terms of what are known as self-concept and personality.

How you perceive yourself and how you feel toward yourself is your **self-concept.** How you interact with others and adjust to your environment, including all the different characteristics that influence your behavior, is your **personality.** Self-concept and personality are interrelated. Your actions toward others are influenced greatly by the way you perceive yourself. Your ideas and feelings about yourself are also determined to a great extent by how others act toward you and by what you believe about their opinion of you.

SELF-CONCEPT

Everyone has a self-concept. You may find it difficult to describe your self-concept exactly. It would be reasonable to ask then, How accurate is my present self-concept? It may be difficult to answer this question realistically because many characteristics and factors are involved. Nevertheless, it can be of value to attempt to gain a better understanding of your self-concept because it can

Quiz Yourself

When I ask for advice or assistance, I feel _____

When I lose in a game or a contest, I feel _____

When I win in a game or a contest, I feel _____

I am usually embarrassed when _____

I feel good about myself when I _____

I am uncomfortable when someone asks me _____

I usually react to criticism by _____

I usually react to a compliment by _____

When I am asked for my opinion on a controversial issue, I _____

Have your answers to these questions changed your self-concept?

help you become the kind of person you want to be, and such an undertaking can be an important factor in your success.

If you were given a list of all possible human characteristics and were asked to check the ones you think describe you, this would help you to understand your self-concept better. Another way to gain insight into your self-concept is to complete sentences such as those in the Quiz Yourself section above. You will likely conclude, however, that in many cases the way you feel or react would depend on the situation and with whom you were involved. Thinking about how your responses will vary according to these variables is also helpful.

Some people, of course, really do not want to understand themselves better. It's like not wanting to look in the mirror because they think they will not be satisfied with what they see. Others adopt a false identity as a substitute for self-understanding. These people may feel more comfortable temporarily but are not doing themselves any good in the long run. Still others are satisfied to identify with someone they admire. Thus a fifteen-year-old music student may identify with her instructor and may try to *be* just like her instead of seeing her teacher as a role model and developing her own individuality as a person and as a musician. Others may identify more with a uniform or with a particular type of career, rather than with their own potential as individuals.

How does self-concept develop? An infant does not have a sense of self. Our self-concepts begin to develop in early childhood, however, and continue to change somewhat throughout life. Our self-concepts are also influenced greatly by the ways others act toward us and by the experiences we have. If young people constantly get the message through words or actions that they do not have much worth, this will affect their opinion of themselves. With such poor self-concepts, they lower their expectations of themselves and, in a sense, fulfill their image of themselves as failures. They tend to blame disappointing experiences on themselves; on the other hand, they are likely to attribute successful experiences to luck. They have a tendency to take general criticisms personally with an "I think he is referring to me" attitude. This is how some people develop feelings of inferiority. On the other hand, if people are treated with respect for their personal worth, even though others may disapprove of some of the things they do, they will develop more positive self-concepts.

We also have a tendency to become the kind of person other people expect us to be. This pertains primarily to those with whom we have ongoing contact in our education, work, or personal lives. Living up to other people's expectations of us in this way is commonly called the "self-fulfilling prophecy."

It should be the goal of all people to perceive and understand themselves as they *are*. Your self-concept should be realistic, but it should also be favorable. The following ideas can help a person maintain a positive self-concept:

- Everyone has worth as a human being.
- You are unique. No one is exactly like you.
- You don't have to be perfect; no one is.
- You have more potential than you will ever develop or use.
- You are capable of loving and being loved.

SELF-ESTEEM

Self-esteem
sense of self-worth.

Your self-concept is thus related to your sense of self-esteem. Unless you develop a sense of **self-esteem** or self-worth, you will be unable to progress toward what Maslow calls self-actualization, a concept that will be discussed in Chapter 3.

Realistic, positive self-esteem should begin at an early age. T. Berry Brazelton, M.D., states:

> If I could give one gift to every child in America, it would be self-esteem, for this is surely a key to happiness. But what exactly is it?
>
> This is how I would depict a child who has high self-esteem: * He feels lovable, so he is open to loving and being loved. * He feels valued for his competence and secure about doing things for himself and others. * He has learned to value praise only when it reflects a genuine accomplishment or learning experience. * He feels worthy enough not to consider doing things that are too far-out or that devalue him. * Being sure of himself, he is not at the mercy of peer pressure; he knows and accepts his limits.
>
> This last quality is referred to by psychologists as a firm "locus of control." A child who has it as he enters adolescence will be able to experiment, but he will also understand the cost of going too far (1).

Even though an early start at self-esteem is critical, self-esteem can also change during the course of one's life, depending on one's experiences. Actually, it is one's evaluations of those experiences that affect his or her sense of self-worth.

PEANUTS

Peanuts reprinted by permission of United Features Syndicate, Inc.

This young gymnast is developing self-esteem as well as honing important physical skills and routines.

Self-esteem also has a direct relationship to one's work. In a survey conducted by *Newsweek,* the following was reported to the question:

How important are the following in motivating a person to work hard and succeed? (Percent saying "very important")

89% Self-esteem/the way people feel about themselves
77% Family duty or honor
49% Responsibility to community
44% Fear of failure
35% Status in the eyes of others (2)

If you are just entering the world of work on a full-time basis, your self-esteem may be a little low or shaky. That is understandable because, in a sense, you will have to prove yourself in this new, important venture.

Kevin is having such an experience in the following account. He recently graduated from a community college in the Northeast and has not yet gained a great deal of confidence in himself as an employee. He had favorable self-esteem as a student and presented himself and his abilities favorably in his job interview, however. A frequent comment made by instructors in his evaluations was that his self-esteem was high but realistic. Below are some of the ways Kevin approached his start with his new job, indicating he had appropriate self-esteem for success.

- Kevin reviewed new experiences he had in the past—in education, sports, and part-time jobs—to assure himself that he could do it again in this job.

- He gained satisfaction from knowing that his employer considered him a potentially valuable employee when he was hired. He evidently had the desired education and personality traits. He admitted, especially to himself, however, that he still had much to learn. He considered his lack of experience a challenge rather than being disturbed by it.

- He had a sense of value and dignity as a person. He was comfortable with himself, without trying to create false impressions. He felt good about himself and therefore was accepted by others.

- He evaluated his progress regularly during the first few weeks. He asked himself questions such as: What have I learned since I've been working here? What can I do better now than when I started? What have I done for someone else? In what way have I proven my worth to the business or organization?

- He had confidence in his ability but was realistic about any limitations he might have had. He worked independently and with confidence following the company's policy for new employees. However, he did not consider himself stupid because he did not know some things about the job or job setting.
- He appreciated favorable reactions to his work but did not depend on them for a sense of well-being and personal worth. He showed appreciation for the assistance, helpfulness, and friendliness of others.
- He didn't try to live up to his highest goals at the beginning. He was conscientious, but reasonable, in his expectations of himself until he could learn the job and procedures.
- He assumed responsibility for his work. If he made mistakes, he acknowledged them, corrected them if possible, and learned from them. He did not feel like a failure if he made a mistake.
- He could accept being shown the best procedure for doing something or being corrected without taking it as personal criticism.
- He realized that positive self-esteem is not overconfident or too self-satisfied in who one is and what one knows. It is a realistic, calm self-assurance in oneself and the situation at any given time.

You might want to use Kevin's experience as a guideline when you begin a new job. If you feel overly anxious about new experiences and somewhat hesitant about your sense of worth, it might help to keep in mind the underlying ideas for gaining and demonstrating positive, realistic self-esteem. Remember, however, that you are a unique individual and may have your own equally valuable ways of expressing positive, realistic self-esteem.

 What would you do? *How would you respond if you were asked in an employment interview, How would describe yourself as a person?*

PERSONALITY

We considered earlier that how we *think* others see us affects our self-concept. This may be quite different from their real opinion of us. People sometimes think of themselves as failures because they mistakenly believe that others look upon them as failures—even though in reality they may be quite capable and are favorably regarded and respected. There are also people who believe that they are regarded more favorably than they actually are. A superiority complex is often accompanied by such a distorted estimation of oneself.

Personality consists of a relatively consistent combination of characteristics that affects how we react to others and our environment. Personality is often thought of as how others would see us and describe us.

The Scottish poet Robert Burns wrote a dialect poem that has a universal message about self-concept and personality. The dialect of his lines can be restated as,

"Oh, if only some Power would give us the gift to see ourselves as others see us. It would from many a blunder free us and foolish notion."

What Do You Think? *Is it always desirable to see ourselves as others see us? Why or why not?*

AS OTHERS SEE YOU

You can expect that each of the people who see you under different circumstances will describe you somewhat differently. Parents, friends, teachers, and employers certainly see an individual differently. Take the case of Yvonne, nineteen years old, who has six older brothers. She has been pampered and protected by her family, who see her as a delicate child. Yet friends in Yvonne's interior decorating class see her as an equal and as having similar abilities and interests. Mr. Narlock, one of her instructors, sees her as a rather immature young woman, but he recognizes that she has talent for color and design. Mrs. Zelinski, the manager of the drapery department where Yvonne works part-time, describes her as knowing about fabrics and decorating but impatient with customers. These people describe Yvonne differently because she reacts to them differently. The various facets of one's personality that are evident at any given time are influenced both by circumstances and by interactions with others.

It is natural and appropriate to act differently in different situations, or to assume the **role,** or type of behavior that is called for in particular circumstances. This does not mean that you are phoney or insincere. Everyone has many roles to play. For example, you may be a student, a brother or sister, a son or daughter, a parent, an employee, a tenant, a club member, a classmate, and a team member. In all these roles you may act somewhat differently, depending not only on your

Role
activity of a person in a particular situation involving personality characteristics that may not be dominant in another situation.

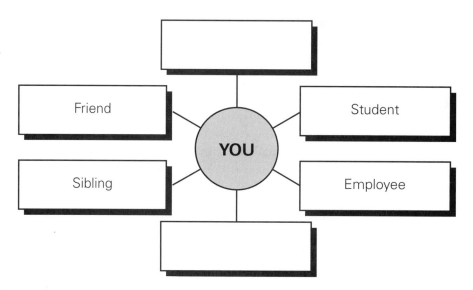

This chart shows different roles in an individual's relationships with others. Can you add any? If so, write them in.

immediate needs, wants, and feelings but also on the total situation. This may cause an onlooker to say, "Susan is not herself tonight." Susan *is* being herself, but she is not acting the way this person expects her to act on the basis of observations of past behavior. It is an indication of a well-adjusted individual to be able to accept the fact that one can act in different ways at different times.

PERSONALITY THEORIES

Several different theories have been developed in an attempt to understand the origin and nature of personality. The major personality theories are psychodynamic, trait, social-cognitive, and humanistic. **Psychodynamic theory** stresses behaviors that are unconsciously motivated. **Trait theory** focuses on both inherited and learned personality characteristics. **Social-cognitive theory** emphasizes learning and experience. **Humanistic theory** emphasizes the individual's ability to determine the kind of person one wants to be. Naturally each of these theories is quite complex. Many psychologists use more than one to form their own beliefs about personality and how it affects our lives and the lives of those around us. Certainly the personality of a particular individual is difficult to define. If someone were asked to describe the kind of person you are, however, he or she would probably describe you in terms of characteristics, or **traits.** Your traits consist of relatively consistent behavior patterns and a style of reacting to situations that others have observed you performing.

THE BIG FIVE PERSONALITY FACTORS

Recent research and writing on personality traits identifies five factors that are evident in some form or degree in each person's personality. Individual personality traits such as those identified above have been combined into categories or factors. These factors, or trait dimensions, are described by R. R. McCrae and Paul T. Costa, Jr., as follows:

Neuroticism (emotional stability)	Worrying versus calm Insecure versus secure Self-pitying versus self-satisfied
Extraversion	Sociable versus retiring Fun-loving versus sober Affectionate versus reserved
Openness	Imaginative versus down-to-earth Preference for variety versus preference for routine Independent versus conforming
Agreeableness	Soft-hearted versus ruthless Trusting versus suspicious Helpful versus uncooperative
Conscientiousness	Well-organized versus disorganized Careful versus careless Self-disciplined versus weak-willed (3)

Psychodynamic theory a theory or belief that stresses unconscious motivation in personality and motivation.

Trait theory a theory that focuses on both inherited and learned personality characteristics.

Social-cognitive theory a theory that emphasizes learning and experience.

Humanistic theory belief in the theory that recognizes some environmental and unconscious influence but emphasizes personal control and responsibility.

Traits personality characteristics.

David G. Myers and others prominent in the field of psychology believe that the determination of these traits is one of the best ways to describe an individual's personality. Myers states, "The Big Five may not be the last word. But it is currently our best approximation of the basic trait dimensions. If you could ask five questions about the personality of a stranger—say, a blind date you were soon to meet—querying where the person is on these five dimensions would be most revealing" (4).

PERSONALITY TESTS

A popular personality evaluation is the Myers-Briggs test. The test is based on an individual's determining his or her preferences in self-description. Results identify a person as having a combination of his or her basic preferences. These preferences relate to:

Extraversion or Introversion

Sensing or iNtuition

Thinking or Feeling

Judgment or Perception

Extravert
person who enjoys being with other people and likes to be involved.

Introvert
person who enjoys solitary activity, often an imaginative person and one interested in art and nature.

Intuition
immediate understanding without conscious attention or reasoning.

An **extravert** prefers activities involving other people, whereas an **introvert** enjoys more solitude and keeps more to him- or herself. Sensing or **intuition** refers to the contrast between using our senses primarily in a practical way as in "I have to see it to believe it" compared to "sensing" something without knowing exactly why. The thinking or feeling contrast is probably more obvious. Thinking is more logical; feeling pertains to a personal, values-oriented way of responding. The contrast between judgment or perception pertains to how one likes to live one's life. Those who prefer judgment like to be more organized, while those who prefer perception are more flexible. (These preferences are described more fully in material directly related to the test.)

According to Myers-Briggs, each person is some combination of these characteristics. Depending on your particular combination of preferences, your personality could be described as a LIFEType. For example, a person would have a ENTP LIFEType if she identified herself primarily with Extraversion, iNtuition, Thinking, and Perception.

Sandra Hirsh and Jean Kummerow elaborate on these basic personality preferences and talk about communication styles, relationship styles, work styles, and career information, as well as other interpretations of each lifestyle combination. They offer the following evaluation to help individuals determine whether they would identify themselves with Judgment or Perception as that segment of their LIFEType. They suggest that,

> [I]n order to further understand the general characteristics of Judgment and Perception, read through the following lists and select those characteristics that better apply to you.
>
> | I am more likely to act like a Judger and: | I am more likely to act like a Perceptive and: |
> | --- | --- |
> | Prefer my life to be decisive, imposing my will upon it. | Seek to adapt my life and experience to what comes along. |

Work for a settled life, with my plans in order.	Keep my life as flexible as possible so that nothing will be missed.
Prefer to reach conclusions. Use words such as *should* and *ought* liberally, on myself and others.	Prefer to keep things open. Use words such as *perhaps, could be,* and *maybe* in regard to myself and others.
Enjoy finishing things. Desire to be right, to do the right thing.	Enjoy starting things. Desire to have many experiences and miss nothing.
Regiment myself and be purposeful and exacting.	Be tolerant and adaptable.

These are followed by expressions like "what others might say when you've overused your Judging" and "what others might say when you've overused your Perception (5).

You have been given a small sampling of what would be involved in identifying your LIFEType and how it might be useful to you. One of the Psychology in Practice projects at the end of the chapter relates to learning more of this test for understanding yourself and other people of different lifetypes better. An understanding of the combination of these preferences is intended to help one lead a more productive, rewarding life.

Business and industry also use psychological tests for another reason: to make better decisions regarding who should be hired and who should be promoted into supervisory or management positions. Occupational Psychometrics of Minnesota offers testing services that include items relating to general aptitude, emotional stability, motivation, personality factors, work ethics, honesty, and attitudes. This testing service also recommends that job applicants request to see the results of any tests they are asked to take. The *Worklife Career Newsletter* discusses psychological testing of job applicants:

> Many employers and employment agencies use tests to help choose staff. You may think such testing is an unreliable indicator of your real self. Many a good applicant withdraws their application when advised that a series of tests has to be completed. Remember, however, that employers who use tests as part of their selection procedures do so because they consider them important. Nothing will be achieved if you want to work for an employer, yet decline to undertake their tests (6).

Keep in mind that certain types of questions cannot be asked in interviews and job-related psychological tests. These pertain to age, personal or family status, and disabilities, for example. These issues will discussed in Chapter 12.

Many different types of psychological tests have been developed and their use has become more common in recent years. Those who design and interpret such tests should remember that people are unique and complex individuals, not simply a particular personality type.

 What Would You Do? *What would you do if you were asked by a prospective employer to take several tests to be considered for employment?*

DIFFICULT OR DIFFERENT?

It is often difficult for people who are very different in some ways to work together or to live together. They may look upon themselves as *incompatible*—as having personalities that are so much in contrast that they cannot get along with each other. It is questionable, however, whether most problems involving personality clashes arise because of incompatible traits, or because people are unwilling to accept one another as *different*, rather than *difficult*. Bruce and Gary entered a business partnership together but soon found that it was difficult to work with each other. Bruce was a perfectionist, but Gary was more concerned with quantity than quality and didn't give much attention to details. Neither may be the type of person who would be successful in the business; on the other hand, perhaps either of them could be successful alone or with another person with whom he had more in common. As business partners, however, they found that they were incompatible. Perhaps you know of examples of persons who were good friends but found that sharing an apartment or entering a business together did not work.

Other people, however, may only be different; this is not a problem in itself. Association with many different kinds of people makes life interesting and meaningful. Understanding the motives, values, and habits of others leads to tolerance, and tolerance leads to harmony and mutually satisfying relationships. This subject is discussed further in Chapters 6 and 12.

What Would You Suggest? *A friend is looking for someone with whom to share an apartment. She wants to be sure that she and the person are enough alike to avoid major conflicts. She has asked for your advice. What would you suggest?*

HOW DID YOU GET TO BE YOU?

What you are is more important than how you became what you are, but efforts at self-understanding and personality improvement usually include a question such as, How did I become what I am?

IN THE BEGINNING

Your understanding of how you got to be what you are is related to your belief in your origin. Do you believe that you are solely a creature of evolution, or that you are a creature of a supreme being? Charles Darwin's theory of evolution was considered extremely radical in the mid–nineteenth century, when he concluded that higher forms of life evolved from lower forms. However, more and more religions have come to accept the theory of evolution as being compatible with a belief in a divine creator of human beings. Many people rely on their religion to help them understand themselves better as human beings and as individuals.

Are personality traits inherited or do babies develop their traits from the environment?

HEREDITY OR ENVIRONMENT?

If you have some of the same personality traits as your parents, does that mean you inherited them genetically or did you acquire the traits from living with them? If you and your siblings, having the same parents, were raised in the same home, why aren't you more alike? Or did you learn, to some extent, to be the kind of person you are from someone else? And to what extent are you the kind of person *you* decided you wanted to be?

We don't have exact answers to all these questions, but we are learning more about how personality develops and to what extent it can be modified or changed. Because each person is unique and has at least some self-control, attempts to understand personality will always remain somewhat of a mystery and will always be interesting and challenging—and important. Understanding ourselves and others requires basic knowledge of personality and a consistent attempt to understand any particular individual.

There is increasing evidence that numerous personality traits have a genetic origin. This statement does not mean that there is a specific personality gene. It is more likely that several genes from our complex genetic structure are involved. One of the ways that the role of heredity has been studied has been in the comparison of personality characteristics of adult identical twins who were separated at birth or very early in life and grew up in different environments. (These twins were not deliberately separated for purposes of a study, however, because that would have been unethical.) The University of Minnesota has done the most extensive studies of such identical twins to determine what characteristics they have in common, beyond what might be considered coincidence. The results of the studies show that these twins display more similarity in traits than would be found in fraternal twins or siblings (7).

Other studies have shown that persons who were raised in adoptive homes have more personality resemblances to their birth parents than to their adoptive parents. The characteristics that seem to be inborn are often referred to as **temperament.**

Temperament
predetermined ways of reacting to the environment.

There is also evidence that interaction with the world around you, or the environment, affects personality development. S. E. Wood and E. G. Wood go further in explaining the difference between *shared* and *nonshared* environments. They refer to shared environments as "those environmental influences that tend to make family members similar." Nonshared environments are "influences that operate in different ways among children in the same family"(8). The birth order of children in a family, as well as changes in family lifestyles, is believed to affect children's personalities. Numerous other factors within the family, school, and other situations can influence a person's personality development .

What does this mean to you and what you want to do with your life? Very few would take the stand that, I am what I am and there's nothing I can do about it. Studies by Robert R. McCrae and Paul T. Costa, Jr., state that personality traits become relatively stable after the age of thirty, however. Does this mean that a personality is fixed at that point and cannot be changed? Do many people become adjusted to who they are and comfortable with their behavior, and they make no effort to change? It is unlikely that one would want to change his or her personality drastically or would even be successful in doing so, but we should be able to modify behavior related to traits that cause us problems. A person who is naturally aggressive, for example, can learn to use aggression in constructive ways. We should also be able to develop traits, such as tolerance, for example, to improve our relationships with others.

The interaction of the multiple factors influencing personality is expressed by Maureen O'Hara of the Association for Humanistic Psychology as follows:

> Of course we do not start with a blank sheet and we do not work in an empty void. We craft ourselves drawing from the experience we have, the views others have, the symbols, values, stories and patterns of life of our community. Who we become emerges in a conversation between our biological limits and our interactional experiences in specific relationships.
>
> The human self is, then, properly understood as a relational self. We come to frame and to know who we are—what matters to us, what brings us a sense of significance and fulfillment, what we need, what we believe, who we belong to, what we will commit to—in other words where we will draw the boundaries of our identity, within relationships with other people trying to do the same thing (9).

STAGES IN SELF-DEVELOPMENT

Stage
recognizable type of behavior that is characteristic of a fixed period in a process of development.

The individuality of every human being begins at conception and continues throughout life. There would not be much to study on the subject of personality, however, if human beings didn't have similarities as well as differences. Some similarities are basic needs and wants. Others are behavior similarities called stages. A **stage** is a recognizable type of behavior that is typical of a person over a limited period of time. Two-year-olds, for example, are likely to experience a negative stage. If Andy's father tells him to drink his milk, he may push it aside; if his mother tells him to come to her, he may run off in the opposite direction. This is an indication that Andy is developing a mind of his own, a step in the process of becoming an independent person, even though it may be disturbing to his parents.

When children begin to use the words *I* and *me,* self-identity becomes evident. But by the time they start school, they have a distinct image of themselves as individuals. Later, when they experience the physical and emotional changes of puberty during adolescence, they have a stronger need to identify themselves as distinct persons. Rebelliousness in teenagers is not so much psychological warfare with their parents and the world as it is the result of an internal struggle to become independent individuals.

Sally, a high school sophomore, insists on choosing her own friends because she knows whom she likes and she has her own ideas about who is acceptable company. This can be disturbing to parents, who as a result are experiencing less influence, but it is a natural step in self-development. More will be said on this subject in Chapter 13.

SEXUALITY

Sexuality
state or sense of being male or female.

What does it mean to be male or female? How does **sexuality** affect your self-concept? How does it affect your personality and your relationships with others? How does it affect your roles in society and even your opportunities? It is essential to one's identity to consider these questions, even though there may be wide differences in answers to them. We can gain further understanding from Letha Scanzoni in her book *Sexuality*. She says, "Sexuality encompasses so much more than sexual anatomy or sex-role attitudes. It has to do with our entire *being* as body-spirit creatures. It involves our self-image, our body image, our self-esteem" (10).

Unisex
characteristic appropriate for either sex.

The term **unisex,** meaning appropriate for either sex, is used to describe hair fashions, clothing, and numerous other articles and services. However, this classification is limited. Society must still recognize certain male and female differences. At the same time, changing societal attitudes and changing roles have lessened the differences.

Heterosexual
quality of being attracted to persons of the opposite sex.

Most human beings are **heterosexual,** or interested in the opposite sex. Part of the initial attraction is curiosity. Part of this attraction may be the result of hormone reaction; part of it may be perceptual, or what appeals to one's eye. However it is explained, it is unlikely that sexual attraction between opposites will ever be understood completely or will ever disappear from human experience.

Homosexual
quality of being attracted to persons of one's own sex.

A person who is sexually attracted to members of his or her own sex rather than to the opposite sex is **homosexual.** Why are some human beings homosexual? In spite of relatively new scientific evidence, there are still numerous and conflicting reasons given. The recent research shows that there is an actual difference in the brain structure of homosexuals, which appears in the hypothalamus, the part of the brain that regulates heart rate, hunger, sex drive, and sleep. The first evidence of this difference was revealed in studies of the brains of homosexual males (11). This difference in the hypothalamus, however, isn't necessarily the sole cause of homosexuality—still regarded as a very complex human characteristic. Many believe that it is determined by a combination of factors: biological, psychological, and social. It is believed, by most homosexuals as well as many others, that they did not choose their sexual preference. Apart from how they developed the preference, that is their orientation and they want to be accepted for what they are.

Homosexuality has received much attention in recent years. Some of this has resulted from protests both by and against homosexuals. People who are attracted to members of their own sex are beginning to be treated with more acceptance, however. In 1973 the American Psychiatric Association decided to stop classifying homosexuals as sexual deviants in need of treatment. The Association now considers homosexuality to be a "sexual orientation disturbance" which should be treated only if the person desires to change. Most homosexuals concede that they are not average, but they also maintain that they are not abnormal.

It is important that an individual receive some sexuality education in preparation for associations and relationships with others. One major objection to such education in public schools, however, has been that there might be too much emphasis on the biology of sex without enough emphasis on sexuality or the total experience of sexually related behavior.

INTEGRATE: SELF AND PERSONALITY

People play numerous roles in a lifetime, react to other individuals differently, and have conflicting forces within themselves and toward others. Yet they are striving to establish and maintain an integrated self-identity and personality. Although a type of behavior appropriate at a picnic would be different from that appropriate at a formal wedding, a person can act appropriately at each and yet remain unified and stable. A person is an integrated individual if there isn't too much difference between how he perceives himself and how others see him and between both of these and his ideal self, or the kind of person he would like to be.

WATCH THAT ID!

Sigmund Freud, one of the most influential scientists to study human behavior, believed that there are three forces within you that determine what you do. He called these forces the *id, ego,* and *superego.* An interaction of these forces results in what a particular person does or does not do (12).

Id
according to Freud, a person's most basic urges.

Freud explained the **id** as an unconscious force that includes your most basic urges. There are many things you want to have or do. Some of these are things to eat or wear or use or experience. If you were an animal, whose rule of life is survival of the fittest, you would just take what you wanted without regard to moral standards, laws of society, or consideration for other people. What you want might be fruit in the supermarket, a neighbor's new car, or sex experience. The id wants immediate satisfaction.

So what *do* you do? Our crime rates indicate that many people attempt to take what they want regardless of laws, behavior standards, or others' rights. Most people, however, have better self-control. The force that keeps you from having

Superego
according to Freud, judicial force within a person that prevents the id from ruling behavior.

Ego
according to Freud, the kind of person you are and what you do, as a result of the interaction of the id and superego.

your id rule your behavior is your **superego.** This force can be compared to what is called a *personal code of behavior or conscience.* Your id wants something, and your superego may determine that it isn't acceptable—resulting in a conflict. Without ever having studied human behavior, you would be familiar with this type of conflict. You were born with the basic urges that are related to the physiological needs discussed in Chapter 3. An individual develops a conscience or control over behavior, however. It is important to recall that people do control their own behavior and are, therefore, responsible for what they do.

What happens when the id signals "do" and the superego signals "don't"? Some people do; others don't. It depends on the interaction of these personality forces and the degree to which one has developed self-control. What kind of person you are or what you do is what Freud called the **ego.** The interaction of the id and superego results in the development of the ego, or your *self.* This is *you.* As an example, a friend buys camping equipment. Even though it is just what you've been wanting, you neither walk into a store and help yourself to similar equipment nor take away your friend's. Your id wants the equipment, but your superego determines that certain means of acquiring it are not acceptable. Your ego determines to go without the equipment another year until you can afford it.

ONE IS THREE?

Oliver Wendell Holmes, an early American doctor and writer, expressed the theory that whenever two people are engaged in a conversation, there are actually six different individuals involved (13). For example, when John and Thomas have a conversation, it really involves John's John (his self-concept); the real John (known only to his creator); Thomas's John (Thomas's perception of

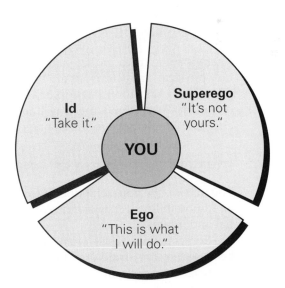

This is a diagram of the Id, Ego, and Superego, according to Freud.

John as a person); as well as the corresponding three Thomases. This makes even a simple conversation a complicated activity. But it also sheds light on why we often misunderstand one another.

In actuality there are as many Johns and Thomases as there are people who know them. But if these images are more or less consistent, the person is probably quite stable. If there is not too much difference between how you see yourself, how you would like to be, and how others see you, you have it together as a person.

PERSONALITY CHANGE

Do you remember this quotation from *Alice in Wonderland*, "I knew who I was when I got up this morning but I must have changed several times since then." This quotation has an element of truth to it. We all change—not only from year to year but even from day to day. Indeed, to develop in any way is to change, and that is a continuous process. Knowing oneself, then, is an ongoing challenge.

Personality change over a period of time can take two courses. Change can just happen as a result of many influences without one's being aware of what is happening. A second way is that changes can be caused, or at least directed, by an evaluation of what one is and through decisions about what one wants to be. Our main concern is with this second type of change.

RESISTANCE TO CHANGE

There is a normal resistance to change that is in conflict with a normal desire for variety, new experience, and personal growth. This resistance is part of psychological self-preservation, similar to physical preservation. A person may not want to make the adjustment to a changed personality characteristic, even if the change is perceived as an improvement. It is often more comfortable in psychological as well as physical respects to stay as one is.

"I've Got to Be Me" is the title of a song that was popular many years ago. There is some truth in that statement; yet it is not entirely accurate. Most hereditary physical characteristics are fixed. Attitudes, values, and personality traits, on the other hand, don't have to be or don't have to remain the way they are. The comment "Well, that's the way I am" is a statement that one does not intend to change, but it is not proof that one cannot change.

EVEN I HAVE FAULTS?

The maxim "Be yourself" doesn't mean that you should remain as you are; that is an impossibility. It means that you should develop according to your own potential and interests.

Some people resist even attempting to see themselves as they really are because they are afraid they will not like what they see. It is more comfortable not to recognize a personal weakness or fault if there is no intention of doing something about it.

The first step in purposeful personality improvement is to analyze your characteristics or traits. You will want to identify what you would consider strengths, but you will also recognize weaknesses, which are the specific targets for change. There are numerous personality self-analysis quizzes that can be interesting and somewhat helpful, but most of them should not be considered complete or entirely accurate.

Phoniness, bluffing, and showing off are often caused by feelings of inferiority. A person who puts on an act to impress people in most cases really feels like a nobody. Trying too hard to be somebody can hinder personality development. One *becomes* a unique personality; one does not acquire a personality.

Just becoming more aware of yourself and your behavior toward others will reveal some weaknesses. Being more observant of other people's reactions to you will also give you clues about whether you are irritating or offending them in some way. However, if you pay too much attention to how other people are reacting to you, rather than paying attention to the other people themselves, you are only adding the fault of excessive self-centeredness. There is no magic formula or instant recipe for personality improvement. Personality growing pains include some frustrations and failings.

MAY I KNOW YOU?

Getting to know and understand others can be even more difficult than understanding yourself. A person who does not open up to other people may be considered unfriendly. Yet the real reason for the person's behavior may be quite different. The word *personality* comes from the Latin word *persona,* meaning "mask." The person who has a sense of personal worth is not fearful of criticism or rejection from others and does not try to hide from others or pretend to be something he or she is not. In his book *Why Am I Afraid to Tell You Who I Am?* John Powell explains that people hesitate to reveal themselves completely to others because they fear they won't be accepted, fearing that "If I tell you who I am, you may not like who I am, and it is all I have" (14). Such hesitancy to remove one's mask, to reveal one's ideas and feeling—both good and bad—keeps people from attaining self-identity and from having meaningful relationships with others.

There are also variations in the way we perceive the personalities of others. We may think that a person is consistently in a good mood and that another person is very moody, with considerable variation in the way he or she feels and

Frank and Ernest

acts from one time to another. We may even be disappointed in ourselves at times, thinking, "Why did I do that? It wasn't like me." We can learn to understand ourselves and others better, and we can sometimes predict what another person will do or say in a given situation. However, we should also expect occasional surprises.

PERSONALITY AND JOB SUCCESS

Various levels of rank and authority exist among employees in job situations. Workers find that some other employees are less experienced than they are and others are old-timers with more experience. Still others have more seniority. And some may not have been with the company as long as they but, at the same time, have more authority and higher pay.

There are many causes of layoffs and unemployment, but more people who are fired or terminated from jobs lose them because of personality characteristics rather than because of inability to do the work. Walter Neff in *Work and Human Behavior* speaks of a "work personality" and describes it as "personal characteristics that the individual brings with him into the work situation—his motives, feelings, attitudes, emotions, preconceptions, and values" (15). Some people refuse to follow instructions or take orders. Others are frequently absent from the job or are continually negligent about safety. Still others may be jealous about any advancement another employee may achieve. The real reasons for losing a job or losing out on a raise or promotion are not always specifically stated, but undesirable personality traits are common causes.

Those who understand themselves and their position at work in relation to others are of value to both themselves and employers. Among the people who are capable at their work, those who can work harmoniously with others and the public come out ahead. Modern career education and job training programs recognize the need for the development of the total person in addition to the acquisition of knowledge and skills.

Some of the personality characteristics generally considered important in job success are the following:

- *Responsibility:* Employers seek and value employees who follow through with what they are expected to do and take proper care of equipment and supplies.
- *Ambition:* Employees not only should be willing to earn their pay, but should also be willing to do whatever is necessary to get a particular job done.
- *Ability to relate well to others on the job:* This includes both coworkers and those in management. It involves interest in others and good communication skills and the ability to work in teams.
- *Presenting a favorable image to the public:* Not all jobs require direct contact with customers, but all employees in some way represent the business or organization to the public.
- *Honesty and loyalty:* These characteristics require an interest in the company and respect for others' rights and their property.

- *Emotional stability:* Employees should be able to accept constructive criticism without getting too upset and should be able to handle frustration without losing their tempers.

The preceding characteristics are important in the job market today, both in getting a job in the first place and in advancing within a business or organization. Job recruiters and personnel directors may have their own ways of evaluating the personality of a job applicant or an employee, but we may be certain that they are concerned with personality as well as career-related qualifications. It may surprise you that some employers not only want qualified, mature, conscientious employees, but they also are interested in whether candidates have a sense of humor. This is often associated with a sense of flexibility and the ability to adjust, which is important in today's world of work. A sense of humor is not the same as goofing off or horsing around, but rather the ability to recognize human weakness in oneself, an occasional harmless error, and the unexpected in situations. Note that several of these personality characteristics considered important to job success are the same as those recommended by SCANS in Workplace Knowhow, discussed in Chapter 1. The importance of personality characteristics will again be emphasized in Chapters 9 and 14.

Summary

Your individuality is a combination of self-concept and personality. Your self-esteem, or sense of self-worth, is also important to your well-being and success in life. Having positive self-esteem can be important in beginning a new job, for example.

Several theories have developed attempts to understand the origin and nature of personality. The major theories are psychodynamic, trait, social-cognitive, and humanistic. The Big Five trait theory is widely recognized today in describing the characteristics of individuals. This theory is based on five factors: emotional stability, extraversion, openness, agreeableness, and conscientiousness.

You can expect that different people who see you in different settings will have different perceptions of you and will describe you somewhat differently.

Several psychological tests have been developed to assist in understanding oneself and others. One of the most popular is the Myers-Briggs test, through which a person can identify his or her LIFEType by determining preferences pertaining to extraversion or introversion, sensing or intuition, thinking or feeling, and judgment or perception.

Our personality and our self-concept are affected substantially by whether we are male or female and by the nature of our sexual attraction to others.

Freud claimed that three factors influence behavior—the id, the unconscious force that includes basic urges; the superego, or the personal code of behavior or conscience; and the ego, or the kind of person you are and what you do, as a result of the interaction of the id and superego.

Increasing evidence shows that both heredity and environment play major roles in the development of personality. Human beings also have the ability to modify or change some traits, or behaviors related to them, that may be causing problems for themselves or others. It is also possible to develop or strengthen traits that will allow you to be more of the person you want to be.

PSYCHOLOGY IN PRACTICE

1. You might expect that friends and acquaintances who know and see you in different situations would describe you somewhat differently. Make a list of the following characteristics and their opposites: talkative or quiet, excitable or calm, forgiving or unforgiving, cautious or careless, trusting or suspicious, humorous or serious, organized or disorganized. You may add to the list if you like. Give a copy to several people who you believe will be honest and ask them to check the characteristics they believe best describe you. Also ask each person describing you to add several characteristics he or she believes describe you. Remember that everyone has both personality strengths and weaknesses. Compare the descriptions, identify what you believe to be weaknesses, and determine how you might modify those characteristics or related behaviors. (If you believe you cannot accept what others may say, do not accept this Psychology in Practice challenge.)

Personality characteristics are important in job success. Employers are looking for more than specific job-related skills in evaluating potential employees and promoting desirable candidates.

One's uniqueness as a person is based on one's particular combination of personality traits, the degree to which one has each trait, and how the trait becomes evident in behavior. You will see a close relationship between personality and the topics in Chapter 3.

Key Terms

Self-concept
Personality
Self-esteem
Role
Psychodynamic theory
Trait theory
Social-cognitive theory
Humanistic theory
Traits
Extravert
Introvert

Intuition
Temperament
Stage
Sexuality
Unisex
Heterosexual
Homosexual
Id
Superego
Ego

Learning Activities

Turn to page LA-5 to complete the Learning Activities and Enrichment Activities for this chapter.

2. We know that people who are different are not necessarily being difficult. Nevertheless, we can sometimes be annoyed by different behaviors. For a week, keep track of things that other people do that annoy you. Determine what you believe to be the reason for your annoyance in each case. Share your findings with a group of two or three students. Discuss reasons for your annoyance, and how you and the others have handled similar situations in the past. Will you do anything differently in the future?

3. Look up additional information on the Myers-Briggs personality test, referred to in the chapter, and find out how a person could take this test to determine his or her combination of preferences. Or, if you prefer, find similar information on some other personality test.

Endnotes

1. T. Berry Brazelton, M. D., "Five Secrets for Self-Esteem," *Family Circle*, February 23, 1993, p. 48.

2. "America Seems to Feel Good About Self-Esteem," *Newsweek*, February 17, 1992, p. 50.

3. Robert R. McCrae and Paul T. Costa, Jr., "Clinical Assessment Can Benefit from Advances in Personality Psychology," *American Psychologist*, September 1986, p. 1002.

4. David G. Myers, *Exploring Psychology*, Worth Publishers, New York, 1996, p. 389.

5. Sandra Hirsh and Jean Kummerow, *LIFETypes*, Warner Books, Inc. New York, 1989, pp. 53–54.

6. "Interview Tip: Psychological Tests," *Worklife Career Newsletter*, Career Development Resources, (http://www.ozemail.com.au/~worklife/news-ltr.html#item2, June 2, 1997, p. 2.

7. T. J. Bonchard et al., "Sources of Human Psychological Differences: The Minnesota Study of Twins Reared Apart," *Science*, October 1990, pp. 223–228.

8. Samuel E. Wood and Ellen Green Wood, *The World of Psychology*, Allyn & Bacon, A Simon & Schuster Co., Needham Heights, MA, p. 461.

9. Maureen O'Hara, "If Not Now, When?" *Vital Speeches*, November 1, 1992, p. 43.

10. Letha D. Scanzoni, *Sexuality*, The Westminster Press, Philadelphia, PA, 1984, p. 13.

11. J. M. Bailey and R. C. Pillard, "The Innateness of Homosexuality," *Harvard Mental Health Letter*, January 1994, pp. 4–6.

12. Sigmund Freud, *New Introductory Lectures on Psychoanalysis*, James Strackey (ed. and trans.), W. W. Norton & Company, Inc., New York, 1964.

13. Oliver W. Holmes, *The Autocrat of the Breakfast Table*, Henry Altemus, Philadelphia, PA, 1899, p. 52.

14. John Powell, *Why Am I Afraid to Tell You Who I Am?* Argus Communications, Chicago, IL, 1969, p. 20.

15. Walter S. Neff, *Work and Human Behavior*, Aldine Publishing Company, New York, 1985, p. 154.

Motives and Values

3

I've never been afraid to fail. I think I'm strong enough as a person to accept failure. But I can't accept not trying.

Michael Jordan

LEARNING OBJECTIVES

After completing this chapter, you should be able to do the following:

1. Identify the four types of motivational conflicts and give an example of each.

2. Explain the psychoanalytic, behavioristic, and humanistic theories.

3. Explain theories X, Y, and Z and how they affect the workplace.

4. Distinguish between physiological needs and psychological wants.

5. Explain Maslow's hierarchy of needs.

6. Differentiate between intrinsic and extrinsic motives.

7. Identify methods of motivating others in a work situation.

8. Describe how one might motivate oneself.

9. Define values and discuss different kinds of values.

10. Identify universal values.

A basic principle of psychology is that behavior is caused—a statement that may raise more questions than it answers. For example, why does one parent desert the family while another works extra hours to provide for the family's needs? Do we personally have different reasons for similar behavior? Is there more than one reason for some particular action? Are you always aware of the reasons for what you do?

BEHAVIOR IS COMPLEX

U nderstanding what motivates people to behave as they do is obviously not simple. Nor are motivations always known or understood even by the persons involved. **Motivation** is a combination of ideas, needs, wants, feelings, or conditions that cause us to act in a certain way. This combination also keeps changing. Is it any wonder that we sometimes think, "Now, why did I do that?"

Motivation
combination of the forces causing a person to act in a particular way.

Each person shares basic needs and many wants with other human beings. If this were not true, we could study human behavior only by examining one individual at a time. We could not set up principles, or general laws, about human behavior. Fortunately, though, we do share common needs and wants. This not only makes it possible for us to study human behavior as a whole, but also makes it easier to satisfy our needs and wants, to understand others, and to share experiences.

Behavior
activity; what a person does.

Human beings sleep, read, work, and mate, as well as engage in many other activities. In fact, **behavior** is anything and everything a person does. Your behavior at any given time may be physical, mental, or emotional, although most actions are a combination of all three.

Overt behavior
activity of an individual that is observable to others.

Covert behavior
activity of an individual, usually mental or emotional, that is not observable to others.

We must be careful not to assume that **overt behavior,** or what can be observed, is the total response. If you were to ask, "What was Roberta's reaction to hearing the news?" and were told, "She got up and walked out of the room," you would have a description of overt behavior. It would be more difficult, but probably more important, to know what Roberta thought and felt. Did she get up and leave because she was offended? Or did she want to use a telephone in the next room? Was she frightened or upset? Or did she leave for some other reason? **Covert behavior,** behavior that is not apparent to the observer, must be considered also in trying to understand the behavior of others.

CAUSE AND EFFECT

The scientific principle of cause and effect applies to human activities. Many misunderstandings about the causes and effects of behavior result from trying to simplify the complex behavior of the highest form of life—the human being. People are naturally curious. We want answers to our questions. We feel more secure when we understand why things happen. We should remember, however, that human behavior is not easily understood.

In earlier times people often accepted false or simple answers to their questions rather than having no answers at all. But as the study of human behavior has become scientific, many false ideas and explanations have been discarded. Except in isolated, technologically undeveloped parts of the world, for example, people no longer believe that thunder and lightning are caused by angry spirits.

Superstition
illogical belief based on ignorance, sometimes related to good or bad luck.

Many early attempts to explain life's occurrences resulted in superstitions. A **superstition** is an illogical belief based on ignorance, sometimes related to good or bad luck. Many superstitions—such as knocking on wood, avoiding black cats that may cross your path, and not opening umbrellas inside a house to prevent bad luck—are recognized as meaningless. Even so, people sometimes still carry them out in a lighthearted way.

Instinct
inborn, unlearned behavior, shared by all members of a species.

Early psychologists explained much of human behavior in terms of instincts. The most famous psychologist to take this view was William James, who is often considered the father of American psychology. An **instinct** is an unlearned or inborn type of behavior shared by all members of a species. The term is applied more accurately to animals than to human beings. For example, animals instinctively prepare for the birth of their young. Some animals instinctively know how to swim. Today the word *instinct* is seldom used to refer to human behavior; and when used, its meaning is usually not literal. For example, one might say that a successful salesperson "instinctively" recognizes a potential buyer. But this ability is not really an instinct, for the salesperson has had to learn to develop the skill.

CONFLICTS

Conflicts
opposing motives or goals.

Since many forces act on us at one time, we often have **conflicts,** or motives that are opposed to one another. You will readily agree that you want some things but do not want others. A conflict arises when things we want and things we don't want come together. You likely also have had the experience of wanting to do two different things, but realizing you could do only one of them.

Such conflicts make choosing necessary. This can often be difficult. You have to decide not only what your needs and wants are but also how important they are. You must be willing to pay the price for what you want; choosing may include time, effort, and money, as well as going without something else. Sometimes you must accept the undesirable along with the desirable. Although it may help in making your decisions to get information and opinions of others, you must remember that what might be an advantage for one person could be a disadvantage for you, or vice versa.

The four basic types of conflicts—approach-approach, approach-avoidance, double approach-avoidance, and avoidance-avoidance are discussed below.

APPROACH-APPROACH The term *approach* means that a person desires an available object or goal. The availability of two desirable goals or courses of action presents an approach-approach conflict. Although either goal is attainable, you cannot have both. A choice must be made between the two. This type of conflict is sometimes referred to as a "can't lose" situation: Whichever choice is made in this type of conflict, the individual gets something that he or she wants. For example, Charles has to decide what to do during his vacation. He has been invited to visit friends in Ohio, where he used to live. He would also like to go camping and sightseeing with a coworker who will be on vacation at the same time. He must choose between the two attractive vacation plans. Betty also has an approach-approach conflict pertaining to her work. She has been offered a job working as a

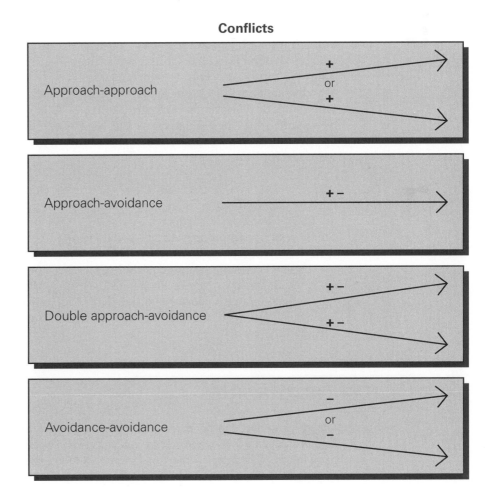

Conflicts

sales representative in an insurance office and also one as an assistant buyer in the housewares department of a large department store. She must decide which of the two available, desirable jobs she would prefer.

APPROACH-AVOIDANCE In an approach-avoidance conflict a person tries to obtain something desirable while avoiding something undesirable that goes with it. It is a case of "take it or leave it," or accepting the undesirable with the desirable, or going without something you want. For example, Randy has been offered a grant to continue his education. He naturally would like to have part of his educational expenses paid, but he doesn't like the condition that, to receive the grant, he must live in a specified housing unit. Becky wants to spend her vacation in a distant state visiting her sister, but she doesn't want to spend the day alone while her sister works. You might be able to suggest some activities for Becky even in a city with which she is unfamiliar. Keep in mind that the undesirable characteristics of conflicts can sometimes be changed. Also, something that might be a major avoidance factor for one person might be considered a minor factor by someone else.

DOUBLE APPROACH-AVOIDANCE Another type of conflict presents two approach-avoidance situations, of the sort described previously in the approach-avoidance conflict. David, a young person who has completed specialized education and is ready to go to work, faces this type of conflict. He has two job offers, both of which have desirable and undesirable features. One job is in a location David likes, but it offers little opportunity for advancement. The other job offers opportunities for growth and advancement, but living expenses in the area are very high. In this type of conflict there are often several advantages and disadvantages to both choices. David must carefully consider his needs and wants and his present and long-range goals. He must evaluate both opportunities to determine which choice offers greater advantages than disadvantages for him.

AVOIDANCE-AVOIDANCE Have you ever felt that you had to choose between two things, neither of which you wanted or wanted to do? This is an avoidance-avoidance conflict. A person in this type of situation may have a "can't win" feeling. For example, a patient may be told by a physician that she must have surgery or live a very restricted life. Neither choice is attractive. Yet one choice is usually less undesirable than the other. It is important not to give up hope in such a situation or get so discouraged that the best decision is not made. Even in an avoidance-avoidance conflict, one choice is usually better than the other. You will see relationships between conflict situations and problem solving in Chapter 7.

HUMAN BEHAVIOR THEORIES

Motivation can be explained according to different basic beliefs or theories. Three of these theories are referred to as psychoanalytic, behavioristic, and humanistic. They are sometimes referred to as the "three forces" of psychology, with humanism, the most recent theory, referred to as the third force. A complementary approach is Douglas McGregor's theory X and theory Y. Each of these theories will be explained further.

PSYCHOANALYTIC THEORY

Psychoanalytic theory
motivation theory that emphasizes unconscious influence on behavior.

The **psychoanalytic theory** is associated primarily with Sigmund Freud and emphasizes unconscious motivation in behavior. You will recall that Freud's ideas about personality based on the id, ego, and superego also involved the unconscious. Freud and others who followed his thinking and work believed that much of human behavior is caused or affected by earlier experiences that were so frightening or otherwise disturbing to individuals that they were unconsciously pushed back into the mind and "forgotten" by the conscious mind. These experiences still continued to affect a person's dreams and behavior, however. Although there is less emphasis on the unconscious in explaining motivation and behavior today, the theory has not been discarded entirely. Dreams are evidence that you have an active unconscious mind. Experiences of which you are no longer consciously aware affect not only your dreams but probably also your motivations and behavior in some ways today.

BEHAVIORISTIC THEORY

Behavioristic theory
motivation theory that emphasizes the influence of the environment and learning on behavior.

Stimulus
anything that excites a need or want within a person producing a reaction or response.

Response
reaction; behavior that results from a specific stimulus.

Behavior modification
approach to improving behavior through a system of rewards or withholding of rewards.

Positive reinforcement
favorable response to behavior; reward.

Negative reinforcement
action that causes an undesirable experience to stop.

Punishment
receiving an undesirable reaction to behavior.

Extinction
elimination of a behavior that is not positively reinforced.

The person primarily associated with the **behavioristic theory** today is B. F. Skinner. This noted psychologist believed that our behavior is determined by our experiences and is controlled by our environment. He referred to this type of cause and effect as the stimulus-response chain (1). A **stimulus** is anything that excites a need or want within a person and therefore causes a reaction, or **response.** The chain is made up of a sequence of stimuli and responses. Each response produces a change in the environment, which then becomes the stimulus for a new response. The continuation of this process results in the chain. When you are introduced to someone by a friend, for example, you say hello or some other appropriate greeting. That person responds to you. This becomes a stimulus to you for further conversation or activity.

You may be familiar with the term **behavior modification.** In very simple terms, the behaviorists say that people do what they do because of what happens to them when they do it. This includes the idea that an individual will continue behavior that provides a favorable response or **positive reinforcement.** We often think of positive reinforcement in terms of reward or satisfaction. Since behavior repeated over a period of time becomes a habit, we can in time influence the development of a favorable trait in an individual.

We should be familiar with several other terms associated with the behavioristic theory. Negative reinforcement is often assumed to mean the opposite of positive reinforcement, or punishment. This is not so, however. **Negative reinforcement** is an action that causes an undesirable experience to stop. If you find that a certain type of situation gives you a headache, and you discover there is something you can do to avoid or change that situation, you will do it.

You are no doubt familiar with the idea of **punishment** as something happening to you that you do not want; therefore, you are likely to avoid the behavior that causes the undesirable reaction. An additional type of stimulus-response basic to behaviorism is **extinction,** which means that a certain type of behavior will cease if there is no favorable response to it. That is why we are sometimes advised to ignore the undesirable behavior of others rather than to try to change it.

HUMANISTIC THEORY

Humanistic theory motivation theory that recognizes some environmental and unconscious influence but emphasizes personal control and responsibility.

Intrinsic motivation causes a person to do something for the experience itself.

Extrinsic motivation causes a person to do something for external reward.

It is generally accepted that we have unconscious influences on our behavior and that we are also affected by our environments and others' reactions to us. Many who study human behavior, however, have found neither the psychoanalytic theory nor the behavioristic theory of motivation to be satisfactory in itself. Even if these two theories were combined, many felt that something essential was missing. Because of this, the **humanistic theory** developed. This theory not only recognizes unconscious and environmental influence, but also emphasizes conscious, personal control over one's own behavior. Abraham Maslow is one of the principal psychologists associated with the humanistic theory. You will learn more about him later in this chapter.

Humanism includes belief in both intrinsic and extrinsic motivation. **Intrinsic motivation** causes a person to do something solely because it is a good experience and gives an individual satisfaction just in the doing of it rather than for some other reason. **Extrinsic motivation** is based on rewards or incentives not directly related to the activity itself.

Let's consider examples of these two types of motivation. Barry is a mechanic because he finds personal satisfaction in that kind of work. He often works on cars for his friends in his spare time, simply because he enjoys doing it. In addition to her job as a middle manager, Brenda reads historical novels because she is interested in changing lifestyles and challenges. Both of these people have intrinsic motivation. On the other hand, Fritz isn't particularly interested in his work as an electrician and therefore works primarily for external rewards, or his paycheck and benefits. All three may do good work and be valued employees, but enjoying one's work is obviously an extra benefit.

Since most of us will have to earn a living, we must be practical and concerned about rewards and benefits for our work and other efforts. The best

Intrinsic and Extrinsic Motivation

Intrinsic Motivation	Satisfying and Stimulating Work
Extrinsic Motivation	Wages and Benefits
Intrinsic and Extrinsic Motivation	Stimulating, Satisfying Work *plus* Wages and Benefits

type of job or other activity, of course, includes both intrinsic and extrinsic motivation. The more reasons we have for doing something, the more motivated we will be.

THEORIES X, Y, AND Z

Douglas McGregor, a professor of industrial management, developed Theory X and Theory Y. Theory X is based on the traditional belief that people don't like to work and would do so only if they are threatened in some way. Management assumes employees would avoid work if possible, and therefore they attempt to control workers and "make them work." **Theory Y** is based on the assumption of natural interest in work as a satisfying experience (2).

Theory Y
based on one assumption and natural interest in work as a satisfying experience.

William Ouchi, who studied both American and Japanese companies, has proposed adding Theory Z to McGregor's X and Y theories. Outstanding features of Theory Z are involvement of employees in group decision-making and long-term employment built on loyalty and trust. Employees typically receive bonuses if the company does well (3).

It isn't likely that any company or business uses any one of the theories exclusively, but there has been a definite move away from Theory X in the world of work. (Herzberg's motivation-maintenance theory and the expectancy theory will be discussed in Chapter 9.)

NEEDS AND WANTS

Many terms are used to refer to the factors that lead people to action. In reading and speaking, we often find the terms *needs, wants,* and *motives* used interchangeably. It is more accurate, however, to say that needs and wants lead to motives and behavior to satisfy them. There are many ways to classify needs and wants. Basic needs can be grouped into just a few broad categories. But lists of a particular person's wants could be very long.

Physiological
pertaining to the functioning of the human biological system.

PHYSIOLOGICAL NEEDS AND DRIVES

Physiological refers to the functioning of the human biological system. The human body must have basic human needs satisfied to function. A **drive** is the urge resulting from a physiological need that causes the individual to seek satisfaction. Human beings have a hunger drive, for example, that is activated when the body needs food. Other human drives involve thirst, sex, and the needs for oxygen, sleep, and pain reduction.

Drive
urge resulting from a physiological imbalance that causes a person to seek satisfaction of a specific need.

Behavioral Chain

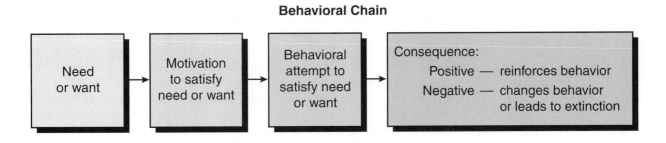

PSYCHOLOGICAL WANTS

Psychological wants
experiences a person
desires for comfort and
happiness.

Strictly speaking, a person has physiological needs for survival as well as **psychological wants** for comfort and happiness. But it isn't always easy to separate a need from a want. Children need love to grow into well-adjusted adults, for example. Studies show that a lack of love and attention can also affect physical development. People also need recognition to motivate them to develop their abilities and to do their best work. Certain things are needed to be comfortable or happy or to achieve another goal. In this respect, today's wants have a way of becoming tomorrow's needs. For example, when electricity first came into use in the home, it was considered a luxury. Now most families think of electricity as a necessity.

What Do You Think? *Can you make a clear distinction between what you need and want? Is it possible for something to be a need to one person but to be only a want to someone else?*

MASLOW'S HIERARCHY OF NEEDS

Hierarchy
grouping persons or
items by order of importance.

Physiological needs
basic requirements for
human survival.

Security or **safety needs**
items or experiences that
give us a sense of security.

Belongingness
feeling included and
involved.

Esteem
self-assurance; feeling of
personal worth.

Self-actualization
the development of one's
abilities and potential.

Abraham Maslow, a pioneer of humanistic psychology, developed a theory concerning a **hierarchy** of basic needs (4). This theory states that humans have needs that have priority, or an order of importance in satisfaction.

According to Maslow, the first human concern is for survival, or satisfaction of **physiological needs.** If necessary, humans would devote all their time and energy to maintaining their very existence. Since it is possible for most of us in today's society to maintain life, or to satisfy physiological needs, without too much difficulty, we soon become concerned with many forms of **security** or **safety needs.** These concerns affect decisions about everything from national defense to personal health. Indeed, there is an almost endless list of items that can be acquired and used to protect ourselves and increase our sense of security.

Maslow believed that **belongingness** and love needs concern an individual only after physiological needs and safety needs are satisfied. However, some of the concern for security also involves our desire to protect our loved ones as well as ourselves. For example, some would risk our lives in an emergency to save others.

Esteem is listed fourth in Maslow's hierarchy of needs. Some people have much more self-esteem, or a feeling of personal worth, than others. Maslow maintained that if people have met their physiological, safety, and belongingness needs, they show more concern for self-esteem. There may be exceptions to this, but it could explain much human behavior. Nearly every large city has a homeless population who barely satisfy their needs for existence, seem to have no sense of belonging, and neither give nor receive love. Can they really be expected to care about self-esteem? If they do not appreciate themselves as persons, they are likely also unconcerned about the disapproval of others.

Self-actualization, or the development of one's potential, is not fully achieved by many people because it is difficult to satisfy the first four levels of needs. It takes both time and effort to satisfy physiological, safety, belongingness, and esteem needs. However, there can be degrees of achievement in self-actualization. A person may develop skill in aviation, electronics, cooking, farming, or whatever, while still not reaching his or her full potential. Self-actualization is achieved only when a person has both the opportunity and desire to develop to the fullest extent possible. Whether or not all other needs must be satisfied before we can achieve self-actualization, it is believed that few people actually become what they might be. This raises questions, of course, about just what a person's potential is. You can gain some understanding of your potential through trial and error, through aptitude and interest tests, and through increased self-knowledge. It is likely that we all have some potential that we will never realize we have or will never develop.

Let's take a look at how Maslow's hierarchy of needs would apply to two young men who are beginning their work careers. Ted and Rob have just graduated from Jefferson Technical College, where they have been friends for two years. They have both been hired by companies in the same town and decide to live together. They were both looking forward to meeting new people, becoming familiar with a new city, and acquiring work experience at their new jobs.

Rob and Ted first sought to satisfy their physiological needs. They use part of their salaries to buy food and pay for a place to live. This attention to physiological or survival needs is often taken for granted. Most of us who are prepared for the world of work can expect to meet our needs.

Next, Ted and Rob turned to their security and safety needs. They have agreed to furnish their apartment with the bare essentials as they have educational loans to pay off, but they want an apartment in what they consider a safe area. They agree to a modest lifestyle so that they can afford such an apartment.

Maslow's Hierarchy of Needs

Hierarchy of Needs from *Motivation and Personality* 3rd edition by Abraham H. Maslow. Copyright © 1954, 1987 by Harper & Row Publishers Inc. Copyright 1970 by Abraham H. Maslow. Reprinted by permission of Addison Wesley Educational Publishers Inc.

They also appreciate being provided with an excellent health insurance package by their respective companies. These factors contribute to their need for safety and security.

Their need for belonging is to some extent satisfied by their friendship. They also have families with whom they will keep in touch, and they expect to become involved in outside activities. They talk about the possibility of meeting people at company-related activities, at places of entertainment around town, and at a local church they are planning to join.

Both Ted and Rob have begun to satisfy their needs for self-esteem. Graduation gave each a sense of accomplishment. Their ability to get good jobs in their fields of study has also contributed to their self-esteem. Their reviews of their interview portfolios, including letters of recommendation from their instructors and others, assures them they are qualified to enter the workforce.

Seeking self-actualization for Ted and Rob, as for all of us, will be a lifetime process. Embracing this process can keep life interesting and challenging. These two young men are confident in themselves and in their potentials, and they are enthusiastic about gaining more experience in the real world of work. They realize they will have to keep up with technological and other changes, but they are looking forward to new experiences and challenges. They are actually a lot like other young people, perhaps very much like you, satisfying their needs at each level of Maslow's hierarchy.

SELF-ACTUALIZING PEOPLE

Maslow and other psychologists have found that certain characteristics are common among people who make the most progress in developing their potential abilities. Such people, for example, are realistic. They are aware of their own abilities, strengths, and weaknesses. Indeed, a person cannot develop an ability until he or she is aware of having that potential.

Self-actualizers also seem to respond quickly and positively to inspiration. They recognize opportunities and make use of them. They are sensitive to their surroundings and have a sense of urgency in responding. People who are not self-actualizers do not experience life in this way.

Another characteristic of self-actualizing people is their concern for problems outside themselves. They are basically unselfish people. Many scientists who have developed cures for diseases have devoted their lives to the service of humanity. Other high achievers can be found in government, education, and other areas of service to society.

Self-actualizers also enjoy a certain amount of privacy, which allows them to pursue their special interests. The development of one's abilities usually involves long hours of hard work or practice. People must usually narrow their interests to develop greater understanding or skill in one area.

These achievers have the further characteristic of appreciating the common, ordinary things of life. This frees them to a large extent from concern with the materialistic world, which could make great demands on their time, energy, and financial resources.

MOTIVATING OTHERS AND YOURSELF

It is difficult to motivate others. How successful has someone else been, for example, in trying to persuade you to do something that you didn't see any reason for doing? Motivating others begins with understanding their needs and wants. Self-motivation is related to personal enjoyment and satisfaction or specific goals that a person believes are attainable. Self-motivation begins with knowing what you want.

MOTIVATING OTHERS

The idea of motivating others is often misunderstood. Some believe that attempting to motivate another person is another form of manipulation. This belief can be disturbing because no one wants to be manipulated or have someone else pull his or her behavioral strings.

Why would one person want to motivate another person anyway? Let's consider some of the situations where motivating another may be for the other person's benefit. Parents, for example, want their children to become responsible, independent individuals, but they must guide them in this process. The behavioristic theory of motivation is widely used in family situations. Parents may reward children for acceptable behavior or performance or punish them in some way if their behavior or performance is unacceptable. Physical punishment is generally undesirable and should be avoided. Withholding a reward or denying an expected privilege can be a more effective form of punishment. The humanistic approach, or encouraging others to develop their potential, can also be

Do you consider it someone's responsibility to motivate you, or are you self-motivated?

effective in families. Much of this type of motivation may be by example. Parents as role models will be discussed in Chapter 6.

Instructors also attempt to motivate students to do their best in their preparation for satisfying and productive lives. This kind of motivation is certainly for the benefit of the students and society. Coaches and leaders of various groups consider motivating others an important aspect of their roles. More on leadership will be discussed in Chapters 9 and 14.

In many cases when one person is trying to motivate another to do something, it is for their mutual benefit. A business benefits from productive employees. In most situations employees benefit as well. Rewards may not always be immediate or they may not be extrinsic in terms of specific material rewards, but productive workers benefit in the long run. James D. Bell, an associate dean at Texas State University advises in a speech entitled "Working and Living," "Don't expect instant recognition or instant reward. And don't necessarily leave your employment because people do not seem to notice. Life is a marathon, not a 100 yard dash. Expect that persistence and commitment will lead to recognition and reward" (5).

Since work takes up so much of our lives, it is important to understand how motivation affects work. One of today's incentives for employees is performance pay. In *Maximizing Employee Productivity*, Robert E. Sibson indicates that there must be a clear definition of performance. His definition is: "Pay for performance means more pay for better performance on an assigned job. Everyone should be expected to perform to standard and acceptable levels of work after they have training and the required experience. That level of performance gets market pay. Performance above standard gets higher pay" (6). Numerous other work incentives, however, are both extrinsic, such as performance pay, and intrinsic, such as interesting, meaningful work.

Ranking the following list of work-related factors from 1 to 12 (1 for most important) can help you determine your priorities in a job.

There is no correct way to rank the items because the values of individuals will differ, and priorities may change from one time to another. It is unlikely that job security would be rated number 1 by everyone in your group or class. During

---

Rank Your Work Priorities

Rank

Good pay _____

Opportunities for performance bonuses _____

Good fringe benefits _____

Job security _____

Interesting, meaningful work _____

Opportunity to develop new abilities _____

Opportunity to contribute to decisions _____

Up-to-date, adequate equipment and materials _____

Recognition for work well done _____

Opportunity for advancement _____

Effective communication with management _____

Day care _____

---

periods of heavy unemployment or serious problems within a particular business or industry, however, job security may become the primary concern of all employees.

We can motivate others if we can show them how to satisfy their needs and wants. Consciously or unconsciously, we are all constantly attempting to satisfy our own needs and wants, but we may not always know what another person's needs or wants and values are, or the person may not always be aware of his or her needs and wants. Determining the needs, wants, and values of potential customers and then showing those customers how they can be satisfied through the purchase of a product or service is a major factor in marketing and advertising. Companies spend millions of dollars each year on customer and product research to learn how to satisfy the needs and wants of their potential customers.

It is difficult in all areas of business and life to know what another's needs, wants, and values are. Our reasons are not always selfish. A person may want what is best for one's family or for society as a whole, for example. In their book, *Thank God It's Monday!*, Kenneth Cloke and Joan Goldsmith see motivation to work this way: "We believe we all need meaningful work in our lives, as a way of bringing our talents, skills, and abilities to higher levels of perfection and as a way of giving something back to the people and the society we live in" (7).

 What Do You Think? *Can you think of any reason why some people might not be interested in employment that offered extra pay for performance?*

SELF-MOTIVATION

Do you consider it someone's responsibility to motivate you? Is it enough for you to go to class or to your job and to wait for someone there to motivate you? If you are like most people, the answer is probably no. If you understand your needs and wants and they are important enough to you, you are self-motivated.

© Universal Press Syndicate, Inc.

Most of us assume the primary responsibility for finding how to satisfy our needs and wants. And this can be done when external conditions are less than desirable.

This person is self-motivated. His own drive to succeed compels him to work hard in his chosen career in electronics.

Denis Waitley, author of *Psychology of Success,* tells us, "It has often been thought that motivation, like gasoline to a car, can be pumped in from the outside through pep talks, rallies, or sermons. These can provide encouragement or inspiration for a person to act, but the person has to have the *desire.* Lasting change can happen only when the individual understands and feels the need inside. The person must want the reward in order to be motivated" (8).

If you don't think you have made enough progress toward your goals, it might be a good idea to examine the reasons. Do you know what you really want? This does not mean that you will never change your mind, but it does mean that you have a realistic understanding of yourself, your potential, and your opportunities and that you do have some goals. What factors have stood in your way thus far? What are you willing to do or give up to obtain what you want? You must keep in mind the choices to be made because of the type of conflicts discussed earlier. To become more self-motivated, follow this basic formula:

1. Decide what you want to do or achieve.
2. Find out what you have to do (with respect to education, experience, financial planning, or whatever).
3. Determine what you have to do without, or what you have to give up, to accomplish your goal.
4. Begin, or take the first step toward achieving your goal.

Deciding on a goal may take a great deal of thought and investigation. There may be many steps along the way. These steps become subgoals that have their own order of priority. But once you are self-motivated—once you have decided that what you want is worth the cost in terms of time, money, and effort—you will have little difficulty in taking those first steps.

Willpower
determination to establish and observe priorities in situations involving motivational conflicts.

Many people think of their own motivation in terms of **willpower.** Have you ever really thought about what willpower is? Do you have willpower to do one thing but not to do something else? Do you have more willpower than you used to have? Does someone else have more willpower than you do? You can probably understand why willpower has also been referred to by some as "won't" power.

The best way to increase your willpower is to decide what you really want. It is less humiliating to admit, "I just don't have any willpower," than it is to say, "I wish I could make up my mind about which of these conflicting things I really

© *Universal Press Syndicate, Inc.*

want." But both statements have almost the same meaning. What you want must also be a realistic goal. The goal need not be easy, but you must believe that it is possible for you to attain it.

We must also lead a healthy life so that we have the physical energy to work toward achieving a goal, but many people have shown that they can accomplish more when they are enthusiastic and confident about the success of a project.

What Would You Do?   *What would you do if you wanted to maintain a productive working relationship with a coworker, but you felt that the person was trying to manipulate you?*

CONTROL OR INFLUENCE?

People control their own behavior (unless, of course, they are under the influence of drugs or hypnosis). It is very rare for one person to be able to control another. In most cases adults are responsible for their own actions.

VALUES

From our discussion of motivation thus far, you can gain some idea of how complex human behavior is. We have also recognized that we cannot have everything we want or avoid everything we do not enjoy. It is also apparent that

Motives and Values   **61**

there are some things we want to *be* and there are some things we want to *have,* or possess.

Value
worth of something to an individual or a group.

The degree to which a person wants something is its **value.** You read earlier in this chapter that security is a basic need. Although everyone wants some sense of security, it is clearly more important or more valuable to some people than to others. And even people who value security highly do not agree about what makes them feel secure. For some, security may relate mostly to money. For others, security may involve close family relationships, education, or religion. Many people want all these types of security. For them, the order of importance is itself a matter of values. The extent to which values may differ is shown by the following:

> Two women were visiting a small village in a developing country where medical help was not available. There they saw a missionary washing the body of a leper. One woman turned to her companion and said, "I wouldn't do that for a million dollars." The missionary looked at the woman with a calm expression and replied, "Neither would I."

CLARIFYING VALUES

Values clarification
attempt to understand one's values and their relative importance to oneself.

Values clarification is an attempt to understand our values and their relative importance to us. This attempt at understanding can help us examine our behavior and decide whether what we do is consistent with what we say is important to us. Many people say that something has great value for them, but their behavior does not bear that out. For example, most people would put their health high on a list of values, yet they continue to do many things that are harmful to their health. People who do not have a clear sense of their values are often confused and purposeless and, therefore, not self-motivated. You should also keep in mind that you have somewhat different values at different times in your life. Parents may have some values that their children do not have, for example. You can gain a better understanding of your own values by ranking those on page 63 according to their importance to you. The one that is most important should be ranked 1, and so on.

KINDS OF VALUES

Tangible
real, material, or perceptible.

You may have noted that the values listed are not things that can be purchased, although they may involve such items. A material object that can be touched, and often purchased, has a **tangible** value. Tangible objects are of value to us to the extent that they satisfy our needs or wants. Al may be looking at fishing equipment, a piano, and a typewriter. The monetary value of these objects depends on their price tags, but their value to Al is determined by his needs and wants. In the same way, a glass of water may have great value to someone who has had nothing to drink for two days. Marlene may put great value on her watch, even though it wasn't expensive. And a painting, which has little practical use, may be prized highly by someone interested in art. People may be willing to work or save a long time to obtain the tangible things they value highly. Or they may value an object only for its resale value to obtain something else that they need or want.

Rank Your Personal Values

Rank

A comfortable life (a prosperous life) _____

Equality (brotherhood, equal opportunity for all) _____

An exciting life (a stimulating, active life) _____

Family security (taking care of loved ones) _____

Freedom (independence, free choice) _____

Happiness (contentedness) _____

Inner harmony (freedom from inner conflict) _____

Mature love (sexual and spiritual intimacy) _____

National security (protection from attack) _____

Pleasure (an enjoyable, leisurely life) _____

Salvation (eternal life) _____

Self-respect (self-esteem) _____

A sense of accomplishment (making a lasting contribution) _____

Social recognition (respect, admiration) _____

True friendship (close companionship) _____

Wisdom (a mature understanding of life) _____

A world at peace (freedom from war and conflict) _____

A world of beauty (beauty of nature and the arts) _____

Intangible
having no material or perceivable characteristics.

Many other values in life are **intangible;** that is, they are not material. Examples of intangible values include freedom, beauty, love, respect, and morality. You may have heard people say, "The best things in life are free." The list of values that you were asked to rank contained many intangible values.

Everyone has both tangible and intangible values. Some people, however, may be interested mostly in acquiring possessions. Others may direct their lives toward acquiring knowledge, happiness, or some other intangible value.

According to Milton Rokeach, values also may be classified as being either terminal or instrumental. *Terminal* values are "desirable endstates of existence that people strive for". Examples include a world at peace, equality, brotherhood, eternal salvation, mature love, inner harmony, and a comfortable life. *Instrumental* values, on the other hand, pertain to "desirable modes of conduct," such as honesty, forgiveness, independence, and competence (10).

INFLUENCES ON VALUES

Many influences begin to interact in the development of a person's values early in life. These include family, friends, religion, school and textbooks, entertainment, and the media. To some extent, values are generational or attributed to a particular age group. You may be part of what is referred to as Generation X—those born between 1965 and 1977. The use of the term came from Douglas Copeland's 1991 novel, *Generation X.* Today, this group is in their twenties and thirties. If you do not belong to this generation you may be a baby boomer or a mature. Margot Hornblower in *Time* refers to

Generation X and the two preceding it as, Boomers, Matures, and Xers. Her article states: "A generation is forged through common experience. The cohort described as 'matures,' born from 1909 to 1945, was shaped by the Depression and World War II. 'Boomers,' born from 1946 to 1964, grew up in affluence: economic progress was assumed, freeing them to focus on idealism and personal growth. Young Xers, however, lurched through the recessions of the early 80s, only to see the mid-decade glitz dissipate in the 1987 stock market crash and the recession of 1990–1991" (11).

Identified values of generations depend on who is describing them. The young at any time are more idealistic, restless, and adventurous than their parents. Baby boomers are probably more interested in security and more appreciative of the values of education today than they were when they were in their twenties. Generation Xers are described as disoriented, cynical, and irresponsible by some and as optimistic, tolerant, and peace-seeking by others.

Our values change somewhat as we become adults, become independent, and become parents, or as a result of other important changes in our lives. Differences in values can result in communication problems and can interfere with family relations, work, education, and society.

We would probably agree that we would like to have our values understood by others; this preference suggests that we should also try to understand their values. The least one can do is at times to say in effect, "That is not important to me, but I recognize that it is important to you. I don't even understand why it is important to you, but I believe that it *is* important to you."

Besides the many forces we have already considered, other factors can influence your values. Advertisers try to influence you to value or want their products more than a competitor's products. Society at large (which is often referred to as "they") also influences you. Consider how easily new styles and fads are accepted. Even people who are confident that their values are independent are influenced by what others currently accept and value.

Regardless of what our values are or how they have developed, our values are our own. Others use various types of influence to try to get us to change our behavior, but they cannot control our values, or what is most important to us. A distinction between external influence and individual choice is expressed by Richard Thornburgh, former Attorney General of the United States. He explains,

> Sometimes we think of laws and values as the same. They're related, but they're not the same. We establish laws to codify certain rules and standards that allow us to live together as peaceful people. But it's our values that inspire our laws—not laws that establish our values. Laws tell us what we *must* do. Values summon us to what we *should* do (12).

Although values do not change easily or readily, our values do change somewhat as we progress in life, as was indicated earlier. In fact, not only do individual values change, but the values of society as a whole change with the times.

We will find that when we are enthusiastic and confident but still realistic about projects and goals, we are more likely to experience success. You will recall that we considered the need for balance in our lives in Chapter 1. Claudette MacKay-Lassonde relates to this in stating: "I think balance is the key to personal fulfillment. Having it all is a vague and ultimately meaningless goal. You have to decide what is most important to you, accept the costs, and go after it. Realize that you can't have it all. But you can have what you value most" (13).

UNIVERSAL VALUES

Several values are common to people in most parts of the world. These are referred to by Rushworth M. Kidder as *universal human values:* "Interviews with two dozen 'men and women of conscience' reveal eight common values that can guide a troubled world through a tumultuous future." He identifies these values as love, truthfulness, fairness, freedom, unity, tolerance, responsibility, and respect for life (14).

The more self-confident you are and the better you understand yourself and know your priorities, the easier it will be to live and work by your values—as long as they do not interfere with the values of others.

Summary

Motivation is a combination of internal and external forces that cause individuals to act as they do. Although all behavior is motivated or caused, behavior is extremely complex. Not all elements of the cause-and-effect relationship can be known, even by the individual.

Three human behavior theories are commonly used to explain motivation: behavioristic, psychoanalytic, and humanistic. Behaviorism emphasizes the effects of environment, psychoanalytic theory emphasizes unconscious motivation, and humanism recognizes environmental and unconscious influence but emphasizes conscious decision making and self-control.

Theories X, Y, and Z offer approaches to behavior at work. According to McGregor, Theory X is based on the assumption that humans will avoid work, if possible. Theory Y is based on an assumption of natural interest in work as a satisfying experience. More recently, Ouchi has added Theory Z. Theory Z emphasizes worker involvement in decisions and long-term employment as important motivating factors.

There are many ways to classify motivational forces. At the simplest level, people have physiological needs and psychological wants. A more complex classification is found in Maslow's hierarchy of needs, which states that people have needs of various degrees of importance. In this theory, physiological needs or survival are most important, followed by safety, belongingness and love, esteem, and self-actualization. Self-actualization needs are met only after the other four needs are satisfied.

We also face motivational conflicts in life; that is, we want some things and experiences but want to avoid others. The four basic types of conflicts are approach-approach, approach-avoidance, double approach-avoidance, and avoidance-avoidance. An understanding of these four types of conflicts can help a person make better decisions in life.

PSYCHOLOGY IN PRACTICE

1. Identify a person you believe to be a self-actualizer. Ask that person to share with you experiences in developing his or her potential. Also ask the person about any failures or major disappointments and how he or she reacted to them.

2. Look up additional information on behavior modification and how it is used today to change the behavior of individuals. Compare your findings and your points of agreement or disagreement on its effectiveness with two other members of your class. You might want to share your discussion with the class.

3. Attempt to determine the major influences in the development of your present values. Ask yourself whether you believe all the influences have been positive ones. Think about how you might avoid negative influences on your values in the future.

Understanding both self-motivation and the motivation of others helps us understand behavior. Employers, for example, value self-motivation but are also concerned with how to motivate their employees to work productively. It is widely believed that people can control their own behavior but can only influence the behavior of others.

Values clarification is an attempt to understand one's values and their relative importance. Values can be classified as being tangible or intangible and as terminal or instrumental.

The values of individuals and even of societies change somewhat over time. Nonetheless, there are universal human values.

The needs and values of individuals affect how they perceive their environment, other people, and experiences. An understanding of the needs and values of others can help you appreciate their point of view. Factors that affect perception and the principles of perception, presented in Chapter 4, will provide insight into the relationship between motivation and perception.

Key Terms

Motivation
Behavior
Overt behavior
Covert behavior
Superstition
Instinct
Conflicts
Psychoanalytic theory
Behavioristic theory
Stimulus
Response
Behavior modification
Positive reinforcement
Negative reinforcement
Punishment
Extinction
Humanistic theory

Intrinsic motivation
Extrinsic motivation
Physiological
Drive
Psychological wants
Hierarchy
Physiological needs
Security or safety needs
Belongingness
Esteem
Self-actualization
Willpower
Value
Values clarification
Tangible
Intangible

Learning Activities

Turn to page LA-9 to complete the Learning Activities and Enrichment Activities for this chapter.

Endnotes

1. B. F. Skinner, *The Behavior of Organisms,* Appleton-Century-Crofts, Inc., New York, 1938, p. 32.

2. Douglas McGregor, *The Human Side of Enterprise,* McGraw-Hill, New York, 1960.

3. William Ouchi, "William Ouchi on Trust," *Training and Developmental Journal,* December 1982, p. 71.

4. Abraham H. Maslow, *Motivation and Personality,* 2d ed., Harper & Row, New York, 1970, p. 35. By permission of Harper & Row, Publishers, Incorporated.

5. James D. Bell, "Working and Living," *Vital Speeches,* April 17, 1997, p. 413.

6. Robert E. Sibson, *Maximizing Employee Productivity,* AMACOM, New York, 1994, p. 163.

7. Kenneth Cloke and Joan Goldsmith, *Thank God It's Monday!,* Irvin Professional Building, Chicago, IL, 1997, p. 215.

8. Denis Waitley, *Psychology of Success,* Irvin Career Education Division, Chicago, IL, 1997, p. 144.

9. Sidney B. Simon, Leland W. Howe, and Howard Kirschenbaum, *Values Clarification,* Hart Publishing Company, Inc., New York, 1972, pp. 113–114.

10. Milton Rokeach, *The Nature of Human Values,* Free Press, New York, 1973, p. 7.

11. Margot Hornblower, "GREAT Xpectations," *Time,* June 9, 1997, p. 60.

12. Richard Thornburgh, "Law and Values in a Changing World," *Vital Speeches,* January 15, 1991, p. 205.

13. Claudette MacKay-Lassonde, "Let's Stop Fooling Ourselves," *Vital Speeches,* July 1, 1996, p. 571.

14. Rushworth M. Kidder, "Universal Human Values: Finding an Ethical Common Ground," *The Futurist,* July–August 1994, pp. 8–13.

Senses and Perception

4

Some things have to be believed to be seen.

Ralph Hodgson

LEARNING OBJECTIVES

After completing this chapter, you should be able to do the following:

1. Explain the role of interpretation in perception.
2. Give examples of the factors of perception.
3. Identify the function of exterior senses in our lives.
4. Give examples of the principles of perception.
5. Discuss perceptual preferences in learning styles.
6. Discuss learning disabilities as they relate to perceptual differences.
7. Give examples of other senses, including interior senses.
8. Explain and give an example of illusion.
9. State an argument for or against parapsychology.
10. Describe how you can expand your world through ordinary perceptual experiences.

If you were to describe your experiences so far today, to what extent would they involve your senses? Did you hear an alarm go off? Did you taste a fruit juice? Did you smell coffee? Did you listen to a weather forecast or relax to music as you started your day? All our waking experiences involve the use of our senses. Not only our sense organs, but our whole nervous system is involved in such experiences. Most of these perceptual experiences are so ordinary that we do not give them a second thought. A thorough understanding of sensory perception, on the other hand, can be very complex. The actual functioning of the eye and ear, for example, is understood only by specialists. The purpose of this chapter is to understand better the role of perception in our lives and the lives of others, to protect ourselves from perceptual hazards, and to learn to use and appreciate our senses more fully.

Perception
awareness through the senses and one's personal interpretation.

Perception is awareness through the senses followed by interpretation by the individual. The last part of this definition—*interpretation by the individual*—is important to our understanding of perception in this chapter. In a way, each of us lives in his or her own perceptual world. Although we may be surrounded by the same environment, eat the same food, or hear the same sounds and messages, all these experiences will have a somewhat different meaning for each of us. A rainy day can have various interpretations, depending on whether one is a farmer whose crops need rain, a letter carrier who must deliver the mail regardless of the weather, or a family planning a picnic.

FACTORS THAT AFFECT PERCEPTION

Numerous factors are responsible for differences in perception. Apply them to your own experience as they are discussed here.

PHYSICAL ABILITIES AND LIMITATIONS

The abilities or limitations of the sense organs can affect perception temporarily or permanently. What you perceive depends, first of all, on what you are capable of perceiving. Some examples of physical limitations are given below.

This child is relying on her sense of smell to discover her world. She is smelling the flowers. Will she stop to smell the roses as she journeys through life?

IMPAIRED HEARING You may hear inaccurately or may fail to hear something that is said because you are deaf or have hearing damage or impairment. Some people have been deaf since birth; others have become hard of hearing because of exposure to noise or because of age. Some hearing problems may be temporary due to a blockage or an infection. Other problems can be reduced with a hearing aid. Persons who are deaf or hard of hearing can learn to communicate in different ways. These include several types of "total communication," including signs to indicate whole words, ideas, and feelings. Advances in signing techniques and other technological improvements have allowed them to lead full and satisfying lives.

COLOR BLINDNESS It may be difficult to know whether you are perceiving the world around you in the same way that others are. Many people go through most of their lives without realizing they are color blind. They may discover during testing for a driver's license or military service that they have this limitation. A person who is color blind sees differentiations in colors but does not perceive colors in the way most people do.

VISUAL IMPAIRMENT OR BLINDNESS Most people rely on their sense of sight more than any other sense. Those who are visually impaired or blind must rely on other senses to give them information about their world. Technological advances have provided many visually impaired people with the opportunity to use computers in their personal lives and work, however. Computers of the future may be able to see their users and listen to their commands. Advancements in laser technology are also used in surgery to restore or improve the sight of many persons with impaired vision.

ILLNESS A temporary change caused by the flu, a virus, or another physical condition can affect all the other senses. Eyes may become more sensitive to light; the sense of hearing, taste, or smell may be dulled because of a cold; muscles may ache or skin may feel unusually hot or cold. You probably have had most of these experiences.

NUMBNESS FROM COLD TEMPERATURES When your blood does not circulate properly, your sense of touch or feeling is temporarily affected. If you live in a climate where the temperature falls below zero, you are familiar with the numbness of your hands and feet that results from being exposed to cold temperatures. You may temporarily lose feeling in your fingers and toes.

SENSITIVITY TO STIMULI Some people are more sensitive to tones than others are. Perhaps you can hear high notes that others do not detect. Other people may be more irritated by certain types of noise than you would be. Some people are able to identify differences in the tastes of cheeses and wines much better than others. Still others are more sensitive to changes in temperature or pressure. Each of us has a range of sensitivity to stimuli, which can be an advantage or disadvantage depending on the circumstances and our purposes. It may be desirable for us to learn to appreciate eating cereal with less or no sugar, for example, but it may be a disadvantage not to be able to detect contamination of food.

ENVIRONMENTAL CONDITIONS

Not only your sensory abilities but also environmental conditions affect your perception. It is usually the total effect of all environmental conditions, rather than a single stimulus, that affects perception. A few examples of such factors are briefly discussed here.

LIGHTING—INTENSITY AND COLOR Artificial lighting at night, of course, affects what you can see, but types of lighting have different effects. Color is also a factor in total sensory response. For example, a color used as a background can alter the appearance of another color placed in the foreground. One color can appear quite different on different people, depending on the color of their skin, eyes, and hair. Also, our color preferences affect our reaction to foods. Is it possible that you do not like a certain food partially because of its color?

GLARE OF LIGHTS AND THE SUN The glare of the lights of an oncoming car can be temporarily blinding and extremely hazardous. For this reason most people who drive are careful to dim their lights when meeting another vehicle at night. Another example of glare is the sun shining on a lake or on snow, causing discomfort unless you are wearing dark glasses.

FOG AND SMOKE AND STORMS Environmental conditions can also be hazardous, especially at night when ordinary visibility is reduced. It can be a rather eerie feeling to be closed in by fog or smoke, which drastically limits your ability to see and therefore to function normally. Sandstorms, snowstorms, and blinding rain can also be treacherous, and caution warnings should be heeded. One's own judgment must also be a factor.

DISTRACTING NOISES As mentioned in the discussion of the sense of hearing, a particular sound may be a distracting noise to you but not to someone else. Or the same sound may be disturbing or pleasing to you, depending on how you interpret its meaning or what else you are attempting to do at the

Environmental conditions, such as fog, smog, and smoke, can reduce our ability to see and react.

time. Even a favorite television program can be disturbing, for example, if someone else is watching it when you are trying to study for a test or concentrate on a project. Other distracting noises can block out sound. For instance, you may not hear the doorbell or telephone if the volume of your stereo is high.

SETTING OR BACKGROUND An important factor in a photograph is the appearance of the main subject against the setting or background. What is not noticed at the time the picture was taken may become conspicuous later. Perhaps you have heard someone say, "Why didn't I close that closet door?" or "Why didn't I move that old wagon?" Other settings can improve the appearance of something or how it is perceived. For example, the backyard can either add to or detract from the appearance of a house. Background is also an important factor in advertising, where it can be used to make a product or service look desirable.

PAST EXPERIENCE

Your perception is also influenced greatly by your past experience. Recognizing an object can give meaning to something you have never seen before. And whether you immediately like or dislike something or someone can be closely related to your past experience. Although our earlier experiences can give us guidelines for reacting appropriately in new situations, they can also interfere with our evaluating a new situation objectively.

RECOGNITION OF THE FAMILIAR Recognition of what is familiar is a factor affecting how you perceive and how you react to what you perceive. Although the idea is interesting, it could be extremely frustrating if we awoke to a new world every day. You know the way to school or work, what kind of car your friend drives, and where to look for particular items in a store. When you meet a particular animal or person, you may react appropriately with joy, fright, or unconcern. Because of recognition and interpretation of the familiar, much of the activity of our lives becomes simplified and routine and we can concentrate on what is immediately important to us.

ASSOCIATION OF NEW STIMULI WITH THE FAMILIAR If you had never seen or used an electric toaster, it isn't likely that you would recognize one. But knowing what a toaster is, you are likely to associate even the most modern models with your concept of this appliance. This kind of association also works in recognizing what is old because of some similarities to what is new. If you visited a museum and saw a toaster from the 1700s, you would probably recognize it as a device for toasting bread. We form opinions or expectations in new situations by this type of association with what is familiar. If we let a single characteristic form the basis for our reaction, however, this type of association can be harmful. We might assume that a particular person is honest, for example, because she has a resemblance to a person whom we trust, but we may find out that she is dishonest in actual experience.

ASSOCIATION WITH ESTABLISHED LIKES AND DISLIKES During your lifetime thus far, you have developed many likes and dislikes. You may like the color green and dislike purple without being able to explain why. In some cases, at least, such responses are associated with pleasant and unpleasant experiences. If you had to wear a purple jacket that you didn't like for two years, you might have developed a dislike for that color. Or you may meet a person for the first time and immediately like that person for no particular reason of which you are aware. In many such cases you may be making an unconscious association of this individual with someone else you have liked and admired.

SET: NEEDS AND WANTS

Set
predisposition to act a certain way.

Certain perceptual experiences are influenced by what you expect, or are **set** to perceive. What you focus your senses on in the vast perceptual world is also determined by your particular needs and wants.

Frank and Ernest

© 1996 Used with permission of Bob Thaves.

EXPECTATIONS You often see or perceive what you expect to perceive. If someone says to you, "Sit in this chair and just see if it isn't the most comfortable chair you have ever sat in," you anticipate a particular type of experience. You are more likely to feel relaxed than if you had not been told what to expect.

IMMEDIATE NEEDS AND WANTS Another type of set perception pertains to your needs and wants. If you want a new car, you notice cars on the sale lots, on the highway, and in parking lots more than you ordinarily would. If you are thirsty, you may notice a drinking fountain in a park before you become aware of anything else. We have the ability to concentrate on what might satisfy an immediate need, ignoring a lot that would ordinarily come to our attention.

BELIEFS, PREJUDICES, AND VALUES When you meet someone, you may pay more attention to what that person is saying and perceive him or her as an acceptable person if both of you are of the same religion or have similar values. On the other hand, prejudice may be aroused by another characteristic about which you are biased.

ATTENTION FACTORS

Several factors are known to gain and hold attention and are therefore used extensively in advertising and display. They can also be used effectively in talking to a group or in other situations when we desire the attention of others. These are change, repetition, intensity, contrast, and novelty.

CHANGE Lights that flash off and on, for example, capture our attention better than a light that remains on continuously. You will notice a change in the sound of an engine or a signal more than if it maintains the same sound you generally hear.

REPETITION The element of repetition is evident in many television commercials and other types of advertising. Key phrases and the name of the product are repeated numerous times to gain attention and make an impression. We respond to this type of exposure to sights and sounds more than most of us realize.

INTENSITY Intensity is a factor in several types of perception. A sound that one might not pay attention to is made louder; a smell that might go unnoticed is made stronger. We may tolerate a certain degree of pain, but a sudden stabbing pain will usually cause a noticeable reaction.

CONTRAST The factor of contrast is widely used in advertising and in window displays. Dark velvet is frequently used as a background for jewelry because the contrast makes the jewelry look brighter and thus more attractive.

NOVELTY Novelty has always been an effective attention-getter with curious human beings. There are always customers to hear, taste, and see the new and different. Promotion people in every business search constantly for ways to use this attention factor to their advantage.

What Are Your Answers?

1. Divide 24 by $\frac{1}{2}$ and add 16. What is your answer? _____
2. How many animals of each species did Moses have on the ark? _____
3. Take $7 away from $20. How many dollars do you have? _____

Answers are on page 91.

EXTERIOR SENSES

Exterior senses
sight, hearing, touch, taste, and smell; senses that give us information about the outside world.

Interior senses
senses that give us the sensations of hunger, fatigue, and muscle tension.

Sight, hearing, touch, taste, and smell are referred to as the **exterior senses** because they give us information about the outside world. Receptors of these sense organs react to energy in the environment and send signals through the nervous system to the brain. Our **interior senses** give us the sensations of hunger, fatigue, and muscle tension. We already know a lot about our senses from our experiences in living, but there is probably still much more that we may never know. An article by Shannon Brownlee entitled "The Senses" in *U.S. News & World Report* states,

> The human senses detect only a fraction of reality: We can't see the ultraviolet markers that guide a honeybee to nectar; we can't hear most of the noises emitted by a dolphin. In this way, the senses define the boundaries of mental awareness. But the brain also defines the limits of what we perceive. Human beings see, feel, taste, touch and smell not the world around them but a version of the world, one their brains have concocted. "People imagine that they're seeing what's really there, but they're not," says neuroscientist John Maunsell of Baylor College of Medicine in Houston. The eyes take in the light reflecting off objects around us, but the brain only pays attention to part of the scene. Looking for a pen on a messy desk, for example, you can scan the surface without noticing the papers scattered across it (1).

Absolute threshold
smallest amount of stimuli that one can detect about half of the time.

We are also aware of our limitations in our abilities to perceive. There is a limit to how far we can see, for example. The smallest amount of stimuli that one can detect, about half of the time, is known as one's **absolute threshold.** This threshold varies with each sense. A person may have a more acute sense of taste, for example, than sense of hearing. It would naturally also vary from one individual to another. A common example of an absolute threshold is being able to see a candle flame from 30 miles on a clear, dark night. Do you think you could see it? The distance at which you would be able to see such a candle would be your absolute threshold. Here is a brief consideration of some of what we do know about the exterior senses and how they function.

SIGHT

Your visual sense depends not only on the capabilities of your eyes and your general physical condition, but also on the amount of light entering your eye and other environmental factors. You may also be aware that you have a "blind spot," the place where the nerves of your eye come together to form the optic nerve, where you have no vision. Under ordinary circumstances, the blind spot does not cause a problem with our vision.

LIGHT AND DARK DIFFERENCES Your eyes really function differently at night or in dim light than they do during daylight. This is because the *retina,* the membrane at the back of the eyeball, has two kinds of cells. Daytime seeing is done with cells called *cones,* which are located in the center of the retina. Night seeing is done with the *rods,* which are on the outside edge of the retina.

You know from experience that it takes a little while for you to be able to see when you walk into a dimly lit room. If you go out into bright daylight a few hours later, the sun may blind you for a while. Light enters the eye through the *pupil,* the dark circle in the center of your eye; the *iris,* the colored part of your eye, expands or contracts to adjust to degrees of light or darkness. Since it takes a few minutes for one's eyes to adjust to light changes, it is advisable to be cautious when entering a situation with a major light difference.

Our visual sense depends not only on the capabilities of our eyes, but on the amount of light that enters the eye.

VISUAL HAZARDS Some of the most serious visual hazards relate to the operation of motor vehicles because of the speed involved. When a vehicle is moving at 55 miles an hour, it covers 80 feet per second. Good vision and quick reaction time are needed to avoid accidents. Young people rate high in both of these categories. Nevertheless, they have more fatal accidents because they take more risks.

Reaction time is slowed and depth perception distorted when a person has been drinking alcoholic beverages or using other drugs. In fact, alcohol is considered to be a contributing factor in at least half of all fatal traffic accidents. Other drugs also distort perception and judgment, thereby leading to accidents. Even antihistamines, found in some allergy and cold medications, can cause dizziness and drowsiness. The combination of alcohol and other drugs can be even more disastrous than either would be if used alone.

Other accidents are caused by people who have faulty vision at night even though their daytime vision may be normal. Visual perception hazards also result from glare and other environmental factors. Rain, snow, or fog, for example, can reduce visibility to a dangerous degree.

Still other visual hazards arise from glare, inadequate lighting, lack of eye protection against fine particles that can fly into the eyes, misuse of contact lenses, or general poor health. Diabetes, for example, is the leading cause of new cases of blindness in the United States today.

EFFECTS OF COLOR The science of color can be both fascinating and challenging. Margaret H. Vaness in the *Photographic Society of America Journal* explains, "Perception of color is highly personal in the way an individual's eyes respond to light and in the sensation of color in the human mind. The nature of light also plays a role in the perception of color. Three processes are involved: physical, physiological, and psychological" (2). You probably know that color is not in the objects themselves but in light waves entering the eye. In spite of what science tells us about color, however, we will probably dismiss that information and go on "seeing" colors as we always have unless our work involves printing, photography, or other work that specifically involves the creation of color.

You may know that white light is a combination of all colors and that black is the absence of color. The primary colors in light are red, blue, and green. These are the colors used in creating color television. The primary colors in paint, however, are somewhat different. They are blue, red, and yellow. You may know from experience that they can be combined to form other colors.

Colors are also commonly used in language to indicate characteristics of behavior or moods. Note the meaning of color in the following expressions: "She saw red!" "He has a yellow streak." "She looked at my ring with green eyes." "I felt blue yesterday." Colors also have meaning in terms such as *red tape* and *blackball*. What other similar uses of color can you think of?

Color is also an important factor in marketing. Studies have shown that the same product will sell more in one color combination of packaging than in another.

Specialists studying the effects of color have made important discoveries about the efficiency, comfort, and well-being of people in their surroundings. Business and industry have used these studies to relieve stress, reduce accidents, improve production, and contribute to employee satisfaction. Some businesses have allowed their employees to select the colors of office equipment and machines they use. It makes people feel better and makes them feel valued by their employer to be able to choose colors they like. The company is also benefiting because employees that feel good are more likely to be loyal employees.

Colors also have functional uses in businesses, schools, hospitals, and other organizations. A common use of color for functional purposes is lateral shelf filing with different colored folders. Although the colors brighten up the office area, they have a more practical function. In some offices the different colors represent names beginning with different letters; others may represent time periods or departments of the organization. Colors are also used for safety coding and for giving directions to specific areas in a large building. The use of color to convey messages or to provide information is called **color coding.** Along with various shapes and printed information, colors are used in transportation systems to help people find rest areas, hospitals, and other facilities or points of interest. There are endless uses of color coding and also endless possibilities for future use.

Color coding
use of color to convey messages or meaning.

HEARING

The **auditory sense,** the sense called hearing, responds to a world of sound that affects us in various ways. The dull drumming of rain on a roof puts us to sleep, but the blare of an alarm clock wakes us up. We are entertained or relaxed by music or frightened by unexpected loud noises or recognizable warnings. We may be thrilled just by the sound of a loved one's voice. Or we may be turned off by a person with irritating or commanding vocal qualities. Sound also permits us to exchange verbal messages with one another.

Auditory sense
commonly called hearing, responds to a world of sound that affects us in various ways.

CHARACTERISTICS OF SOUND There are many different kinds of sound, but what is sound? Vibrating changes in the air, known as *sound waves*, stimulate the auditory nerves in the ear. Impulses are then transmitted to the brain and are

The Decibel Ratings for Various Common Sounds

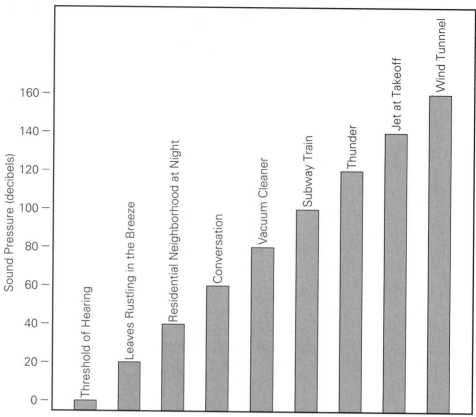

Sound
sensation perceived through the hearing mechanism and caused by vibrations in the air.

Threshold of audibility
point at which one hears sounds.

interpreted as **sound.** The number of vibrations per second is known as *frequency.* Most people cannot detect sounds with frequencies below 20 waves per second or above 20,000 waves per second. The point at which one hears sounds is called the **threshold of audibility.**

Pitch, loudness, and quality are characteristics of sound. *Pitch,* or the highness or lowness of tones, is determined by frequency. A low-pitched voice is more pleasant to most ears than a high-pitched one. *Loudness* is the strength of the sensation received by the ear and sent to the brain and is measured in decibels. *Quality* is a characteristic of musical tone but is also the feature that makes a friend's voice recognizable on the telephone. You know your friend's voice by its distinctive quality.

The difference between noise and music is that noise consists of irregular vibrations at irregular intervals, whereas music has regular characteristics. Any undesired or disturbing sound is also considered noise. A group of young people talking, laughing, and playing music at a party, for example, may cause neighbors to complain that they are making too much noise.

HAZARDS OF NOISE Noise has become a serious problem in today's world. The United States Environmental Protection Agency reports that millions of Americans have suffered some degree of hearing loss because of noise. Dr. Paul Hammerschlag explains:

Noise damage to the ears occurs in two ways, by acoustic trauma or noise trauma. Acoustic trauma is less common and occurs when a sudden, loud noise such as a gunshot creates a sudden pressure wave that damages the inner ear. The damage could be a ruptured eardrum, dislocations of small middle-ear bones, or injury to delicate nerve endings in the inner ear producing hearing loss. Noise trauma results from repeated, long-term exposure to sounds that are loud but not intense enough to cause acute acoustic trauma. Typically noise trauma damages the delicate nerve endings in the inner ear known as hair cells, which rupture and then become dysfunctional (3).

A wide variety of noises bombard our ears in modern society. Jets and helicopters, loud music, construction and street repair, sirens, and combinations of household appliances all take their toll. Such noise not only causes loss of hearing but also creates stress that contributes to accidents, decreased productivity, and irritability. Normal conversation is around 60 decibels in loudness. Sound twice that loud can be harmful or detrimental to hearing. It can also contribute to physical reactions such as headaches and nausea. The Occupational Safety and Health Act (OSHA) has set limits on the amount of noise allowable in a working environment.

The following list provides suggestions for protecting yourself from excessive noise:

- Avoid noisy environments as much as possible. Even if you like loud music, remember that it can damage your hearing.
- Take noise breaks. If you can't avoid noisy environments, get away from the noise at intervals, if possible.
- When purchasing appliances, check their noise level. Manufacturers are responding to customer concerns about noise in the home.
- When renting an apartment or buying a home, check the acoustics and also the general environment at different times of the day and night.

Noise pollution has become a serious problem. It can cause noise trauma, which can lead to ruptured eardrums and hearing loss.

Remember that noise can cause stress and other problems in addition to being hazardous to hearing.

SOUND CONTROL AND USE Scientific control of sound, or *acoustics,* is an important consideration in the construction of auditoriums to eliminate interference or to enhance sounds. Sound is also being reduced or absorbed in offices, factories, schools, and other types of buildings. Even homes are being designed to reduce or control sound.

Some sounds are beneficial, and a background of music in offices and hospitals, and even schools, has proved to reduce tension. This music should be soft and without vocal accompaniment, of course. You have probably had the experience of hearing music while you were on hold on a telephone line. Music in places of business also has the psychological effect of making the listeners feel that someone cares about them and can function as a morale booster.

Science has produced ultrasound, or ultrasonic waves, at vibrations too high to be heard by human beings. Ultrasound is used for several medical procedures. Manufacturers also use ultrasound to detect cracks in castings. Another scientific development is sonar, a device or system using the reflection of sound waves. Two of its many uses are detecting submarines and determining the depth of water in oceans.

 Quiz Yourself on Sound *Sound does not travel in a vacuum. The speed of sound depends on the density of the substance through which it travels. See whether you can match the number of feet per second sound travels through the following three substances:*

_____ *1. water*   *a. 16,400 feet per second*

_____ *2. steel*   *b. 4,700 feet per second*

_____ *3. air*   *c. 1,087 feet per second*

Answers are on page 91.

TOUCH

Cutaneous sense
the sense of touch.

The sense of touch is known as the **cutaneous sense.** Receptors, or cells in the skin that respond to stimuli, give us sensations of heat, cold, pain, and pressure. Each touch sensation affects specific pinpoint skin areas and does not affect other areas. Receptors that respond to cold do not respond to heat, pain, or pressure, for example. Experiments have been conducted to determine different points of the skin that are sensitive to each of the four cutaneous sensations. Doctors and dentists freeze pain receptors in the body so that the patient does not feel pain during treatment or surgery. The term *painless dentistry* has arisen from this practice.

Through the sense of touch one can also distinguish thickness, flexibility, and texture. Experience makes it possible to identify metal, wood, paper, fabric, and plastic by touch alone. The blind often have highly developed abilities to distinguish objects by touch because they must often rely on this sense.

The skin responds to humidity and air movement as well as to temperature and the other sensations mentioned previously. Thus you feel hot, the wind is brisk on your skin, or the high humidity makes you feel uncomfortable. People have learned to control these factors indoors, however. Furnaces, air conditioners, humidifiers, and dehumidifiers help to keep us comfortable and efficient at work or at home.

PAIN Pain is part of life: to be human is to know pain. Some people who have fibromyalgia, muscular dystrophy, arthritis, or frequent migraine headaches experience more pain than others. There is emotional pain as well as physical pain. It is also true that the same condition, such as a toothache or a misunderstanding between friends, can be more painful for some people than others.

A new approach to understanding and reacting to pain has developed in recent years. Dr. John J. Bonica is credited with establishing the nation's first pain clinic in 1960. Since then, pain control centers, including the Pain Management Center at the Mayo Clinic in Rochester, Minnesota, have been started throughout the country. These pain clinics have medical directors and employ several specialists, including nurses, physical therapists, and psychologists.

The basic goal of a pain clinic is not so much to eliminate pain—an objective that is often impossible—but to help a person prevent pain from being the main focus of life. A patient who has been helped might typically say, "I still have pain, but my whole life no longer centers on pain." Such a person has learned to manage pain. Dr. Lorenz K. Y. Ng, a neurologist and psychiatrist at the Washington (DC) Pain Center, is quoted in an article entitled "Coping with Chronic Pain" as saying, "We need to reward wellness—to focus not on relieving pain but instead on restoring function. The focus shifts from passive to active, from cure to care, from pills to skills" (4). Methods used to help people with pain to learn to live more relaxed and constructive lives include physical and occupational therapy, biofeedback, walking, stationary bicycling, relaxation exercises, group therapy sessions, and gradual reduction of dependency on medication.

Although no one wants to live a life of pain, we should remember that pain serves a useful purpose. It tells us that something is wrong. We should attempt to learn the cause of pain, often with professional help. Then it can be determined how to eliminate the cause, reduce the pain, or learn to live with it, if necessary. For those who must live with pain, support groups whose members live with similar types of pain have been helpful to many. Just knowing that you are not alone and that others understand what you are experiencing can mean a great deal.

HUMAN CONTACT It is becoming more evident that some caring physical contact is important to most human beings. Those who say they don't want to be around other people, much less touch them or be touched by them, have probably been psychologically hurt and could be unconsciously protecting themselves from further hurt.

TASTE

Gustatory sense
the sense of taste.

Taste, known as the **gustatory sense,** responds only to stimuli in a chemical state. We cannot taste salt or sugar, for example, until it has been dissolved in liquid. Most tastes also involve smell. Experiments have tested the degree to which people can distinguish between taste and smell when one of the senses isn't working normally. Some people cannot distinguish between an onion and an apple if they cannot see or smell them. Thus taste, smell, and even sight are interrelated in eating. For example, something that has an unpleasant odor or appearance can spoil your appetite or desire to eat. Texture, which involves the sense of touch, is part of the total experience in eating such foods as pudding, a bagel, or peanut brittle. Even hearing can be a factor. The crunchy sound of celery or an apple or the sizzling sound of steak broiling can add interest to eating or spark our appetites. Temperature, too, can affect taste. Chocolate, for example, has more flavor when it is at room temperature than when it is very hot or very cold.

There are four basic tastes: sweet, sour, salty, and bitter. All others are said to be variations or combinations of these. The *taste buds* are groups of cells found in various areas of the tongue, mouth, and throat. Each taste has its particular area of the taste buds. Can you tell from your own experience where these are? What part of your mouth reacts, for instance, when you taste something sour? (The center of the tongue has little or no sensitivity to taste.) Because our tastes differ greatly, it is more reasonable and accurate for you to say that you don't like something than to say that it isn't any good. Other people may like the things you don't like. Thus, your taste is one more expression of your individuality.

SMELL

Olfactory sense
the sense of smell.

The sense of smell is more accurately called the **olfactory sense.** Like taste, smell is experienced only through chemical stimuli. Molecules of gas and vapors in the air enter the nasal passage, where moisture dissolves them. The olfactory nerve cells thus are activated, enabling us to experience smell.

Scientists have discovered that it is primarily the shape of molecules in the air that causes odor. Although it is difficult to classify basic odors, some common ones include camphoric, musty, floral, minty, ethereal, putrid, and pungent. Vapors and gases in the air can travel long distances, and you can be aware of odors that have originated many miles away. Odors are more noticeable at some times than at others, depending on atmospheric conditions. Many factories emit odors that are recognizable to nearby residents.

Olfactory fatigue
adaptation to an odor so that one is less aware of it.

Have you ever walked into a room that had a strong odor and found that after a while you didn't notice the odor so much? This type of sensory adaptation is called **olfactory fatigue.** Although all the senses adapt to continued stimulation of a particular type, the sense of smell is especially adaptive. This can be dangerous! You may be inside a building where there is such a gradual increase in the smell of smoke or gas that you don't notice it immediately. If you do not check out a threatening smell before you become accustomed to it, you may forget it and suffer serious harm.

PRINCIPLES OF PERCEPTION

Perception was one of the earliest subjects in the study of human behavior. Wilhelm Wundt experimented with perception in the first psychological laboratory, established in 1879. Perception is still one of the most important and most interesting aspects of human behavior because we use our senses in some way all the time.

What Is Your Experience?   *What part does smell play in your enjoyment of certain foods? Can you always distinguish smell from taste?*

Our knowledge of how the senses and the nervous system operate and of the factors that affect perception can be combined into principles of perception, or basic rules about how perception functions. Although it is true that we as individuals hear, see, smell, taste, or feel the same things quite differently, there are some general principles underlying what we perceive and why or how. Some of these were included in the discussion of the different senses, although they may not have been stated as such. In addition, six others are explained in the following sections.

CONSTANCY

Constancy means that we tend to maintain established perceptual concepts and images; that is, we have a tendency to continue perceiving something in the same way, even though it may have changed. Even though a particular food you eat frequently has been "improved" and changed slightly, you may not notice the difference. Your friend approaching you from a distance is the same size to you as always. You may not notice something different about your brother's appearance because you have a predetermined idea of what he looks like. It is not suggested that, because of the principle of constancy, we never notice changes in others or in our environment. We know from our own experience that we do. But you have probably also had the experience of not noticing a change that can be explained by the principle of constancy.

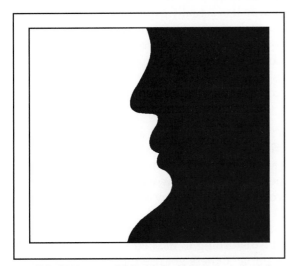

How many faces do you see?

FIGURE-GROUND

The principle of *figure-ground* is involved in much of our visual experience. Every time we focus on a particular thing, the rest of the surroundings becomes background. The wall is background for the clock that you may look at occasionally. If someone comments on the color of the wall, we may pay attention to the wall itself and ignore the clock. If you look at the figure you may recognize one or the other element of the figure-ground image but not both at the same time. We usually notice that which is most meaningful to us or that which looks familiar. The background may distort or emphasize certain figures. Figure-and-ground contrast is used for emphasis in advertising and display. Background may also distort certain features as well as emphasize them.

TOTALITY (GESTALT)

Another principle of perception is often referred to as either the *gestalt* or the *totality* principle. In fact, *gestalt* is a German word that means "unit" or "whole"—several stimuli are perceived as having a relationship to one another in making up a meaningful whole. You hear a melody rather than a series of individual notes. You see a painting rather than individual objects and colors. Parts of a machine are more meaningful if you can see where they belong in relation to other parts and the whole machine. This perceptual principle makes diagrams, blueprints, and maps more meaningful and helps us make more sense out of our work experiences and other activities.

**What Would
You Say?** *If someone should ask you, "How can the whole be more than
the sum of the parts," what would you say?*

CAMOUFLAGE

You are probably familiar with *camouflage* and some of its uses. This principle becomes very important when you are trying to protect yourself from an enemy. You try to blend in with your surroundings so you will not be noticed. This principle can also be helpful in making unsightly, but necessary, objects less conspicuous. Garbage cans can be camouflaged by painting them the same color as the building they are near. As you may have concluded, camouflage is essentially the opposite of figure-ground.

CLOSURE

Closure is the tendency to complete or close the gaps in what is perceived. What you are accustomed to perceiving or expect or want to perceive may be a determining factor here. We might be surprised if we knew how often we actually believe we heard people say what we wanted them to say rather than what they did say! Rumors are also examples of how closure operates in what one hears. Some people (not *us*, of course) may hear part of a statement or conversation and complete it in their minds quite differently from the way it is actually expressed. If this inaccurate version is passed along from one person to another, it becomes even more distorted.

Closure can also involve what one sees. Three persons describing an athletic event may give conflicting accounts of what happened. Yet each person describing the event may be sure of what he or she saw. People not only see what they want to see or expect to see, but they jump to conclusions using partial or inaccurate evidence.

CONDITIONING

Becoming accustomed to an experience is also involved with perception and judgment. You sense the speed you are traveling or estimate the weight of a package because of previous similar experiences. You know where the church chimes are coming from partially because you know where they are supposed to be coming from.

An advantage of *conditioning* is that we become accustomed to environmental conditions that otherwise might be disturbing to us. People can become acclimated to hot or cold weather, for example. Others get used to working in a very noisy situation. It should be kept in mind, however, that becoming accustomed to something does not mean that it may not be harmful. Even though some persons may become conditioned to working in a noisy environment, it can still be harmful to their hearing, for example.

LEARNING STYLES

You have been involved in a broad array of learning experiences in your life as a student thus far. Regardless of your age, it is likely education has changed a great deal in your lifetime. Both teachers and students have many more choices than those of a generation ago, a decade ago, or perhaps even a year ago. You don't always have a great deal of choice in how you are expected to learn, but it can be helpful for you to have some understanding of how you learn best and how you can continue to learn. As emphasized in Chapter 1, we are all expected to be lifelong learners. You will have more responsibility for your learning after you graduate from the present program, but you will have more choice.

The sensory style that maximizes an individual's learning is called **learning style.** A learning style inventory, available in the guidance department of many colleges, can give you some insight on how you learn best. A well-known learning style inventory, developed by D. A. Kolb, refers to four approaches to learning related to *feeling, watching, thinking,* and *doing.* Another learning style inventory might classify a student primarily as a *visual* learner, an *auditory* learner, or a *tactile* learner. A **visual learner** learns best by watching an actual experiment or procedure or viewing a videotape, for example. An **auditory learner** learns best by listening to a lecture or tapes, and a **tactile learner** learns best by doing or practicing a procedure. Although it is important to try to increase our learning ability in all ways, most of us do have natural preferences that can make learning easier, more effective, and more interesting.

Learning style
sensory style that maximizes an individual's learning.

Visual learner
someone who learns best through watching and looking.

Auditory learner
someone who acquires knowledge most effectively by hearing information.

Tactile learner
someone who learns best by doing or practicing a procedure.

LEARNING DISABILITIES

Many people have struggled through years in schools without realizing that they had a learning disability. A **learning disability** is "a disorder that affects people's ability to either interpret what they see and hear or to link information from different parts of the brain. These limitations can show up in many ways—as specific difficulties with spoken and written language, coordination, self-control, or attention. Such difficulties extend to schoolwork and can impede learning to read or write, or to do math" (5).

Learning disability
learning problem that inhibits a person's ability to interpret or link information.

Those who have learning disabilities need not be embarrassed about the disability itself or about taking advantage of opportunities to learn in the most effective way possible. Having a learning disability does not mean that a person has a low level of intelligence. In fact, with appropriate testing, many are found to be average or above average in intelligence. Many people with learning disabilities have high levels of self-motivation and are successful in their careers. According to Janet Lerner in *Learning Disabilities: Theories, Diagnosis, and Teaching Strategies,* an "element common to many definitions of learning disabilities is the identification of a gap between what the person is potentially capable of learning and what the student has in fact learned" (6). Schools are legally required to provide educational opportunities specifically designed around the needs of individual students.

OTHER SENSES

What senses do we have besides the *exterior senses*—sight, hearing, touch, taste, and smell—that receive stimulation from the environment? We also have *interior senses* that involve body needs and sensations such as hunger, thirst, fatigue, and pain. In addition, we have a sense of movement called *kinesthesis,* with receptors in the muscles and joints. A sense of *rhythm* belongs to this type. We have a sense of balance, or *equilibrium,* which is controlled by the inner ear. And we have a sense of *nearness,* particularly important to sightless people, who sense that they are approaching obstacles. (This awareness is the result of changes in vibrations and air pressure caused by people or objects nearby.) Some of us have a better sense of *direction* than others. We also have a sense of *depth,* an awareness of deepness or distance, which is present even in infants.

Our sense of *time* is associated with cues such as daylight and hunger. We can become so interested in what we are doing that we ignore the usual reminders, however, and lose all sense of time. An 8-year-old boy playing baseball after school does not have the same sense of time as the parent who is preparing the evening meal. And who can explain the inner alarm that wakes some people just before the alarm clock goes off, even when it is set for an unusual hour?

ILLUSIONS

Illusion
misinterpretation of stimuli received by the senses.

Some of the foregoing factors and principles are involved in illusions. An **illusion** is a misinterpretation of the stimuli your senses receive. Since illusions are deceiving, they are often deliberately used to create desired effects. People can try to make themselves appear slimmer by wearing vertical stripes. Decorators make rooms look larger with color, wallpaper, design, and furniture arrangement. Makeup and hairstyles can be used to accent a person's best physical features and minimize weak points. It is interesting to try to figure out why your senses deceive you. It is important to keep illusions in mind when you are making major purchases, to guard against being deceived.

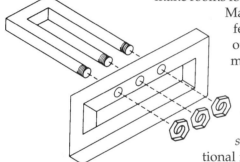

Try to find the source of the middle bar in this figure.

You have also had experience with illusions involving motion. The *"phi phenomenon"* is what makes alternating lights in a sign appear to be a moving arrow, for example. By *stroboscopic motion,* a series of images on film appear as a movie. An additional illusion is called *induced movement.* This phenomenon explains the sensation you sometimes have of moving when you are sitting in a parked car and the car next to you starts to move.

PARAPSYCHOLOGY

Parapsychology
psychological term for extrasensory perception.

Extrasensory perception (ESP)
awareness that does not arise from the ordinary use of the exterior senses.

The field of **parapsychology** deals with psychic phenomena or events beyond normal experiences or happenings. **Extrasensory perception (ESP)** belongs to this realm of psychology. It is the ability to perceive objects or know about happenings without the normal use of the senses. Three types of extrasensory perception are described below.

Telepathy is defined as the ability to transmit ideas from one person to another without any usual means of communication. It is often referred to as "mind reading." Although one occasionally may hear or read about reports of mind reading, it isn't likely that you have the skill or will meet anyone who has.

Clairvoyance is an awareness of objects or their location without the usual use of one's senses. People who are believed to have this ability have been contacted, on occasion, by law enforcement departments or families looking for missing persons. Their success has not been overwhelming; if it were, we would have fewer missing persons.

Precognition is an ability that modern-day prophets claim to have. It is the ability to know in advance that something is going to happen. Many predictions are made every year by people who are credited with having this kind of foresight. Such predictions are often made at the beginning of a new year. Some of these predictions come true, of course. Opinions differ on whether some people have the ability to know accurately what will happen in the future.

Not a type of extrasensory perception but often included with the discussion of telepathy, clairvoyance, and precognition is *psychokinesis,* or mind over matter, because it is an out-of-the-ordinary experience. Some people claim to be able to control or move objects without the usual means of handling them. A person may attest to having the ability to close doors or move a tray of glasses across the room without touching them, for example. As stated by Daryl. J. Bem in *The World and I,* "For many scientists, it is far more sinful to conclude that an effect exists when it does not than to conclude that an effect does not exist when it does" (7). Others argue that extrasensory experience, by its very nature, is unprovable. The debate goes on.

WIDEN YOUR WORLD

To enlarge your perception is to expand your world and enhance your life. Most people are interested in doing that. We would want to be somewhat selective, of course, because we are not looking for more pain or frustration caused by noise or unpleasant perceptual experiences. We can seek new experiences, however, that increase our understanding and appreciation of the world in which we live. Our lives can be a lifelong adventure if we accept the challenge to use our senses more fully.

We can make ordinary experiences extraordinary just by paying more attention to what our senses can tell us. Sometimes we are too busy or too preoccupied to pay attention to the ordinary. At other times we are bored or impatient when we could be enjoying the food we are eating, listening to the sounds of nature or the voices of people we love, appreciating a place to relax when we are tired, stopping to smell the roses or other fragrances along our way, or enjoying the beauty in our immediate environment that we are prone to overlook because of familiarity and habit.

As we progress through life, we may travel to new parts of the world and have numerous and exciting perceptual experiences. In the meantime, however, each new day offers us a wealth of perceptual experiences wherever we are. We always have the abilities and opportunities to widen our worlds.

Reprinted from The Saturday Evening Post.

Summary

Perception consists of stimulation to the senses interpreted by an individual. We should try to understand better the role of perception in our lives and the lives of others, to protect ourselves from perceptual hazards, and to learn to use and appreciate our senses more fully.

Numerous factors can affect perception and make seemingly identical experiences quite different for individuals. These factors include physical abilities and limitations, environmental conditions, past experiences, set: needs and wants, and attention factors. Although it is quite natural to assume that others have the same perceptual experiences that we do, such is not the case.

We have both exterior and interior senses. The five exterior senses are sight, hearing, touch, taste, and smell. Other senses, including interior senses, are a sense of movement, known as kinesthesis, and senses of rhythm, equilibrium, nearness, depth, direction, and time.

Many principles of perception pertain to how human beings perceive. Some of these principles are constancy, figure-ground, totality (or gestalt), camouflage, closure, and conditioning.

How we learn most effectively is determined by our perceptual preferences. Learning styles can be primarily visual, auditory, or tactile.

Learning disabilities are also related to how one perceives. A learning disability is a disorder that affects one's ability to either interpret what is seen or heard or to link information to different parts of the brain. People with learning disabilities can be given specialized help in learning and they can be successful in their lives and work.

Illusions, or misinterpretations of stimuli, can be interesting and useful, but it's also important to remember that we can be deceived by them.

The most controversial realm in the area of perception is parapsychology. Some claim that extrasensory perception (ESP) is a respectable science, some aren't sure, and still others discredit it completely.

PSYCHOLOGY IN PRACTICE

1. Identify ways in which principles of perception apply to your major area of study. (You may want to consult your instructor in your field of study about this.) Remember that perception involves all the senses. Determine whether any of the principles contribute to possible hazards or problems.

2. Use an Internet search engine or the Electronic Library to obtain more information about learning disabilities. Select a particular learning disability, such as dyslexia, and find out how people with that disability can learn more effectively.

3. Obtain more information about OSHA and find out how a particular industry protects its employees from noise and other perceptual hazards. Working in teams of two or three, design an ad for this industry—something to tell employees the company is looking out for them.

How you perceive the world is related in some respects to emotions, the subject of Chapter 5.

Answers to What Are Your Answers? on p. 77.

1. 64. You may have divided 24 by 2. But to divide by a fraction you invert it and multiply. That means you multiply 24 by 2, which gives you 48, and add 16, to get 64.

2. None. It was Noah's ark, not Moses'. This is an example of seeing what you expect to see.

3. You have the $7 you took. The question is, How many dollars do you have? not, How many dollars are left? The question is differently phrased than it usually is, hence the possible confusion.

Answers to Quiz Yourself on page 82.

1. b
2. a
3. c

Key Terms

Perception
Set
Exterior senses
Interior senses
Absolute threshold
Color coding
Auditory sense
Sound
Threshold of audibility
Cutaneous
Gustatory sense
Olfactory sense

Olfactory fatigue
Learning style
Visual learner
Auditory learner
Tactile learner
Learning disability
Illusion
Parapsychology
Extrasensory perception (ESP)
Telepathy
Clairvoyance
Precognition

Learning Activities

Turn to page LA-15 to complete the Learning Activities and Enrichment Activities for this chapter.

Endnotes

1. Shannon Brownlee with Traci Watson, "The Senses," *U.S. News and World Report*, January 13, 1997, p. 59.

2. Margaret H. Vaness, "Color Is Visual Response to Wavelengths of Light," *Photographic Society of America Journal*, September 1996, p. 17.

3. Dr. Paul Hammerschlag, "Learning about Noises To Prevent Loss of Hearing," for the Associated Press, *Wausau Daily Herald*, January 27, 1997, p. 6B.

4. Susan M. Menke, "Coping with Chronic Pain, *Consumers' Digest*, July 6, 1985, p. 33.

5. Sharyn Neuwirth, M.Ed., *Learning Disabilities*, pamphlet, National Institute of Health, U.S. Government Printing Office, NIH Publication No. 93-3611, p. 4.

6. Janet Lerner, *Learning Disabilities: Theories, Diagnosis and Teaching Strategies*, 6th ed., Houghton Mifflin Company, Boston, MA, 1993, p. 13.

7. Daryl J. Bem, "Does ESP Exist?" *The World and I*, August 1994, p. 219.

Emotions

5

Tears are not a sign of weakness, but of being human.

Therese Wilder

LEARNING OBJECTIVES
After completing this chapter, you should be able to do the following:

1. Define emotion.
2. Explain the development of emotions.
3. Give examples of pleasant and unpleasant emotions.
4. Describe the physiological effects of an emotion such as fear or anger.
5. Explain the difference between fear and anxiety.
6. Give suggestions for controlling and using anger.
7. Describe five different kinds of love.
8. Compare envy and jealousy.
9. Describe the effects of emotions in the workplace.
10. Identify the domains of emotional intelligence.

Emotion
complex feeling that begins with some type of mental experience that, in turn, leads to physiological changes and a possible change in behavior.

A robot would make a very uninteresting roommate, coworker, marriage partner, or substitute for a person in any other human relationship. Although robots can have computerized brains, they have no emotions or feelings. Although a robot cannot become angry or jealous, neither can it appreciate you or show you affection.

An essential part of being human is having emotions. An **emotion** is a complex feeling that begins with some type of mental experience, such as a memory, imagination, idea, desire, or awareness of reality or a threat. This leads to physiological changes and possible changes in behavior. Thus, a complex relationship exists among emotional, physical, and mental behavior. No behavior is based on only one of these. Rather, behavior can be mainly physical (such as running), mainly mental (such as working math problems), or mainly emotional (such as cheering at the hockey game). It is more accurate to say that emotion is a particular combination of mental and physical behavior than that it is a distinct type of behavior in itself.

An emotional response, then, begins in the mind and may result in fear, love, or any other emotion that affects our body functioning in some way. You may "get the chills," for example, when a friend tells you about a frightening experience. Or you may perspire when you are in a stressful situation, or your heart may beat more rapidly when you see someone you love.

Further insight into understanding emotion comes from Robert Zajonc, director of the Institute for Social Research. He explains,

> All emotional experiences involve a sudden and vigorous change in the nervous system; we are *always* in a state of emotion, and what we know of emotion is simply a change from one state to another. Some stimuli, such as strong sensory events, are intrinsically capable of evoking emotional reactions. But *any* stimulus can become emotional under particular circumstances: The harmless ticking of a clock is felt as a real threat if we believe it is connected to a bomb fuse (1).

Our emotions play a role in most of our activities as human beings. The abilities to solve problems, adjust to new situations in life, develop relationships with others, and maintain our well-being all involve the emotions or are affected by them.

Since emotions can be an underlying cause for behavior, they are closely related to motivation. Even our perceptions can be affected by emotions. Thus, a basic understanding of emotions is helpful in understanding other areas of our lives.

In some ways it is easy to discuss emotions because everyone has feelings—another term for emotional experience. Yet the attempt to understand emotions can be quite complex, because feelings may be deep-seated and may involve a combination of emotional responses. Emotions also may be difficult to understand because by nature they interfere with clear thinking. An underlying source of emotional experience may even be unconscious.

DEVELOPMENT OF EMOTIONS

How are emotional responses first experienced and expressed? Are some emotional responses inherited, or genetic, as some personality traits are now believed to be? What role does the brain play in an emotional experience? To what extent are emotional responses learned, and how are they learned? As you might suspect, we do not have complete answers to all those questions, but more has been learned in recent years.

Positron emission tomography (PET) brain scans have provided us with more information about the brain's involvement in emotion. A small, almond-shaped area of the brain called the **amygdala** becomes activated when a person responds to a stimulus, a frightening situation, for example. There is also more interaction of various parts of the brain in emotions than was previously known (2). It is likely that we will learn more about emotion through research in the future.

We do know that emotions are part of human experience. All normal human beings seem to develop several emotional responses, even though most emotions are not apparent at birth. Infants show only a kind of general response that later develops into specific emotional responses.

You may have heard it said that newborn infants have two fears: fear of falling and fear of loud noises. These are not real fears, however, because infants have no understanding of any possible danger. They do seem to be startled by noises or by a falling sensation. They show this by flinging out their arms. But such responses can be interpreted more accurately as a disturbance to the nervous system rather than fear. As will be discussed later in the chapter, fears are learned.

Newborn infants also display "emotional" reactions to discomfort caused by hunger, pain, or wet clothing. These first emotion-like responses are basically reactions to unpleasantness. During the first few months of life, infants learn to react to pleasant feelings by smiling, making sounds, or making body movements that indicate a sense of well-being or pleasure. In the first few years they learn more specific responses such as fear, joy, love, and possibly even jealousy.

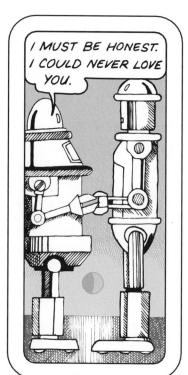

I MUST BE HONEST. I COULD NEVER LOVE YOU.

Amygdala
an almond-shaped portion of the brain that becomes activated when a person responds to a stimulus.

The development of emotions varies somewhat with the individual and continues throughout life. We learn to express our emotions in specific ways that become somewhat automatic. For example, we usually react immediately and in a habitual way to something that frightens us. Such emotional habits are formulated early in life and are carried over into how we react to friends, employers, and others. We learn to control our emotions, as well as personal ways of expressing them, to some extent.

CLASSIFICATIONS OF EMOTIONS

Emotions can be classified in various ways. Some psychologists use the two terms that describe emotions shortly after birth: unpleasant and pleasant. They would classify emotions such as fear, anger, jealousy, envy, guilt, and grief as being unpleasant; love, trust, peace, gratefulness, and enthusiasm would be classified as pleasant.

Others subdivide pleasant emotions into lower and higher categories. "Lower pleasant" emotions are associated with basic physical needs such as eating, exercise, and sex. "Higher pleasant" emotions come from a sense of achievement, from a feeling of contributing to others, and from natural beauty and aesthetic experiences. The higher pleasant emotions involve greater mental reaction, understanding, and appreciation than the lower ones do. For example, people learn to appreciate various forms of art and classical music.

Is it possible to fake an emotional response? To some extent and perhaps, for whatever reason, you may have tried it. The studies of Paul Ekman in his research

A winning pitcher responds to congratulations by his teammates.

report, "Facial Expression and Emotion", claim that it is not entirely possible to fake an emotional response. He reports that anger, fear, and sadness create facial expressions that "contain one or more muscular actions that most people cannot perform deliberately, in addition to muscular actions that are easy for everyone to make" (3). The eyes and voice are also indicators of emotion.

What Do You Think? *Is it advisable to try to determine whether others are trying to fake emotions?*

Are particular emotional responses inborn or hereditary? We do not have a clear answer to this. You will recall from the discussion of temperament in Chapter 2 that some of what makes us who we are is inborn. We have inborn tendencies to react in certain ways to life experiences. Heredity should not be blamed for all our bad behavior, however. We may have a natural disposition to react intensely to frustration, but we can learn to control our related behavior. We cannot really excuse ourselves by saying, for example, "I inherited my grandfather's terrible temper."

You may have read or heard that there are three basic emotions: love, fear, and anger. Those who classify emotions in this way consider all other emotional responses as variations or degrees of these three. Others refer to basic emotions as love, joy, sadness, interest, anger, fear, disgust, and suspense. Even these would be subdivided into dozens of more specific emotional experiences including hate, envy, jealousy, guilt and grief, which are discussed later in the chapter.

Most methods of classifying emotions are too simple. Many experiences are a combination of pleasant and unpleasant emotions. A person who is leaving her present job for a promotion may say, "I have mixed emotions about leaving. I am excited about the new career challenge, but I will miss daily contact with the people I have worked with." You may have had the same kind of feelings at some turning point in your life. Agreeing about how to classify emotions is not as important as understanding how our emotions affect our lives and the lives of others.

Other feelings that we can experience besides the ones already mentioned are annoyance, shame, bitterness, tenderness, loneliness, courage, and resentment. There are probably hundreds more. It is natural for human beings to have a wide range of feelings about themselves, others, and various aspects of their lives.

PHYSIOLOGICAL EFFECTS OF EMOTION

What happens to your body functioning when you are emotional? What changes in your physical being are you aware of when you are angry? How would you describe your total experience when you are thrilled about something that has happened to you? What physical sensations do you have after an intense emotional experience?

Emotional Experience

Mental Experience	Physiological Change	Change in Behavior
▪ Memory ▪ Idea ▪ Desire ▪ Awareness of Reality ▪ Threat ▪ Imagination	▪ Eyes dilate ▪ Heart beats faster ▪ Blood pressure rises ▪ Breathing speeds up ▪ Hormones are released ▪ Mouth becomes dry ▪ Hands perspire	▪ Determined by the emotions and the individual

Actually, anger and fear affect your body in much the same way—by preparing you for "fight or flight." The pupils of your eyes dilate or enlarge, your heart beats faster, your blood pressure rises, your breathing speeds up, hormones are released into your bloodstream, your mouth becomes dry, and your hands perspire. These are typical physical effects of either anger or fear. Since your brain is not receiving its normal supply of oxygen, it, too, is affected. You may not be able to think as clearly and quickly as usual. In fact, people can become so irrational during violent anger that they do things they never would do under normal circumstances.

When the emotional reaction is anger, people are more likely to fight—either physically or verbally—than they usually would be. And because of the muscle tension and energy-giving hormones that accompany anger, a person is able to strike with more force than usual. If the emotional reaction is one of fear, people are prepared for escape or self-defense. People really can run faster when they are scared. They also have more strength in an emergency. You may have read about people who performed "impossible" feats to save themselves or others. One mother was able to lift an automobile off her child, who was pinned under a wheel. The hormones released in her system gave her the strength she needed in the emergency. After an intense emotional experience, one may feel weak. Muscles and limbs may feel limp before the body returns to normal.

All emotions affect our body functioning and sensations in some way. Joy gives sensations of lightness or exhilaration, whereas grief gives sensations of dullness and heaviness. Although an emotional experience begins with a mental experience, even a mistaken idea, there is a physiological involvement in one's reaction.

The polygraph, commonly called a lie detector, measures the physiological effects of emotion. The assumption is that a person cannot lie without changes in body functioning, such as pulse rate or perspiration. This is not necessarily true, however. In fact, most courts do not accept the results of polygraph tests as evidence. Many who have studied the polygraph and its use (and misuse) warn against its weaknesses. It can record only how you are reacting to the test. The polygraph does not know whether a person is lying. Some people may be so nervous about even taking the test that they "fail," and others may be so accustomed to lying that they "pass."

Because of limitations of the polygraph and some misuse, Congress passed the Employee Polygraph Protection Act in 1988. The law makes it illegal to use the polygraph to screen job applicants or investigate employees, with some exceptions.

Nation's Business offers the basic elements of the law as:

> The Employee Polygraph Protection Act prohibits the use of polygraphs for pre-employment screening by most private-sector employers (exempted are security-service firms and pharmaceutical manufacturers, distributers, and dispensers).
>
> The act permits limited testing of employees as part of workplace investigations, but only under strict regulations.
>
> No employer can legally screen employees randomly or periodically.
>
> The act specifically outlaws employers' use of polygraphs, deceptographs, voice-stress analyzers, psychological-stress evaluators, and other devices used to judge a person's honesty (4).

 What Would You Do?   *If you were asked to take a polygraph test, what would you do?*

You are probably aware that the appearance of one's eyes changes with emotional state. When a person is excited or intensely aroused, the pupils widen. When someone is experiencing something negative or dull, the pupils get smaller. This information may be interesting or somewhat useful, but we must always be cautious in using a single factor as a basis for judging the complex reaction of another human being. Tears, for example, can indicate grief, joy, or even that one has been peeling onions.

FEAR

Everyone has experienced the sensation of fear. It is normal, and even sensible, to have fears. Since fear is an unpleasant emotion, you might conclude that people would be better off without it. However, you should recognize that there are very real dangers in the environment, and you are wise to fear them. By recognizing hazards and the threats they pose, you can avoid them and protect yourself.

FEAR OR ANXIETY?

Fear can be exaggerated and can cause needless discomfort and ineffectiveness. But fear can also be realistic and can be directed toward protecting ourselves. A limited amount of tension that produces anxiety or apprehension can help us to perform at our best. On the other hand, anxiety can become a destructive habit. It can interfere with the ability to react realistically and effectively to a situation.

"Stop trembling, Ferguson -- They can sense fear."

Commonweal

Anxiety, along with stress, will be discussed further in Chapter 10. However, it will be helpful to compare fear and anxiety at this point in our study. Note the following differences:

Fear	Anxiety
Reaction to a specific, known, immediate threat	Prolonged concern about a vague, potential type of threat
Intense physiological reaction in preparation for fight or flight	Moderate but continuous physiological disturbance

 What Would You Say? *If a friend of yours commented that she had never had any fears, what would you say?*

CHILDHOOD FEARS

You may no longer fear something you were afraid of when you were a small child. Children perceive their environment differently from adults. They therefore have fears that they will outgrow when they see things differently later in life. For example, small children may be afraid of a dog that is much bigger than they are. Children may also be afraid of thunder and other things they do not understand. They need a sense of security and therefore may fear being alone. Since it is common for human beings to fear the unknown, and since there are more unknowns in a child's experience, children are likely to have more fears than adults.

Conditioning
the association of a
secondary stimulus with
a primary stimulus so
that one eventually
reacts to the secondary
stimulus alone.

Some fears result from associations known as **conditioning.** A person becomes afraid of something that is associated with an original fear. A child who has to climb some stairs to the residence of someone who abuses him while his parents are away may become frightened of climbing any stairs by the association of those experiences. Childhood fears that have resulted from such conditioning can be very difficult to dispel because the original fear stimulus is not always known. Often adults have fears they do not really understand. Some such fears are the result of conditioning; the associations made earlier in life are no longer remembered.

LATER FEARS AND ANXIETIES

Another time of life that presents a whole new set of fears is adolescence, or the teen years. During this time, tremendous physical and psychological changes make an adolescent feel insecure. Individuals are more self-conscious during the teen years than at any other age. Therefore, they may have fears about their abilities and the impressions they make.

As adolescents enter young adulthood, they are also likely to experience a sense of insecurity, this time as a result of the independence they desire. Along with independence comes anxiety about career success and a future lifestyle. These experiences will be discussed further in Chapter 13.

Adults are likely to have both fears and anxieties but should be able to recognize them for what they are. Adults generally are better able to deal with their particular fears or anxieties. Some do, however, develop anxiety disorders, which will be discussed in Chapter 10.

CONTROLLING AND USING FEARS

It has been mentioned that many childhood fears are simply outgrown. Others can be overcome with the help and understanding of parents or other adults. A child who has learned to fear dogs, for example, can unlearn that same fear by a series of nonthreatening, pleasant experiences with a puppy or grown dog.

When people recognize what they are afraid of, they can take steps to protect themselves. For example, someone afraid of automobile accidents can take steps to reduce the threat of accidents. Someone else, perhaps fearful of the injury to children from idle machinery, can remove from reach some of the dangerous equipment. People can also remove themselves from danger. A person in a hazardous job who recognizes his or her fear can control that fear by seeking a less dangerous job.

Some people who have performed acts of courage readily admit that they were afraid but—in spite of their fear—performed the dangerous acts because they felt they had to. Still other types of courage involve constant risks, such as exposure to possibly harmful elements in research or the hazards inevitable in law enforcement. People choose to take such risks for personal reasons or because of dedication to a cause.

Here are some suggestions about how to deal with or overcome fears:

■ Admit that you have fears.
■ Do not be ashamed of or apologize for your fears.
■ Understand your fears as specifically as possible. Try to identify exactly what it is that frightens you.

- Realize that fears can help you protect yourself from real dangers.
- Remember that the actual threat in a fearful situation is often exaggerated.
- The more competent you become in taking care of yourself, the fewer threats you will face and the fewer fears you will have.

"Do the thing you fear" is recommended for those who are afraid to resume a particular kind of activity because of a recent accident. The longer a person waits to go back to normal activity after an accident, the greater the chance that the fear will magnify and that future behavior will be affected. It is important to remember, though, that a person should never be forced to do what he or she fears. Forcing is likely to deepen the fear and make the problem even worse.

What Do You Think? *Do you think anyone reacts to danger without fear? Can you give examples to support your answer?*

PHOBIAS

Phobia
an abnormal fear; a fear out of proportion to the situation.

Phobos
Greek word meaning "fear."

Hemo
Latin word for "blood."

Hemophobia
fear of blood.

Agoraphobia
fear of crowded places.

Agora
Greek word for "marketplace."

Claustrophobia
fear of confined places.

Practically everyone has at least one abnormal, illogical fear. Such fears, which are out of proportion to any actual threat, are called **phobias.** Phobias can range from relatively mild, but disturbing, fears to severe phobic anxiety. This term comes from the Greek word **phobos,** meaning "fear." **Hemo** is from the Latin word for "blood," for example, so **hemophobia,** is a fear of blood.

One of the most common phobias is **agoraphobia,** from the Greek word **agora.** It literally means "fear of the marketplace." It is not so much a fear of crowded places but of any place that can cause anxiety in the individual. These are usually public places with which the person is unfamiliar or uncomfortable for some reason. *The Journal of the American Medical Association* (JAMA) notes, "Phobias are common, increasingly prevalent, often associated with serious role impairment, and usually go untreated" (5). **Claustrophobia,** which is fear of confined places, is another common phobia.

TREATMENT OF PHOBIAS

The basic idea underlying most treatment for phobias is to expose the person gradually to the anxiety-causing situation until the person begins to feel more comfortable. It is also important in such therapy that the individual with the phobia consent willingly to the treatment; otherwise, anxiety may be increased, rather than decreased. The length of time that one is involved in the anxiety-producing experience can be increased gradually. A person with agoraphobia, for example, may sit in one's own yard with a friend watching other people go by; on another day, she may take a short walk down the block with someone she feels comfortable with; at a later time, she may go around the block; she can gradually go to familiar places close to home with someone else until she begins to feel comfortable enough to go away from home alone. Overcoming a phobia is not simple, but it is important to realize that most phobias can be overcome with the desire and time to do so. Some individuals can even overcome

Quiz Yourself on Phobias See whether you can determine the definition of the following phobias. Write the letter of the definition next to the phobia it describes.

_____ 1. Androphobia

_____ 2. Claustrophobia

_____ 3. Hydrophobia

_____ 4. Acrophobia

_____ 5. Gynephobia

_____ 6. Phobophobia

_____ 7. Thanatophobia

_____ 8. Pyrophobia

a. Fear of height

b. Fear of fire

c. Fear of being afraid

d. Fear of closed spaces

e. Fear of men

f. Fear of death

g. Fear of water

h. Fear of women

Answers are given on page 115.

"You gotta' admit, Bernice, your fear of flying makes it darned hard to get to Capistrano every year."

Reprinted from The Saturday Post with permission.

phobias on their own. Their feeling that they are in control helps reduce anxiety for them.

ANGER

How do you feel when you are angry? What do you do? Anger and the ways of expressing anger—like other emotional responses—are learned. Children who have temper tantrums, for example, have learned that such behavior gets them what they want. If the behavior continues to be effective, they will learn to utilize temper displays as adults.

CONTROLLING AND USING ANGER

Anger can be suppressed, displaced, and destructive, or expressed openly, directly, and constructively. Anger is ordinarily thought of as a negative, unpleasant emotion, and it can be a very destructive force. Many people feel frustrated today because they believe problems in society are out of control. They are angry and are expressing these feelings in destructive ways. Anger, for whatever reason, is often suppressed or held in by persons who either feel it is wrong to be angry or are afraid of the consequences of expressing their anger. In other instances, it is expressed in an inappropriate direction or displaced. If people did not make some attempt to control their anger, there would be much more violence in the world than we have now. Because violence and aggression are increasing, it seems that many people are not trying to understand and control their anger—or, at least, are not very successful in their attempts.

Controlling anger or any other emotion can be carried to extremes, however. A person may become so filled with repressed emotion that illness or an outburst of irrational behavior results. To avoid this, we can exercise some control over how we react to whatever causes us to become angry. Many of us would admit that we are more disturbed by trivial inconveniences than we should be.

The following list offers suggestions about how to react to frustration and use anger for constructive purposes.

- Learn to understand yourself and what bothers you to the point where you become angry about it. Then find out what you can do about it—and do it. Learn to solve problems. Chapters 6 and 7 will help you improve your ability to do this.

- Calm down after you have become angry. Give your body a chance to return to normal. Then exercise to relax tense muscles. Instead of slamming doors and breaking items, take a walk, do some manual work, or engage in other physical activity. In the past, physical labor was a way to work off emotional tension. Automatic machines now perform much of the manual labor of the past, and that could be one reason why many people today are so tense. To provide more opportunity to vent anger with physical activity, some people may choose to do yard work, clean the house, or wash the car. In that way two goals are achieved: the anger is vented and a chore is done.

- Concentrate on something else. Occupy your mind with something that demands your attention. Do something that gives you pleasure or satisfaction. Substitute a pleasant emotion for the unpleasant emotion. A hobby, special interst, or volunteer work can be of value at emotional times. Hobbies require action and give a sense of satisfaction.

People who are frequently (some almost constantly) frustrated and angry are endangering their own well-being. Anger and hostility cause stress, which can be related to high blood pressure and other health problems. This topic will be discussed further in Chapters 10 and 11.

Anger is a feeling of frustration that results from a situation that is not the way we think it should be or that we believe to be wrong or unfair. Some people become angry most often with other people. Others are more likely to be angered by machines that don't work or by items or information they can't find. People are more likely to become angry when they are tired or hungry or are upset for some other reason. You may have found this to be true from your own experience. Keeping this in mind may help you when responding to other people who are frustrated and angry.

Feelings of anger are to be expected at times in people who are seriously involved in their work and care about what is happening or not happening. Anger, like fear, can be reasonable and even a desirable emotional response if it is channeled constructively. If nothing bothered people enough to make them frustrated or emotionally upset, much less would be accomplished in our schools, businesses, and communities.

Aggression can be described as behavior intended to hurt someone or to violate the rights of others for one's own advantage. Although aggression is a major problem, there is no complete agreement on the causes and therefore on measures to reduce it. Some say that certain individuals are born to be aggressive; others say that aggression is caused by biochemistry and that it can be influenced significantly by drugs or even by diet. Probably the greatest number say that aggression is learned and these people emphasize preventing children from learning aggression. There are many examples of individuals who are abused, grow up with a poor self-concept, and become aggressive toward others and toward society in general. People who have a realistic, positive self-concept aren't as likely to cause problems deliberately for others.

Many argue that violence on television has prompted aggressive behavior in the young and emotionally immature. Some people have difficulty distinguishing between fantasy and reality. Parents, television producers, educators, and other interested groups are working to reduce the potentially harmful effects of television on such viewers.

Some individuals haven't learned, and may never learn, how to relate to others. Such aggressive individuals, particularly young people, are often referred to as bullies. Hara E. Marano, in a *Psychology Today* article entitled "Big. Bad. Bully," states that bullies

> . . . perpetually attribute hostile intentions to others. The trouble is, they perceive provocation where it does not exist. That comes to justify their aggressive behavior. Say someone bumps them and they drop a book. Bullies don't see it as an accident; they see it as a call to arms. . . . That allows them a favorable attitude toward violence to solve problems. Whether they start out there or get there along the way, bullies come to believe that aggression is the best solution to conflicts" (6).

Much aggression seems to be caused by frustration. The individual, then, strikes out at others in an attempt to release this frustration. Victims of the aggressive behavior may have nothing to do with the cause of the frustration, however. Sometimes the cause of the frustration is within the individual. He or she may have a desire for control or power, which often results from an underlying feeling of insecurity and a need for acceptance.

LOVE

Every human being desires to be loved. People would be happier and the world would be more peaceful if a discussion of love were not needed—if everyone knew what love was from personal experience. Probably all of us are aware, however, that there are different kinds of love, including self-love, humanitarian love, family love, friendship, romantic love, and love of God or a higher power.

Self-love
a positive, realistic self-concept and favorable self-esteem.

Egotist
one who is excessively concerned with him- or herself.

Humanitarian love
concern for other human beings.

Self-love, or having a positive realistic self-concept and favorable self-esteem (as discussed in Chapter 2), is the foundation for all the other types of love. How we feel about others is determined primarily by how we feel about ourselves. We cannot accept others, trust them, and learn to love them unless we have a sense of self-worth. Self-worth is not what some might call egotism. An **egotist** is centered excessively on him- or herself. Such persons are boastful and usually consider themselves superior to others. A person with self-love values him- or herself and in turn values others. People who do not feel good about themselves have difficulty establishing loving relationships with others. We love ourselves first, learn to love others, and help them to grow in their own self-love.

Humanitarian love is caring about and having concern for other human beings. These human beings include those we do not know personally, in our communities, our country, and in other parts of the world. People demonstrate humanitarian love when they care about people who are suffering from hunger, oppression, earthquakes, floods, and other unfortunate circumstances, for example. Some people become actively involved in trying to lessen such suffering in the world; others donate to organizations, such as CARE, that work to promote the well-being of people worldwide.

Family love
personal caring toward and among family members.

Family love is personal caring toward and among parents and children, siblings, and members of one's extended family. There are many definitions of family in our society today and there can be love for one another in all of them. Family love is a type of love that everyone should be able to know from personal experience. Unfortunately, there are individuals whose families feel no love for one another or who no longer have families in the true sense of the word. Some of these people, however, have relationships with others who are like family to them. Most people, therefore, can identify with family love.

Friendship
a relationship with another characterized by a bond of mutual understanding, sharing, and affection.

Friendship is a relationship with a person with whom you have a bond of mutual understanding, sharing, and affection. Friendship is voluntary; you choose your friends. We may care about friends in different ways, depending on differences in age or sex, for example. You may consider the old man across the street your friend and may have deep affection for him. You probably have a best friend who is your own age and gender for whom you care deeply and in whom you confide. Friendships with members of the opposite sex can also be **platonic,** or nonsexual. Perhaps only those involved in such a relationship can really understand it, but it is friendship, nonetheless. A friend accepts us for who we are and stands by us when we are not in the best mood or are having difficulty. Whatever the degree or type of mutual affection between you and others, there can be no substitute for friendship.

Platonic
nonsexual.

Romantic love
a deep and committed caring and sharing, involving sexual attraction.

Romantic love is what is usually referred to when a person declares, "I am in love." It probably is possible to find more quotes on love than on any other subject. Fiction, poetry, movies, love letters, and personal diaries abound with examples and variations of romantic love. From these and from the testimony of people who believe they know what romantic love is, the following characteristics are frequently mentioned: trusting and being honest with one another; sharing fears, burdens, and disappointments, as well as pleasures and joys; working at a compatible relationship, including making concessions and compromises; maintaining a rewarding sexual relationship but understanding that it is only part of their sharing with one another; accepting one another's individuality and giving one another the space and freedom to grow; and regarding one another as a special friend.

Love of God or a higher power
recognition of and commitment to a higher power.

Love of God or a higher power is important in the lives of millions of people. It is central in the lives of many. A common element seems to be recognition of a source of power and love higher than oneself. For many people, this love of a higher power affects all the other kinds of love because it has an impact on self-love, humanitarian love, family love, friendship, and romantic love.

HATE

Love
an intense emotional attraction that involves caring and respect.

Probably the most negative emotion of all is hate. It is the opposite of love, yet it has characteristics in common with love. To **love** means to care deeply for a person and to wish that person every good. To **hate** means to dislike a person intensely and to wish that person harm. Both emotions require a deep

Hate
an intense dislike.

involvement with another person. In fact, there are times when people feel as though they hate someone they love. However, this could be described more accurately as resentment for being hurt.

Hatred does not seem to have any useful purpose. In fact, it can have harmful effects—even on the person who hates. The time and energy spent hating someone could be used for a constructive purpose. And hatred can be damaging to a person's overall well-being. A person may rightly be disgusted or angry with the behavior of someone else, but it is always difficult to justify the desire to harm another.

OTHER EMOTIONS

People can experience a wide range of emotions besides the ones already discussed. Other emotions that deserve our attention are envy, jealousy, guilt, and grief.

ENVY

Envy
wishing you could have what someone else has or be what someone else is.

Envy is wishing you could have what someone else has or be what someone else is. People who are envious experience displeasure at the success, happiness, or achievement of another. They may avoid doing anything that would help those they envy—even if they also ultimately harm themselves. Without doubt, envy can be considered a negative emotion. It usually does the envious person as much harm as it does the person envied. People who have a favorable self-concept are more concerned with their own self-development than with a useless feeling such as envying someone else.

JEALOUSY

An emotion with some of the same characteristics of envy is jealousy. The basic difference between the two is that the jealous person already has what is desired but is afraid of losing it. Jealousy, then, results mainly from feelings of insecurity. A person who is afraid of losing the love of another person may even act in such a negative, suspicious way that he or she causes the very loss that is feared. It is not a good feeling to be jealous; neither is it good to feel that someone else is needlessly disturbed about what we say or do.

How does one work on excessive feelings of jealousy? Even though jealousy is considered a negative emotion, it is natural and understandable to a degree. There is a difference, also, between being interested in what another person is doing and investigating for our own sense of security. Since jealousy is anxiety about a relationship, the following suggestions could be helpful.

- Work on developing a more positive self-concept. This is easier said than done, but all of us have personal worth and deserve to feel good about ourselves.
- Do not allow any one individual to become the only important person in your life. You can be involved in numerous types of activities and meet many interesting people.
- Remember that there are different kinds of love. There is a difference between platonic love (friendship with a person of the opposite sex) and

Quiz Yourself on Jealousy

Do I feel as if our relationship is threatened if my best friend tells me (he or she) is going to a social event with someone else? _____

Do I feel as if our relationship is threatened if my (boy friend, girl friend, or spouse) tells me about an interesting person (of my own sex and age) whom (he or she) met recently? _____

Do I feel as if our relationship is threatened if my (boy friend, girl friend, or spouse) compliments someone on (his or her) appearance or achievement? _____

Do I become suspicious and feel threatened if I don't know where my (friend, girl friend, or boy friend) is or what (he or she) is doing most of the time? _____

Do I have a tendency to give my (boy friend or girl friend) "the third degree" about where (he or she) has been or what (he or she) has been doing if I have been out of town for a few days? _____

Do I feel unloved and uncertain of our relationship if my (boy friend, girl friend, or spouse) does not tell me frequently that (he or she) loves me? _____

Do I insist on knowing what my (girl friend, boy friend, or spouse) has been talking about if I see (her or him) talking to a person of the opposite sex? _____

Yes answers to more than one of the above questions are an indication that you should work on eliminating feelings of jealousy.

romantic love. It is also true, however, that friendship can grow into romantic love.

- Realize that a meaningful, lasting relationship must be based on trust. A general feeling of mistrust toward others may indicate a lack of confidence in oneself. It may also be related to disappointing experiences we have had with others that have no connection with our present relationship.
- If possible, get to know the person or persons about whom you are jealous. You will gain a better understanding of the situation and may also find them to be friendly and interesting.
- Don't feel sorry for yourself or look for sympathy. This can be more damaging than supportive to a relationship. Become a more interesting person.
- Talk about your feelings instead of pouting or making accusations and threats. One could say, "I felt really uncomfortable when you seemed to ignore me while you were talking to Jeff after class."

Jealousy in work relationships can also be self-destructive. It interferes with a person's self-confidence and productivity, and it can cause disharmony in the work environment.

What Would You Suggest? *If someone you know quite well and like talks as if he's jealous of his friend and asks for your opinion, what would you suggest?*

GUILT

Guilt is an emotion directed toward oneself rather than toward others. In a sense, we are all guilty. Each one of us has made mistakes and may even have done something on purpose that we shouldn't have done. Or we may not have done some things we should have done. It is usually of value—for oneself and others—to admit our wrongdoings and to attempt somehow to make up for them. But it can be useless, and even harmful, to exaggerate our wrongdoing and to live with constant feelings of guilt. "Nobody knows how much suffering, and even tragedy, has been triggered by needless feelings of guilt, one of the commonest, yet most powerful, emotions that rule our lives," says Lester David in an article from *Family Health* (7).

It can be even more intolerable for an individual to harm another person severely and to *lack* any feelings of guilt or remorse. It is an individual's responsibility to establish a realistic sense of right and wrong and to know what guilt *is*, without being overshadowed by it. Nothing is more useless than trying to undo what has been done. We can, however, use our feelings of guilt to stimulate ourselves to correct our mistakes and to become better persons.

GRIEF

The emotion of grief is based on a keen sense of loss, usually associated with the death of a family member or other loved one. That type of loss is the most difficult emotional experience most people encounter. In today's society where death is spoken of more openly, we have a better understanding of grief and how we can deal with our own losses and support others. Although it is difficult to know what to do or say when we want to express our sympathy to someone experiencing grief, the most important thing is to let people know that we care and support them as friends anyway we can.

In addition to grief associated with loss through death, other types of separation can also cause great emotional pain. Divorce, even when it is a preferred change, can cause grief for either or both partners. Even a baby weaned from the breast or bottle may experience a sense of loss. A high school athlete who graduates and is no longer part of the team, or a family that moves to another city, away from friends, may experience a sense of loss that can be classified as grief. Since these types of experiences require further understanding and adjustments, they will be discussed again in Chapter 10.

EMOTIONS IN THE WORKPLACE

If a person is living with a strong emotional experience such as grief, anger, or fear, for example, he or she will be affected by that emotion continually, not just where and when it can be expressed appropriately. We may not express what we are feeling when we are at work as much as we do in privacy, but it is affecting us and very likely also our work. Sharon Nelton, in a *Nation's Business* article "Emotions in the Workplace," states,

> Not so very long ago, business owners and managers believed that emotions—their own and their employees'—were to be left outside the company gate. Not anymore. . . . Business people and researchers are beginning to find that when understood and managed wisely, emotions can enhance a business. But if they go unacknowledged or are misunderstood or mismanaged, they set a business back (8).

Even coworkers who have little else in common may be experiencing the same emotion at some time. Sharing emotions in the workplace is important. It allows people to understand each other better and to feel empathy for one another. Grief, as discussed earlier, may be one example. The best time to acknowledge the person's loss is the first time that you see him or her. You may do this by simply saying, "I'm so sorry" while taking the person's hand or placing your hand on his/her shoulder. If you do not have daily contact with the person, a personal note can be an important way to acknowledge the person's grief without offering too many words of advice. Although emotions in the workplace can create problems, people who care about their work and one another will be more satisfied and productive.

How can managers themselves capitalize on the value of emotions in the workplace? In "The Emotional Side of Management," in *Industry Week*, Tom Brown has the following suggestions:

> Managers can do at least three things to widen their skills at dealing with emotions. First, they can learn to recognize and accept their *own* emotions. This will immediately create greater empathy with the people they are dealing with. Second, they can do more listening and rapport-building with the people they are working with. Third, they can start to *trust* that the answers will emerge as they explore and acknowledge the problems. This means giving up control. Often our need to control is driven by fear and insecurity in the first place (9).

EMOTIONAL INTELLIGENCE

Emotional intelligence has recently been closely related to success in life. In fact, it seems to be more important than basic IQ or other types of ability. Much of the focus has been on the work and writings of Daniel Goleman. In his book, *Emotional Intelligence*, Goleman refers to the earlier work of Peter Salovey and John D. Mayer, and he identifies the five main domains of emotional intelligence:

1. *Knowing one's emotions.* Self-awareness—recognizing a feeling as it *happens*—is the keystone of emotional intelligence. The ability to monitor feelings from moment to moment is crucial to psychological insight and understanding. An inability to notice our true feelings leaves us at their mercy. People with greater certainty about their feelings are better pilots of their lives, having a surer sense of how they really feel about personal decisions from whom to marry to what job to take.

2. *Managing emotions.* Handling feelings so they are appropriate is an ability that builds on self-awareness. It includes the capacity to soothe oneself, to shake off rampant anxiety, gloom, or irritability—and the consequences of failure at this basic emotional skill. People who are poor in this ability are constantly battling feelings of distress, while those who excel in it can bounce back far more quickly from life's setbacks and upsets.
3. *Motivating oneself.* Marshaling emotions in the service of a goal is essential for paying attention, self-motivation and mastery, and creativity. Essential self-control—delaying gratification and stifling impulsiveness—underlies accomplishment of every sort. And being able to get into the "flow" state enables outstanding performance of all kinds. People who have this skill tend to be more highly productive and effective in whatever they undertake.
4. *Recognizing emotions in others.* Empathy, another ability that builds on emotional self-awareness, is the fundamental people skill. People who are empathetic are more attuned to the subtle social signals that indicate what others need or want.
5. *Handling relationships.* The art of relationships is, in large part, skill in managing emotions in others. Social competence and the specific skills involved are the abilities that undergird popularity, leadership, and interpersonal effectiveness. People who excel in these skills do well at anything that relies on interacting smoothly with others (10).

EMOTIONS CAN ENRICH LIVING

Are most of our feelings negative or causes of displeasure? It would seem that way, from the amount of emphasis that has been put on anger, fear, envy, grief, and other such emotions. Although these emotions would fall into the unpleasant category, some of them—such as anger and fear—can also be useful. Appropriate reactions to these two emotions can contribute to a fuller, more enriched life.

We can also have feelings of contentment and peace. These feelings occur when we have no major frustrations and are comfortable with ourselves and our lives. We can at least occasionally experience joy, that total sense of well-being sometimes referred to as a "natural high," when an experience or situation is all we might hope it to be.

To enjoy life you should also understand your moods, or periodic shifts in how you feel. You know, for instance, that the way you feel affects the way time seems to pass. If you are depressed, time seems to pass very slowly. On the other hand, if you are enthusiastic about what you are doing, time seems to pass quickly. You can almost measure how much you are getting out of life by the pace at which hours, days, and years seem to pass. Whenever people, young or old, say that the days just fly by and they never get all the things done that they would like to do, it is likely that they are emotionally stable and able to solve their problems to their satisfaction.

There can be so much emphasis on controlling emotions and on what not to do with regard to unpleasant emotions that a person may be tempted to suppress all emotion and become robotic. But life consists of laughter and tears, emotional ups and downs. We will not experience the satisfaction, and even joy, of achievement if we are not willing to take some risks. We would miss

These basketball players demonstrate fear and anxiety about their anticipated loss.

opportunities to improve our personal lives and situations in our workplaces and communities if some things did not frustrate, or anger, us enough to move us to constructive action. *The person for whom life is an exciting experience has learned how to make the joys of living far outweigh the disappointments.*

Summary

Emotions make the difference between human beings and machines, between living and merely existing.

Basic emotions are sometimes classified as love, fear, and anger. Other classifications also focus on joy, sadness, interest, disgust, hate, envy, jealousy, guilt, and grief.

Emotions can also be divided into two broad categories: pleasant and unpleasant.

The physical effects of emotions are evident in fear and anger. For example, the pupils of the eyes enlarge, the heart beats faster, blood pressure rises, breathing accelerates, hormones are released into the bloodstream, digestion slows down or stops, muscles become tense, the mouth becomes dry, and the hands perspire. These physical effects, causing a decrease in oxygen to the brain, can result in irrational behavior.

Fears are learned and therefore can be unlearned or overcome. Many childhood fears result from a lack of understanding or from conditioning. These fears can be eased as time passes. Fears carried over into later life, however, can be more difficult to overcome. Fears that are out of proportion to the actual threat involved are known as phobias. Understanding the basis of fears and phobias is the first step to overcoming them.

Everyone experiences a degree of anger, at least occasionally. Anger can be harmful to oneself and to others, but it can also motivate and lead to constructive behavior.

Love, one of the basic emotions, is an important part of our lives. The different kinds of love include self-love, humanitarian love, family love, friendship, romantic love, and love of God or a higher power.

Envy and jealousy are emotions that cause problems for ourselves and others. Envy is wishing you could have what someone else has or be what someone

PSYCHOLOGY IN PRACTICE

1. Read an article or a book about a particular emotion and how it affects one's life. Develop several personal guidelines for enriching your life through emotional experiences.

2. Over a three-day period, keep track of pleasant and unpleasant emotions in others. Note how people express these emotions and how others react to them. Plan a role-play with another student to present to the class. Have the class evaluate the expression of emotions.

3. Collect information on current use of the polygraph. Infotrac in the library or a search engine such as Infoseek on the Internet should be a good place to start.

else is. With jealousy, a person already has what he or she wants but is afraid of losing it.

People in the workplace at times experience difficult emotions and should be responded to accordingly. Emotions such as interest and enthusiasm can have a positive effect on one's work.

Emphasis has recently been given to the importance of emotional intelligence in attaining success. Five related main domains are knowing one's emotions, managing emotions, motivating oneself, recognizing emotions in others, and handling relationships.

With understanding and appropriate control and expression, emotions can enrich our lives. Our study of emotions in this chapter should be helpful in learning about attitudes in Chapter 6.

Answers to Quiz Yourself on page 104.

1. e	**3.** g	**5.** h	**7.** f
2. d	**4.** a	**6.** c	**8.** b

Key Terms

Emotion
Amygdala
Conditioning
Phobia
Phobos
Hemo
Hemophobia
Agoraphobia
Agora
Claustrophobia
Self-love

Egotist
Humanitarian love
Family love
Friendship
Platonic
Romantic love
Love of God or a higher power
Love
Hate
Envy

Learning Activities

Turn to page LA-19 to complete the Learning Activities and Enrichment Activities for this chapter.

Endnotes

1. Robert Zajonc, "The Face as Window and Machine for the Emotions," *LSA Magazine,* University of Michigan, Fall 1990, p. 17.

2. "Anatomy of Apprehension," *Science News,* November 9, 1996, p. 301.

3. Paul Ekman, "Facial Expression and Emotion," *American Psychologist,* April 1993, p. 390.

4. "How to Cope with the Polygraph," *Nation's Business,* December 1989, p. 36.

5. William J. Magee, "Agoraphobia, Simple Phobia, and Social Phobia in the National Comorbidity Survey," *The Journal of the American Medical Association,* April 10, 1996, p. 1064L.

6. Hara Elstroff Marano, "Big. Bad. Bully," *Psychology Today,* September/October 1995, p. 54.

7. Lester David, "The Many Faces of Guilt," *Family Health,* July 1977, p. 22.

8. Sharon Nelton, "Emotions in the Workplace," *Nation's Business,* February 1996, p. 54.

9. Tom Brown, "The Emotional Side of Management," *Industry Week,* May 1, 1995, p. 36.

10. Daniel Goleman, *Emotional Intelligence,* Bantom Books, New York, 1995, p. 43.

Attitudes

6

Optimism, when applied to our lives, cleanses the mind of unhealthy thoughts. And, of course, unhealthy thoughts quickly take away the joy, peace, and even the health of life.

Norman Vincent Peale

LEARNING OBJECTIVES

After completing this chapter, you should be able to do the following:

1. Identify five areas that can influence the development of attitudes.
2. Discuss how attitudes and behavior are interrelated.
3. Compare optimism and pessimism.
4. Explain the use of surveys in determining the attitudes of a group.
5. Identify common causes of prejudice.
6. Discuss how the government has tried to deal with discrimination in the workplace.
7. Identify important work attitudes.
8. Explain how it is possible to change attitudes.
9. Describe how your body language can give clues about your attitudes.

Attitude
disposition, or readiness to act, involving both thinking and emotions.

Apathy
an attitude of lacking interest; lack of concern about events or circumstances.

Rational
the quality of being reasonable or logical.

Probably nothing is more fundamental to what you are and what you do than attitudes. An **attitude** is a readiness to act; it involves both thinking and emotion. It is a tendency to respond in a particular way to an object, a person, a group, or even an idea. A person can hold many attitudes, and they can be favorable or unfavorable. Even not caring at all about something is an attitude, called **apathy.**

We have a tendency to believe we are more **rational,** or thinking, than we probably are. In other words, most of us tend to believe we use our minds more than our feelings in reacting to other people, situations, and events. What we think affects how we feel, and how we feel affects what we think. An attitude or a reaction may seem to be based on reason but in reality may be based largely on an emotion such as fear or jealousy. What we feel can become so interwoven with what we think that we may be unable to understand our response to a particular person, event, or thing.

In a discussion of a controversial issue such as capital punishment, you would probably hear statements such as "I think deliberately killing another person is always wrong" or "I feel each state should have the right to make its own laws." People often interchange the expressions "I think" and "I feel" when expressing their attitudes. However, it would be more accurate to say, "My attitude is . . . ." This wording would indicate that both the ideas and the feelings of the speaker are involved. We should try to understand the difference between our thoughts and our feelings, and we should say what we mean.

Note also that even our thinking is not always clear and logical. Even if we could always separate our feelings from our thoughts or beliefs, the result might not be sound thinking. There are many different reasons why we think or believe as we do. And there are many reasons why we feel as we do.

INFLUENCES ON ATTITUDES

The many attitudes you now have were learned. They were acquired over a period of time, and they were influenced by at least five different factors: family, peers, role models, experience, and culture.

FAMILY

You did not inherit your attitudes, even though the members of a family often have similar ideas and beliefs. For example, the members of a family may have similar attitudes about exercising or about watching television. This happens because children learn their attitudes from their parents. Of course, parents do not say, "Today we are going to teach you an attitude about television." Instead, attitudes develop in a more gradual and subtle way. Neither the child nor the parents may even be aware that an attitude is being taught. Suppose, for example, that the parents say things like, "I'm too busy to watch the junk on television. It rots your mind." Their child will learn a different attitude about television than if they say, "I really enjoy watching television after a hard day. It gives me a break and helps me to relax."

Children learn by watching others and imitating them. If parents and older children hold strong attitudes about something, a young child is likely to develop similar attitudes. Many attitudes are learned in the home. Your feelings about spending or saving money or about treating older people politely are likely to be influenced by your family life. Also, your family is particularly influential when it comes to religious and political attitudes.

PEERS

Peer
a member of one's own age group.

Although your family will doubtless have a lasting effect on how you think and feel about many things, it is seldom the only strong influence on your attitudes. By the time children reach adolescence, other people their own age—their **peers**—become an important influence on their attitudes and values. Because young people during these years are psychologically breaking away from their families, being accepted by peers becomes extremely important. Thus, the attitudes of most young people are affected at least for a while by friends and

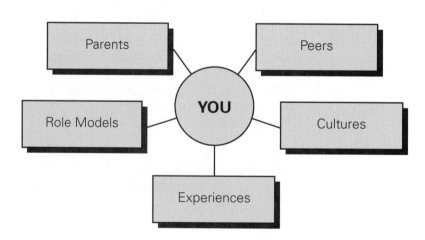

acquaintances of their own age. More will be said about the influence of both family and peers in Chapter 13.

ROLE MODELS

Role model
an older person whom one emulates.

Every child has a **role model**—an older person he or she admires and would like to emulate. A young person's evaluation of such a role model might not be realistic, but whatever he or she thinks the person is and stands for affects the development of his or her attitudes and behavior nonetheless. Sometimes the role model is an older brother or sister, a parent, or other relative. At other times the person might be a television personality or an athlete. One doesn't have to be especially talented or famous to be a role model. It should also be noted that those who are models or examples for others aren't necessarily displaying attitudes and behaviors that are desirable. They appeal to young people for various reasons.

Many people who are role models for younger persons are not even aware of their influence. It can even be awesome to think that someone else wants to imitate us. Even suspecting that we may be someone's role model might inspire us to examine our attitudes and behavior.

EXPERIENCE

Your direct experience also influences your attitudes. If you have had many bad experiences in a particular situation, you are likely to develop a negative attitude toward it. For example, if Roger has had poor luck fishing on Perch Lake several times, he is likely to have a negative attitude toward fishing there. On the other hand, if Louise has had fun every time she has visited her friend in Denver, she will doubtless develop a favorable attitude toward that city as well as toward her friend. These are examples of how experiences affect our attitudes.

The type of work we do can also influence our attitudes to some extent. This is especially true if the work limits our contact with other people. A marriage counselor, for example, who works mostly with couples having problems, may develop unrealistic, negative attitudes toward marriage. Since most jobs limit the types of experiences we have, our attitudes often are affected by our

Role models inspire us and influence our life goals.

occupations. However, we should not assume that all people who hold particular jobs have similar attitudes. It is a mistake to think that, for example, all teachers or all salespeople or all plumbers have similar attitudes.

CULTURE

Another influence on attitudes is the culture in which one grows up. People in different parts of the world traditionally have had different attitudes toward family relationships, work, education, leisure time, and death, for example. In the global community, discussed in Chapter 1, we now have a more multicultural society, and there is an attempt to preserve some values and customs of one's heritage as well as to appreciate the attitudes and values of others. An article in *Time* entitled "Beyond the Melting Pot," notes, "During the 21st Century racial and ethnic minorities will collectively outnumber whites for the first time. The 'browning of America' will affect every aspect of society" (1). New attitudes will develop and some changes of attitudes will be required if we want to live in harmony with one another.

ATTITUDES AND BEHAVIOR

Understanding attitudes is valuable because they are closely related to behavior. You will control your own behavior better if you understand the attitudes that affect what you do. You also will understand the behavior of others better, and you will be better able to predict what someone else might do in a certain situation. Finally, by understanding your attitudes, you can see how others are trying to influence your behavior by attempting to change your attitudes.

Attitudes are sometimes expressed openly in various types of discussion groups or in conversations, but more often they are revealed only indirectly. It is important to understand attitudes because certain attitudes can lead to certain types of behavior. Thus we act toward others according to what we assume about their attitudes. For example, if someone believes you have an attitude of trust toward others, that person will expect you to enter into relationships more readily than would a person who is suspicious of others.

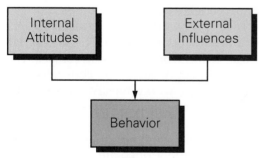

Even though attitudes usually precede behavior, they can also result from behavior. Behaving or acting in a certain way can lead one to develop a particular attitude. For example, if you make a special effort to accept other people—even though they may have characteristics quite different from yours—this effort can lead you to become more tolerant. In the same way, by acting enthusiastically about your work or some other activity, even though you may not feel that way at first, you can develop an enthusiastic attitude.

Attitudes and behavior do not always agree. What you say and do may contradict what you think and feel. A phrase as simple as "thank you" can be sincere

or it can express sarcasm and discontent. Your expressions and gestures may emphasize or contradict the actual words you are using. Thus, you may agree to work on your day off, even though you had other plans and think the request is unfair. Disagreement between attitudes and behavior will be discussed in more detail later in this chapter.

The relationship between attitudes and behavior can be confusing because they influence each other and we may not always know exactly how that influence works. Since attitudes *do* affect behavior, it is helpful to know the attitudes of others. Remember also that others are "reading" your attitudes and are reacting to you accordingly.

In Chapter 3, we discussed the difference between controlling and influencing others. If you agree that we can only influence, not control, the behavior of others, you can see that it is even more difficult to control what others think and feel. Someone in authority may have considerable influence over what others do (and don't do) in a particular situation. Such a person may be able to encourage or discourage certain types of behavior. But a person who says, "I insist that you respect me," will get nowhere. Respect is an attitude. It is based on our opinion of another person and on our feelings toward that person. Although an attitude of respect or disrespect is reflected in what we do, no one can force us to have that attitude. People may be able to influence our behavior, but they cannot control our thoughts and feelings.

POSITIVE AND NEGATIVE ATTITUDES

Pessimist
a person who habitually displays negative attitudes toward life in general and toward specific events.

Optimist
a person who habitually displays positive attitudes toward life in general and toward particular events.

A common way of classifying attitudes is to think of them as positive or negative. People who habitually display negative attitudes toward their jobs and the world are called **pessimists.** Those who see the brighter, more positive side of life are called **optimists.** In reacting to the same experience, both types will perceive it differently. Thus, a pessimist might consider a job transfer to be an undesirable change that probably will cause disappointments and problems. An optimist, however, would see the situation as a new opportunity and challenge. In both cases, attitudes affect the person's perception.

In fact, a job transfer probably will cause some problems, such as finding a new place to live. But an optimist focuses on the desirable aspects of the situation, and a pessimist pays more attention to the negative aspects. Very few people view themselves as pessimists. Most people tend to believe that they are viewing the situation as it really is.

An appropriate theme for attitude improvement might be "Accentuate the positive; eliminate the negative." Examples of positive attitudes are tolerance, enthusiasm, optimism, confidence, and conscientiousness. Examples of negative attitudes are revengefulness, pessimism, suspicion, apathy, and uncooperativeness. We must first recognize our negative attitudes if we want to eliminate them.

Low self-esteem can contribute to negative attitudes toward oneself as well as toward others and the world in general. Cherie Carter-Scott coined the term *negaholism* and describes it as "a syndrome in which people unconsciously limit their own innate abilities, convince themselves that they can't have what they want, and sabotage their wishes, desires, and dreams" (2). Although it isn't likely that your attitudes are that self-defeating, it is important to keep in mind that our attitudes do affect our behavior and what we achieve in our lives.

Joseph T. Martorano and John P. Kildahl relate a fictional example of negative thinking in their book, *Beyond Negative Thinking,* in the following anecdote:

> A traveling salesman gets a flat tire on a dark, lonely road and then discovers that he has no jack. He sees a light in a farmhouse. As he walks toward it, his mind churns: "Suppose no one comes to the door." "Suppose they don't have a jack." "Suppose the guy won't lend me his jack even if he has one." The harder his mind works, the more agitated he becomes, and when the door opens, he punches the farmer and yells, "Keep your lousy jack!" (3).

You can choose to be an optimist. Advantages of developing a more positive attitude are further explained by Martin E. P. Seligman in *Learned Optimism.* He maintains,

> Life inflicts the same setbacks and tragedies on the optimist as on the pessimist, but the optimist weathers them better. As we have seen, the optimist bounces back from defeat, and, with his life somewhat poorer, he picks up and starts again. The pessimist gives up and falls into depression. Because of his resilience, the optimist achieves more at work, at school, and on the playing field. The optimist has better physical health and may even live longer. Americans want optimists to lead them. Even when things go well for the pessimist, he is haunted by forebodings of catastrophe" (4).

It is easier for most people to control what they say or do than to control their attitudes. Although attitudes and behavior affect each other, acting in a particular way can gradually affect how one feels. As mentioned earlier, by acting enthusiastically about your work or about other activities—even though you may not feel that way at first—you can develop an enthusiastic attitude toward them. You also can lessen feelings of discouragement by working at something constructive or creative. If a certain aspect of your work becomes discouraging, the time spent on more satisfying tasks can help restore a positive, confident attitude.

ATTITUDE SURVEYS

Various types of surveys to determine attitudes of society in general, or a segment of society, are common. Partial results of such a survey were reported in *American Demographics:*

> . . . according to recent surveys conducted by Gallup, CBS News/The New York Times, ABC News/Money, NFO Research, and Yankelovich Partners for Time and CNN: 71% of Americans say they are dissatisfied with the way things are going in this country, but 74% are satisfied with the ways things are going in their own lives; just 25% of Americans say future generations will be better off than people are today, but 55% believe their children will be better off then they themselves are today (5).

Similar attitude surveys are periodically conducted about freedom of the press, abortion, foreign aid, education, and other current issues. Although there are different ways of structuring a survey, many are set up like the self-evaluation called "Quiz Yourself on Your Attitudes Toward Smoking". This self-evaluation contains only a few typical questions; therefore, it would not necessarily be an accurate determination of your attitudes. Although there are no right or wrong answers to these questions, notes at the end of the chapter will be helpful in interpreting your responses. Additional questions concerning attitudes and possible attitude change will be found later in the chapter.

Remember that attitudes are what one thinks and feels and are not behavior. Although an attitude often leads to behavior similar to that attitude, there can be various explanations for a person having a particular attitude. A person who does not smoke, for example, may still be opposed to certain regulations to restrict smoking.

Quiz Yourself on Your Attitudes Toward Smoking

Determining your response to each of the following questions can give you a better understanding of attitudes in general and your attitudes on this particular issue. This is a self-evaluation, but you may want to compare your attitudes with others in the class.

1. *Should smoking be prohibited in all public buildings?*	Yes	Not sure	No
2. *Does everyone have a right to smoke where he or she chooses?*	Yes	Not sure	No
3. *Do some people have the right to ask others not to smoke?*	Yes	Not sure	No
4. *Are you in favor of an increased tax on cigarettes to help pay for health insurance?*	Yes	Not sure	No
5. *Are your attitudes toward smoking the same as that of your friends?*	Yes	Not sure	No
6. *Are your attitudes toward smoking influenced by either your smoking or nonsmoking behavior?*	Yes	Not sure	No

Notes on Quiz Yourself on Your Attitudes Toward Smoking are on page 139.

PREJUDICE

Prejudice
prejudgment made without adequate information.

Prejudice is an attitude that seriously affects the lives of many people. The word **prejudice** means "judging before"; it is prejudging without having adequate information or reason. We develop attitudes over time without being fully aware of why we think and feel the way we do. Or we may develop an attitude as a result of a single especially favorable or unfavorable incident. In either case such attitudes may lack justifiable foundations.

As you know, it is possible to be prejudiced either in favor of something or against it. If an employer believes that the only people qualified to work for her are those who graduated from her alma mater, she is prejudiced in favor of these graduates. If another employer believes that all people who belong to a certain religion are unreliable, he is prejudiced against this religious group. In both cases, prejudice or prejudgment is being made by the employers without adequate information.

The word *adequate* is an important part of the definition of prejudice. In reality it is necessary to prejudge every day. You decide to buy a new product without knowing exactly how well it will serve your purposes. You may ask a new acquaintance for a date without knowing exactly how the person will act. You may enroll in flight school without knowing whether you have the aptitude or even a realistic desire to learn to fly. However, the more information you have about a product or a person, the greater the chance that your prejudgment is sound. Whether a given amount of information is adequate for making a prejudgment depends on the amount of information that is available, the difficulty or complexity of the activity, and the seriousness of the consequences.

STEREOTYPING

Stereotyping
attitude that assumes all members of a particular group are alike.

"Men are all alike." "Teenagers all act the same." "All salespeople are alike." These statements are examples of **stereotyping,** or assuming that all members of a particular group conform to the same pattern and react in the same way. Although members of a group often have characteristics in common, there is no group in which all members are alike.

WHAT CAUSES PREJUDICE?

Why do so many people prejudge without adequate information? There are several reasons. Common causes of prejudice are lack of information, misinformation, fear of the unknown, lack of understanding, and blind loyalties. Some prejudices arise from a basic feeling of inferiority. Thus, people may try to make themselves look and feel better by making others appear inferior to them.

Prejudiced people usually hold very strong opinions. They are likely to have a number of prejudices because they are narrow-minded and often are not interested in acquiring adequate information. This makes it difficult to reduce prejudice. Since prejudice is an unsupported attitude, prejudiced people cannot be expected to be reasonable about examining their attitudes. They are also often insecure and distrustful in their relationships with others.

Most people try to justify their prejudices by devising what they think are acceptable reasons for them. One difficulty in eliminating prejudices is that the cause of the prejudice lies within a person.

The following questions were among those posed by *Christopher News Notes* as a self-examination on prejudice:

How do I react when I hear about an example of racism? Do I seek revenge?
Do I see all people of a particular race in a bad light because of the actions of a few?
Do I welcome others of different races or backgrounds?
Do I respect the languages and customs of others?
Do I know the contributions various races and ethnic and religious groups have made to this country?
Do I join in negative remarks about a person or persons of a specific racial, religious, or ethnic group or do I refuse to participate? (6)

DISCRIMINATION

Discrimination
behavior that is usually unfair and harmful toward an individual because he or she belongs to a particular group.

Prejudice is an attitude; **discrimination** is behavior. Discrimination is behavior—usually unfair and harmful—toward an individual because he or she belongs to a particular group. A person may be discriminated against because he or she is a Democrat, a Methodist, a Native American, a manager, a union member, a homosexual, or a member of any other group; for example, she may be discriminated against because she is a female. People are also discriminated against because they are too old or too young, too thin or too fat, or too anything. Discrimination ranges from simple avoidance to verbal criticism to hostility and violence. There are laws against discrimination in housing, employment, club membership, school attendance, and many other areas. However, problems often arise in efforts to adhere to these laws. Consider the following example.

> The Reliable Construction Company had neither employed a female construction worker nor had any females applied for work with the company. Karen applied to work for the company when it was looking for thirty workers to build a new community health center. Because the building was funded in part by federal money, the superintendent of the project was fearful of losing the contract if he showed gender discrimination in hiring workers. As a result, he reluctantly hired Karen. However, she discovered by the end of the first week on the job that none of the male construction workers wanted to work with her. In an effort to make Karen quit, the superintendent assigned her more than her share of heavy manual labor.

Affirmative action
government guidelines that require businesses receiving government contracts to hire representative numbers of minorities.

Reverse discrimination
preferences given to minorities, thereby discriminating against the majority race and gender.

Attempting to eliminate discrimination has been a complicated process. In 1965, President Lyndon B. Johnson signed an executive order establishing **affirmative action** guidelines. These guidelines required businesses receiving government contracts to hire, or at least attempt to hire, representative numbers of women and minorities. The first affirmative action program also provided for greater enrollment of minorities in colleges and universities. Other organizations and institutions developed plans to give those who had been discriminated against in the past new opportunities in employment and education.

New problems arose, however, including charges of **reverse discrimination** against white males. Preference given to minorities, who were often less qualified, resulted in discrimination against those who had not been discriminated against in the past. As a result, in 1978, the Supreme Court heard a reverse discrimination case and ruled that a California medical school discriminated illegally against Allan Bakke, a white male, in favor of minorities. The Court did not rule against affirmative action as a whole, however. There have been numerous other reverse discrimination cases involving employment as well as educational opportunities since that time.

Affirmative action has become very controversial in recent years. As with other controversial issues, there are firm believers on both sides. Those who oppose the continuation of affirmative action claim that preferential treatment is unfair and, at best, no longer needed. Most of those who support continuation of affirmative action acknowledge that there have been and still are problems, but that the program needs modification rather than abandonment. Jeff Dickerson states in *The Atlantic Journal*

> The trouble is that the school officials and proponents of preference never acknowledged that affirmative action was temporary. It needed an expiration date, even after a few decades of trying to right centuries of discrimination. Our legal principles demanded that at some point we accept and be judged by one, nonracial standard (7).

Obviously laws cannot eliminate discrimination completely. Such attempts, along with efforts to avoid and reduce attitudes of prejudice, improve the equality of opportunity for all, however.

A basic social problem is the elimination and prevention of prejudice itself, rather than concentrating only on control of the results of prejudice. Because of better educational opportunities and a more mobile population in which people come into contact with many others, some kinds of prejudice have decreased. There is probably far less religious prejudice, for example, than there was a generation ago.

Keep in mind that we all use reasonable discrimination in making choices every day. Whenever we choose one thing over another, we are discriminating. Some of it may be unwise but not unfair to others. It is unfair discrimination resulting from prejudice or self-interest that is a serious social problem.

William B. Allen, then Commissioner of the U.S. Commission on Human Rights, gave a speech in 1991 in which he declared that we must learn to "live in a world, in a country, where people can see black, white, and anything at all, without seeing a problem, where people can refer to color because color is no longer an issue" (8). Chapter 12 will give us a greater understanding of how we can all accept and value one another.

WORK-RELATED ATTITUDES

How do your attitudes affect your work? How do they affect your education (which, for the time being, *is* your work)?

Because most people have to work whether they like it or not, people have a wide range of attitudes toward their jobs. To the question, How do you like your job? typical replies might be:

I'm glad I am able to work and that I have a job.

I couldn't ask for a job I'd like better; it's a real challenge.

It's okay, I guess; I've never thought much about it.

I like my job. If I didn't like it, I would try to find one I did like.

Who likes any job? Work is work.

I don't like the work itself so much, but it's a good company and I like the people I work with.

You might say, "If I do my job, what difference does it make what my attitude is?" The answer is that your attitude toward your job affects the quality of your work. If you don't take pride in your work, your performance may not meet the requisite standards. In specialized fields, in which many people may work on the final product, a careless attitude by one person can cause the final product to be inferior. An expensive motor can be rejected because it has one flaw caused by one person who didn't care.

How your attitude influences others is noticed by your boss and by others who are in a position to affect your future. Arlo may think, "I have kept my job for fifteen years, so I must be considered a good employee." However, he may never know what opportunities or benefits he has missed because someone decided he did not have the right attitude.

A widely used book by those who realize that positive attitudes are important on the job is Elwood Chapman's *Your Attitude Is Showing.* He tells us, "A positive attitude is essential to career success for many reasons." He then goes on to say that:

■ When you are positive you are usually more energetic, highly motivated, productive, and alert. Thinking about negative things too much has a way of draining your energy. Put another way, a positive attitude opens a gate and lets your inner enthusiasm spill out. A negative attitude, on the other hand, will keep the gate closed.

■ First impressions are important on the job because they often have a lasting effect. Coworkers you meet for the first time can be said to have little radar sets tuned in to your attitude. If your attitude is positive, they receive a friendly, warm signal, and they are attracted to you. If your attitude is negative, they receive an unfriendly signal, and they try to avoid you.

■ A positive employee contributes to the productivity of others. A negative employee does not. Attitudes are caught more than they are taught! Both negative and positive attitudes are transmitted on the job. They are picked up by others. A persistently negative attitude, like the rotten apple in the barrel, can spoil the positive attitudes of others. It is very difficult to maintain a high level of productivity while working next to a person with a negative attitude.

■ Coworkers like you when you are positive. They like to be around you because you are fun. This makes your job more interesting and exciting, because you are in the middle of things and not on the outside complaining. When you are negative, people prefer to stay clear of you. A negative person may build good relationships with a few other people (who are perhaps

Universal Press Syndicate, Inc.

negative themselves), but such a person cannot build good relationships with the majority of employees.

- The kind of attitude you transmit to management will have a great deal to do with your future success. Management constantly reads your mental attitude, even though you may feel you are successful in covering it up. Supervisors can determine your attitude by how you approach your job, react to directives, handle problems, and work with others. If you are positive, you will be given greater consideration when special assignments and promotion opportunities arise (9).

WHERE WORK ATTITUDES BEGIN

Attitudes toward work begin very early in life—long before a child is expected to work. As with other types of attitudes, children are influenced by their parents' attitudes toward work. Today, however, outside influences also begin at an earlier age than in the past. Children in elementary schools are learning more about careers and career choices, and such information is provided in depth in high school. The goal is to encourage realistic attention to career opportunities over the years, as well as to promote the development of constructive attitudes toward work. Recognition of the fact that work is a major part of life should not be something that comes as a shock upon graduation from high school.

After deciding what you want to do in the way of work, the next step is to prepare yourself for it. Most jobs today require some specialized training. Many young people who have dropped out of high school "to get a job" have found that there aren't many jobs for which they are qualified. In addition, they cannot foresee working a lifetime at the unskilled jobs that are available. Perhaps a negative attitude toward school caused them to drop out and seek a job. But a realistic encounter with the job market may cause a change in attitude that will result in further occupational education and training.

After you prepare yourself through education and training for a particular type of work, the next step, of course, is actually to get the job. You must be not only personable and persuasive but also skilled enough at a particular type of work to get the job, and then you must do the job well enough to keep it. Both you and your employer must be interested in developing your skills so that your value to the company increases. Attitude is an important factor throughout. Being able to do a particular type of work is expected, but that is only the beginning of your evaluation as an employee.

Some students in vocational and job training programs are impatient with courses that do not seem to train them directly in their major skills. But experience has shown that those who have favorable attitudes toward themselves, other people, and life in general become the most sought-after employees. It is not unusual for an employer to say something like, "Let people with basic skills and constructive attitudes come to our company, and we'll give them the special training and opportunities they need. People who have the right skills but negative attitudes soon become a nuisance to us—and often discredit themselves."

IMPORTANT WORK ATTITUDES

Managers and personnel directors consider attitude more important than any other factor when hiring and promoting employees. John Lippert, a *Detroit Free*

In the workplace, positive attitudes are the most important factor in employee promotion and success.

Press labor writer, states that managers "are more interested in what you are willing to do than in what you know" (10). Richard L. Weaver II, in a speech entitled "Attitude, Not Aptitude, Determines Altitude," maintains that "You can have the loftiest goals; you can have the highest ideals; you can have the noblest dreams; you can have the richest ideas; but remember nothing works unless you do! It is, indeed, attitude, not aptitude, that determines altitude" (11).

What are some of the attitudes employers look for? Below is a list of some of them.

LOYALTY TO THE COMPANY Loyalty begins with interest and caring. Personnel managers naturally expect that employees are interested in satisfying their own needs, but they look also for people who will show an interest in and feel loyal to the company. Employees are expected to have a high regard for the company or organization they work for, without being negative about competitors or past employers. A person can be interested in the company from the beginning of employment and have intentions of being loyal, but a feeling of loyalty and pride in the organization you work for usually takes some time.

WILLINGNESS TO WORK Although it would seem obvious that someone looking for a job wants to work, employers know this is not always the case. An employer is not likely to hire someone who answers the question, "Why do you want to work for our company?" by saying, "Well, I need something to do," or "I could really use the money."

WILLINGNESS TO LEARN Students completing work-related courses have the right to feel competent and to believe they are qualified for a job in the area of their major. You are being naive, however, if you do not realize that you still have much to learn. New employees must be willing to learn about the functioning of a particular business or industry. They must be willing to become more skilled through practice and to benefit by association with those who have more experience. Willingness to learn includes receptiveness to constructive criticism. We cannot learn if our attitude is that we have nothing to learn.

WILLINGNESS TO WORK WITH OTHERS Teamwork is required in today's workplace. Although individuals may have different skills and responsibilities, it is only when everyone is working together toward common goals that the company or organization is productive and profitable. Also, situations may arise that require temporary substitutions or helping out beyond one's immediate responsibility. Although union contracts or licensing may limit what employees are allowed to do outside their own jobs, an overall attitude of helpfulness makes the organization run more smoothly and improves morale.

RESPECT FOR SUPERVISORS, COWORKERS, CUSTOMERS, AND CLIENTS Respect is an attitude rather than a behavior. It consists of what one thinks and feels toward others. No one can demand that you respect him or her, for example. What others can do is demand that we treat them the way they want to be treated or accept the consequences over which they have control. Remember the discussion of control and influence in Chapter 3? Respect should not involve believing that others are superior human beings with greater human rights. It recognizes the dignity and needs of others and our relationship to them under specific circumstances. Respect recognizes the uniqueness of each individual and accepts his or her ways—as long as this does not interfere with the rights of others or with the organization's productivity or goals.

POSITIVE ATTITUDES TOWARD CHANGE You will recall (or you can review) several types of change related to the world of work discussed in Chapter 1. Although some resistance to change can be expected, especially when we are not sure how it will affect us, change is inevitable in all aspects of life. Change can require new learning and some adjustments; it can also keep our work lives interesting and challenging. There aren't very many people today who would be willing to do the same repetitive job for twenty-five or thirty years, as was often the case in the past. Not only can we be receptive to change but we can be among the most valued employees who help bring it about.

These are some of the attitudes most frequently mentioned by employers. A person needs the skills to do the job, but it has been said, "Attitude is more important than aptitude." It is easier to teach individuals something new if they have the attitudes discussed above.

What Would You Suggest? *If a good friend asked you, "How can I improve my attitude toward my work?" what would you suggest?*

CHANGING ATTITUDES

We would be much less concerned about attitudes if it were impossible to change or to influence them. Even so, it can be a frustrating experience to try to change the attitudes of others.

People change their attitudes only after they perceive situations differently. This change doesn't ordinarily happen easily or quickly. But to believe that attitudes cannot be changed is a negative attitude in itself.

Earlier in this chapter you were asked to examine your attitudes toward smoking restrictions. Following are a few more questions pertaining to attitude change. As with the questions pertaining to smoking, there is no way to score your responses accurately. Notes at the end of the chapter will help you evaluate your responses.

Quiz Yourself on Attitude Formation and Change *The following are questions to consider in an examination of your attitudes. They require careful thought, but your answers can be helpful in understanding your attitudes.*

1. *Do I resist new ideas or change?*	*Yes*	*Not sure*	*No*
2. *Is it difficult for me to admit I am wrong?*	*Yes*	*Not sure*	*No*
3. *Am I tolerant of the ideas of others? Do I really listen to and consider their opinions?*	*Yes*	*Not sure*	*No*
4. *How long have I held particular attitudes? Have my attitudes become habits?*	*Yes*	*Not sure*	*No*
5. *Have I recently had new experiences or acquired new information related to certain attitudes?*	*Yes*	*Not sure*	*No*
6. *Are my attitudes affecting my studies, my work, and my relationships with others?*	*Yes*	*Not sure*	*No*

Notes on Quiz Yourself on Attitude Formation and Change are on pages 139–140.

ATTITUDES CAN CHANGE WITH TIME

Attitudes, like values, can be expected to change over time. In part, this change results from having new experiences and developing new understanding. As Mark Twain put it: "When I was a boy of fourteen, my father was so ignorant, I could hardly stand to have the old man around. But when I got to be twenty-one, I was astonished at how much he had learned in seven years!"

One parent recalls a conflict of attitudes between herself and her parents when she was a teenager. Evidently they disagreed about how much independence the girl should have at the age of 16. She recalls thinking, "When I get to be a parent and have a 16-year-old daughter, I will allow her as much independence as she wishes." Now, as a parent, she can remember her earlier attitude, but she no longer thinks and feels that way. Because of her age and new point of view, her attitude has changed.

The attitudes of most older adults are relatively stable. They may not change much for the rest of a person's life. There are several reasons for this. Some older people may simply be stubborn. Others may have more knowledge than younger people but are not continuing to learn at the same pace as younger people, so their attitudes may not be challenged so much. Their attitudes at this time may be the result of earlier changes. They have become satisfied now with their ideas and feelings on many subjects. They have established their ideas about politics, religion, economics, and many other subjects, and they are not likely to change. This is called *cognitive consistency*. Many married couples over the years maintain similar attitudes and values. Avshalom Caspi, who conducted a study of couples, explains that they did not *grow* more alike; instead they *remained* moderately similar in attitudes and values across 20 years. He believes shared experiences such as work, recreational, and religious activities maintain similarities (12).

In addition, older people may not have as much contact with as many different people as they did when they were younger. They have settled down socially, so there are fewer people influencing their attitudes. Finally, the attitudes of older people may become so much a part of what they are that to change their ideas and feelings would be damaging to their sense of security. We will look at this idea more closely in Chapter 10.

WHERE DOES CHANGE BEGIN?

If a change in either attitude or behavior is desired, where does one begin? Most often it is suggested that attitudes be changed first, since they tend to result in certain kinds of behavior (as discussed earlier). But some people say that attitude changes should begin with a behavior change. This, they say, will encourage a more natural, permanent behavior change.

ATTITUDES AND PERSONALITY

Since attitudes are underlying factors in our reactions to others, they must be closely related to our personalities—our typical ways of expressing what we think and feel. However, personality involves how we behave or act as a result of our attitudes. A person may think that other people are basically honest and may feel no threat from them. Therefore, he or she will act toward others in a relaxed, trusting manner.

There are many ways to describe someone's attitudes and behavior. We may consider a person to be outgoing, sincere, considerate, self-centered, stubborn, suspicious, belligerent, humane, defiant, inflexible, enthusiastic, and so on. The willingness to change one's attitude is related to one's basic personality. A person who has a poor self-concept may be influenced more easily than someone who is confident, for example. Other people may be narrow-minded or stubborn and may be unable or unwilling to see things from another point of view. Again, we can see the relationship between attitude and perception.

What Do You Think? *Can one regard one's own unwillingness to change as loyalty or dedication and yet regard someone else's unwillingness to change as stubbornness? What do you think?*

AGREEMENT BETWEEN ATTITUDES AND BEHAVIOR

Not only do attitudes and behavior affect one another but it is important for an individual's attitudes and behavior to agree or to be in balance. Sometimes two attitudes can be in conflict with one another, or attitude and behavior can be in conflict. When such a conflict exists, a person is said to be experiencing *cognitive dissonance*. A person can become so disturbed that either the attitude or behavior has to be changed.

For example, a person may have a charitable attitude and yet never really do anything to help others. Such a person either has to perform charitable acts or admit to not really being charitable. Another person may have favorable ideas and feelings about being clean and orderly but still be careless about personal appearance and possessions. To feel comfortable, this person must change either the behavior or the attitude about order and cleanliness. In a sense, it is important not only to practice what you preach but also to practice what you believe. You sometimes can be frustrated by a situation or by your overall lifestyle without quite realizing that the problem is caused by a conflict between your attitudes and behavior.

MOTHER GOOSE & GRIMM

**What Would
You Do?** *If you came to the conclusion that you had conflicting beliefs
and behavior about a subject important to you, what would you
do?*

DRASTIC EXPERIENCES

Although attitudes do not change readily after a person reaches adulthood, sometimes a single drastic experience can cause complete attitude reversal. Someone who has never bothered using seat belts, for example, may see a tragic accident that changes that attitude for life. Or someone may be skeptical about the value of a proper diet until the onset of a medical condition changes that attitude. Most of us, however, do not have to face such drastic situations, so our attitudes may change only slightly and gradually unless we make a serious effort to change them.

OUTSIDE INFLUENCES

Some common methods of changing attitudes are used in advertising, sales promotion, and other persuasion techniques. One technique used in advertising is called **association.** A product or service is shown with something else we already accept, or it may be presented by a celebrity to persuade us to transfer our favorable attitude toward that person to the product being sold. We would like to believe that we make up our own minds, but advertisers know they have tremendous opportunities to influence our attitudes and buying behavior. Indeed, they spend millions of dollars trying to do so.

Association and other persuasion techniques can be used by any group or individual seeking to change attitudes. The efforts may be aimed at the general public, at a smaller group such as a club, or at an individual. As an individual, you should be aware of such techniques and what those who use them are trying to accomplish.

The most extreme method of changing attitudes is called **brainwashing.** Brainwashing is an attempt to change a person's thinking and feelings completely, causing him or her to reject former loyalties and adopt a new point of view. Brainwashing has occurred mostly in prison camps during wars, but cult groups and others have also been accused of using the technique. The basic principle involved is to isolate the individual from what was previously meaningful and important. Next, the person's basic needs are not satisfied until the new attitude is accepted. Only then is the person permitted to sleep or eat. This technique obviously requires that the brainwashers control the environment totally. In such circumstances it is difficult or impossible for the individual to realize what is happening or to resist the influence being exerted. Of course, people vary in how readily they react to such influences and pressures, but the process seems to be very effective with some people.

Association
the relating of something new with what is already accepted.

Brainwashing
an attempt to change a person's thinking and feelings completely, causing him or her to reject former loyalties and adopt new beliefs.

WHAT'S YOUR ATTITUDE?

On what basis do you judge the attitudes of others? Some people openly express their beliefs and ideas in various types of discussion groups and in conversation. Others may have similar attitudes but do not share their ideas and feelings readily.

For most people it is easier to share ideas than feelings. There are some, however, who are willing to express their feelings, at least to a few other persons. The willingness or unwillingness to share thoughts and feelings was discussed in Chapter 2.

In many instances attitudes are revealed by indirect clues, such as facial expressions and body posture, often referred to as body language. Our thoughts and feelings are revealed in these ways even when we do not realize it. Attention or lack of it is also an expression of attitude. If you have a negative attitude about an experience you are having, it probably shows in some way. It is important to realize, however, that facial expressions and body language can be misinterpreted. Thus, someone who is simply not very expressive may be considered apathetic or even aloof. We are not always accurate in determining the attitudes of others, yet we often react toward them as though we knew what they believe and feel. This chapter should have made it clear that attitudes are difficult to determine or change. A little tolerance goes a long way—on the job and in every aspect of living.

Summary

Attitudes influence us more than we realize. An attitude involves both what we think and what we feel about a person, an object, a situation, or an idea.

Attitudes are learned. Major influences on the development of attitudes are your family, peers, role models, experience, and culture.

Behavior and attitudes are interrelated. Certain attitudes usually result in similar behavior. But it is also possible for behavior to lead to the development of an attitude.

One way to classify attitudes is to see them as positive or negative. Those who are usually cheerful and positive toward work and life are called optimists; those who habitually display negative attitudes are known as pessimists.

Attitudes of a specific group or of society in general can be measured with surveys. An understanding of the attitudes of a group may lead to appropriate action.

Prejudice is prejudging without having adequate information. Common causes of prejudice are lack of information, misinformation, fear of the unknown, misunderstanding, blind loyalties, or a basic feeling of inferiority. Discrimination is unfair treatment that results from prejudice. In 1965, the government established affirmative action guidelines to attempt to hire representative numbers of women and minorities. In some cases this practice led to reverse discrimination against white males and to other problems.

Work-related attitudes develop very early in life. The attitudes of your parents and your teachers as well as your part-time work experiences have undoubtedly influenced your attitudes toward work. Desirable work attitudes include willingness to work, willingness to learn, a desire to work with others, loyalty, and respect for supervisors, coworkers, customers, and clients. It is also important to have positive attitudes toward change.

Attitudes become relatively fixed as a person becomes older, but they can be changed through self-understanding, motivation, and sincere effort.

PSYCHOLOGY IN PRACTICE

1. Try to identify a group against which you might have been prejudiced. Find out as much about the group and several of its members as you can. Does your evidence indicate that your beliefs have sound support, or can you see ways that you were, or still are, prejudiced?

2. Work on having a more positive attitude toward everyone you associate with and all your experiences for at least three days. Either share the results orally with the class or write a brief description of the results.

3. Working in a small group, choose two current controversial issues and discuss what you believe to be important influences on your attitudes toward them.

In the process of examining our attitudes and how they affect others as well as ourselves, it is worthwhile to examine our body language. Indirect clues such as facial expressions and body posture can reveal our attitudes. Our attitudes affect everything we do. They even affect our ability to think and solve problems, the subject of Chapter 7.

Notes on Quiz Yourself on Your Attitudes Toward Smoking

Although there are no right or wrong answers, the following notes may be helpful in interpreting your responses. You may want to compare your responses with other members of the class or friends.

1. Since smoking is now prohibited in federal buildings and many other public buildings in some states and communities, there is support for this position. Even some people who smoke may be opposed to smoking in public buildings. Others may disapprove of smoking but do not wish to prohibit others from smoking under certain conditions. Do you think your attitude is related to whether or not you smoke?

2. A yes answer to the question indicates a disregard for the rights of others. Most people today would probably answer no to this statement.

3. Those who answer yes to this question will often qualify it according to the place and conditions involved. Most would agree one has the right to ask others not to smoke in their automobiles and homes. Laws prohibiting smoking and policy of the establishment would be additional factors. The well-being and rights of individuals affected would also be factors. Some smokers, in referring to a public place not restricting smoking, would respond, "If my smoking bothers you, you can move." Would this be your attitude?

4. Since nonsmokers would not have to pay the tax, it is likely those who disapprove of smoking would favor the tax. Other nonsmokers, as well as smokers, would consider the tax an unreasonable way to discourage smoking. They might claim that smoking and its effects, in most cases, should not be controlled by government.

5. The question pertains to how attitudes are acquired. Consider the influence your friends or peers have on your attitudes. Also consider, of course, the influence you may have had on their attitudes.

6. This question pertains to the relationship between attitudes and behavior. They affect one another.

Notes on Quiz Yourself on Attitude Formation and Change

The following notes are intended to give you a better understanding of attitudes. There are no right or wrong answers to the questions.

1. Since we are living in a rapidly changing world, we should be willing to at least examine our attitudes to determine if they are still valid or appropriate. A change in behavior can often lead to a corresponding change in attitude. Since it is easier for most of us to change what we do than to change what we think or feel, some changes can begin with how we act.

2. Being unwilling to admit that we are wrong usually indicates a weak self-concept. This unwillingness can keep us from being open-minded, from learning, and from examining our ideas, feelings, and behavior. We are thus not being fair to ourselves as well as to others.

3. Lack of tolerance leads to some of the same problems as resisting change. Lack of tolerance of others is often due to an inferiority complex. This, of course, is also related to a poor self-concept. When people feel good about themselves, they are more accepting of others.

4. The longer one holds an attitude, the more difficult it can be to change. What we think and how we feel, as well as what we do, can become habits. And we know that habits can be difficult to change. The first step in changing a habit is becoming aware of it and its possible negative effects.

5. Although we need not examine our attitudes on a daily basis, we should be willing to adjust our ideas and feelings if new experiences or information warrant it. New experiences include an evaluation of the experience. People who hesitate to have new experiences are leading lives that are not as interesting as they could be.

6. Since our attitudes affect our studies and work, we can improve what we accomplish in these areas by developing more optimistic, constructive attitudes. Nobody enjoys being around others who consistently display negative attitudes. Such attitudes can definitely interfere with our relationships with others, which includes relationships at work.

Key Terms

Attitude	Prejudice
Apathy	Stereotyping
Rational	Discrimination
Peer	Affirmative action
Role model	Reverse discrimination
Pessimist	Association
Optimist	Brainwashing

Learning Activities

Turn to page LA-23 to complete the Learning Activities and Enrichment Activities for this chapter.

Endnotes

1. Mehta S. Naushad, Sylvester Monroe, and Don Winbush, "Beyond the Melting Pot," *Time*, April 9, 1990, p. 28.

2. Cherie Carter-Scott, *Negaholics: How to Recover from Your Addiction to Negativity and Turn Your Life Around*, Villard Books, New York, 1989, p. 18.

3. Joseph T. Martorano and John P. Kildahl, *Beyond Negative Thinking*, Insight Books, New York, 1989, p. 207.

4. Martin E. Seligman, *Learned Optimism*, Alfred A. Knopf, Inc., New York, 1990, p. 207.

5. Cheryl Russell, "Are We in the Dumps?" *American Demographics*, January 1995, p. 6.

6. "Healing the Hate: What You Can Do About Racism," *Christopher News Notes*, July/August 1990.

7. Jeff Dickerson, "Numbers Tell the Story," *The Atlantic Journal*, July 8, 1997, p. A08.

8. William B. Allen, "Why I Am Still Black," *Vital Speeches*, May 1, 1991, p. 430.

9. Elwood N. Chapman, *Your Attitude Is Showing*, *A Primer of Human Relations*, 8th ed., Prentice-Hall, Upper Saddle River, NJ, 1996, pp. 21–22.

10. John Lippert, "Winning Résumés Reflect a Can-Do-Attitude, Bosses Say," *Detroit Free Press*, June 10, 1994, p. 1A.

11. Richard L. Weaver II, "Attitude, Not Aptitude, Determines Altitude," *Vital Speeches*, May 15, 1993, p. 480.

12. B. Bower, "Adult Attitudes: Share and Share Alike," *Science News*, February 22, 1991, p. 116.

Thinking and Problem Solving

7

A person who never made a mistake never tried anything new.

Albert Einstein

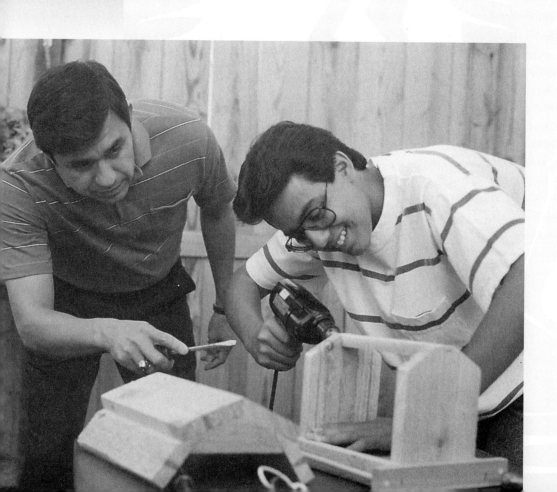

LEARNING OBJECTIVES

After completing this chapter, you should be able to do the following:

1. Contrast right-brain and left-brain functioning.
2. Identify and define the stages of cognitive development.
3. Describe the different intelligences according to Gardner and Armstrong.
4. Define the three stages of memory and give an example of each.
5. Identify factors that contribute to learning and memory.
6. Describe abilities involved in using common sense.
7. Apply the problem-solving guidelines to a realistic problem.
8. Describe characteristics common to creative thinkers.
9. Describe two kinds of work-related problem-solving groups.
10. Compare intuition and insight as they relate to problem solving.

Think! When you think, what really happens in your brain? You might answer, "I never thought about it." If you have thought about it but still don't know what is happening in your brain when you think, you are not alone. Although more has been discovered about the brain and its functions in recent years, it still is not known exactly how our brains perform when we remember, solve problems, or imagine new experiences. Fortunately, we can do these things without having to control or understand the processes consciously. However, we can learn to think more logically, remember more accurately and for longer periods, and think more creatively. This ability could remove some of our frustration and make our lives more interesting.

The term *cognition* is frequently used in discussions of learning and thinking. It can be defined as the mental activity involved in processing, storing, and retrieving information.

Richard E. Mayer, in *Thinking, Problem Solving and Cognition*, explains that thinking includes three basic ideas:

1. Thinking is cognitive, but is inferred from behavior. It occurs internally, in the mind or cognitive system, and must be inferred indirectly.
2. Thinking is a process that involves some manipulation of or set of operations on knowledge in the cognitive system.
3. Thinking is directed and results in behavior that "solves" a problem or is directed toward a solution (1).

What Mayer is saying can be interpreted as: Since we don't know what other people are thinking, we infer, or suppose, what they are thinking by their behavior. We use knowledge in the process of thinking. And finally, there is purpose to thinking. We think about a situation to decide what to do or how to solve a problem. We need mental ability to gain knowledge but we wouldn't have much to think about without knowledge. If you are serious about your present education and continued learning, you must be interested in gaining more knowledge and improving your ability to think and solve problems.

A **problem** involves a situation that offers a choice of actions, and it therefore requires a decision about what should be done. A young person graduating from high school, for example, must decide whether to get more education or look for a job. Or a job opens up for someone who then faces the problem of getting there each day. The choices may include using public transportation such as a bus or train, driving, joining a carpool with other employees, or moving within walking distance of the job. If young parents work outside the home, they then have the problem of child care. The parents can share the responsibility if they work different hours, they can find a child care center that suits their needs, or they can explore other possibilities.

Problem
a situation that offers a choice of actions and requires a decision.

YOUR INCREDIBLE BRAIN

The human brain is considered the most mysterious mechanism in the universe. The structure of this organ is complex and contains millions of neural connections. Its specialized parts control speech, vision, and other senses and all human activities. The functioning of the brain may never be understood completely, but knowledge and understanding are continuously increasing. We can at least be assured that it does function and serves us in remarkable ways. We are concerned here primarily with mental abilities related to thinking and problem solving.

FUNCTIONING OF THE BRAIN

Forebrain
the part of the brain primarily involved in thinking and problem solving.

Cerebral cortex
the portion of the forebrain that gives us the ability to speak, think, solve problems, learn, and remember.

Corpus callosum
connection of network fibers in the brain that allows the hemispheres to interact.

Although every part of the brain is essential to leading a normal life, it may help us to understand the brain's role in thinking if we recognize that there are structural divisions known as the forebrain, midbrain, and hindbrain. The **forebrain** is involved primarily in thinking and problem solving. The **cerebral cortex** of the forebrain gives us the ability to speak, think, problem solve, learn, and remember. It consists of two hemispheres that have numerous folds, or fissures, resembling a walnut. The two hemispheres are connected by a network of nerve fibers called the **corpus callosum,** which is essential to the interaction of the hemispheres or the functioning of your total brain. The illustration on the following page shows a simplified cross-section of the brain and the locations of the forebrain, midbrain, and hindbrain.

RIGHT-BRAINED OR LEFT-BRAINED?

Right-brained
dominance by the hemisphere of the brain involved in creative abilities.

Left-brained
dominance by the hemisphere of the brain involved in reasoning, language, and mathematical ability.

Considerable attention has been given in recent years to whether a person is basically **right-brained** or **left-brained.** This designation pertains to the dominance of either the right hemisphere or left hemisphere in various functions. Studies have shown that the left hemisphere is more involved in language, reasoning, and mathematical ability; whereas the right hemisphere is more involved in our creative abilities. The right hemisphere is believed to be more holistic, specializing in forming mental images or maps. The left hemisphere, on the other hand, might provide specific instructions for following the map. The right hemisphere forms an overall image of a person; whereas the left hemisphere would be more involved in noting specific features of the person's face and remembering his or

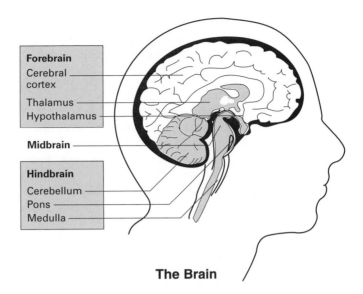

The Brain

her name. Although the two hemispheres of the brain do have these and other differences, this discussion is oversimplified. The interconnections between the two hemispheres makes it possible to coordinate the functioning of the brain so that all abilities are used in harmony. Since we do not have external controls, or switches, to operate our brains, it is reassuring to know that the brain itself knows

Right-brain/Left-brain Functions

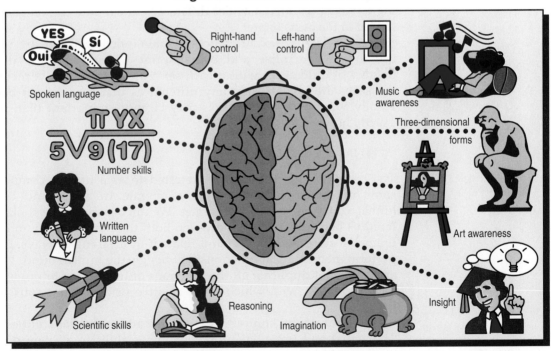

"Illustration," from THE BRAIN by Richard Restak, M.D. Copyright © 1984 by Educational Broadcasting Corporation and Richard M. Restak, M.D. used by permission of Bantam Books, a division of Bantam Doubleday Dell Publishing Group, Inc.

how to function. The illustration on the preceding page shows specialized functions of the hemispheres of the brain. Would you consider yourself primarily a right-brained or a left-brained person?

GENDER DIFFERENCES IN THE BRAIN?

Are there differences in the brains of males and females that affect the way they think? Do males and females have different kinds of mental abilities? The questions have been asked for generations, but we still don't have all the answers. Many people, generations ago, just "knew" without need of scientific proof, that the answer was, "Of course men and women think differently." A generation ago, many females, particularly feminists, strongly objected even to suggestions that they weren't the same as males, except for obvious physical differences. But scientists search for the truth, even if it isn't what others hope they find. They admit that studies aren't always in agreement and that the truth is difficult to establish.

What are these scientists saying today about sex differences in the brain? There is limited recent research that points to some differences. Doreen Kimura, who has studied the subject extensively, has written an article in the *Scientific American*, in which she attributes differences to the effects of sex hormones in brain organization. These occur so early in life, she says, "that from the start the environment is acting on differently wired brains in girls and boys." She notes further, "Major sex differences in intellectual function seem to lie in patterns of ability rather than in overall level of intelligence (IQ)" (2). Men, on the average, are better at spatial tasks, following a route, and on mentally manipulating an object in some way. Women, on the average, are better at language skills, recalling landmarks on a route, and at some manual tasks requiring precision, according to recent research. Gender differences in communication styles will be discussed in the next chapter.

In considering sex differences in brain functioning, we are again cautioned not to overgeneralize and oversimplify. There are many differences and degrees of differences within each sex. Also, similarities in mental abilities of the sexes are greater than any differences that have as yet been identified. Finally, what each of us thinks may be more important than understanding exactly how we think.

A HUMAN COMPUTER?

The brain has sometimes been referred to as a human computer. Although some humans know how computers operate, we are still not certain how the human computer, or brain, operates. We can observe some similarities and differences between the two, however. Both the human brain and the electronic brain can store information and relate it in meaningful ways. Computers can perform mathematical functions that boggle the human mind. Yet the computer still cannot duplicate all the functions of the human brain. It does not have an imagination with which to be creative or an unconscious with which to dream.

Without doubt, computers will have additional capabilities in the future. The actual and potential problem-solving abilities of computers, similar to what would be considered intelligence in humans, is called **artificial intelligence**—a fascinating but still highly speculative subject. Danny Hillis, in

Artificial intelligence the ability of computers to solve problems.

an article entitled "Can They Feel Your Pain?" in *Newsweek,* shares his views in saying,

> Although I believe that we will someday build thinking machines, I am much less confident that we will ever really understand the process of thought. This may sound like a contradiction. How can we build a mechanism that does something that we do not understand? Actually, we do it all the time. Anyone who has written a complicated computer program realizes that there is a difference between understanding the parts and understanding the consequences of how they interact. Even a state-of-the-art computer like Deep Blue can surprise its designers. Computers a few decades from now will be thousands of times faster and more complicated. Their thoughts will be correspondingly more difficult to predict and understand (3).

Advances in any technology are not accomplished by people who are quick to say, "It can't be done." Although most people do not expect computers to surpass the intricacies and range of mental abilities of the human brain, they recognize that artificial intelligence will continue to become a reality.

 What Would You Suggest? *If you could make a suggestion to computer scientists for an ability you would like a computer to have, what would it be?*

STAGES OF COGNITIVE DEVELOPMENT

Cognitive characteristics related to mental development.

The Swiss psychologist Jean Piaget studied extensively the development of mental ability and identified four stages of **cognitive** or mental development. These stages are shown with some of the characteristics of each stage in the following list:

Sensorimotor Stage (birth to 2 years)
Develops *self*-awareness as being separate from the rest of the world; recognizes objects and realizes that objects do not cease to exist when they are out of sight.

Preoperational Stage (2 to 7 years)
Develops some ability to remember and look forward to future events; pays attention to only one or two characteristics of an object rather than all (a 3-year-old child, for example, may think of an orange in terms of its color only, ignoring that it is also round, slightly rough, tasty, and fragrant); is not capable of mentally retracing a series of steps to reach a conclusion.

Concrete Operations Stage (7 to 11 years)
Can retrace thoughts; can consider more characteristics of objects; is capable of looking at a problem in different ways; can retain understanding of amount or mass even though shape may change (can understand, for example, that an amount of liquid remains the same when it is poured from a bottle of one shape to one of another).

Formal Operations Stage
(12 years and up)

Can consider various solutions to a problem; can ponder consequences of action; can use reason and logic in problem solving; can think about **abstractions,** or ideas that are not directly related to specific objects (can think of the idea of justice without relating it to a specific situation) (4).

Abstractions
ideas that are not directly related to specific objects.

The age ranges for each of the stages are average and may vary with individuals. We can see, however, that the ability to do various types of thinking is developmental. This factor is important in elementary education, but should also be useful to parents or anyone else associated with children. Children who are encouraged to use their mental abilities as they develop and who are allowed to solve some of their own problems are learning to become more effective problem solvers as adults. They learn to solve difficult problems by first solving fairly simple problems. Thus ability to solve problems depends both on development of mental abilities and on learning experiences. By the time young people begin high school, they have developed the ability to evaluate possibilities for their futures.

INTELLIGENCE OR INTELLIGENCES?

Does a person have a certain degree of intelligence or does he or she have degrees of different kinds of intelligences? It used to be thought generally that intelligence pertained to how "smart" a person was without recognizing different types of mental ability. We now know that intelligence varies not only in degree but also in kind from one person to another. Two people may have the same **intelligence quotient (IQ),** or score on an intelligence test, and yet their ability to solve particular kinds of problems or perform certain tasks may be quite different. One person may be good at word meanings and relationships; another may be outstanding in mathematics.

Intelligence quotient
a score on an intelligence test.

Howard Gardner in *Frames of Mind* discusses the "prerequisites of an intelligence." He says, "To my mind, a human intellectual competence must entail a set of skills of problem solving—enabling the individual *to resolve genuine problems or difficulties* that he or she encounters and, when appropriate, to create an effective product—and must also entail the potential for *finding or creating problems*—thereby laying the groundwork for the acquisition of new knowledge" (5). He identifies different kinds of intelligence as *linguistic, musical, logical-mathematical, spatial, bodily-kinesthetic,* and *personal* (6). Linguistic intelligence pertains to the ability to use and understand language. A person having this type of intelligence reads and writes with ease and may also be adept at learning new languages. Musical intelligence may pertain to learning to play a musical instrument or interpreting and perhaps even composing music. Logical-mathematical intelligence is related to solving problems that involve step-by-step reasoning or mathematical relationships. Spatial intelligence helps a person visualize three dimensions, for example, in reading blueprints. Bodily-kinesthetic intelligence pertains to mastery over the motions of one's body, which could be evident in gymnastics or dexterity required in one's work. Personal intelligence refers to understanding of oneself and understanding of others. A person may have several of these intelligences or may excel in one while being only average or below average in others.

Thomas Armstrong, in his book, *7 Kinds of Smart,* divides Gardner's personal intelligences into *interpersonal* (the ability to understand and work with other people) and *intrapersonal* (the intelligence of the inner self). Armstrong concludes, "If I can leave you with any single message concerning the theory of multiple intelligences, it would be that *each person possesses all seven intelligences and has the ability to develop each one to a reasonable degree of proficiency*" (7).

Today there is less emphasis on the measurement of mental ability and more concern with motivation and learning opportunities. Your desire to learn, in most cases, is more important than your score on an IQ test. The extent to which one learns and develops her or his abilities depends also, in large measure, on the environment in which one lives. If Angela grew up in a family that followed and discussed current events, she is likely to have more motivation to develop her mental abilities than someone whose family has lived only in their own small world of interests and problems.

LEARNING AND MEMORY

Learning
the acquisition of knowledge, the understanding of facts and principles, the development of skills, or the shaping of attitudes and values.

Memory
the ability to retain knowledge.

Sensory register
the stage of memory during which we are aware of something.

Short-term memory
memory that lasts a short period, as long as we need it.

Working memory
temporary storage of information.

Y̵ou have been learning since you were born, and you will continue to learn all your life. Learning results in a relatively permanent change in behavior. We must consider all types of behavior, however, including physical and emotional as well as mental. **Learning** may involve the acquisition of knowledge, the understanding of facts and principles, the development of skills, or the shaping of attitudes and values. An educated person has developed learning in each of these areas. Career education programs are usually planned carefully to include all types of learning.

There are many ways to learn besides taking formal courses. We can learn from experience, from observation and listening, and from independent study. Activities of the human brain that show evidence of learning include interpreting, recognizing, associating, and recalling. Rhonda, for example, interprets the dark screen on a television set as a burned-out transistor, thus giving meaning to clues that she perceives. On examination of the set, she recognizes, or identifies, the transistor that is burned out and needs replacement. She associates, or compares, the present task with a similar lab activity. She recalls, or remembers from previous learning, where the transistor for replacement is located. The brain may perform these four activities in any order or even all at once.

Memory is the ability to retain, or hold, knowledge or learning and to retrieve it. Like most mental activities, it is more complex than we might expect, even though you have had considerable experience in remembering—and in forgetting. There are three stages in the memory process. The first stage is referred to as **sensory register** and lasts only a fraction of a second. In this stage, we are aware of something to which we may or may not want to give additional attention. You are using sensory register when you scan a newspaper, for example, looking for a particular item. The second stage is referred to as **short-term memory** and can last less than a minute or as long as we immediately need it. It involves information we want to use for a brief time. You may look up a number in the telephone directory, for example, and remember it only long enough to dial it. This is the type of memory also referred to as **working memory.** According to Alan Baddeley, a recognized authority on memory, "The term working memory refers to a brain system that provides temporary storage and manipulation of the information necessary for such complex cognitive tasks as language comprehension, learning, and reasoning" (8).

Long-term memory
the ability to recall information on demand.

Semantic memory
memory of learned information.

Procedural memory
memory of learned skills.

Episodic memory
memory of personal experiences or observations.

Recall
to retrieve information from memory.

Recognize
to remember information with the aid of a sensory cue.

Relearning
to relearn material previously retained in memory.

Learning involves the third stage, or **long-term memory.** We not only want to learn certain things, but we want to be able to recall them at appropriate times. Long-term memory consists of three basic types of memory: semantic, procedural, and episodic. **Semantic memory** consists primarily of what we have learned, including facts and knowledge. Much of what you are learning in your classes becomes part of your semantic memory. **Procedural memory** pertains to skills you have learned. You learned to use a keyboard, for example, to be able to use your computer for word processing. You have doubtless learned how to use equipment in your major area of study. Both semantic and procedural memory are important in our education. **Episodic memory** pertains to our personal experiences or observations. You remember many experiences you had as a child, for example. We add to our episodic memory as we go through life.

To **recall** something from your memory, without clues, can be more difficult than to **recognize** an idea or information with the aid of a sensory stimulus to your sight, sound, taste, touch, or smell. For example, if you were asked the capital cities of the fifty states of the United States, you might find it difficult to recall all of them. But if you were given a matching exercise with the states in one column and the capital cities in another, you would likely do much better.

Other evidence of the function of memory can be seen in **relearning.** Even when previous learning cannot be recalled or is recognized only faintly, it is easier and faster to relearn the material than it was to learn it in the first place.

When people say that they have a poor memory, they are often speaking as though nothing can improve their memory. Memory is an ability that can be

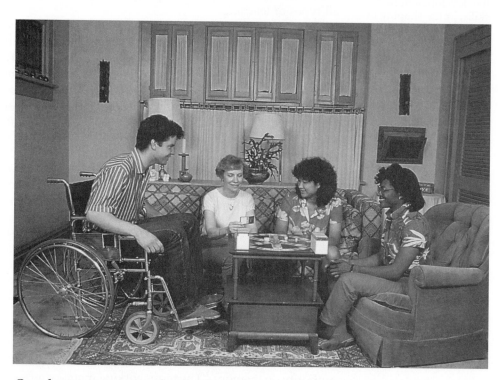

Our short-term memory lasts only as long as we immediately need it—to win a game or to look up a phone number in the phonebook.

Stages in the Memory Process

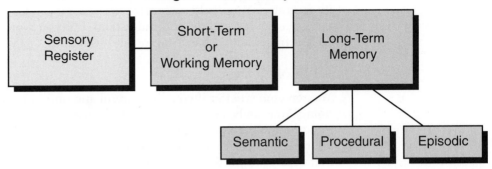

developed and improved. Danielle Lapp in *(Nearly) Total Recall*, discusses principles of good retention. She refers to these as relaxation, awareness as a key to selective attention and observation, image-association, personal comments, organizing by categories, and reviewing and using what we want to remember (9). You will recognize most of these factors in the following discussion of contributors to learning and memory.

THE WALL STREET JOURNAL

"I'm not good with names, but I never forget a Web site."

Cartoon Feature Syndicate.

CONTRIBUTORS TO LEARNING AND MEMORY

We remember only a small part of what we learn. Many factors determine what we learn and how well or how long we remember it. The more factors involved in a particular learning experience, the better it will be remembered. A few of these factors include motivation, meaningfulness of skill or material, attention, association, and repetition.

MOTIVATION

How well you learn and remember depends greatly on your reasons for doing so. If you are quite confident that your learning skills will help you get the kind of job you want, you are likely to learn well. You remember the name of a person to see about getting a job if you really want the job. Or you remember your friend's birthday because that person is special in some way. When you have reasons for remembering something, you are also likely to make use of the following additional factors.

MEANINGFULNESS OF SKILL OR MATERIAL

It is easier for you to remember something if it makes sense to you, if you understand what you are trying to learn. Something learned by strict memorization, or *rote learning,* is often not understood and, therefore, cannot be applied and is easily forgotten. You could memorize nonsense syllables that have no meaning for you or formulas you do not understand, but you would not remember them as well as material that has meaning and usefulness for you.

ATTENTION

You remember better if you give careful and undivided attention to what you are doing. You can be so involved mentally in a project or work that is interesting or important that you are quite unaware of other things taking place around you. A young man who is concentrating on troubleshooting an engine may not notice that others are putting away tools or that he is hungry; he may not even hear a whistle blow. But when he does leave his work and later returns, he will remember what he has already tried and tested.

ASSOCIATION

When you use association, you relate what you want to recall to something else easily recalled. You often can remember the names of people if you associate them with the way the people look, or the kind of work they do, or the place where you were or the thing you were doing when you met them. You may not recognize Joan's cousin, whom you met only once, unless you see her with Joan, whom you know well.

There are many interesting—and sometimes silly, but effective—ways to remember by association. You may have relied on the following rhyme to help you remember how to spell some words:

> *i* before *e*, except after *c*
> or when sounded like *a*
> as in *neighbor* and *weigh*

Mnemonic device
a memory aid relying on association such as letter recognition.

Such a technique, called a **mnemonic device,** is intended to assist memory. Another mnemonic device is the word *HOMES* for remembering the Great Lakes: *H*uron, *O*ntario, *M*ichigan, *E*rie, and *S*uperior. Do you know of other such memory aids? Why not develop a mnemonic device of your own for something you want to remember?

REPETITION

Performing an activity over and over in the same way helps you to learn and also to remember what has been learned. It was mentioned earlier that you remember your friend's telephone number because you have reason to remember it. Another factor that helps you remember the number from day to day is using it often. Mentally going over a procedure, as well as actually doing it, helps one to remember. The use of repetition, or practice, is one of the techniques involved in on-the-job training programs. Trainees, for example, often learn how to operate a machine by repeating the process several times. When people set up their own practice sessions, they find that spaced, shorter sessions give them better results than longer practice periods. A person practicing information processing, for example, will show greater improvement from practicing an hour a day for six days than from practicing six hours one day but none the next five.

Another type of repetition that aids memory is known as *overlearning.* To overlearn is to review mentally or orally what you have already learned to ensure greater retention. Although it may not be interesting to review what you already know, experiments have shown that it is an effective memory technique. Students who review their mathematics equations every week will easily remember them throughout the course.

Many books and articles have been written on improving memory, and many gimmicks are advertised as being useful for that purpose. Remember, however, that you are the one who has to improve this ability. Techniques can be learned and can be useful, but success depends largely on the factors we have just considered.

What Do You Think? *Would you agree with, "The more you know, the easier it is to learn more"? Why or why not?*

EXPERIENCE AND COMMON SENSE

The knowledge or skill gained from being engaged in an activity is referred to as *experience.* We can learn from experience how to solve problems and also how to avoid problems. Experience teaches us not to repeat an activity that has brought undesirable results. Yet it is impractical for us to experience everything firsthand. Some things are obviously best learned through the experience of others. From their experience we learn not to risk swimming alone in unknown bodies of water because of current and depth hazards, for example. Neither do we knowingly test the consequences of lighting a flame near explosive vapors nor expose ourselves unnecessarily to radiation or high-voltage lines.

A common difficulty in benefiting from the experience of others is the great amount of conflicting suggestions and advice available. When you want to change jobs, buy a car, or even arrange for a date, you can usually get more advice than you can use or may want. On the other hand, advice based on the experience of others can save time, money, pain, and even your life. To profit from this source of experience, you must be able to evaluate suggestions and decide what advice you can use and in what way you can use it.

Every normal human being possesses a type of problem-solving ability known as common sense. A definition of **common sense** might be the ability to make use of past experience to prevent or avoid a problem or to react to a situation that demands immediate attention. According to this definition, a person using common sense is better able to:

Common sense approach to problem solving involving reason and use of what has been learned in the past to solve new, similar problems.

- Identify danger and take necessary precautions for the protection of life
- Identify possible hazards to equipment or property
- Consider probabilities in cause and effect
- Engage available human resources
- Make appropriate use of available tools and materials—improvising, if necessary

As learning experiences vary from one individual to another, so do uses of common sense in any given problem situation. Common sense might be credited with solving the following problem in the Question Box that follows.

What Would You Suggest? *A truck became wedged in an underpass. Most of the suggestions offered by bystanders involved damage to either the underpass or the truck. What would you suggest? A workable solution is on page 165.*

It would be worthwhile for everyone to remember that others do not have the same type or degree of common sense that he or she has. People cannot be expected, therefore, to react to a problem in the same ways. It can be very frustrating to a new person on a job to be expected to know how to handle situations with which he or she has no knowledge or experience. Although it is true that those who live and work in similar environments often have similar common sense, many problems require more than that type of everyday problem-solving ability.

GUIDELINES TO PROBLEM SOLVING

The following guidelines to problem solving can be helpful to a person in a situation requiring analysis, evaluation, decision, and action, when an immediate solution is not required.

Define the problem.

Look at the total situation.

Identify problems related to the major problem.

Determine possible causes of the problem and related problems.

Consider as many solutions as possible.

Consider sources of advice and assistance.

Evaluate plus and minus factors of each solution.

Decide on a solution.

Take the first active step.

Reevaluate the effectiveness of the solution.

Each of these guidelines is discussed on the following pages, along with some specific examples. A similar approach and procedure can be used to solve your own problems.

DEFINE THE PROBLEM

This first step in problem solving is often the most difficult but is also the most important. Defining the problem is difficult because many people do not look at themselves or their situations objectively. They are likely to blame someone else for their troubles or to emphasize the wrong factor. Thus to really solve a problem, you must determine all the facts and conditions as distinctly and clearly as possible.

LOOK AT THE TOTAL SITUATION

The gestalt principle of perception, discussed in Chapter 4, applies to this early stage of problem solving. Although the situation may be complex and you may not be able to deal with all aspects of it at the same time, it is helpful to see the total picture. You must relate the various aspects of the situation to the overall problem by looking at the total situation and determining what things you can—and want to—change.

IDENTIFY RELATED PROBLEMS

A complex problem usually includes several interrelated smaller problems. These problems could pertain to time, money, energy, motivation, abilities, or relationships with others. Such problems must be identified and assigned an order of importance in solving the main problem. Also, solving one of the minor problems sometimes leads to solving the major problem.

DETERMINE POSSIBLE CAUSES

In a situation involving a complex problem, it is not always simple to distinguish between cause and effect. In fact, an effect of one problem may cause another problem in the total situation. The following questions must be considered at this stage of problem analysis: If two things are happening in sequence or at the same time, is one related to or causing the other? Is an identified cause of a problem the sole cause or only one of a number of causes? What may at first seem to be the obvious cause may not be the underlying cause of a problem at all. All possible cause-and-effect relationships must be considered.

CONSIDER AS MANY SOLUTIONS AS POSSIBLE

Visualize your problem as being solved. Compare your situation now with what you want it to be. Then consider as many ways as possible to arrive at the desired change in your situation. Think of as many possible solutions as you can before deciding which to use. The first solution that comes to mind may not be the most effective. You might use individualized brainstorming as discussed later in this chapter to think of solution possibilities.

CONSIDER SOURCES OF ADVICE AND ASSISTANCE

For many reasons it is often advisable to seek advice and assistance in problem solving. Because it is difficult to see yourself and your problem objectively, someone else can often help you define your problem more accurately. Also, because of special knowledge or experience, others may be able to suggest solutions that you would fail to consider on your own. Not to be overlooked, either, is the moral support you can receive in making your decision and taking necessary action. Students, counselors, and financial aid personnel, found in nearly every community and technical college, can also help with both academic and personal problems. Advice from your family and friends, who have a special interest in you, is also worth consideration. A further value of sharing your problems with others is that often, in just talking about a situation, you view it in a different perspective and may come up with your own solution.

What a person does in this step of problem solving depends on the particular problem, on the types of advice and assistance available, and on the preferences of the individual. It is not suggested that you run for help whenever you encounter some difficulty. But it can be just as unwise to ignore available sources of advice and assistance.

This couple is solving an important problem—they are seeking information to double-check their telephone billing statements.

EVALUATE PLUS AND MINUS FACTORS OF EACH SOLUTION

The approach-avoidance conflicts discussed in Chapter 3 were really situations presenting problems. It may be a good idea at this time to review these conflicts. Almost every decision you can make has both positive and negative factors or characteristics. How you weigh these factors depends on your circumstances and values. What might be a plus factor to one person could be a minus or at least a neutral factor to you. The cost of buying a computer, for example, may be a minus factor to one person, whereas to another a computer would be well worth the immediate cost or possible payments. The plus factor of its usefulness could outweigh the minus factor of cost. It is essential to keep your needs, abilities, and values in mind in evaluating possible solutions. One should also consider the effects of a decision on others and one's relationships with them. Note the involvement of motivational conflicts discussed in Chapter 3.

DECIDE ON A SOLUTION

After thoughtful consideration and investigation of all the previous guidelines in problem solving, you must decide which solution you believe would be most effective and practical. Not only must a solution work, but it must also be practical in terms of the time, cost, and effort involved. If you are having serious trouble with your car, for example, the most effective solution to your transportation problem may be to buy a new one, but that may not be practical in terms of your financial situation.

TAKE THE FIRST ACTIVE STEP

When a solution has been decided upon, you must take action to put the solution into effect. The first step in this procedure should be taken as soon as possible or practical. For example, if you decide that you will contact a credit union about a loan, look up the telephone number or address and make the contact as soon as possible.

REEVALUATE THE EFFECTIVENESS OF THE SOLUTION

Some decisions in life are somewhat more permanent, such as getting married or buying a house. Others also have a degree of permanence, for example, attending a particular school, starting a new job, or even buying a car. It is difficult but not impossible to make changes after action has been taken in light of such decisions. In many other situations, it is relatively easy to reevaluate or change a decision if a solution proves ineffective. It is important in such cases to follow through by reevaluating solution effectiveness. A person who makes a practice of evaluating decisions and their results not only solves problems more effectively but also foresees and prevents additional problems that others may overlook.

CREATIVE THINKING

To be *creative* is to be imaginative and original in developing new works of art, products, services, uses of materials, or ways of doing things. Creative thinking is not a new approach to problem solving. An example from ancient times involves Hammurabi, king of ancient Babylon, who was concerned about getting people to a water supply. He solved the problem by realizing that it would be more practical to find a way of getting the water to his people. Through this type of thinking and problem solving, the concept of a canal was developed.

You may have noticed that many new foods, styles, materials, and processes are not completely original but are combinations or variations of things already familiar in some form. Other innovations simply make things smaller or larger than they were. The minicalculator is an example. Another is the adult-size tricycle used by older people who do not feel secure on a bicycle or a moped.

Everyone can do creative thinking and problem solving. We can all learn to use the abilities of our right brain more fully. We can learn to perceive characteristics and relationships that otherwise would go unnoticed by others. Creative thinking is not just a magic bursting of ideas in the minds of especially gifted individuals. Even though some people have more natural creative talent than others, we can all be creative in some ways.

To be creative is to be original. The objectives of creative people are usually to express themselves, to make life more interesting, and to seek improvements in their surroundings. The world is constantly presenting its inhabitants with new problems, and human beings are also constantly seeking new or better solutions to old problems. Some of the best future solutions will be the result of creative thinking.

CHARACTERISTICS OF CREATIVE THINKERS

Although creative thinking is not as structured as traditional problem solving, creative people have demonstrated that they have several characteristics in common. If we want to become more creative, it may help to try to develop these characteristics.

QUESTIONING ATTITUDE Creative thinkers wonder why things are the way they are and how they might be changed and improved. New ways of doing things, after all, are often just variations or adaptations of old ways. Two stimulating questions used by creative workers are, How can present methods be changed or combined for an improved effect? and What materials can be substituted for those that are costly, scarce, ineffective, or dangerous in some way? Individuals who consider such questions frequently in their work and other activities find that they are generating new ideas. Periods of waiting can be used to perceive one's environment in new ways, boring tasks can become stimulating, work can become highly challenging, and all of life can become extremely rewarding.

SELF-CONFIDENCE To be creative means, in a sense, to be different. Creative people are looking for new ways to do things. Their ideas and even their products are often criticized by others who are less imaginative or who are reluctant to change their ways. This resistance does not bother creative persons. They have confidence in their individuality and in their ability. When they do make mistakes or develop "duds," they can laugh at themselves and try something else. They are not embarrassed or stifled by criticism from others and can evaluate their work's worth. They are their own critics to a large degree.

FLEXIBILITY It doesn't disturb creative people as much as it does others if things go wrong. They can adapt to new methods and even think of better ones. They can go without what others might consider necessities or substitute new uses for existing products. Neither do they feel the need to function according to fixed schedules. Variations in when and how they do their work, if within the requirements of the job, help them to break out of fixed patterns of time and procedure. They are generally less disturbed by what others may consider inconveniences.

ABILITY TO CONCENTRATE Creative thinkers give their undivided attention to their projects. They may sometimes appear inattentive, but their minds are occupied with the task at hand, and they are not distracted by other environmental stimuli. People who have developed the ability to concentrate may at times be totally unaware of their surroundings.

PERSISTENCE Many people who are creative explain that they cannot be creative at will. This is partly because the unconscious mind is involved in the creative process. Some creative people become familiar with the problem and what

---

 What Would You Say? *If someone were to ask what you considered the outstanding characteristic of a creative person, what would you say?*

---

they want to achieve. Then, they let the problem rest, giving their unconscious minds an opportunity to solve it.

There are many variations in how creative people work. Sometimes they get an inspiration for a complete piece of work or project at once. Or creative people may develop ideas as they get further into their work. In any case, creative people do not give up easily, do not lose confidence in their ability, and make fuller use of both their conscious and unconscious mental abilities than most of us do.

Quiz Yourself on Connecting the Dots

The problem is to connect all the dots by drawing no more than four straight lines without lifting your pencil or pen from the paper.

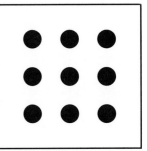

The answer is on page 165.

BRAINSTORMING

Brainstorming
group creative thinking involving a period of wild, uncritical generation of ideas.

Creative thinking can also be done by a group. One type of group creative thinking has been made popular by Alex Osborn and is called **brainstorming.** With this approach, a group of people get together and spontaneously pool as many ideas as possible about a given problem. Following are Osborn's rules for a brainstorming session during the period when ideas are being presented:

- Criticism is not allowed. This will come later when the ideas are evaluated.
- The wilder the idea, the better. It is easier to discard or modify ideas than to think of new ones.
- Quantity is more important than quality—the more ideas, the better.
- Combinations and variations of ideas are welcome. One idea can lead to another. Some brainstormers refer to this association of ideas as "hitch-hiking" (10).

It is also profitable to engage in your own brainstorming to solve some of your problems. Simply follow the rules for brainstorming, jotting down ideas as fast as you can think of them, without evaluation or self-criticism. Then look at your ideas more critically to see whether any of them have merit.

LATERAL AND VERTICAL THINKING

Edward de Bono, a well-known British author of works on thinking and problem solving, has developed a type of problem solving that he calls *lateral thinking*. This type of thinking involves taking different viewpoints and approaches to problem solving. Sometimes we have difficulty solving a problem because we are viewing it in the same way we have approached similar problems in the past. Lateral thinking is different from *vertical thinking,* or logical thinking, which proceeds step-by-step in a given direction.

A writer who attended one of de Bono's lateral thinking seminars describes the following problem often used by de Bono. What would your explanation be?

 Quiz Yourself *Three worms, a mother, father, and baby worm, crawl partway up a little hill and then crawl into it at different points. Upon coming out on the other side, the baby worm looks back and says, "I see only two holes." (11)*
Check de Bono's explanation on page 165.

The writer quotes de Bono in saying, "Whatever you're thinking about, there will be things you'll take for granted." A lateral thinker does not take for granted things that interfere with different approaches to solving a problem.

Another example used by de Bono pertains to the fish-processing industry in England. The old way of filleting fish was to pull the meat from the bones. One day a worker suggested that the process be reversed. His suggestion was tried and it worked, and removing the bones from the meat became the improved method.

In brainstorming, discussed earlier, lateral thinking is used in the first part of a session to break out of mental ruts and to generate new ideas. Vertical thinking is then done to see whether any of the ideas will work. Many problems in business and industry have been solved this way. The method has also been used to improve products and develop new processes.

GROUP PROBLEM SOLVING

There are numerous types of group problem solving and several factors involved that determine their effectiveness or ineffectiveness. Brainstorming as a method of group creative problem solving was discussed earlier. Brainstorming is not used regularly, but it can be effective in finding new ways to achieve an objective or solve a problem. If you have not already tried brainstorming, you are encouraged to do so. Many find it an effective and creative problem-solving technique.

QUALITY CIRCLES

Quality circles are another type of group that includes problem solving. They originated in Japan and were widely adopted by business and industry in the United States in the 1980s. Essentially a **quality circle** included both employees and management from the same work area who worked together to improve quality and production and to solve work-related problems. Participation was voluntary.

Quality circle
a problem-solving group in which employees and managers in the same work area share ideas to improve quality and production and solve work-related problems.

Theoretically, quality circles had many positive characteristics. They have been declining in use, however, in recent years. According to a study reported in the *Journal of Social Psychology,* reasons for this have been lack of support from top management, lack of commitment from workers, lack of problem-solving skills, member turnover, nature of the task, lack of support from staff members, and lack of data and time (12). Quality circles, which evolved from principles developed by William E. Deming, are now being replaced by his total quality management principles and practices (13). Teams in the workplace are more common today and are generally considered effective in attaining mutual goals. Teams in the workplace will be discussed in Chapter 9.

COMMITTEES AND TASK FORCES

Committee
group of people working for a common goal or toward a common end.

Standing committee
a committee that has a permanent status and several functions, although membership may change over time.

Ad hoc committee
a committee set up to perform a particular task and dissolved when the task is completed.

Task force
members of an ad hoc committee, coming from different backgrounds, with some special interests or experience related to the task.

Groupthink
a situation that results when members of the group suspend their own better judgment to achieve agreement.

Frequently in a work situation, groups are referred to as **committees.** Two general types of committees are standing committees and ad hoc committees. A **standing committee** has permanent status and several functions, although membership may change over time. A standing committee is concerned with ongoing objectives and problems related to its general purpose. An **ad hoc committee** is set up to perform a particular task and is dissolved when the task is completed. Members of the ad hoc committee, often referred to as a **task force,** usually come from different backgrounds but have some special interest or experience related to the task. Some committee or task force meetings with members at different locations are conducted by means of electronic interaction without people coming physically together. This technology saves travel time and expense, but it has disadvantages as well. It is difficult to know when to contribute and it is impossible to evaluate nonverbal communication, for example.

Meeting time can be more efficient if members know what the agenda is ahead of time. Frequently members are given the opportunity to suggest agenda items. Receiving an agenda before the meeting shows that some planning has taken place and also gives those attending some lead time to prepare for more meaningful participation.

Anyone who has much experience with meetings will attest that they can be ineffective for various reasons. There is also the possibility of groupthink. **Groupthink** results in poor decision making when members of the group suspend their own better judgment to achieve agreement. Some members of the group may sit back and abandon evaluative listening instead of participating in reaching the best conclusion (14).

EFFECTIVE PROBLEM-SOLVING GROUPS

What are the characteristics of effective problem-solving groups?

- Group members have either volunteered or agreed to work with the group.
- Group members are familiar with problem-solving guidelines.
- The current problem or issue is understood by all members.
- Group members have some knowledge and perhaps experience related to the problem or are willing to learn and become involved.
- The atmosphere is relaxed and members feel comfortable about their roles.
- Everyone is an active participant. No one dominates the discussion.
- Members listen to one another and carefully consider what others suggest.
- Criticism of ideas is positive and constructive.
- Individuals respect one another and basic human relations skills are practiced.
- The group leader is an effective communicator and is accepted in his or her role by members.

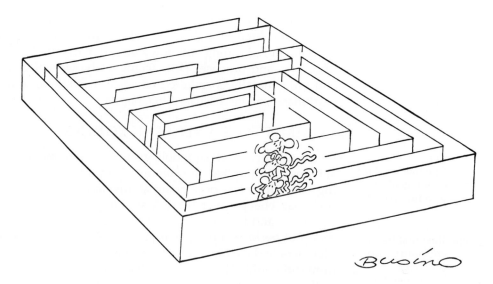

" OKAY, TURN RIGHT AND THEN RIGHT AGAIN
AND WE'LL BE OUT. . "

In addition to being knowledgeable about problem solving and being accepted by group members, the group leader should be highly motivated about the purposes of the group, be tolerant and fair, and encourage participation of all group members. It is also his or her responsibility to keep discussion and activity relevant to the subject and objective at hand. Leadership qualities will be discussed in more detail in Chapter 14. Many of the above characteristics of effective problem-solving groups will apply to the functioning of teams, discussed in Chapter 9.

INTUITION AND INSIGHT

Intuition
immediate understanding without conscious attention or reasoning.

Intuition is often associated with a decision to react to a problem situation. It is that sudden feeling that you know what to do without fully understanding why. It is coming to a conclusion without following the usual guides for reasoning and problem solving. Intuition is often referred to as a "gut feeling" about what to do. While intuition is not entirely reliable, many insist that it should not be ignored. It is can also be described as an unconscious interpretation of related experiences in the past. It has been said that when we err by using intuition, we were following a "bad hunch."

Insight
judgment based on knowledge and experience.

Insight is often difficult to analyze or explain but nevertheless can affect making judgments and decisions. Insight is usually thought of as being based on knowledge, experience, and understanding that would give more validity to a conclusion. Perhaps you have had the experience of mentally wrestling with a problem for quite a while and all of a sudden, the solution pops into your head. "I've got it!" might have been your reaction. Insight involves the unconscious relationship and interpretation of several factors. It is often referred to as wisdom. The more knowledge and experience one has, the more likely he or she is to have insightful solutions to problems.

LIFE AND PROBLEM SOLVING

Problems are a part of life. You have already faced many problems in your life and you undoubtedly face some right now. You will become more effective—and, therefore, happier—if you become a better problem solver.

There are variations from person to person in what is perceived as a problem, what can be considered as possible solutions, and what is selected as the best solution. Individual needs, abilities, opportunities, and values all influence one's decision and course of action in solving problems.

You may think that if you could remove all problems from your life, you would be a happier person. And it is true that fewer health, financial, family, or social problems would make life more secure and satisfying. Constant effort is being made by individuals and society, therefore, to prevent or solve such problems.

Not having any problems, however, would essentially leave you with no choices in life, which would be dull and uninteresting. In fact, life consists of a constant stream of problems, some of which are not really undesirable. Sometimes we even create problems for the enjoyment or challenge of solving them. Athletic contests, puzzles, and many games are problems that have been created for the purpose of trying to overcome the obstacles and "win."

We will be able to continue to learn as long as we live, barring brain injury or disease. Our brains will not wear out or use up their potential for "storing knowledge" or developing understanding. And we can learn to use our mental abilities more fully and creatively. Although the full extent of our mental abilities is not known, it is suspected that we use only a portion of our brain power. This does not necessarily mean that we are mentally lazy, but it does suggest that we have mental abilities we have not yet learned to use or are not using effectively. Most of us have greater mental potential than we will ever develop or use to our advantage.

Take a problem-solving approach to life. Not only will your life become safer and more financially sound, but it will be more challenging and interesting.

Problems are part of life, and you can become more productive if you learn to solve problems effectively and creatively.

What Do You Think? *It has been said that good judgment comes from experience—and that experience comes from poor judgment. To what extent do you think parents, teachers, and employers should allow others to make mistakes in learning to solve problems and develop good judgment?*

Summary

People can learn to develop and use more of their mental abilities despite the fact that they do not understand completely how their brains function.

A problem is a situation in which some change is desired, there is some choice of possible solutions, and a decision must be made about what action to take. Since life brings problems for all of us, effective living consists of effective problem solving. A person who learns to think and reason effectively in solving problems will lead a stimulating and productive life.

Research indicates that the right and left hemispheres of the brain have specialized abilities but that they function together in a whole-brain system. Recent research also seems to confirm that there are sex differences in the biology and functioning of the brain. Both of these brain-related subjects are controversial, however.

According to Jean Piaget, ability to think and problem-solve is developmental. He has identified four stages of this development: sensorimotor, preoperational, concrete operations, and formal operations. Abilities range from the recognition of objects in the sensorimotor stage to abstract thinking in the formal operations stage.

It would be more accurate to refer to human intelligences or kinds of mental abilities, rather than intelligence in general. According to Gardner, kinds of intelligence are linguistic, musical, logical-mathematical, spatial, bodily-kinesthetic, and personal. Armstrong divides personal intelligence into interpersonal and intrapersonal.

Memory is the ability to retain knowledge or learning. Three stages in the memory process are sensory register, short-term memory, and long-term memory. There are three basic types of long-term memory: semantic, procedural, and episodic. Mental activities involving learning and interpretation are recognition, association, and recall. Factors that contribute to learning and memory are motivation, meaningfulness of skill or material, attention, association, and repetition.

PSYCHOLOGY IN PRACTICE

1. Check your school or community library for a book or videotape on memory. Select a resource that explains the "loci," "peg," or a similar method for improving one's memory. Use one of these methods to remember something you are currently studying in one of your courses or in your work.

2. Brainstorming can be fun, and it is also very effective in problem solving. If you belong to a club or some other organized group, suggest that the group brainstorm how to raise money to go on a trip or to a convention.

3. Identify six problems or related parts of one problem someone might have that involve health, finances, a family situation, or work. List them according to the order in which you think they should be solved. If you think some have equal priority or must be solved at the same time, explain why.

A degree of common-sense problem-solving ability results from experience in living. People have developed common sense when they can identify danger and take necessary precautions for the protection of life, identify possible hazards to equipment or property, consider probabilities in cause and effect, engage available human resources, and make appropriate use of available tools and materials—improvising, if necessary.

People can solve problems more effectively if they employ the following guidelines to problem solving: define the problem, look at the total situation, identify problems related to the major problem, determine possible causes of the problem and related problems, consider as many solutions as possible, consider sources of advice and assistance, evaluate plus and minus factors of each solution, decide on a solution, take the first active step, and later reevaluate the effectiveness of the solution.

Although creativity is generally thought of as a talent, anyone can become a more creative thinker. Characteristics of creative thinkers are a questioning attitude, self-confidence, flexibility, ability to concentrate, and persistence. A popular type of creative problem solving is known as brainstorming. This type of creative thinking, in the first phase, stresses quantity rather than quality of ideas, expression of wild ideas without criticism, and combination of ideas. In the second phase, these ideas are evaluated to determine whether they are workable.

Quality circles, popular in the 1980s, have been declining in use and are being replaced by total quality management principles and practices. Teams have become part of the workplace. Committees and task forces are frequently used to solve problems and accomplish objectives.

Intuition and insight can also be useful in problem solving. Intuition is a sudden, inexplicable feeling of knowing what to do. Insight is based on knowledge, experience, and understanding and is often referred to as wisdom.

You will find that what you have learned in the chapters thus far will serve as a useful basis for the next chapter, "Communicating Effectively."

Answers to What Would You Suggest? on page 154

One bystander suggested letting some of the air out of the tires. The height of the truck was thereby lowered and the vehicle moved out without damage to the truck or underpass.

 Solution to Quiz Yourself on Connecting the Dots on page 159.

Many people assume that they have to draw a square formation or that the lines may not fall outside the dots. There are also other possible solutions. Can you think of any?

Answers to Quiz Yourself on page 160

According to de Bono, the baby worm can't count. An effective lateral thinker does not make assumptions that would narrow thinking—in this case, the assumption that the baby worm could count.

Key Terms

Problem
Forebrain
Cerebral cortex
Corpus callosum
Right-brained
Left-brained
Artificial intelligence
Cognitive
Abstractions
Intelligence quotient
Learning
Memory
Sensory register
Short-term memory
Working memory
Long-term memory

Semantic memory
Procedural memory
Episodic memory
Recall
Recognize
Relearning
Mnemonic device
Common sense
Brainstorming
Committees
Standing committee
Ad hoc committee
Task force
Groupthink
Intuition
Insight

Learning Activities

Turn to page LA-27 to complete the Learning Activities and Enrichment Activities for this chapter.

Endnotes

1. Richard E. Mayer, *Thinking, Problem Solving and Cognition,* W. H. Freeman and Company, New York, 1992, p. 7.

2. Doreen Kimura, "Sex Differences in the Brain," *Scientific American,* September 1992, p. 119.

3. Danny Hillis, "Can They Feel Your Pain?" *Newsweek,* May 5, 1997, p. 57.

4. Richard I. Evans, *Jean Piaget: The Man and His Ideas,* E. P. Hutton and Company, Inc., New York, 1973, pp. 15–27.

5. Howard Gardner, *Frames of Mind: The Theory of Multiple Intelligences,* Tenth Anniversary Edition, Basic Books, New York, 1993, pp. 60–61.

6. Ibid, pp. 73–276.

7. Thomas Armstrong, *7 Kinds of Smart: Identifying and Developing Your Many Intelligences,* Penguin Books, New York, 1993, p. 221.

8. Alan Baddeley, "Working Memory." *Science,* January 1992, p. 556.

9. Danielle C. Lapp, *(Nearly) Total Recall,* Stanford Alumni Association, Stanford, CA, 1992, pp. 141–143.

10. Alex Osborn, *Applied Imagination,* Charles Schribner's Sons, New York, 1963, p. 84.

11. Kevin McManus, "How to Think Sideways," *Forbes*, December 20, 1982, p. 152.

12. Thomas Li-Ping Tang, Peggy Smith Tollison, and Harold Dean Whiteside, "The Case of Active and Inactive Quality Circles." *The Journal of Social Psychology*, February 1, 1996, pp. 57–58.

13. Dan L. Costley, Carmen Santana-Melgoza, and Ralph Todd, *Human Relations in Organizations*, West Publishing Company, Minneapolis/Saint Paul, MN, 1994, p. 399.

14. Irving L. Janus, *Groupthink: Psychological Studies of Policy Decisions and Fiascoes*, Houghton Mifflin Company, Boston, MA, 1982, p. 9.

Communicating Effectively

Do more than exist—love
Do more than touch—feel
Do more than look—observe
Do more than hear—listen
Do more than listen—understand
Do more than talk—say something

John Rhoades

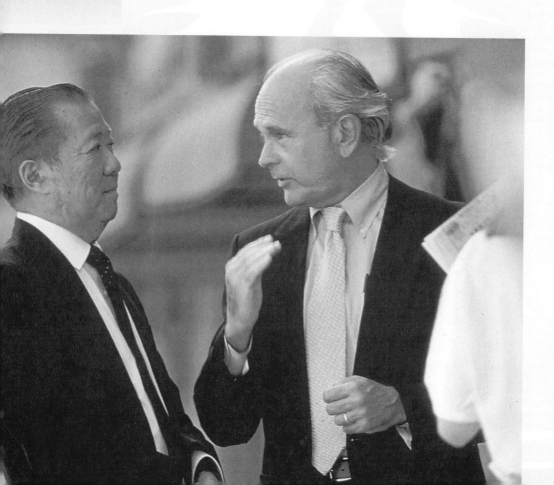

LEARNING OBJECTIVES

After completing this chapter, you should be able to do the following:

1. Identify the components of communication and explain how they interact.
2. Discuss how one's listening skills can be improved.
3. Explain how nonverbal communication contributes to the communication process.
4. Discuss what a person seeking a job can do to prepare for a job interview.
5. Identify factors contributing to effective group participation.
6. Explain the Johari window and the effect the open area has on other areas.
7. Describe the levels of interpersonal relationships and explain how they affect communication.
8. Define assertiveness and give guidelines for being assertive.
9. Identify barriers that interfere with effective communication.

Communication in some form is essential to all interpersonal relationships. Human relations and communications are interlinked in whatever we do in our personal lives and in our work. We are always communicating with those around us. Even silence and body movements convey messages. We share personal thoughts, concerns, questions, and feelings by using different types of communication.

In our personal lives and in the workplace, communication enhances our relationships and facilitates our activities. Nearly every employer, when asked to identify skills desired in potential employees, will have communications skills as a priority. You probably recall from Chapter 1 that Workplace Skills for the 21st Century also included communication skills. You may want to review the competencies and the skills recommended by the *SCANS Report of America 2000* occasionally as you proceed in this course because they are critical to success in the world of work today and in the future. A section of Chapter 9 deals more specifically with communication in the workplace.

COMPONENTS OF COMMUNICATION

What constitutes effective communication? A simple answer might be a message is sent, received, and interpreted as the sender intended. It's a little more complicated than that, however. Several components are involved in a communication transaction. Of course, there must be a *sender, receiver,* and *message,* each with a *purpose.* But there are also the *channel,* or means of communicating; the *environment; situation;* and *feedback. Barriers,* or interferences, are not a necessary part of the transaction but they are part of it nonetheless and must be recognized. Each of these components can also consist of related factors. Let's take a look at the interaction of these components in the communication process.

It would be difficult to determine whether any component of communication is more important than the others because they are all part of the process. There is no communication without a receiver, for example. Sometimes the message is the most important, as when lifesaving instructions are given during a crisis. Because of celebrity status or some other distinction, sometimes the sender receives the most attention. In most cases, it is important for us to consider the relative significance and interaction of all the components.

SENDER/RECEIVER

Let's assume that senders and receivers are human beings even though the message may be contained temporarily in an electronic device or some other channel. We know from our study of Chapter 2 that we all have a self-concept that affects

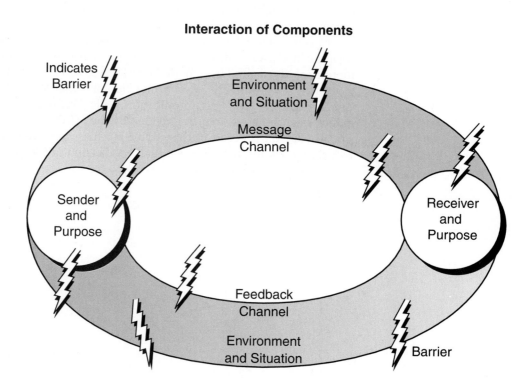

Interaction of Components

everything we do, including how we communicate. The way you communicate is part of your personality and, to some extent, is a habit. Some people are soft-spoken and do not reveal their feelings readily in their voices and facial expression. Some people can communicate their feelings better in writing than they can in person. We can all learn to be more expressive and to become more interesting, influential communicators, however.

What kind of persons deserve your attention? Why do you deserve the attention of others? One of the most important characteristics related to these questions is integrity. **Integrity** is the underlying honesty or dependability of an individual. A person is said to have integrity if there is consistency between what he or she says and does. A person without integrity soon encounters difficulty in finding people who will pay attention to what he or she wants to communicate.

A person who lacks integrity probably also lacks **credibility,** or believability. It is possible, however, for a person to have credibility, even though he or she might not be honest or sincere. Some persons may be dishonest in their intentions but still be so convincing that others fall for their line or scheme. Fortunately most people are not trying to take advantage of us, but it would be naïve to think that everyone is honest and unselfish. Knowing individuals well enough to know that they have integrity will bolster their credibility. Also, if others know we are persons of integrity, we will have more credibility with them.

The knowledge and experience of individuals also contribute to their credibility and effectiveness in communicating. Unless a person knows what he or she is talking about, the effect of communication may not only be meaningless, it could even be harmful. We have more confidence in a medical technician who has had experience with our problem than in one who is inexperienced. A safety director, for example, probably has not experienced firsthand all the accidents that he is concerned about in safety communications. However, he knows safety regulations and precautions, and it is likely that he has had experience in responding to accidents.

The knowledge both senders and receivers have of one another also affects the interchange of information. Is the sender an authority on the subject? How much does the receiver already know? How much do they want or need to know?

We may now be more aware of the influence of attitudes on what we do and on the reactions of others because we studied Chapter 6. Attitudes of both senders and receivers toward one another and toward the subject, message, and situation will all affect the outcome of communication. Positive, open attitudes contribute to success in communications as well as to all of life's endeavors. Additional factors may affect the interaction between sender and receiver.

MESSAGE

What is communication without a message? Can communication occur without a message? A command of language and vocal skills aren't of much use without something to communicate. The message also needs to be understood by the receiver. Anyone striving for success today should be able to use language skills. We should practice using the various forms of communication to achieve clarity and correctness. We are expected to know the technical language for our specialized area of work, but we must also remember that customers, clients, and patients are not likely to be familiar with such technical terminology. It is also important to avoid language that may be offensive to any of our receivers.

Integrity
underlying honesty or dependability of an individual.

Credibility
believability; having others believe your message.

PURPOSE

Both the sender and the receiver should have a purpose. Much communication can be frustrating if purposes are not clear. From the sender's point of view, purposes may be to *inform, instruct, persuade, support, be social,* or *entertain.* People at work may be informed about a workshop they could attend. When they are given an explanation and demonstration on how to use new equipment, the purpose would be to instruct. The purpose would be to persuade if a member of a work team attempted to get coworkers to adopt his plan for designing a product. The purpose to support is most often used in our personal relationships, in helping others deal with difficult situations. Giving support may also be appropriate on the job, however, in encouraging a person to achieve a goal, or being empathetic toward a person experiencing disappointment at not receiving a promotion, for example. An additional purpose of communication is to be social—to gain and give pleasure through conversation and sharing. And the purpose of communication can be to entertain, even though that is not a purpose for our consideration here. Some of these purposes, and a few additional ones, are discussed on pages 174–175.

ENVIRONMENT

Environment includes your location and the related circumstances. Much of it has to do with your physical comfort. If you are listening to a speaker, it could also pertain to the area and to acoustics. The environment can also affect how we feel and our willingness to communicate. You may have entered offices and meeting areas, for example, that appear cold and unattractive or comfortable and relaxing. These have psychological effects on how we feel and how we communicate.

Children often communicate honestly and directly.

SITUATION

The situation in a communication transaction is unfortunately often overlooked but it can be crucial to effectiveness. Situations involve the relationship between senders and receivers, attitudes, and other psychological factors. A person may want to make a suggestion in a meeting, for example, but may refrain if a person who is expected to criticize is present. Others may help us feel at ease and encourage our participation. Situations pertain to such questions as: Who else is there? How do you feel about one another and the message? What's happening? Paying attention to the situation may make the difference between a message being received and accepted or becoming lost in the process.

CHANNEL

Channel
the means of relaying a message.

Holography
a laser technology that allows an image to be re-created.

The **channel** is the means of relaying a message. It can be important in terms of time, cost, or effectiveness. A particular channel may even be the preferred means of communicating by an individual. The standard types of communication were speaking and writing, but there are many variations of these in today's world. Some people are more effective in face-to-face communication, others prefer the phone, and still others may choose a more formal, written channel. E-mail has become one of the most popular electronic forms and is widely used in both business and personal communication. Websites and chat rooms on computers have opened up whole new realms of communication. Interactive television offers another technologically sophisticated channel. Communicating with others anywhere by three dimensional **holography,** whereby the image of a person is produced by laser light, will also be an optional communication channel in the future.

E-Mail is one of the most popular new channels of communication in both business arenas and personal ones.

FEEDBACK

Feedback is important to effective communication. We like to know, in some way, whether our intended receiver or receivers got the message. It is not only a courtesy to respond, but it is often essential to the achievement of objectives. Feedback is important in any form of communication, however. We should expect and be alert to feedback when we are the senders, and we should return appropriate feedback when we are the receivers. Nonverbal communication, discussed later in this chapter, is also significant in feedback. Effective communication often follows a continuing cycle, rather than consisting of just a message and feedback to that message.

BARRIERS

Barriers can affect any of the components in numerous ways and will be discussed as a separate topic at the end of the chapter.

LISTENING

Hearing
how we physically experience sound.

Listening involves much more than just hearing. **Hearing** is how we physically experience sound. Sound waves stimulate our ear mechanism, and messages are thus relayed to the brain. We may hear many sounds daily to which

Listening
a voluntary action that involves paying attention and interpreting sound.

we do not pay attention or listen. Hearing some sounds may be involuntary, as when we hear thunder. **Listening** is voluntary and involves paying attention and adding interpretation to the sounds we hear. Listening does not always require the same amount of effort. If we hear the sound of a siren, it may not be difficult to determine what it means. Listening to a lecture, on the other hand, may require our undivided attention.

REASONS FOR LISTENING

Why do we listen? Several reasons for listening are considered below:

- *To gain information.* We listen to the news on our radios or television to keep abreast of world events and to learn about local happenings. We also gain information in our classes and from many different sources at work. Gaining information is usually only the first step in learning, however.

- *To understand or comprehend.* We need to understand how we can use information we receive. We need information about the use of computers but we also want to comprehend the possibilities of the Internet. We also need to comprehend the instructions given when we learn a new skill.

- *To evaluate.* Evaluating a message is sometimes referred to as critical listening. Raymond Zeuschner in *Communicating Today* states, "Critical listening means taking information and looking at it carefully. It means being able to analyze the content and form of the message so that you make informed

Members of this group listen attentively to one another as they share ideas for a project.

decisions about the value of the information for you" (1). It is not meant to find fault, necessarily, but to determine the accuracy and possible uses of what another person is saying. We may be listening to someone explain a new procedure for cleaning equipment and may be evaluating the new procedure compared to the old. We should get in the habit of listening critically, even when it is not our responsibility to make an immediate decision. We form opinions by listening critically. We often follow through with a decision and action when we have listened to evaluate. While we listen to a presentation on student housing, for example, we may listen for a comparison of costs, location or bus routes, and lease stipulations.

- *To be courteous and/or to show empathy.* We can go to extremes and allow other people to take up valuable study time with meaningless chatter, but we can also listen to others when we sense that it is important to them to be able to talk to us. As valuable as our time may be, often one of the kindest things we can do for others is to give them a little bit of our time and listen to them. We are using empathy, as defined in Chapter 5, when we try to understand what others are experiencing and how they feel, and listen to them.

- *To be social and share.* Friends listen to one another in the course of sharing, also discussed in Chapter 5. You may call a friend or stop by to visit with no other purpose than to see one another and talk. But such talk also involves listening, doesn't it? People like other people who are interesting and who are also good listeners. We also listen to one another as family members, even though some of us may not listen as much or as carefully as we might. It is important to know that we have someone who cares about us and will listen to whatever we have to share.

- *To relax and be entertained.* When we listen to entertainment, we may be enjoying a speaker at an awards dinner or program, or we may be listening to an entertainer or to music, live or through a medium such as television. For many, listening to something pleasant is also a means of relaxation.

What Would You Say? *If a person tells you something as if it were a fact and you believe it to be an opinion, what would you say?*

CHECKLIST OF ACTIVE LISTENING SKILLS

You may gain some insight into what kind of a listener you are by evaluating yourself in terms of the characteristics listed below. Circle the number that you believe best describes your listening skills. Circle 1 if you are very weak in a skill, 2 if you are somewhat weak, 3 if you consider yourself average, 4 if you are quite strong, and 5 if you are very strong.

- I determine the value of listening for me in each situation.   1   2   3   4   5
- I focus on the present subject and situation.   1   2   3   4   5
- I try to determine the speaker's purpose.   1   2   3   4   5

■	I do not get distracted by the speaker's appearance.	1	2	3	4	5
■	I do not let the use of language interfere with meaning.	1	2	3	4	5
■	I have taken care of physical needs so I am comfortable.	1	2	3	4	5
■	I give visual attention to the speaker.	1	2	3	4	5
■	I ask questions as needed for clarity, if permitted in the situation.	1	2	3	4	5
■	I take notes, when appropriate, to stay focused on the subject.	1	2	3	4	5
■	I try not to be distracted by environmental factors such as noise.	1	2	3	4	5
■	I keep an open mind and avoid jumping to conclusions.	1	2	3	4	5
■	I focus on main ideas rather than supporting facts and examples.	1	2	3	4	5
■	I do not argue mentally with the speaker instead of listening.	1	2	3	4	5
■	I do not try to do other things while listening.	1	2	3	4	5

If you have checked mostly 3s, 4s, and 5s, you have active listening skills. Persons who have all 4s and 5s may not be accurately evaluating their skills. The purpose of the checklist is for you to evaluate your skills rather than to obtain a particular score. Some of the statements in the checklist are oversimplified; therefore, there will be exceptions. It would be beneficial to discuss some of the statements with class members or friends. It may be true, at least for you, that you can do other things while listening, especially if you are listening to music. The checklist can make you aware of some habits that may keep you from being a more effective listener.

CONSEQUENCES OF POOR LISTENING

It may be an incentive to improve our listening skills if we consider some of the consequences of poor listening. These negative effects can pertain both to ourselves and to those to whom we are (or should be) listening. One of these involves loss of confidence. We may not only lower our self-confidence and self-esteem when we make an error due to poor listening, but others may also lose confidence in us. These errors could result in loss of customers due to delays or in receiving the wrong service or products. Time and materials can be wasted. Frustration can run rampant and jobs may even be lost. Poor listening can also lead to rumors that, in turn, contribute to confusion, negative emotions, and bad decisions. We probably aren't aware of all the problems that are caused by poor listening.

 What Do You Think? *Can you think of any additional consequences of poor listening?*

SUGGESTIONS FOR BETTER LISTENING

Diane Bone notes in *The Business of Listening*, "Most of us are not good listeners. We listen at about 25 percent of our potential, which means we *ignore, forget, distort,* or *misunderstand* 75 percent of what we hear" (2). You can judge for yourself to what extent you believe Bone's percentages apply to you, but we can all benefit by improving our listening skills. One thing we can do is to adapt our listening to a particular situation. It makes a difference, for example, whether we are talking to friends or family members, with whom we can interact freely, or whether we are involved in a job interview. It also makes a difference whether we are in a communication situation involving only one other person, or whether we are part of an audience listening to a speaker. There are no hard and fast rules for being an effective communicator because all the components of the communication transaction are involved, and each component consists of its own variables. It is important, therefore, to be flexible and to adjust our listening to what we believe the speaker's purpose to be, to our purpose in listening, and to the situation.

THE WALL STREET JOURNAL

"Could you repeat that? I was just desperately wishing I was somewhere else."

Cartoon Feature Syndicate

NONVERBAL COMMUNICATION

Do actions really speak louder than words? It is estimated that nearly half of all communication is nonverbal. While estimations may differ, it is certain that nonverbal communication is an integral component of the communication process. Oral communication, or what we say and how we say it, is closely affected by nonverbal aspects of communication such as appearance, facial expression, body language, personal distance, and posture. Nonverbal communication can add to the meaning of the message or reveal the feelings of the speaker. Some nonverbal signs, such as smiles, handshakes, and waves, seem to have a universal meaning; others can be interpreted in many ways, depending on the person and the situation. All the elements of communication, both verbal and nonverbal, should be combined into an integrated communication experience for both the speaker and the listener.

APPEARANCE

Appearance is considered an important component of nonverbal communication, especially in the workplace. First impressions, such as those gained at job interviews, when our intended listeners do not know us personally, may be formed with a great deal of emphasis on appearance. Before you have had the opportunity to say anything, your appearance has already told something silently about you. What does appearance normally include? Admittedly it includes some of the factors over which we have no control, such as our height and physical characteristics. Most of what constitutes your appearance, however, is within your control. We also accept that, in the workplace, it is important to wear appropriate attire for the work we do.

Appearance is an expression of how we want to present ourselves to others. Our impression of what that means, however, may not be the same as how others perceive it. Consider again the factors that affect perception discussed in Chapter 4.

FACIAL EXPRESSIONS

Facial expressions can be very communicative, especially when they pertain to emotions, as discussed in Chapter 5. We may or may not be aware of what our facial expressions communicate to others. Spontaneous feedback in the form of facial expressions is often more revealing of our reaction and its intensity than our words.

The most expressive features of nonverbal communication are the eyes. Looking directly at another person can indicate interest or a desire for attention. Not looking at those we are talking to is usually interpreted as lack of confidence in ourselves, lack of interest in others, or even that we cannot be trusted. A steady, concentrated gaze, or stare, however, can indicate displeasure.

In addition to how we communicate with our eyes, other types of facial expression also affect our communication. Smiles, frowns, looks of surprise, bewilderment, and fear, for example, convey messages to others.

The way you position your body in relation to others affects the way your message is perceived.

Proxemics
the spatial distance between people.

BODY LANGUAGE

Body language is most evident when we are relaxed and talking comfortably with friends, when we use our whole bodies to communicate. If we concentrate on what we are saying, give our attention to others, and have a sincere desire to communicate, it is natural to use gestures for clarification, directions, or emphasis. The way we walk, sit, or stand also suggests our attitudes about ourselves, others, or what is happening. We often relay messages with our bodies without being aware of them. A person who slouches or leans continuously on furniture or equipment suggests lack of motivation or interest in what he or she is doing. If we want to be considered confident, energetic, ambitious, and interested in what we are doing and in others, we will indicate this in our posture, both sitting and standing, and in how we move and walk. In interpreting any nonverbal communication, it is helpful to know the context of the situation and the other person or persons involved.

PROXEMICS

Proxemics, or spatial distance between persons, plays an important role in communication, especially comfort levels. Individuals who are in close personal relationships will generally feel more comfortable in close proximity to one another than they would with strangers or business acquaintances. Also, a certain amount of respect can be shown for people of authority by maintaining distance when communicating. Different types of people may prefer different amounts of personal space, and they may feel uncomfortable and even back up if their space is diminished.

Different cultures also have customs involving personal space. Often one will be able to tell if the distance is acceptable to both parties by the degree of relaxation and other nonverbal clues.

Everyone, both consciously and unconsciously, uses nonverbal communication. We should try to become aware of how we communicate ideas and information in this way and how we interpret the nonverbal communication of others. On the other hand, it is important to realize that nonverbal communication can easily be misinterpreted. Crossed arms, for example, are believed by some to indicate a defensive attitude or a firm position in a disagreement. For some people, however, crossing arms is a comfortable position and may not have a particular relationship to what is happening or to a person's attitudes or feelings. Nonverbal communication is usually spontaneous and may not be a conscious effort to portray a particular meaning.

We can become more aware of our posture, distance, expressions, and movement, however, when communicating with others. The more relaxed we feel when we communicate, the easier it will be for us to breathe naturally and for our muscles to relax, allowing us to be more effective speakers or listeners. When we are relaxed, both our verbal and nonverbal communication will less likely be misinterpreted.

COMMUNICATING TO GET THAT JOB

Seeking a job, writing a résumé, drafting specific cover letters, preparing for an interview, participating in an employment interview, and follow-up require various types of communication skills. People who are alert to what is happening in the economy, in businesses, and in their particular field of interest are more likely to hear about or learn of job opportunities. Many persons receive jobs with a particular business or company as a result of a referral from a current employee. Keep in mind that ongoing businesses and companies are continually hiring new employees to replace those who retire, move, are fired, or lose their jobs for other reasons. In spite of downsizing, or cutting down on the scope of business and number of employees, many companies are frequently hiring. Companies want the best employees they can get just as job-seekers want the best jobs they can get. It takes effective communication skills on the part of both companies and potential employees to make the right match.

YOUR RÉSUMÉ

Some owners or managers of businesses do not require a résumé. They may make a decision based entirely on a job application, a brief interview, and references. Even if you think you may not need a résumé, however, it is recommended that you prepare one and have it available. It gives you a picture of your objectives, educational background, work experience, and related achievements that you might overlook unless you think about them seriously and put them in writing. If you are taking a written communications course as part of your education, you may be required to prepare a résumé and cover letters written for specific companies. If this task is required, take advantage of the opportunity to identify and organize your skills, strengths, and talents.

A résumé may be difficult to prepare, but it is easier to do so under the guidance of an instructor than to write it on your own. Of course, it is important to keep your résumé current. Preparing your résumé on a computer gives you the advantage of easily making changes or additions.

Classified ads, computerized job searches, and other sources of information about available jobs often say "Send Résumé." Your résumé is the first impression a prospective employer has of you and if he or she doesn't like your résumé, you will not be contacted for a personal interview. It is worth your time and effort, therefore, to prepare an accurate, complete, and good-looking résumé.

THE JOB INTERVIEW

You may participate in several job interviews in the process of getting your first full-time job in your chosen career. At some point you may have the opportunity to be an interviewer or part of an interviewing team. In addition to the job or employment interview discussed here, other types of work-related interviews will be described in the next chapter.

The **job interview** usually occurs between a personnel director or company representative and a job applicant. Each party tries to gain and give information by asking questions, answering questions, making statements, and careful listening.

Job interview
a face-to-face question-and-answer session to determine a person's suitability for a job.

A job interview is often the determining factor in whether a person is hired. In a job interview, the interviewer is trying to assess the kind of person you are and whether you have the motivation and enthusiasm to achieve in the position you are seeking.

We usually experience a certain amount of anxiety in preparing for an interview. What will they ask me? What should I wear? What should I tell them about myself? Job applicants ask themselves these kinds of questions as they prepare for an interview. Preparing helps to relieve tension and helps us to be ourselves. While it is impossible to predict what an interviewer might actually ask or say, some questions and topics are common to many interviews. Your skills and educational experience will probably be discussed, even though they are also part of your résumé.

Your strengths and weaknesses, likes and dislikes, should be considered when preparing for an interview. One commonly asked question is, "What is your greatest weakness?" This question is difficult to answer but it is best to acknowledge some weakness. A student who has just graduated may say that she doesn't have related work experience, but that she has excellent training and is looking forward to applying her education to her work and gaining experience. In this way she takes a positive approach to the question. We all have weaknesses, but we can continue to improve ourselves and accept suggestions regarding weaknesses.

What are your skills, goals, hobbies, and interests? Do you have any special talents and achievement? Have you been involved in activities in school or in your community? What are your goals? Where would you like to be in five or ten years? Why are you interested in working for our company? Do you work best alone or with others? How do you feel about working overtime? These are some additional questions that merit consideration and thought in preparation for an employment interview.

The job interview is often the determining factor in whether a person is hired. An individual must have the required training qualifications, but beyond that, the prospective employer tries to determine what kind of person you are. Employers evaluate your qualifications, recommendations, attitudes, appearance, and both oral and nonverbal communication and try to determine whether you will be reliable and trustworthy and whether you will be able to get along with other employees. More workers who are fired from their jobs are probably released for personality traits than because of inability to do the work.

Some apprehension regarding the interview process is caused by myths, according to C. R. Krannich and R. L. Krannich. They have identified what they believe to be common **myths,** or mistaken beliefs, pertaining to job interviews. Several of the myths are listed below, along with what they believe to be the reality of each situation.

Myths
mistaken beliefs.

Myth: The candidate with the best educational skills and experience will get the job.
Reality: Employers hire individuals for many different reasons. Education, skills, and experience are only a few of several hiring criteria. If they hired only on the basis of education, skills, and experience, they would not need to interview candidates. Such static information is available in applications and résumés.

Myth: Once I submit my application for a job, the proper thing to do is to wait until I hear something from the employer.
Reality: Waiting is not a good job search strategy. It is perfectly acceptable to call the employer within two weeks of submitting your written materials to ask when you might expect to hear about the final selection. Employers often fail to inform candidates whether or not they are still under consideration. It is to your advantage to get a definite yes or no rather than waste your time doing nothing else in anticipation of being called for an interview.

Myth: While waiting in the office for the interviewer, I should just sit and wait to be called.
Reality: Your job interview begins as soon as you walk through the office door. Since you will be under observation, do something positive that can be observed and reported. For example, if the secretary or receptionist is not too busy, ask some friendly and interesting questions about the organization. You may get some important information that will help you in the interview. If the waiting area has some magazines or literature on the organization displayed, pick up and browse through the more relevant and serious literature.

Myth: I should wait for the interviewer to take the initiative in asking questions.
Reality: Let the interviewer initiate the first question, but you must also take the initiative in asking questions of the interviewer. An interview is a two-way communication situation in which both parties are attempting to exchange useful information. If you don't take any initiative, you will be seen as someone lacking initiative.

Myth: My major goal in the interview is to get the job.
Reality: Your major goal should be the same as the interviewer's—to gain useful information from which you can make a decision about joining this organization. If you make this your goal, the interview will become more like a friendly, two-way dialogue rather than a stressful inquisition. Both you and the interviewer will go away with the information the two of you need to make the right decisions (3).

Getting a job can be one of the most important challenges of your life. Make every effort to communicate effectively throughout the entire process.

GROUP PARTICIPATION

Group participation can give you an opportunity to contribute to an effort or a cause that requires the input and talent of many individuals. "The whole is greater than the sum of its parts" is true of group activity. Effective communication skills are essential to meaningful participation and achievement of a group's goals.

ORAL PRESENTATIONS

The ability to speak to a group is a valuable skill. You may have already made such presentations. You may be expected to speak to a group as part of your job, but such experience can well be thought of as an opportunity to strengthen your communication skills, to contribute to group goals, and to influence others. Many employees are promoted within businesses and other organizations largely because of their communications skills.

An oral presentation at work could be a report to a work group or an explanation of what your department is doing to increase efficiency. Although you may feel some apprehension about the presentation, you can do a commendable job with some basic knowledge, preparation, a little practice, and self-confidence. Some of the background questions you should consider for such an experience are: What else is on the agenda or program? What will precede or follow my presentation? How much time am I allowed for the presentation?

Location is another factor to consider. Your presentation may take place in a familiar work or meeting location, or it you be in a place unfamiliar to you. Even if the location is familiar, you should check out its condition ahead or at least at the beginning of the presentation. If possible, move aside any equipment that you will not be using. Remove distractions such as material written on a chalkboard or other visuals left by an earlier presenter. If you plan to use visual aids that require lighting or electricity, note where electrical outlets are and determine whether you will need an extension cord. If you are using slides, for example, note whether lights can be dimmed. Determine whether you need assistance with equipment, lights, or handouts.

Visual aids can contribute to the total understanding and impression of your presentation. Some of the more common types of visual aids include actual objects, models, graphics, photographs, or computer-produced materials. Give careful consideration to the type of visual that would be obtainable and appropriate for the group. Visual aids serve many functions. They help hold attention by adding variety, provide for visual learning styles, offer reinforcement to verbal explanations, and serve as guides to the presenter.

It will probably help if you don't think of your presentation as giving a speech. Public speaking causes anxiety for most of us because we don't have much of that type of experience. Rather think specifically about what you will be doing. You will be sharing knowledge, ideas, and probably experience with others who you can expect will be interested. If you think of the components of communication as they relate to your purpose, the experience will be more meaningful for you and those to whom you are making a presentation.

In addition to using visual aids as guidelines, notes can be helpful. Except in cases of extremely technical material, a presentation should not be read. Even if you do read, reading should be meaningful and should include some eye contact. If you choose to use cards, write on only one side, print larger than you would ordinarily, and try not to refer to the cards more than is necessary. Do not worry about making a mistake. Everyone makes mistakes. It's how you handle a mistake, without getting flustered, that is important.

RESPONDING TO QUESTIONS

Sometimes you must answer questions and address comments during a presentation itself. The problem, however, may be that you won't cover your prepared material. If possible, let group members know that you will answer questions after the presentation.

If it is not already part of your program, a course in oral communication would be an excellent preparation for many future experiences, both on the job and in other activities. Practice in a class or in a real situation helps a person increase self-confidence, develop organizational skills, and practice critical thinking. These abilities are part of all our communication and human relations interactions. Toastmasters International is an example of a group that helps its members continue to improve their communication skills.

INTERPERSONAL COMMUNICATION

We communicate with people differently in form and in content, depending on our relationship with them. It would not be difficult to think of three different people with whom we have different types of relationships. How well we know a person and the amount of trust we put in our relationship with that person are factors that affect how we communicate with them.

TYPES OF RELATIONSHIPS

An *acquaintance* is someone with whom we exchange verbal and nonverbal greetings and other social expressions. "Hello, have a nice day. How are you doing?" are examples of communication exchanges we may have with acquaintances. Whether we see these people only once or several times, our relationship and communication with them usually does not go beyond this initial level.

Once we exchange initial greetings with others, we may be interested in getting to know them better. *Associates* are people that cross our paths because of a common experience. Coworkers, other students in a class, and church members may be associates. We usually communicate with associates about our commonality or regarding a particular topic. We generally see them at a certain time, in a certain place, and on a regular basis. We become associates.

Friends are people with whom we make voluntary connections. Most friendships develop over time. Factors that lead to friendship are common goals; similar personality characteristics, background, interests, and values; and even similar difficulties and sorrows. Through communication we find out what we have in common and become friends.

Friends have an understanding of one another that goes beyond ordinary means of communication. In fact, friends often have an accurate idea of how we feel without our telling them. Empathy, or understanding to the best of our ability what another person is experiencing, is easier with friends. Indications by others that they are at least attempting to understand what we are undergoing can support us in many aspects of our lives. It's valuable to know that others support you, even when they are unable to understand a particular experience or when communication is difficult.

Intimacy develops as we reveal more of ourselves to another person. Intimacy is based on trust. We are willing to share our fears, hopes, dreams, likes, and dislikes because of this trust in a friend. When we get to know someone on an intimate level, much nonverbal and verbal communication is shared and understood more easily. We need to continue to be careful listeners, however, because intimate friends share things that are very important to them and are often difficult to talk about if they have a high emotional component.

GENDER DIFFERENCES

We are becoming increasingly aware of gender differences in communication styles. We need to be careful, however, of stereotyping or making assumptions that men and women will communicate in a certain style just because of their gender. Recent research has confirmed that there are some basic differences in male and female communication styles that, if understood, can improve communication between the genders.

John Gray, author of *Men Are from Mars, Women Are from Venus,* states, "Men mistakenly expect women to think, communicate and react the way men do; women mistakenly expect men to feel, communicate and respond the way women do" (4). He discusses gender differences in several communication areas and situations. For example, he believes that men prefer to work out problems by themselves, while women prefer to discuss their problems. He also suggests ways that men and women can communicate with one another with greater understanding and fewer hurt feelings.

What Do You Think? *From your own experience, do you agree that there are differences in gender communication styles?*

YOUR JOHARI WINDOW

You know some things about yourself that other people don't know, right? Could there also be some things that others know about you that you don't know about yourself? You are even more complicated than that. This idea of "Who knows what about you?" can be understood better through the Johari Window, designed by Joseph Luft and Harrington Ingham. The word *Johari* was formed from their two first names. The four areas of the window, as shown below, represent four areas of who you are in terms of what is known or unknown about you (5).

If you follow both the vertical and horizontal identifications of the areas of the window, it can be interpreted as the following:

Open area	Known to self; Known to others
Blind area	Not known to self; Known to others
Hidden area	Known to self; Not known to others
Unknown area	Not known to self; Not known to others

The following example will add to our understanding of these areas. Brad wanted the promotion to sales manager very badly. The promotion, however, was given to Karen, who had two years less experience with the company than Brad. Karen and several others knew that Brad wanted the job (open area). It was also commonly known that Brad probably wouldn't get the promotion because he talked too freely about confidential company business matters. Brad, however,

	Known to self	Not known to self
Known to others	1 Open	2 Blind
Not known to others	Hidden 3	Unknown 4

The Johari Window

was not aware that this was a problem standing in his way (blind area). Brad had hoped that Karen would leave the company and join a competitor before this promotion came up, although she had never mentioned this to anyone (hidden area).

Brad is actually jealous of Karen, but he is unaware of this. Brad has repressed his feelings of jealousy because it is unacceptable to him to be jealous of another person's success (unknown area). At the department meeting, in fact, Brad congratulated Karen on the promotion and pledged his cooperation (open area again). One's unknown area could also refer to one's potential that neither the individual nor others are aware of.

The Johari Window can be used as a means of increasing self-awareness and improving relationships with others by sharing who we are. This is often referred to as self-disclosure. J. C. Pearson and P. E. Nelson, in *Understanding and Sharing,* have the following to say: "Self-disclosure includes statements a person makes about himself or herself that another person would be unlikely to know or discover." They go on to say, "Self-disclosure is important for two reasons. First, it allows us to establish more meaningful relationships with others. Second, self-disclosure allows us to establish more positive attitudes toward ourselves and others" (6). Self-disclosure would be involved in the intimacy level of the relationship discussed earlier. Disclosing information about ourselves will usually allow others to be more comfortable in doing the same, and relationships will grow.

The degree to which we share ourselves with others differs with respect not only to those with whom we are sharing but also to who we are as individuals. The more self-confidence we acquire, personally and in our careers, the more open we will be with others. We will have less need to be self-protective and defensive. Naturally, as mentioned earlier, we don't need or want the same degree of openness with everyone. As we enlarge one area of the window, other areas become smaller. The large window (square) is representative of who we are as a person.

 What Would You Say? *What would you say to a person who asks you a question, the answer to which you do not care to share with that person?*

ASSERTIVENESS

Assertiveness
protecting your rights in a situation without harming others or abusing their rights.

Aggressiveness
asserting your rights in a way that takes advantage of others.

Ideas about assertiveness vary. Some people consider it a threat; others consider it a challenge. It is most accurately thought of in terms of rights. **Assertiveness** refers to protecting your own rights in a situation without intending to harm or to abuse the rights of others. Some people confuse assertiveness with aggressiveness, but there is an important difference. **Aggressiveness** refers to taking advantage of other people, thus abusing their rights. (Being aggressive can also mean being ambitious and a go-getter in a competitive sense, but that is not the meaning intended here.) Assertiveness is related to aggressiveness because assertive people do not allow themselves to be victimized by the aggression of others.

What Would You Do? *If you thought someone was aggressive in his or her actions toward you, what would you do? How would you classify your reaction?*

If you believe sincerely that others take advantage of you, what can you do about it? It isn't easy to protect yourself without sometimes taking advantage of or hurting others. But you are entitled to protect yourself as much as possible from being hurt by others, intentionally or unintentionally. A maxim worth applying is "Try not to hurt anybody, including yourself." Here are some guidelines for being assertive without being aggressive:

- *Know yourself.* As discussed in Chapter 2, self-knowledge and self-understanding go beyond the mere facts of who you are. They are essential to meaningful living and in developing rewarding relationships with others.

- *Accept yourself.* You are unique. Recognize this fact and appreciate it. This does not mean that you cannot grow or that you cannot improve yourself. But you should not be dissatisfied with yourself to the point where you feel inferior or worthless. If you have trouble accepting yourself, others are less likely to accept you. If you are comfortable with yourself, you will have more satisfying relationships with others.

- *Express yourself.* The inability to express what you think and feel can lead to a kind of victimization. You can learn to say what you like or don't like— and what you want to do or don't want to do—without antagonizing others. We should always be considerate and tactful, even though our actions may sometimes be disappointing to others. Others may not be happy when you don't give in to their ways, but that may be because you are interfering with their aggressiveness. **Discretion,** or good judgment, is always important in our relations with others.

Discretion
good judgment.

- *Expect respect.* There is truth to the idea that people react to you largely according to what you expect. We should show that we care about ourselves. We can show by the way we dress, walk, and act toward others that we expect respect as another human being. Expecting respect does not mean we consider ourselves superior to others. It is based on a sense of equality. We recognize that there are situations in life and work where others have authority over us, but that does not make them superior to us as human beings.

- *Respect others.* If we treat others as we would like to be treated, we show them respect. In reality we can act respectfully without feeling respect, which is an attitude. But if we care about others and their concerns, we will treat them with the type of consideration we want for ourselves.

- *Suggest reasonable solutions or alternatives.* We should let people know that we are interested in improving total situations rather than in merely defending our own rights. When workloads are inequitable, for example, the department is not functioning as well as it could. Assertiveness is striving for consideration and fairness.

BARRIERS TO COMMUNICATION

Countless factors can become barriers to or interferences in our ability to communicate effectively. These barriers are not always the same, nor do they affect all people in the same way, but we all experience them in our attempts to communicate. A review of the diagram of the communication transaction, presented earlier in the chapter, will reveal that all components can be affected by barriers. The transaction as a whole can also be affected by barriers.

Although we are not able to eliminate or overcome all barriers, communication will be easier and more effective if we are aware of them in our interactions. The following is a discussion of some of the more common communication barriers.

THE WALL STREET JOURNAL

"Stop diving underwater when I'm talking to you."

Cartoon Feature Syndicate.

DISTRACTIONS

Distractions such as noise, people walking around, or other activity can make it difficult to both speak and listen. Other distractions may be associated with appearances of the sender or the message itself. In fact, anything that diverts our attention from the communication process is a distraction.

PHYSIOLOGICAL CONDITIONS

Physiological conditions such as fatigue, illness, or hunger can lessen our effectiveness both as a sender and a receiver. Although in a work situation we may be required to be as effective as possible under these circumstances, it is important to recognize them.

PSYCHOLOGICAL FACTORS

Psychological factors affect everything we do, including communication. These factors may be related to mistrust, loneliness, self-concept, or our emotional state. Anxieties may contribute to our thoughts being elsewhere. Values and needs can interfere with mutual understanding. Personality characteristics and attitudes toward any of the components can also create barriers.

PERCEPTUAL DIFFERENCES

Perceptual differences or individual interpretations of persons, places, and things may cause additional communication problems. The many factors involved in perception, discussed in Chapter 4, also affect communication. Principles of perception such as constancy and closure may prevent a complete and realistic interpretation of what we see or hear.

LANGUAGE PROBLEMS

Language related to culture, education, work experience, and life experiences can cause numerous problems. These language barriers may involve vocabulary, accent, slang, or vulgarity. The ability to use language should include adaptability to what can be understood by and is acceptable to receivers.

CHANNEL CHARACTERISTICS

Channel characteristics can also present barriers. Some examples include the tone of a speaker's voice, a dislike of certain communication methods such as e-mail or voice mail, confusing or unnecessary written messages, inability to hear or understand some audio transmissions, or a multitude of other problems or personal biases. Some of the barriers are related directly to the channel itself, such as a lack of privacy or malfunctions, and others are related to individual responses to them.

Eliminating or overcoming barriers to communication will definitely improve the process. Our primary focus in becoming more effective communicators, however, should be on what we can do in a positive sense. Becoming a better communicator can be a lifelong challenge, and no ability is more valuable in harmonious, productive human relationships.

Summary

Several components make up a communication transaction: the sender, receiver, message, purpose, environment, situation, channel, and feedback. There are also barriers that can affect any component or the process as a whole.

Listening is a vital communication skill. Most of us are not as effective at listening as we could be. There can be serious consequences to poor listening. We can evaluate our listening skills and work at becoming better listeners.

Nonverbal communication plays a greater role than most of us realize. Appearance, facial expression, body language, and proxemics are some aspects of nonverbal communication. They add meaning to communication, but we should be cautious when interpreting them in others. We should also be aware of negative messages we may be sending by means of nonverbal communication.

Communication plays a major role in getting a job. Your résumé creates a first impression and should be correct and neat. Careful preparation for a job interview should include consideration of questions that may be asked. In addition, a follow-up contact expressing appreciation and inquiring about a possible employment offer is recommended.

Group participation, both on and off the job, requires communication skills. Workers today can expect to make oral presentations to groups. Preparation, self-confidence, and basic communication skills contribute to successful presentations.

Many of our daily communication activities are in interpersonal relationships, which include acquaintances, associates, and friends. Intimacy develops as we become willing to trust and share with others.

New emphasis today is being placed on differences in gender communication styles. We must keep in mind, however, that we communicate with individuals.

PSYCHOLOGY IN PRACTICE

1. Evaluate your listening skills using the Checklist of Active Listening Skills provided in this chapter. Compare your evaluation with that of a friend and discuss the differences. Determine a strategy for improving at least one of your listening skills.

2. Ask a person who is a member of a committee in a work situation about the purpose of the committee and his or her opinion of the committee's effectiveness. Also ask this person to describe his or her role as a committee member.

3. Observe the proxemics in your own communication experiences for three days. Note the differences in spatial distance depending on your relationship with the person and the purpose of your communication. Have you ever felt like backing away from someone you thought was intruding on your personal space?

The Johari Window helps us to understand who we are in terms of what is known or unknown about us. The four window areas are open, blind, hidden, and unknown. It is advantageous for most people to enlarge the open area.

Effective communication in many of life's situations requires assertiveness, or protecting one's rights without violating the rights of others. Respect for oneself and others is one of the characteristics of assertiveness.

In spite of skills and the best of intentions, there will always be barriers—distractions, physiological conditions, psychological factors, perceptual differences, language problems, and channel characteristics—to communication.

Anyone can become a more effective communicator. The advantages of communication skills will become evident in the next chapter, "Human Relations at Work."

Key Terms

Integrity	Proxemics
Credibility	Myths
Channel	Job interview
Holography	Assertiveness
Hearing	Aggressiveness
Listening	Discretion

Learning Activities

Turn to page LA-33 to complete the Learning Activities and Enrichment Activities for this chapter.

Endnotes

1. Raymond Zueschner, *Communicating Today,* 2nd ed., Allyn and Bacon, Boston, MA, 1977, p. 48.

2. Diane Bone, *The Business of Listening, A Practical Guide to Effective Listening,* rev. ed., Crisp Publications, Menlo Park, CA, 1994, p. 7.

3. C. R. Krannich and R. L. Krannich, "Interview Myths and Realities," *EEO BiMonthly, Equal Employment Opportunity Career Journal,* December 31, 1993, pp. 4–8.

4. John Gray, *Men Are from Mars, Women Are from Venus,* HarperCollins Publishers, New York, 1992, p. 10.

5. Joseph Luft, *Group Processes: An Introduction to Group Dynamics,* Mayfield, Palo Alto, CA, 1970, pp. 11–12.

6. Judy C. Pearson and Paul E. Nelson, *Understanding and Sharing,* 5th ed., Wm. C. Brown Publishers, Dubuque, IA, 1991, p. 192.

Human Relations at Work

9

We would rather have one man or woman working with us than three merely working for us.

F. W. Woolworth

LEARNING OBJECTIVES

After completing this chapter, you should be able to do the following:

1. Compare two different motivation theories related to work.
2. Define job enrichment and identify its effects.
3. Give an example of how emotions affect workplace relations.
4. Explain how loyalty and trust are related to employer-employee relations.
5. Describe some of the benefits of positive coworker relations.
6. Discuss ways of handling customer complaints.
7. Give an example of a work-related situation requiring an ethical decision.
8. Describe three different types of conflict resolution.
9. Identify advantages and possible problems related to team functioning.
10. Compare formal and informal channels of communication at work.
11. Define sexual harassment in the workplace.
12. Discuss the difference between being a friend and being friendly.

A re you a different person at work than at home or wherever else you may be? Probably not. Why, then, a separate chapter, "Human Relations at Work?" We know that psychology is the study of human behavior, which certainly involves attempting to understand one another and our interactions with others wherever we may be. There is much more diversity in the workforce, as well as in society as a whole, than ever before. This diversity presents both challenges and opportunities in human relationships. The nature of this diversity, its effects, and potential advantages for everyone will be discussed in depth in Chapter 12.

In this chapter we will extend our knowledge and understanding of what we have already studied to improve human relations in the workplace. This study can be valuable to you in your future career. If you already have work experience, you can personally relate to the content of this chapter and you can make valuable contributions to the class.

John D. Rockefeller (1839–1937) made a fortune in the oil business and was one of the most successful men in the United States in his lifetime. He once said, "I will pay more for the ability to deal with people than for any other ability under the sun." He obviously knew the value of harmonious, productive human relations in the workplace.

In Chapter 2, you read about roles we assume in different situations. The following statement was made: "It is natural and appropriate to act differently in different situations, or to assume the role or type of behavior that is called for in particular circumstances." Since it is fairly obvious that a situation at work is different from one at home, in school, or in a community setting, it is expected that our behavior would be at least somewhat different. We have a boss or supervisor (unless we are self-employed), coworkers, and customers or clients, and certain things are expected of us to earn our pay and possibly other benefits. Topics that relate to work situations will be discussed in this chapter.

You will be reminded at different points of the relationship of previous chapters to human relations at work. Although relating chapters to one another has been a feature of this book throughout, there will be even more such references in an attempt to make our work more satisfying and rewarding.

There are human relations problems in job situations that one can learn how to solve or respond to appropriately. We may also be able to prevent some problems from developing if we improve our ability to apply basic principles of human relations.

Robert A. Baron and Paul B. Paulus, in *Understanding Human Relations: A Practical Guide to People at Work,* state:

> Human Relations is concerned with the factors that help and hinder effective relationships in the work environment. Indeed, one of the most basic assumptions is as follows: In order to have an effective organization, we must provide for effective, satisfying relations between the people in it. Consistent with this point of view, human relations generally concentrates on two major goals: (1) increasing our understanding of interactions between individuals, and (2) developing practical techniques for enhancing such relations (1).

MOTIVATION TO WORK

The psychoanalytic, behavioristic, and humanistic theories of motivation were discussed in Chapter 3. It might be helpful to review these as we discuss again the motivation to work.

Numerous other theories can be identified, some of which have developed from perceived weaknesses in theories existing at the time. One of these theories frequently associated with the workplace is Herzberg's two-factor theory (2). Herzberg identified two sets of outcomes related to job satisfaction as **hygiene factors** and **motivation factors.** Hygiene factors, also referred to as maintenance factors, pertain to avoiding and eliminating conditions that cause workers to be dissatisfied with their jobs. These factors are not directly related to the work itself but might include the work environment, relationships with supervisors, or other outcomes or factors related to extrinsic motivation.

Hygiene factors
factors pertaining to avoiding and eliminating conditions that cause workers to be dissatisfied with their jobs.

Motivation factors
factors related to outcomes that increase job satisfaction.

Herzberg's Two-Factor Theory

Hygiene (Maintenance) Factors	Motivation Factors

Work environment	Recognition for work well done
Relationship with supervisor	Opportunity for advancement
Pay/fringe benefits	Enjoyment of work

Motivation factors, on the other hand, are positive and are related to outcomes that increase job satisfaction. These factors would include recognition for work well done, opportunities for advancement, and enjoyment of the work itself. These factors are more directly associated with intrinsic motivation.

Lilly M. Berry and John P. Houston, in *Psychology at Work: An Introduction to Industrial and Organizational Psychology,* point out that, even though research hasn't given a great deal of support to Herzberg's theory, it has influenced organizations and managers to redesign jobs "to make work more interesting and challenging, and to increase responsibility and opportunities for achievement" (3). Various interpretations and applications of this theory can be beneficial to both companies and employees in different ways. Becoming aware of conditions that dissatisfy workers and of other conditions that promote satisfaction, if acted upon constructively, can do a great deal to improve human relations in the workplace.

The expectancy theory is another motivational theory applied to the world of work. The **expectancy theory** refers to employees' motivation to do what they have to do to get what they want. It is based on three basic assumptions: (1) the employees believe they have the ability and means to do the work, (2) the rewards or gains are worth the effort, and (3) the rewards will be forthcoming if the work is satisfactorily completed. Managers must keep in mind, however, that all employees do not want the same rewards or results and that a particular result, such as a promotion, is more important to some individuals than to others. It is not only important for managers and supervisors to attempt to understand individual employees, but it is also important for employees to understand themselves and their values. A practical approach to the expectancy theory is to ask, "Is it worth it to me?" The accompanying illustration contributes to an understanding of the expectancy theory.

The need for achievement, referred to in textbooks as *nAch,* is also frequently associated with work motivation, but it, of course, would apply to other facets of one's life also. David McClelland is the psychologist primarily associated with this theory, although others have also had input into the theory and its application (4). According to this theory, individuals have different levels of a need for achievement. Those with a high level of this need set high standards for their own performance, like activities and work that challenges them, and are more persistent in working toward achieving goals. They are self-motivators and are naturally highly valued by employers. Fear of failure is sometimes in conflict with a need to achieve. For example, those who are motivated primarily by a fear of

Expectancy theory
a motivational theory based on the assumption that individuals believe in their ability to do work and that the rewards are forthcoming and worthwhile.

Expectancy Theory

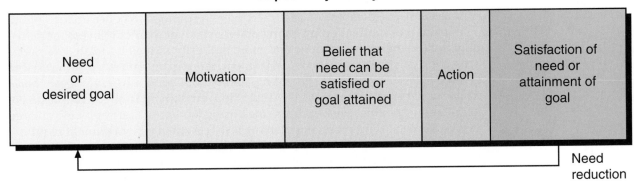

Need or desired goal	Motivation	Belief that need can be satisfied or goal attained	Action	Satisfaction of need or attainment of goal

Need reduction

failure often will study only as much as necessary to avoid failing a course or will work only as hard as necessary to avoid losing their jobs. Those with a high level of need for achievement, on the other hand, are more concerned with meeting their own high standards of performance than they are about failing.

Maslow's hierarchy, discussed in Chapter 3, is related to all human behavior because we are always attempting, consciously or unconsciously, to satisfy our needs. Every level of the hierarchy, from satisfying survival needs to achieving self-actualization, can be applied to both why people work and satisfactions from work. Those who achieve self-actualization, or development of their potential through their jobs, not only enjoy their work more than the average person, but they enjoy life more because so much of one's lifetime is spent working. Preparing yourself for a type of work that you expect to find challenging is the first step, but people with a high level of need to achieve, as discussed above, would also be likely to develop a high degree of self-actualization in various careers. Liking one's work is related to one's attitude and motivation as well as to the work itself.

Can too much attention be given to satisfying one's need for recognition and esteem according to Maslow or to Skinner's emphasis on positive reinforcement? A warning related to satisfying such needs is expressed by Robert J. Samuelson in a *Newsweek* article entitled "The Trophy Syndrome." He says,

> Everyone likes praise. At the age of 6, an extra pat on the back is helpful. A few trophies are no big deal. Our problem is that we perpetuate childish customs. Praise given too easily or too lavishly is worse than none. Trophies are worth something only if they are earned, not bestowed (5).

Samuelson's observation might be applied to recognition given at work as well as to numerous other types of experiences in our lives. On the other hand, some would say recognition is lacking or too scarce in the workforce. It depends on the company or organization and numerous other factors.

 What Do You Think? *Do you think medals, plaques, trophies, and bonuses are given out too freely in today's society? Support your response with an example, if possible.*

JOB ENRICHMENT

In recent years, business and industry have responded to better understanding of employee motivation by giving at least some of their employees more freedom in how their jobs are done and more authority in making related decisions. This approach is known as job enrichment. An explanation of *job enrichment* is given by R. V. Dawis, R. T. Fruehling, and N. B. Oldham in *Psychology: Human Relations and Work Adjustment*. They say: "Job enrichment is not accomplished by job rotation (moving workers from one boring job to another) or by job enlargement (simply adding more monotonous tasks). Rather, job enrichment requires a radical redesign of the job to make greater use of a person's abilities (6). Realistically it must be recognized that not all aspects of a job or work can be made more challenging nor can all workers be relied on to assume more responsibility. But job enrichment has not only increased satisfaction in many instances, it has also improved productivity and employer-employee relations.

EMOTIONS IN THE WORKPLACE

How do emotions fit into workplace relations? However that question might be answered, as long as we have human beings in the workplace, there will also be evidence of emotion. Your understanding of pleasant and unpleasant emotions, physiological effects of emotion, and constructive use of emotions from Chapter 5 should be helpful in understanding the effects of emotions in the workplace.

CARING

Although unpleasant emotions and expressions of them are more evident in the workplace, pleasant emotions should not be overlooked. Caring about what we are doing and about other people we work with or for involves our emotions, even though there are different degrees of caring and it may be expressed in different ways. Our discussion at the beginning of the chapter about situations and circumstances calling for different types of behavior applies not only to caring but also to expressions of other emotions on the job. If you don't care about what you're doing, you'll never be good at it. Well-adjusted workers also care about their coworkers, customers, supervisors, managers, and themselves.

People become angry when they are frustrated. In the workplace, it's important to use anger constructively and to think carefully about how you react to a situation that makes you angry.

ANGER

People become angry when they are frustrated—when others aren't acting the way they think they should or things aren't going the way they want them to. We want to keep in mind that becoming disturbed isn't necessarily bad. If you didn't care about yourself, the quality of work you do, or even whether you keep your job or not, you wouldn't experience much frustration. But is that what you want in your work experience?

How can we apply the suggestions given in Chapter 5 for using anger constructively in workplace situations? One of the suggestions pertained to understanding what causes you to become angry and to becoming a better problem solver. If a coworker borrows a tool, for example, and does not return it, what should you do about it? You are justified in not wanting to be taken advantage of, but what can you do to solve the problem?

First, we should give ourselves time to calm down, if we do feel angry, and to decide how to react to the situation. You can remind the person to return the tool (it is possible that he or she forgot), inform the person that you need it for yourself in the future, and possibly suggest that the person purchase or requisition his or her own tool. In other words, you can use your frustration to solve the problem and to prevent frustration in the future rather than to become angry.

If you do become angry, your anger could be suppressed, which is not healthful, or it could be expressed destructively, which could cause a problem with coworker relations. It could even cost you your job or an opportunity for promotion. You should note that trying to solve the problem and avoid similar instances in the future is an assertive, rather than an aggressive, response to the situation.

If we experience frustration with our supervisor because we did not receive recognition for extra work or are upset because what we thought was a reasonable request was not granted, we have a different type of situation. Naturally our decision on how to react depends on the type of communication and relationship we have with him or her. (Employer-employee relationships will be discussed later in the chapter.)

If we cannot or don't resolve the problem, we are likely to use the coping mechanism called displacement—taking out our frustrations on someone else not involved in the cause of our frustration. Displacement might also be used as a psychological defense when we are disturbed by an encounter with a patient, customer, or client, depending on the nature of our work.

FEAR

How would you associate McGregor's Theory X with fear in the workplace? Do you recall, from Chapter 3, that Theory X was based on the belief that most people don't want to work and will do so only if they feel threatened? Although fear of losing one's job due to this type of threat is not as common as it once was, many in today's world of work fear losing their jobs for other reasons.

Many Americans have been losing their jobs due to their companies being acquired and/or downsizing, going out of business, reducing production, or moving to another location. Uneasiness about job security is worse if communication within the company is poor and employees are confused about what might happen next. This type of uneasiness can interfere not only with the quality of work, but also with all types of human relations within the company. Such negative feeling can also be reflected in relations with customers and others not directly involved.

JEALOUSY

The important thing to remember about jealousy is that it springs from a feeling of insecurity. This is true whether it pertains to a relationship with a special person in our personal lives or whether it pertains to a situation at work. People who feel insecure, either in their jobs or in their relationships with coworkers, have a tendency to be overly sensitive to being slighted. They may be also discontented with the advancement or achievement of others and are often unrealistic in thinking they were more deserving. Jealousy can cause friction that is disruptive to harmony within a company or organization and can interfere with benefits of job enrichment and job satisfaction. If the situation is such that someone is jealous of you, the best way to react is with confidence in yourself and honesty, without being accusing or argumentative. Otherwise we are allowing the jealous person to interfere with our ability to control ourselves and take advantage of opportunities available to us.

EMPLOYER-EMPLOYEE RELATIONS

An important aspect of employer-employee relations is that both parties understand what is expected in their relationship. Although most people would admit we are all equal as human beings, situations may temporarily put another in a position of authority. Examples are law enforcement officers dealing with citizens, instructors and students, and employers and employees. In a sense we all have "bosses" who have rights in terms of what to expect of us under mutually understood, and often agreed upon, conditions.

INTERVIEWS

Interviews, in addition to the employment interview (discussed in Chapter 8), also involve employer-employee relations at the workplace. The **appraisal interview** occurs after a certain amount of time on a job, generally every six to twelve months. The purpose of the appraisal interview is to review an employee's performance, recognize strengths and achievements, examine goals, and look for ways to improve weaknesses or areas of difficulty.

Appraisal interview
an interview that occurs after a prescribed amount of time on the job (usually 6 to 12 months) to review an employee's performance to date.

The **counseling interview** is held for the purpose of problem solving. For example, a supervisor may counsel an employee on tardiness, the use of alcohol, or proper work attire. It may include a review of company policy, clarifications of expectations, or other matters related to improving one's well-being and performance. A counseling interview need not be viewed as a reprimand. Employees themselves may request such an interview to seek advice or assistance in solving problems. An employee may seek assistance in solving personal problems as well as those that pertain directly to work.

Counseling interview
an interview that occurs when an employee has a problem.

The **exit interview** occurs when an employee leaves a job or company. The interview may include reasons for the employee's termination or a discussion of why the employee is voluntarily leaving. It can often prevent having an employee leave a company with misunderstandings or bitter feelings. Counseling may be offered to help the individual who is leaving to improve her or his opportunities in finding another job.

Exit interview
an interview that occurs when an employee leaves a job or company.

KNOW MANAGEMENT STRUCTURE

Knowing the management structure of the company or the organization for which you work helps you to know who has authority over you and what authority you yourself may have. This depends somewhat on the size of the company

Frank and Ernest

or organization, but other factors are also involved. It also depends on the philosophy of the company about how authority should be distributed. In a centralized organization, all important decisions are made by those in top management positions, for example. It is the responsibility of department supervisors to see that the decisions are carried out. There is a trend today toward decentralized organization, however, where top management delegates much of the decision making to employees at lower levels.

In many companies, employees have the opportunity for input into decisions. It is recognized today that those doing the actual work can contribute valuable input to company policies and practices. This is one of the reasons for the emphasis on teams in today's world of work. A common term for this kind of organizational structure and functioning is **participatory management.**

Participatory management
management style that allows employees to have input into decision making.

If you know who has what authority, you can make appropriate referrals in difficult problem situations. If you know how much authority you have, you can avoid frustrating others with problems that you should be handling yourself. An essential element of effective employer-employee relationships is to know not only who your boss is but what he or she expects of you.

LOYALTY AND TRUST

Loyalty
standing up for and behind your company and your coworkers.

Loyalty has always been valued in employer-employee relationships. **Loyalty** can be defined as standing up for and behind your company and those you work with. You believe in them and you make that evident by how you talk and how you act. Loyalty, however, does not come as easily today as it did when jobs were more secure. It is harder to maintain loyalty in a world of work that has numerous economic problems and challenges. Employees have difficulty being loyal to a company who, they fear, may lay them off next week. Middle management and even those at the top of an organization may feel insecure in their own jobs. As long as we work for a company, however, we should be as loyal as we reasonably can.

Trust
faith, placing reliability upon.

Loyalty and trust go hand in hand. Both are essential elements of employer-employee relationships. **Trust** has to do with honesty and reliability between employers and employees. We may hear more about lack of trust than having

Company loyalty means that you stand up for your company and your coworkers.

trust, just as we always hear more about problems than desirable situations. We may also hear more about employers and managers who are not reliable in following through on their commitments because they have more power than employees. It is essential, however, that employees also be trustworthy in any organization. A great deal of damage can be done by employees who are not honest and reliable in what they say and do.

What Would You Say? *If a coworker has a habit of speaking negatively about the company, how would you respond?*

LABOR UNIONS AND MANAGEMENT

Both employers and employees admit to having difficulties with one another over union negotiations, contracts, and possible grievances. A *union* is a group of workers who bargain collectively with management on issues such as working conditions, working schedules, seniority rights, wages, fringe benefits, and whatever issues are important to that particular group. Contracts are not only in the interest of workers, however. Contracts are negotiated by representatives of management and representatives of employees, and both attempt to obtain agreements favorable to them and to the organization.

Some employee associations are also unions, but they may have other purposes in addition to the negotiable items mentioned above. They may be interested in safety factors, educational and training opportunities, service to the community, or assistance to members in need, for example. Some labor unions also have similar objectives.

In today's world of work, employers and employees recognize the reality of organized labor and in most cases can work out equitable agreements without damage to their relationship. If this isn't possible, all the effort put into improving employer-employee relations can be lost when it comes time to negotiate a new union contract. Strikes are not as common as they used to be, for several reasons—two being that both management and labor unions recognize that strikes are costly for everyone and also that negative feelings develop that may never heal.

Another reason is related to the effects of the media and public opinion on both management and unions today. This phenomenon is explained by D. Benton and J. Halloran, in *Applied Human Relations: An Organizational Approach.* They say:

> No longer can unions or management count on blind support from their members or employees. So many aspects of labor problems have been brought to public attention, that union employees cannot help but know the effects of their proposed actions even before they are taken. Workers are forced also to take public reaction into account now because the public, through television, may know about the strike or walk-out even before some of the workers do, and public reaction will be instantaneous. In the past, news of strikes wasn't heard until the following day or by word of mouth. Public sympathy for a strike for higher wages or increased fringe benefits cannot be gained by simply making the facts known, no more than management can get the public on its side by claiming low profits and increased costs (7).

Mediation
process of bringing groups with opposing views together to resolve differences.

Mediator
an unbiased third party that helps parties resolve differences.

Arbitration
a hearing in which both cases present opposing viewpoints along with supporting facts and evidence.

An additional reason for fewer strikes today is that mediation and arbitration are more commonly used to settle management/union differences. **Mediation** is a process whereby both groups are brought together with a **mediator,** or unbiased third party, who tries to help the parties settle their differences. Both management and employees must agree to mediation following their impasse, or inability to come to an agreement between themselves.

If an agreement cannot be reached through mediation, the issues of disagreement may go to **arbitration.** With this procedure, a hearing is held in which both sides present their cases with supporting facts and evidence. The arbitrator then studies what both sides have presented, considers similar agreements and settlements, and, in due time, returns a written decision in favor of either management or the union. Both sides must have agreed to accept this decision before the arbitration process begins. Arbitration is costly and, for all practical purposes, one side loses. Therefore, if an agreement cannot be reached in contract negotiations, agreement is often reached through the mediation process without resorting to arbitration. Variations in these procedures depend on existing contracts and the laws of the state where the parties reside.

Trust between employers and employees, discussed earlier, must survive contract negotiations if favorable relations are to be maintained between contract negotiations. Both management and employees will admit that this is a difficult challenge. To negotiate in "good faith," with the intention of reaching an equitable agreement, can help to maintain trust and respect for one another. Because of complex economic conditions, unions have had to become more conservative in what they request in negotiations. If they want their employers to stay in business and want to keep their jobs, they must share their concern in making a profit. Work teams and employee-involvement programs are also accomplishing some of the cooperation formerly sought by unions.

COWORKER RELATIONS

When employees have positive feelings toward one another, they enjoy their jobs more and morale is usually higher. There is more respect for one another's rights and property, and absenteeism is lower. With high company spirit and a feeling of job togetherness, employees hesitate to miss work except for very good reasons. Individuals realize that if they are not there to do their share of the workload, their coworkers will be inconvenienced and often overworked. They will not want to do this unnecessarily to people they care about. They will come to work more dependably because they feel a bond with their coworkers.

Also, since employees generally enjoy association with their coworkers, they miss their company when they are not there. S. Strasser and J. Sena comment on this in their book, *Work Is Not a Four-Letter Word*. They contend,

> One of the great joys of work has nothing to do with money, power, or prestige; it has to do with people. It is the pleasure derived from meeting people, building relationships, forming friendships, and experiencing companionship; it is the enjoyment and good feeling we get from working with others and sharing with them our thoughts and feelings, our hopes and fears.
>
> For numerous people, however, the joys derived from socialization at work are minimal or nonexistent. Instead of interacting with others, these individuals remain isolated, alienated, and estranged. Instead of building relationships, they build walls that separate themselves from colleagues. Sometimes the isolation is unwittingly self-imposed; sometimes it is imposed upon them. In either case, the enormous personal and professional benefits obtained from connecting with others—the exhilaration of comradeship—is denied, and work becomes a sterile, lonely experience (8).

Social facilitation
liking your coworkers.

Liking the people one works with is known among industrial psychologists as **social facilitation.** Many employees may have limited opportunity to talk to others while actually doing their work, but they still enjoy being among their coworkers and talking to them before and after work, during their lunch period, and during breaks. It has been found that a ten- to fifteen-minute break twice during the working day does not interfere with the amount of work produced. In fact, in many cases, even with less total time spent working, production has increased because people can be refreshed physically and mentally in even a short period of time and return to work with new vigor and increased motivation.

Businesses and industries that recognize the value of social facilitation sponsor bowling teams, arrange parties, and provide other social events outside working hours. These activities may be considered fringe benefits, as indeed they are, but management benefits also by establishing bonds among employees and between themselves and their employees. The company benefits in terms of improved attitudes, increased loyalty, and improved productivity. Additional aspects of coworker relations will be considered in the chapter section on Teams at Work.

CUSTOMER OR CLIENT RELATIONS

We all have had the experience of being customers or clients, and many of us have had experience with serving others in job situations. The most important thing to remember about customers or clients is that they are human beings like us. They do not suddenly turn into another kind of being when they are seeking a product or service.

WHAT CAN YOU OFFER?

A customer, or a potential customer, appreciates recognition. If a person is a regular customer, it helps to greet him or her by name. Even if you do not know the person's name, you can offer an appropriate greeting such as "Good morning" or "Good afternoon." Some people want immediate attention, others may want to look around, but everyone—except a shoplifter—appreciates recognition.

You can project friendliness in your attitude and total behavior, as well as in what you say. Many people shop at certain stores or do business with particular companies because, in addition to offering good service, the people they deal with are friendly. Friendliness makes a person feel that you are interested in him or her as an individual, not only as a customer or possible source of profit.

In addition to friendliness, helpfulness is important when serving customers. As human beings, customers have normal needs and wants, and you should try to identify an individual's particular need at the moment. If you are attentive and perceptive, there are several ways you can identify the person's need. One good way, obviously, is to ask how you can help. Observe what the person is looking at or seems to be looking for. The overall behavior of customers may indicate whether they are in a hurry and want help or are interested in browsing on their own. The better you understand people in all situations, the better the chance that you can be really helpful to a customer.

People seeking goods or services are also seeking reliability. They want to deal with people they can trust. Most people in business depend heavily on repeat business and steady customers. Customer or client relations, therefore, should be sincere and trustworthy. The product or service and everything connected with it should match claims about it.

HANDLING COMPLAINTS

In spite of efforts to offer high-quality products and services, there will always be some dissatisfied customers. The following suggestions should be considered in responding to customer complaints. Remember, however, that customers are individuals and situations vary. There is no absolute best way to respond.

- Listen. Just talking (sometimes yelling?) about his or her dissatisfaction may cause the customer to calm down. You should also be alert to discovering how the customer perceives the product or service and the situation.

- Ask questions. This action shows that you are interested in the person and in knowing more about the situation. You can't make a judgment or even explain the complaint to a supervisor unless you have the facts.

- Do not accuse the customer or be too quick to admit fault on your part. If you say, "There must have been some misunderstanding," or "Perhaps there has been some mistake," you are being attentive to the customer, but are still withholding a conclusion on what actually happened.

- Don't lose control of your temper. No matter how angry the customer is or how abusive his or her language may be, you are expected to be rational and courteous. Your calmness may have a quieting effect on the customer.

- Assure the customer that you will do whatever you can to correct the situation or satisfy the customer. Follow through on your word.

- Refer the customer to the manager (unless you are the owner of the business) if that is the store or company policy. But give the customer attention first, so he or she does not feel like a victim of a runaround.

- Expect some complaints. Remember that dealing with dissatisfied customers is part of your job. Most customers with complaints will continue to do business with you or the company you work for if they feel they have been treated fairly. Also, keep in mind that customers are more likely to tell others about their bad experiences than about their good experiences. In the long run, your reputation and future business for the company are at stake.

- Be courteous. Everyone likes to be shown courtesy and appreciation. "I appreciate your bringing this to my attention," or "I'm sorry for your inconvenience," can make a significant difference in customer relations and in handling complaints.

ETHICAL STANDARDS AND RELATIONS

Ethics
standards of right and wrong behavior.

Ethics, or standards of right and wrong behavior, are based on fundamental beliefs about what individuals and organizations stand for, and what they will do or not do because of these beliefs. Many professional groups have their own ethical standards, in writing at least. The medical and legal professions, government, education, and many businesses have ethical codes, for example. If individuals are known to seriously violate these codes, they may be expelled from professional membership or lose their jobs. Unethical practices by some members of these groups are a major societal concern today. An association with a code or even taking an oath does not guarantee honest, ethical behavior.

Small businesses and individuals also have ethical standards. What is right or wrong is not determined by the size of the group to which one belongs. For those who are not concerned about honesty and fair treatment of others, however, unethical practices are sometimes easier to disguise or hide in large organizations or governmental bodies. Some individuals also rationalize, or make excuses, for their unethical behavior. They convince themselves, for example, that "everyone is doing it."

What is considered ethical is not confined to what is legal. It is relatively easy to find out what is legal and what the consequences are. We, or others, may not always know whether something illegal is involved in a particular transaction, however. We may not know, for example, that a coworker is stealing company tools. Then let's suppose he offers to give you some of them, which you could use. Do you accept them? Do you question your coworker about where he got them? Do you report him to management? These situations involve making ethical decisions.

Some people make a distinction between what they consider ethical behavior in their personal lives and in their work. They would not cheat a friend, for example, but they might overcharge a customer. Over time, an individual's reputation and the reputation of a business are developed by the perception of their practices related to ethics. But with most individuals, how they feel about themselves and their relationships with others is of greater importance. They still must realize that others may have different standards, however.

Our daily lives are affected by ethics whether we realize it or not. We would be foolish to believe everything anyone tells us about a product, service, or treatment. We would be equally foolish, however, not to believe anything others tell us. So we have to make judgments. And others make judgments about our integrity, or basic honesty, in their relations with us.

 What Do You Think? *What do you think is the primary cause of unethical practices in the world of work today?*

CONFLICT, COMPETITION, OR COOPERATION

How do conflict, competition, and cooperation fit a discussion of human relations at work? Some say they want to avoid conflict, they expect competition, and they seek cooperation. Each of these can be productive, however. Let's consider briefly each of these types of human interation and their effects on our work.

CONFLICT

Conflict is a clash of opposing ideas, interests, or activities. Although it is realistic to expect some conflict in our work, people generally want to avoid conflict or hope to resolve it without harm to feelings or productivity. It is not so much the conflicts themselves that cause problems or promote progress but the means by which they are resolved. Those who work with conflicts describe three types of conflict resolution.

LOSE-LOSE In this type of conflict resolution, neither party is satisfied with the results, and negative feelings become stronger. The conflict isn't really resolved. It becomes similar to smoldering ashes that readily flare up if given a little fuel. Conflict can be a cause of anxiety that interferes with our well-being and performance on the job. Aggressiveness, as discussed in Chapter 8, can be associated with conflicts. When people are working against each other in a cut-throat way, both individuals and organizations suffer.

WIN-LOSE Someone gets his or her way in this type of conflict, as the name suggests. However, in many cases the loser becomes defensive and looks for the opportunity to win the next round. In a work situation, the win-lose approach to conflict resolution is similar to "I'm the boss, so do it my way or look for a job somewhere else." Most bosses and managers today know that causing fear of losing one's job is not the best way to motivate employees.

WIN-WIN Can both sides in a conflict win? The idea with this approach is to resolve the conflict so that both sides benefit as much as possible and there is mutual understanding of why whatever solution is agreed on is best. This type of conflict resolution requires cooperation and effective communication, but results warrant the effort.

COMPETITION

Competition is trying to gain something that another person or persons are also trying to gain. There is rivalry in competition, but it can spur motivation and productivity rather than being a negative force. Most of us grow up with a sense of competition in many areas of our lives—winning the game, getting better grades, getting the job, getting the promotion.

Businesses are in competition with one another. This competition can be healthy for them as well as for the economy and individuals. Competition can bring out the best in both individuals and organizations.

COOPERATION

Cooperation is working together to achieve a common goal or common purpose. Our society needs competition, but we also need cooperation to get our tasks completed and to reach our goals.

When we recognize our own strengths and weaknesses, along with those of others, we can determine the best ways to cooperate, or work together to achieve

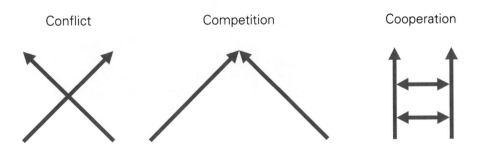

Conflict   Competition   Cooperation

what one person cannot do alone. In a group situation, success is a result of each person's depending on the others to use their abilities well.

Cooperation is important in our personal lives also. A cooperative attitude, an acceptance of ourselves as well as others, helps us to work together as teams. All those involved in cooperative efforts should feel comfortable expressing their needs, ideas, and values so that they will not be lost in the interest of others or in a group effort.

TEAMS AT WORK

If and when you are anticipating a job interview, be prepared for questions such as: What experience have you had working as a member of a team? How would you describe yourself as a team player? What do you see as the purposes and advantages of teams in the workplace?

If you don't have a ready answer to the last question now, keep the question in mind as team functioning in the workplace is discussed. You should also note how important understanding others, communication skills, and application of human relations guidelines are to productive team functioning.

Those who have not studied psychology often think human relations is simply being friendly and considerate, but there is much more to it than that. In fact it can be one of the most complicated subjects you'll ever study because it involves not only the behavior of others, but also your own behavior. And both

The members of this team listen to one of their own make a presentation.

of these are somewhat unpredictable. We cannot improve our ability to understand human relations in teams unless we first know something about human behavior; about team structures, purposes, and functions; and about how we might function as a member of a team.

The idea of people cooperating at work to accomplish objectives and solve problems is not new. There has been a new emphasis in recent years on the team approach in the workplace, however. Companies and organizations are involved in quality-improvement teams, decision-making teams, and teams or groups of different types to increase employee input and satisfaction and to accomplish common goals.

David W. Johnson, in *Human Relations and Your Career,* points out that conflicts can have positive results:

1. If the two of you can work together, the conflict has been beneficial.
2. If both you and the other person feel better about each other and your jobs, the conflict has been beneficial.
3. If both you and the other person are satisfied with the results of the conflict, the conflict has been beneficial.
4. If the ability of you and the other person to resolve future conflicts with each other has been improved, the conflict has been beneficial (9).

TEAM PURPOSES AND STRUCTURES

Team membership is usually relatively small so that everyone can, and likely will, play an active part. Much of the time team membership is voluntary, but even then some employees sense some pressure to "volunteer." Employees who are interested in their work and in contributing to common goals will usually want to be part of a team, but they still appreciate a choice of teams to which they might belong.

Purposes of teams vary. Some teams are specifically related to work—to accomplish job-related objectives, to problem solve, or to achieve goals not readily attainable by individuals. Other purposes may be to explore and arrange for training and continuing education opportunities for employees and other company personnel. Still other teams might be organized for a specific immediate purpose, such as to determine ways to implement a new policy within the organization.

Team structures also vary. Ronald A. Gunn and Marilyn S. Burroughs in *The Futurist* compare three types of team structures and workspace implications. These team structures are identified as **linear, parallel,** and **circular.** The characteristics of each type follow.

Linear team
a team in which members operate *on* a team rather than *as* a team.

Linear Teams

- Most common type in organizations today.
- Most formal and bureaucratic type.
- Members operate *on* a team rather than *as* a team.
- Fixed roles, somewhat routine tasks, organized around function; process-oriented, and implementation-driven.
- Decision-making power of team leader has narrow focus, limited information access.
- Performance judged and rewards given on an individual basis.

Parallel team
a team in which members contribute their unique special skills toward a particular project or market.

Circular team
a team in which there is little or no distinction between team goals and individual goals.

- Permanent or temporary life span.
- Independent focus allows for operation within conventional office arrangements or some alternatives, like home offices.

Parallel Teams

- Problem solving; focused on a particular project or market.
- Individuals contribute unique, specialized skills toward a combined outcome.
- Team leader has the "game plan," broad information access, more authority and autonomy.
- More training opportunities for team members.
- Individual performance is rewarded.
- Permanent or temporary life span.
- Good candidates for nonterritorial off-space designs, need formal and informal meeting spaces and shared project rooms.

Circular Teams

- Creative, open, democratic; focused on exploring possibilities and alternatives.
- Organized around a group vision with little or no distinction between team goals and individual goals.
- Team leader directs and facilitates members' contributions to team performance; high autonomy and information access.
- Members often train as a unit.
- Group performance is rewarded.
- Temporary life span.
- Prevalent in young, fast-growing organizations where power is decentralized.
- Need open, flexible environments with plenty of space to meet and work together as subgroups, as well as centralized filing, resource, and project spaces (10).

ADVANTAGES OF TEAMS

Not only may teams accomplish their specific purposes but teams can also promote personnel getting to know one another better. There can be numerous advantages to this, but one is that it contributes to a sense of belongingness and loyalty to one another and to the organization.

Members of a team can learn how to work together more effectively, not only in team situations, but on the job where they have individual responsibilities. A spirit of cooperation can develop that contributes to tolerance and helpfulness when needed or appropriate.

If all members of a team are participating, more workable ideas are generated. Ideas that are presented spontaneously can be evaluated from different perspectives. Creative thinking can be stimulated by different people communicating freely with one another. If a number of different problem-solving strategies or models are familiar to the group, better decisions can be made.

A sense of team achievement, of getting things done, can also be an advantage. Teams can accomplish things that individuals cannot. Members of the team also motivate one another so that team members want to be part of the action and a member of the group that solved the problem or achieved the purpose of the team. All of these possible advantages improve morale, which is the prevailing attitude within the company or organization. When morale is high, employees feel good about both their jobs and their relationships with others within the organizations, and are motivated to do their best work.

POSSIBLE PROBLEMS

Most teams function as described under Advantages of Teams, but realistically teams can also have problems. These are not because of what a team is or should be, but are the result of how the team functions. Let's consider some of these possible problems.

Team meetings can be time wasters, which is often the result of individuals not really wanting to be members of the team. They are wasting their time and it reflects on the efficiency of the whole team. Another reason may be lack of understanding of the purpose of the team or the agenda for a particular day's activity. As indicated earlier, this is primarily the responsibility of the team's leader or facilitator. The leader of the team can be an employee, but whoever it is, the person should have some leadership skills.

Some team members seldom participate for whatever reason. One of the values of smaller membership is to make it easier for everyone to have input of one kind or another. It is also the responsibility of the leader to encourage reluctant members to participate by asking them for their ideas or suggestions.

When the team consists of a cross-section of personnel, such as managers and employees from different departments, individuals may not feel free to express themselves openly. Even though managers and supervisors may say, "While we are functioning as a team, everyone has equal status and everyone is free to express his or her opinion," some employees do not feel comfortable criticizing their boss's ideas. They are afraid about possible retribution. And they may be right.

Advantages of Team Functioning		Possible Problems of Team Functioning	
Team Interaction	**Advantages**	**Team Interaction**	**Problems**
	• Contributes to cooperation, belongingness, and loyalty • Contributes to tolerance and helpfulness • Generates more workable ideas • Participants motivate one another • Fosters sense of achievement		• Wasted or poorly used time • Ineffective leadership • Retribution from management • Suggestions not considered or implemented • Conflicts and jealousies • Groupthink leads to illogical decisions

Some team members often complain that their suggestions and solutions are not considered or implemented. Therefore, they do not feel valued as team members or as individuals and lose interest in spending more time and energy making additional suggestions. They say they hear a lot of talk about team input, participatory management, and empowerment of employees, but they don't see it in practice.

There can be conflicts and jealousies among team members, or even between different teams, just as there can be between individuals. An individual may feel that another team member is getting credit for his or her idea, for example. Or a member may feel that he or she is being slighted by the leader. If such were true, this would be unfortunate because it should be a function of the leader to prevent or resolve conflicts and negative feelings among members rather than to add to them.

BECOME A TEAM PLAYER

It is very likely that you will be expected to function as a member of a team in your future work experience. You may even be asked to organize or lead team activity. Following are some suggestions that could be helpful.

Increase your ability to understand and work with people. Even though you may not be aware of any particular problem you have in this respect, we can all improve this ability. As has been discussed earlier in a number of chapters, the workplace will be much more diversified in the future than it has been in the past. Tolerance, acceptance, understanding, and respect are keys to effective human relations on the job today and in the future. These qualities will be especially important in working in teams, where interaction is continuous and more involved, but they are also valuable in all human relations experiences.

Improve your communication skills. All of the suggestions in Chapter 8 pertaining to communication skills are applicable in team situations. Understand yourself and your present communication skills and habits to avoid two extremes: the person who talks too much and the person who sits or stands back and doesn't contribute. It is especially important to improve listening skills—which we all can do. Members of a team cannot build on the contributions of others if they are not listening to one another. Communication at Work is the next section in this chapter.

Develop or improve critical thinking skills. This activity involves other abilities. To think critically about an issue, for example, we need some knowledge about the subject. We also have to be an effective listener (or reader, depending on the situation). Once we know and understand what is being said, then we can examine it critically. This means examining the content for validity, or workableness. In this respect, it is important to be able to distinguish between what is fact and can be verified, and what is a person's opinion. Often these are closely interwoven, intentionally or unintentionally, so that it is difficult to tell the difference. However, a good listener and a critical thinker does not hesitate to ask a person for some factual verification on what he or she is saying. This practice can be overdone and can become a distraction to the whole team, but used with discretion, it is essential to making the best decisions. Examining the practicality or workability of ideas is also an important aspect of critical thinking.

Know the team's purpose, your particular role as a member of the team, and how the team functions. This was referred to earlier but it is essential for each member of the team who desires to make a contribution. In addition to the overall purpose of the team, there should be a specific agenda that is known by all team members for each meeting or activity. Although it is the responsibility of the team leader to make this known, team members should take the initiative to find out, if it isn't apparent. Also, keep in mind that you may become a team leader yourself at some time. Susan Caminiti, in "What Team Leaders Need to Know," offers the following tips for leaders: "Don't be afraid to admit ignorance; know when to intervene; learn to truly share power; worry about what you take on, not what you give up; and get used to learning on the job (11).

Be willing to work or contribute without personal recognition. If you are a team player, it is the ultimate success of the team's objective that is important. This doesn't mean that individuals don't often receive recognition for outstanding contributions within the team, but we should be able to identify with the team's achievement, rather than seeking individual recognition or compensation. If you are a team player, this becomes known eventually throughout the company or organization.

Support other members of the team. This doesn't mean that you should agree with everything they say or propose. As mentioned earlier, this would lessen the effect of the team itself or lead to groupthink. But we should be able to recognize that other members of the team have their particular strengths and contributions and to support them when we do agree or think they are proposing what is best for the team or organization. Those who are insecure and defensive about their own position in the group have the most difficulty supporting others.

What Would You Do?   *If you were a member of a work team that you believed wasn't accomplishing its purpose, what would you do?*

COMMUNICATION AT WORK

Effective communication is important at work because the wrong instructions or misunderstood instructions can result in injuries, damage to equipment and materials, dissatisfied customers, stress, and negative feelings among coworkers or between employees and supervisors. The guidelines discussed in the previous chapter on communication apply to situations at work also. It is important to ask questions, for example, when you aren't sure whether you understand a procedure. This is particularly advisable until you gain experience on the job and until you know how your supervisor wants a task done. After you have some experience, you may have the opportunity to make suggestions on how a procedure could be improved, but it is wise to refrain from making too many suggestions until you have established some credibility as a member of the organization.

SHARING EXPERIENCE AND KNOWLEDGE

Ideally, in today's companies and organizations, everyone has an opportunity for input through teams, as discussed earlier. Everyone can make a unique contribution, even though you may have the same job title and receive the same pay as someone else. It can be especially valuable for older workers—who have a great deal of experience—and younger workers—who usually have the advantage of recent education and training—to pay attention to one another. Everyone can learn from others if he or she is receptive to learning. Nobody knows everything on the job or anywhere else. Asking experienced persons for their opinion or reasonable assistance not only is helpful to a new employee, but it can also contribute to establishing a relationship that can be beneficial to everyone.

OPEN-DOOR POLICY

What is known as the open-door policy in organizations and companies isn't always reality. An *open-door policy* means that employees are welcome to go into a supervisor's or manager's office at any time to discuss a problem or concern or to make a suggestion. Some employees say, "Sure you can go into her office, but she doesn't listen or seem to care." Others may say, "He has an open door, but you're lucky if you can find him in." Whatever the intentions or related problems, the open door does give employees communication opportunities that were not ordinarily available years ago. Just knowing there is an open-door policy, if one believes that it is a reality, makes one feel more comfortable. Naturally, taking the time of a person with many responsibilities should be used with discretion. On the other hand, supervisors or managers who are interested in their employees and their concerns do not wait for the employees to come to them. They are part of team efforts and are visible and available in several ways.

FORMAL CHANNELS

Formal channels
channels of communication that are well-defined and travel either vertically or horizontally.

Vertical channels
channels of communication in which messages are carried from top management to employees.

Horizontal channels
channels used for messages between department heads or other employees at the same level of the organizational structure.

The larger the organization, the more important it is to have **formal channels** of communication. These messages are often written and may have either vertical or horizontal pathways. **Vertical channels** may carry messages from top executives or managers to employees. Although it is not as common, they can also be a means for employees to send information or requests to supervisors. Messages going through a vertical channel may move through numerous personnel levels. The first person an employee contacts is usually one's immediate supervisor. The messages may move from there to others on the communication hierarchy. **Horizontal channels** are used for messages between department heads or other employees at the same level of the organizational structure.

Formal channels may involve the use of telephone messages, e-mail, memos, newsletters, manuals, or other written material. The use of fax and computer scanners have added to the list of ways for sending both written material and visuals. The use of websites is also becoming more common as a means of communication between organizations and businesses. Postal mail is still a major means of communication with businesses. The messages themselves may pertain to items such as team information or reports, information on new company policies or changes therein, instructions for work procedures, changes in responsibilities, or opportunities for continuing education.

INFORMAL CHANNELS

Grapevine
informal, usually verbal, communication that frequently becomes distorted.

There are numerous ways that people communicate informally with one another at work. One of these is called the **grapevine.** A. J. DuBrin, in *Applying Psychology: Individual & Organizational Effectiveness*, describes the grapevine: "The grapevine is the major informal communication in an organization. The term refers to the tangled branches that distort information" (12). Let's suppose that, coming to work some morning, a coworker approaches you with, "Have you heard that . . . ?" You should recognize this as the grapevine in action.

The grapevine is not necessarily an undesirable form of communication. It is a way for employees to know what is going on within an organization without continuous formal notification. Managers sometimes purposely use the grapevine to allow employees to react to the idea of a change in policy, for example, before it actually takes place. If there is too much negative feedback, the policy may be modified or even not adopted. The grapevine should not be the primary means of employer-employee communication, however. There should be open, face-to-face communication on a regular basis—especially when there are issues of major importance or concern.

Rumor, as compared with the grapevine, often has less basis in fact. Very frequently, rumors are negative and cause worries and anxieties among employees. It is difficult to know how rumors get started, but considering all the possibilities for misunderstanding in communication, it is not surprising that rumors develop. During a work break, for example, someone may comment, "I suppose the next thing they will be doing is . . . ." Someone may interpret that to mean that it is in the planning stage and repeat it to others as a foregone conclusion. And the rumor spreads.

Ideally, communication should be accurate and responsive to feedback. Communication will never be without error; however, we can all do our part to make it as effective and as error free as possible.

SEXUAL HARASSMENT AT WORK

What is sexual harassment? How serious is it? What can be done about it? Can it be prevented? Everyone should know the answers to these questions. Those who have been sexually harassed should know what to do about it.

"I still say there are better ways to decide which positions to eliminate!"

© Patrick Hardin.

Others should be aware of how to react if they are accused of sexual harassment. It is a subject that must be taken seriously in society today, not only in the work environment but also in schools and other settings.

Although sexual harassment has occurred in the workplace ever since males and females have been working in the same environment, it has received widespread attention in recent years. The Civil Rights Act of 1964 prohibited sexual harassment in the workplace, but as with other civil rights, it has taken a long time for attitudes and behavior to change. It wasn't until 1986 that the Supreme Court ruled that sexual harassment violated human rights, giving those so abused legal access to protection.

Melissa Rapham and Max Heerman, attorneys in employment law practice, define two kinds of sexual harrassment—quid pro quo and hostile environment. They state, "Broadly and legally defined, **sexual harassment** includes unwelcome sexual advances, requests for sexual favors and sexually motivated conduct, contact or communication." They offer the following definitions: "**Quid pro quo harassment** occurs when sexual activity is made a condition of employment or of receiving employment benefits. For example, if a manager asks a subordinate to have sex—and indicates that a refusal to comply will cost the subordinate a promotion—the manager has committed quid pro quo sexual harassment. A **hostile environment**, which is less blatant and more difficult to define, occurs when an employee is placed in a threatening environment because of his or her sex" (13). Examples of hostile environment harassment could be pressure for a date or staring at a person in a way that makes him or her uncomfortable.

Either sex can be guilty of sexual harassment: Men can harass women and women can harass men. Also, women can harass women and men can harass men. Harassment can come from a coworker, supervisor, regular customer, maintenance worker, or anyone associated with the place of employment. When you begin working for a company, you should familiarize yourself with company policies, including those pertaining to sexual harassment. Many employers have a written sexual harassment policy that is distributed to all employees.

It is the responsibility of the person being harassed to let the offender know clearly that his or her behavior is unwelcome and that it should be stopped. If that does not take care of the problem, it should be reported to the appropriate authorities in the company, school, or other organization.

There are more cases of males harassing females than the other way around, but women do harass males. Males file one-tenth as many complaints with the Equal Employment Opportunity Commission each year as do females. The number of complaints does not give us a true picture, of course. Do all people who are sexually harassed file a complaint? Are females or males more likely to file a complaint?

Sexual harassment
unwelcome sexual advances, or sexually motivated conduct.

Quid pro quo harassment
a form of sexual harassment in which sexual activity is made a condition of employment or advancement.

Hostile environment
a type of sexual harassment in which an employee is placed in a threatening environment because of his or her gender.

What Would You Do?   *If you were being sexually harassed at work by your supervisor, what would you do?*

FRIENDSHIPS AT WORK

any people have become overly cautious about what is considered harassment. Can coworkers give one another a hug on a special occasion? Can you compliment someone on their appearance? Can a pat on the back still be used to show appreciation for a job well done? There are no absolute answers to these questions, but what we should keep in mind is that sexual harassment is unwelcome because *harassment* is part of the definition.

Fear of being accused of sexual harassment should not interfere with sincere friendliness or friendships at work. Just as individuals have different attitudes toward their jobs, they have different attitudes about human relationships at work. Some people want to go to work, earn their pay, and be left alone. They may be very good employees, but they are the exception when it comes to human relations at work.

Enjoying association with one's coworkers was discussed earlier in the coworker relations section of this chapter. When we consider the amount of time we spend at work during our lifetimes compared with time spent in personal relationships, we can appreciate the value of mutually satisfying human relations in the workplace. Even though we aren't likely to be working in the same place and with the same people throughout our working years, those who like people will make new friends easily when change affects their work.

What is the difference between being friendly and being a friend? Although a coworker who is friendly would probably help you out with an immediate, temporary problem, there is no continuing commitment that we find in friendship. The primary characteristics of friendship are understanding, accepting, caring, and sharing. These create a bond that contributes to making one's work a rewarding part of one's life.

Can managers and supervisors have friendships with those they supervise? This is a controversial subject, and the answer depends ultimately on the individuals involved. Some employees might attempt to take advantage of a friendship with a supervisor. "She gets all the favors," according to coworkers. In other cases a supervisor may feel uncomfortable evaluating or correcting an employee who is also a personal friend. This has more to do with the personality characteristics of the individuals involved than with their working relationship, however. On any level of an organizational structure, persons who feel they cannot be friends with others at work probably feel relatively insecure in their positions.

No one, of course, has the time or desire to be friends with a great number of people at work or in other areas of one's life. If we are friendly, friendship will develop quite naturally in time without much special effort.

It is a common experience to have friendships at work with persons we see only in that particular environment or at social activities sponsored by the company. In other cases, a friendship developed at work can carry over into sharing vacation experiences or other types of leisure-time activities. No one wants someone else to give us rules to follow in forming friendships. Our friends are ours to choose.

Summary

Our human relations at work can make a difference in how well we do our work and in how much we enjoy our work. These relations involve supervisors and managers, coworkers, and customers or clients. How we interact with others depends not only on our particular relationship with them, but also on the situation.

In addition to motivational theories discussed in Chapter 3—psychoanalytic, behavioristic, humanistic and x, y, z—three additional theories related to work motivation are Herzberg's two-factor theory, the need for achievement theory, and the expectancy theory. Job enrichment is also used to increase worker satisfaction and provide employers with the benefits of the full use of employee capabilities.

Evidence of emotions can be found in the workplace and is not necessarily undesirable. Caring is important to a sense of achievement, to the quality of the work we do, and to mutually satisfying relationships with others. Unpleasant emotions such as anger can cause problems, but, if understood, can be controlled or used constructively. Fear and jealousy, if not checked, can also cause problems with work itself and with relationships with others.

There are variations in employer-employee relationships today. It is important, therefore, to know the management structure of the company for which you work. Loyalty and trust are also important in employer-employee relationships. Labor unions and management must work together to accomplish objectives and still maintain favorable relationships.

Coworker relations are more relaxed than those between employers and employees. Liking the people one works with is known as social facilitation. Customer or client relations require courteous attention, satisfaction of needs, and, if necessary, handling complaints. Ethical standards and practices are a concern to business, organizations, and individuals today. We should be aware of the

PSYCHOLOGY IN PRACTICE

1. Read an article about one of the human relations subjects discussed in this chapter. Identify the main idea of the article and explain how it can be applied to a situation you have been involved in or know about.

2. Working with a classmate, ask four owners of small businesses or department managers of larger businesses what they consider the most common human relations problem they encounter in their work. Ask them how they handle it. Prepare a group report and present it to the class.

3. Describe an ethical situation (real or hypothetical) pertaining to the career you are preparing to enter. Identify those factors you believe should be considered in making ethical decisions.

ethical standards of those we work for and have contact with, and we should live up to our own ethical standards.

Conflict, competition, and cooperation are part of the world of work, and each can contribute constructively to people working together or in the same line of work. Types of conflict resolution are lose-lose, win-lose, and win-win.

Teams in today's workplace are used to accomplish job-related objectives, solve problems, and accomplish goals not readily attainable by individuals. There can also be other purposes. Three types of team structures are linear, parallel, and circular. There are advantages to team functioning, but there are also potential problems. One should be prepared to be an effective team player as he or she enters, or re-enters, the workplace today.

Communication at work should incorporate the suggestions for effective communication discussed in Chapter 8. The appraisal interview, counseling interview, and exit interview are part of workplace communication activities. There should also be a willingness to share knowledge and experience. An open-door policy by management can contribute to the resolution of problems and concerns of employees. The grapevine should also be recognized as a means of communication at work, even though it is not always accurate.

Sexual harassment has received increased attention in recent years. Everyone should know what it is and how to protect oneself from unwanted sexual attention.

Friendships at work can interfere with some working relationships, but they can also contribute greatly to job satisfaction and enjoyment.

Chapter 10 will include discussion of work-related stress and coping skills.

Key Terms

Hygiene factors	Social facilitation
Motivation factors	Ethics
Expectancy theory	Linear team
Appraisal interview	Parallel team
Counseling interview	Circular team
Exit interview	Formal channels
Participatory management	Vertical channels
Loyalty	Horizontal channels
Trust	Grapevine
Mediation	Sexual harassment
Mediator	Quid pro quo harassment
Arbitration	Hostile environment

Learning Activities

Turn to page LA-39 to complete the Learning Activities and Enrichment Activities for this chapter.

Endnotes

1. R. A. Baron and P. B. Paulus, *Understanding Human Relations: A Practical Guide to People at Work,* Allyn and Bacon, Boston, MA, 1991, p. 2.

2. Frederick Herzberg, *Work and the Nature of Man,* World Publishing Company, Cleveland, OH, 1966; reference in L. M. Berry and J. P. Houston, *Psychology at Work: An Introduction to Industrial and Organizational Psychology,* Brown & Benchmark, Madison, WI, 1993, pp. 85–86.

3. L. M. Berry and J. P. Houston, *Psychology at Work: An Introduction to Industrial and Organizational Psychology,* Brown & Benchmark, Madison, WI, 1993, p. 85.

4. D. C. McClelland, *Human Motivation,* Scott, Foresman and Company, Glenview, IL, 1985.

5. R. J. Samuelson, "The Trophy Syndrome," *Newsweek,* December 21, 1992, p. 45.

6. R. V. Dawis, R. T. Fruehling, and N. B. Oldham, *Psychology: Human Relations and Work Adjustment,* McGraw-Hill Book Company, New York, 1989, p. 297.

7. D. Benton and J. Halloran, *Applied Human Relations: An Organizational Approach,* Prentice-Hall, Englewood Cliffs, NJ, 1991, p. 386.

8. S. Strasser and J. Sena, *Work Is Not a Four-Letter Word,* Business One Irwin, Homewood, IL, 1992, p. 147.

9. D. W. Johnson, *Human Relations and Your Career,* 3rd ed. Prentice-Hall, Englewood Cliffs, NJ, 1991, pp. 221–222.

10. R. A. Gunn and M. S. Burroughs, "Work Spaces That Work: Designing High-Performance Offices," *The Futurist,* March–April, 1996, p. 21.

11. Susan Caminiti, "What Team Leaders Need to Know," *Fortune,* February 20, 1995, p. 94.

12. A. J. DuBrin, *Applying Psychology: Individual & Organizational Effectiveness,* 4th ed., Prentice-Hall, Englewood Cliffs, NJ, p. 339.

13. Melissa Rapham and Max Heerman, "Eight Steps to Harassment-Proof Your Office," *HR Focus,* August 1, 1997, p. 11.

Coping with Stress

10

God grant me the serenity to accept the things I cannot change, courage to change the things I can, and wisdom to know the difference.

Reinhold Niebuhr

LEARNING OBJECTIVES

After completing this chapter, you should be able to do the following:

1. Define stress and eustress.

2. Explain how a person might adapt to an experience in life that would require major adjustments.

3. Identify six job-related situations that require adjustments.

4. Describe stages of relating to the approach of one's own death, according to Dr. Kübler-Ross.

5. Explain how three different coping mechanisms might be used in reacting to trying situations in life.

6. Describe the effects of coping mechanisms.

7. Describe the three characteristics of neurotic behavior.

8. Explain the consequences of the inability to cope.

9. Suggest eight ways to reduce stress.

Adjust
change oneself in response to an unchanging situation.

Coping
solving problems or adjusting to what cannot be changed.

What do you do in a situation that is not the way you would like it to be? Marcy may say, "Change it." Aaron may say, "Accept it." Jerrod may say, "Adjust to it." We have to be able to do all these things, but it can be difficult to decide which is most appropriate in a particular situation.

Even the best problem solvers cannot always get the results they want. Therefore, they must be able to accept what they cannot change or adjust. To **adjust** means changing oneself and one's behavior in response to an unchanging situation. Removing oneself from a stressful situation that cannot be changed is also a form of adjustment. The ability to solve problems, to accept what we cannot change, or to make adjustments, as appropriate, is known as **coping.** This is something we have to do throughout life. Chapter 7 should be helpful in the coping process. Without the ability to cope, our personal lives and those of people in general would be burdened with problems. We would also experience excessive stress and its harmful effects.

WHAT IS STRESS?

Stress
a physiological disturbance or psychological frustration resulting from a person's reaction to physical conditions, unmet needs, or external pressures.

Stressors
sources of stress.

Eustress
positive stress resulting from excitement, enthusiasm, or anticipation of a desired event.

General adaptation syndrome
according to Hans Selye, a three-stage process of reacting to stress: alarm, resistance, and exhaustion.

Stress is physiological disturbance and psychological frustration resulting from a person's reaction to physical conditions, unmet needs, and external pressures, real or perceived. This human condition can also result from a sense of personal inadequacy. Environmental factors, such as noise, crowding, and climatic conditions, are also sources of stress. Sources of stress are called **stressors.** In a very real sense, however, external factors and situations do not produce stress. It is the individual's perception of these and the individual's reaction and inability to cope effectively that cause stress.

Life also provides us with opportunities for "good" stress, or **eustress,** a term used by Dr. Hans Selye, a Canadian scientist who studied stress extensively (1). This kind of stress is created by excitement, enthusiasm, and anticipation of desired circumstances or events. The type of stress to be considered further here, however, is stress according to the opening definition—the kind that causes us problems and therefore requires more of our attention.

Dr. Hans Selye explains that human beings react to stress with three stages of adjustment, which he refers to as the **general adaptation syndrome** (2). These stages are alarm, resistance, and exhaustion. The *alarm* stage involves physiological changes similar to those associated with emotion. The heart beats faster, hormones are released by the endocrine glands, breathing becomes faster, muscles tense, pupils dilate, blood sugar level increases, and digestion slows. The body's resources are becoming mobilized.

During the *resistance* stage, there is an effort to cope with the stressful situation. If the cause of the stress is removed or is handled in a satisfactory way, body functioning returns to normal. If stress continues over time, *exhaustion* is experienced, with the person becoming less able to deal with the stress constructively. The illustration shows the stages of the general adaptation syndrome.

Chronic stress can interfere with the body's immune system and can contribute to psychosomatic illness, headaches, or other physical problems. Knowing more about stress and how to avoid or react to it can help in protecting ourselves from possible ill effects.

General Adaptation Syndrome

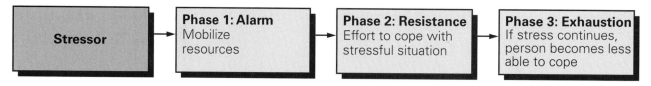

MAJOR ADJUSTMENTS IN LIFE

As long as we live we will have to cope with change. Even though some of the changes will be desirable, we will still need the ability to adjust. Some of the situations during our lifetimes that will challenge our ability to cope are discussed in the following sections. Although each of us may not personally experience all of them, we will be faced with situations with which we must cope throughout our lives.

EARLY EXPERIENCES

Leaving the security of the mother's womb and entering the entirely different environment of the outside world is the first major adjustment a human being must make. This experience was much more traumatic in previous generations than it is today. Instead of being spanked into a new world of bright lights, many infants today are born in much friendlier birthing rooms with the father present to give support to the mother and to welcome his child into the world. Immediately after birth, the newborn is laid against the mother's body so that both may experience a sense of warmth and security—the beginning of their bonding.

For many children, the next major change may involve absence from the parents for hours at a time while they work. Day-care centers have been established almost everywhere, including places of employment of a parent, where trained personnel care for and teach children from infancy to school age. Most children adjust quickly to this change and even enjoy their experiences at these centers.

For other children, the beginning of school is the first time they are away from home for any length of time. Parents' attitudes and examples of older brothers and sisters influence how well a young child makes this adjustment. Even at this early age, a child's self-concept affects how this new experience is approached.

There are other reasons why young children sometimes have to make adjustments. There may be a change of position in the family with the arrival of a new brother or sister. For a first child who has been the center of attention, this adjustment can be quite difficult. Hospitalization during the early years can be another situation that requires adjustments. Today, both parents and the hospitalized child receive special attention to make this adjustment as pleasant as possible.

This mother realizes that love and a sense of security are important.

PEANUTS reprinted by permission of UFS, Inc.

ADOLESCENCE

Adolescence
teen years of life.

Puberty
the physical development during adolescence that makes one capable of reproduction.

The teen years, or **adolescence,** are filled with complex psychological and physical changes. The young boy or girl must adjust to the physical change of becoming an adult, known as **puberty.** Some young people are very self-conscious about their body changes. They may also have relatively low self-esteem, and therefore acceptance and approval are important to them. They need to have the opportunity to communicate their feelings and to feel that they are understood. They have this need even though parents may feel that their adolescents do not want to communicate with them and are even somewhat rebellious. When there is too much adolescent-parent conflict, some young people leave home; others are asked by their parents to leave or are "kicked out." Some troubled teens turn to drugs or even suicide. They do not realize that help is available and that they can learn to manage their lives.

Adolescents must cope with increased responsibility and independence. Even though young people may regard these changes as desirable, there are likely to be some confusing and disturbing times for them. They must strive to achieve individual development while being influenced strongly by their peers.

Although there are numerous difficulties in leaving childhood and approaching adulthood, the teen years can also be exciting and challenging. In fact, many teenagers do not experience major problems and conflicts. For both them and their parents, their transition to adulthood is a positive experience.

INDEPENDENT LIVING

Many young adults today are living on their own while they attend school or after they have taken a full-time job. They often share apartments or, in some cases, a house. If you are living this way, you know about the adjustments that are required. Along with added independence comes the responsibility of running a household, including cooking, cleaning, and paying the bills. To do this, young adults must learn coping skills; they must manage both time and money. There also may be adjustments in learning to live with other people who have different habits and values.

In speaking of their experiences in independent living, many young adults tell of unexpected problems, such as noise complaints from the people downstairs or plumbing problems. They can also frequently laugh about some of their "challenges" such as trying to live three days at the end of the month on two dollars or using too much soap in the automatic washing machine at the laundromat. You may have heard the expression, "Experience is a good teacher." Someone else has responded, "Considering what it costs, experience *should* be a good teacher." The main idea is to keep learning through experience that is not too costly or harmful to oneself or others.

MARRIAGE

When a couple marry, there are more adjustments than are immediately obvious. Each person must give up some independence and must consider the needs and wishes of another person in making decisions. On the other hand, it is easier to accept disappointments if the person you love is pleased or benefits in some way. It is also easier to adjust to changes involved with your job or other activities when you have the support of an understanding marriage partner.

One obvious adjustment required in marriage involves the use of money. The young couple probably has saved to make basic purchases for their home; they may also have received gifts to meet other needs. But the day-to-day and month-by-month expenses of maintaining a home can bring unexpected problems and bills. An important requirement in making these adjustments is to avoid blaming each other for problems.

Other adjustments in married life involve personal habits and shared living space. The use of time may result in too much togetherness or too little privacy. Relationships with each other's friends and family also require both persons to adjust.

When "two become three," more adjustments are required. A couple may want children and may rejoice when their first child is born, but there will still be some major adjustments to make. Although these can be difficult or sometimes disturbing, patience and caring can increase the love and joy in the home—and can ease the problems of coping.

Some couples who have been married for years claim they have never had a quarrel. This is unlikely; it certainly cannot mean that the couple has never had a disagreement. No two people think and act exactly alike. Instead, one person probably has continually given in to the other. This approach may maintain a peaceful marriage, but it is not likely to be a happy one.

When two human beings care about themselves and about the many things that happen in life, they have differences. People have emotions, and feelings are not always expressed with appropriate control. In a good marriage, both partners should be able to express themselves, either rationally or, sometimes, emotionally. Each person should also be able to admit making a mistake and say, "I'm sorry." It isn't the disagreement or how it develops that is important, but how it is settled. Disagreements can be worked out satisfactorily through a problem-solving approach, or settled by compromise or thoughtful consideration of the other person.

DIVORCE

When a marriage does not last, there are new adjustments to make. Even when a separation or divorce is desired by both partners, the actual experience can be complicated and difficult. There are not only the legal aspects of divorce but also the social and emotional ramifications of returning to single life. For example, friendships can become awkward or lost, and family celebrations can become strained. There can also be emotional trauma involving a sense of failure or even guilt. Each divorce is different just as individuals are different, but even in the best of circumstances, adjustments must be made. These often take time, effort, and sometimes counseling.

Divorce can be especially difficult for children. Kevin Chappell in *Ebony* states,

> In today's climate of sky-high divorce rates (one out of every two marriages ends in divorce), more and more spouses are trading in the "I dos" and the "until death do we part" for phrases like 'custody,' 'visitation' and 'child support.' While experts say it's hard enough to negotiate co-parenting arrangements when a splitting couple is on speaking terms, when a marriage ends with the child being caught in the middle of name calling and court battling by emotionally racked parents, the separation could result in serious mental anguish for the child (3).

In spite of such situations, however, the emotional as well as the physical well-being of children is usually important to both ex-spouses. They realize that children must understand that they are not responsible for their parents' decision, and both parents encourage the children to love and respect the other.

ILLNESS OR DISABILITY

Fortunately, not everyone has to make the crucial adjustments that involve coping with the effects of a major illness or disability. Probably only those who have had this experience, or those living or working directly with people who have, can understand how difficult these adjustments are. There is much more involved than simply adjusting to a different kind of activity or to limited activity. One's previous activities affect the problems of adjustment. An athlete, for example, may have more difficulty in adjusting to a disability than a person whose work and interests require less physical activity.

Attitude toward the total situation is important in the adjustment process. Brad, who broke both legs in an automobile accident, keeps asking, "Why did this have to happen to me?" Amy, who had a similar accident, expresses a different attitude: "I'm fortunate that I'm alive—that my chances of walking again are excellent."

JOB-RELATED ADJUSTMENTS

A person who likes other people, who can get acquainted easily, and who has human-relations skills has valuable job-related assets in these traits. People function and work in groups in much of our modern world, and harmony is extremely important for production. Liking your boss, coworkers, and work is a factor in reducing stress in the workplace. If you are not disturbed by irritations and tensions, you can give more attention to your work and will have a better safety record. Stress contributes to numerous problems. For example, the cost of work-related stress can run into billions of dollars a year. Problems caused, or at least made worse, by stress are excessive absenteeism, decreased productivity, disgruntled workers, conflicts between employees or between employees and their supervisors, fatigue, and other physical or psychological problems. Businesses and other organizations are therefore concerned about reducing stress in the workplace. The Northwestern National Life Insurance Company, for example, has developed a workplace stress test to determine stress levels of employees. The items on the test require workers to react to topics such as training procedures, workloads, workspace and equipment, layoff practices, and benefits (4).

Employee assistance programs for dealing with stress and other problems will be discussed in the next chapter. Some of the job-related situations often associated with stress are discussed in the following sections.

THE NEW EMPLOYEE

When beginning a new job, a person has several adjustments to make at once. This can be frustrating to the conscientious person who begins the job with good intentions. Most companies and businesses have some type of job orientation that helps new employees become acquainted with their employer, coworkers, and job. This may be just an interview and a walk around the department, or it may be an extensive program of on-the-job training lasting several weeks.

Some of the things a new employee will want to know are, Who is my boss? From whom do I receive instructions? If I work for more than one person, do their standards and expectations vary? What are the priorities when work accumulates? How can I avoid misinterpretations of instructions? What supplies and equipment are available?

A new employee may also have questions pertaining to work done by workers on another shift, use of equipment and tools, break and lunchroom policies, absenteeism, safety measures, or union policies. Becoming a part of the company or business will require related adjustments.

A few suggestions to a new employee may be:

- Be friendly; introduce yourself to others.
- Be willing to learn; observe; listen.
- Be yourself but try to adjust to company and employee policies and practices.
- Be patient; it takes time to adjust to a new situation and responsibilities.
- Show appreciation to those helping you get started in various ways.
- Maintain your self-confidence; you will soon feel comfortable in your job and as part of the organization.

What Would You Suggest? *If a friend confides in you that she is having difficulty adjusting to a new job, what would you suggest?*

WORKING HOURS

Working shifts is a common employment situation that may require adjustment. Many night workers have had to learn to sleep during the day while other people are at work. A job with rotating shifts poses a particular adjustment challenge; as soon as a person adjusts to one shift, a change must be made to another.

Some people may have great difficulty in adjusting to anything except a traditional workday. It is now recognized that some people are basically day people and others are night people. Each person seems to feel and function best during some part of the twenty-four-hour day. If employees and the companies they work for recognize this and have some flexibility in scheduling working hours, everyone can benefit.

An increasingly popular concept of time spent on the job is called **flextime.** Under this arrangement, employees can choose their own hours to work as long as they establish a schedule. A schedule may consist of working a split shift or starting earlier or later than usual. There are usually certain "core hours" when everyone is expected to work, but flexibility is allowed in scheduling around these hours. Many large companies and businesses are satisfied with the results of flextime. People plan their schedules according to other responsibilities, transportation arrangements, or personal interests. This recognition of individual needs has resulted in greater commitment to work responsibilities and, in many cases, greater productivity.

Flextime
a practice in which employees choose the hours they work.

CHANGES IN SUPERVISION AND PROCEDURES

You may have become well adjusted to your job and total work situation only to be faced with changes in supervision and procedures. A new supervisor means a different person, and new human relationships always require adjustments. In another instance, the management of a company may plan and adopt new policies and procedures. Many of the actual changes, however, are made by their employees. It can be particularly difficult to accept and adjust to changes that are decided by someone else and that you do not understand. This is one of the reasons why management and labor often work together to determine necessary changes and to make smooth adjustments.

JOB CHANGE

It is estimated that a young person starting out in the working world today may change jobs six or seven times. Each of these new situations will call for many adjustments. Young people may stay with the same company and be promoted to another position or even transfer to a new location, or they may go to work for another company or for themselves. It is not unusual today for a person to receive new training to enter a different line of work. Many of tomorrow's jobs do not exist today. Career education is concerned not only with what you learn but whether you continue to learn and to adjust to changes in your work.

It is common for a change in employment to require moving to a different location. Relocation may automatically require many changes and adjustments, including selling and buying a home, changing schools, finding new care providers, and establishing oneself and family in a church and in the community. Maintaining contact with friends and family left behind can help the adjustment to the many changes.

Status quo
the existing conditions or environment at a certain time.

Changing the **status quo,** or existing conditions, is always disturbing, even when most aspects of the change in work and location are desirable. Better adjustments can be made when those affected are informed ahead of time about changes to be made or opportunities offered. Companies and organizations are becoming increasingly helpful in assisting employees who are moving to find housing and solve problems related to the new experience. They frequently offer assistance in helping a spouse find suitable employment in the area. The adjustments to a job change take time, and all involved need patience and resourcefulness.

UNEMPLOYMENT

Unemployment, for whatever reason, is another situation that calls for adjustments. These adjustments can relate to factors such as income and spending, self-esteem, relationships with others, use of time, further education or retraining, and personal responsibilities.

Unemployment compensation and other types of insurance can prevent unemployment from becoming a financial disaster. If there is another income in the family, that money will likely have to be budgeted more closely. Spending, even for necessities, may have to be restricted. This requires understanding and willingness to make adjustments by all family members.

Suppose you have lost your job or could sometime in the future. It is not pessimistic to recognize that job security is not as assured as it was in earlier years. If you do lose your job, you may be somewhat embarrassed, even if your unemployment is no fault of yours. Talking about your problems with friends and others who are interested can release tension, lead to temporary solutions in meeting responsibilities, and ease other adjustments. Others may also be able to give you leads to another job.

You will also have to adjust to a change in those with whom you have daily contact. You may miss some of your coworkers. You may also have more contact with other members of your family. If you are married and your spouse works, you may have additional responsibilities pertaining to household chores and child care. Whatever your particular situation, adjustments will have to be made in related changes in human relationships. These adjustments can be trying, especially when added to other aspects of unemployment.

How to use extra time constructively can be an additional challenge. You can become very discouraged and may feel useless unless you can occupy yourself in satisfying activity. You may want to catch up on some well-deserved rest and relaxation. You may also adjust to unemployment by actively job hunting, learning new skills, making home repairs, or helping others. Not having to maintain the schedule required of your former job may be welcome and give you flexibility in other activities. Yet it is advisable to develop a schedule that will provide you with a sense of purpose and accomplishment. At least planning what you will do each day, even if each day's activities vary, will keep you feeling better both physically and mentally.

Options for additional education and retraining are available to people at all age levels today. The class you are taking now doubtless is made up of individuals from various age groups and work-related backgrounds. It is common to return to school for many different reasons. An injury may prevent a person from continuing in former work, a change in lifestyle may give a person the time that he or she didn't have earlier, a change in responsibilities may require preparing for employment, or a person may need retraining for a new line of work because of loss of a job. Many adults going back into education may lack self-confidence at first, but most soon realize that they can still learn, and their motivation usually makes them highly successful students.

It is important for an unemployed person to evaluate his or her current total situation. Drastic, impulsive decisions should be avoided. In some cases a person may decide to sell his or her home and move to another part of the country where the employment situation is more promising, but that should not be done without careful consideration of all factors involved. Above all else, unemployed persons should keep confidence in themselves and their potential and be realistic and responsible.

RETIREMENT

It comes as a surprise to many people that they must adjust to retirement, but retirement can be another difficult adjustment in one's life. Unless they have prepared for their days of free time by developing new interests or can participate in activities in which they can make a contribution, retired persons may experience disappointment and serious maladjustment. New types of activity must replace their former work if retirement is to be enjoyed.

You probably know of people who have made relatively smooth transitions into retirement and perhaps others who had some difficulties. This topic is not discussed in more detail here because many readers of this book are not close to that stage of life. Remember, however, to prepare for your retirement and to expect to make some adjustments when the time comes. In the meantime, for those of you soon to enter the workforce as full-time employees in careers you have chosen, look forward to many years of challenging, satisfying work. Remember self-actualization at the peak of Maslow's heirarachy in Chapter 3? Your best opportunity to develop your potential is likely to be through your work.

DEATH AND DYING

For the vast majority of people, adjustments to death and dying will be the most difficult. Coping with death must occur on both a mental and an emotional level. This coping pertains to one's own death as well as to the deaths of others.

I AM MORTAL

Children today are not sheltered so much from death as they were in the past. One reason is that adults themselves are learning to cope with death more effectively. Therefore, they can be more realistic in helping children to understand both life and death. Even the death of a pet can often be used as an opportunity to help a child learn that living things die.

Quite early in life, one learns that human beings die. One must come to say, "I am a human being; therefore I will die." That is the mental aspect of recognizing and accepting death. A person can say, "I am mortal," however, without learning to deal with death on an emotional level. It is natural to fear the unknown and to avoid involvement with what is feared, yet it must be done.

Acceptance of death in a personal sense takes time. Even if we accept the idea of death and our own mortality, we may regard our own death as extremely remote. This is not to suggest that we should be thinking continually about death or dying. But we should not avoid the issue either. We must accept it as a reality. Then we can give attention and energy to experiencing life more fully.

ACCEPTANCE OF DEATH

Dr. Elisabeth Kübler-Ross has contributed notably to our understanding of the psychological aspects of dying. After interviewing hundreds of dying patients, she concluded that there are five stages to approaching one's own death. According to Dr. Kübler-Ross, dying patients generally go through these stages, or some variation of them, between the time when they learn about a terminal illness and the time they die (5).

The first stage is *denial.* The dying person refuses to believe that death is near. Relatives and friends may also try to deny the inevitable, either to protect the dying person from the truth or because they cannot accept the truth themselves. The second stage is *anger.* Once the reality of dying has been recognized, the person reacts in protest and anger, asking "Why me?" The patient may be angry with doctors and nurses, with relatives, and even with God. A person in this stage of approaching death may express anger at anyone who is well and at anyone who tries to help.

After the anger stage, for most people comes a period of *bargaining*—either with God or with whatever power the person believes in. Such bargains take the form, "If I get well, I will lead a better life" or "If I could only live until . . . I would dedicate my life to . . . ." The actual bargains depend on the values, past experiences, and personality of the individual. Some claim that their bargaining, to some extent, was successful, but in most cases the dying persons realize that bargaining does not work.

Depression is the stage following bargaining. By this time the patient realizes death is near, but emotional acceptance is not yet possible. It is heartbreaking to lose a loved one, but it can be many times harder for the dying person to cope with the idea of losing everyone and everything on earth. The opportunity to express this loss can be helpful to the patient. Those who care about the dying person should be willing both to talk and to listen.

The fifth and final stage of dying is *acceptance.* The dying person learns to accept death without undue fear and bitterness. Just how a person reacts in this stage varies with the individual. Some want to do whatever they can as long as they are able. They may want to see friends and relatives. Others may wish to spend more time alone or with someone close, to prepare for the death they have now accepted.

Critics of Kübler-Ross claim that the stages are not that predictable or do not necessarily occur in a particular sequence. Nevertheless, she can be credited with bringing the formerly taboo subject of death and dying into the open so that greater understanding could develop and feelings could be expressed.

Since people have different personalities, live their lives differently, and have widely different beliefs about the purpose of life, it can be expected they would also have different attitudes and behaviors related to death. One's age is also an important factor in reaction to approaching death. Elderly people are usually realistic about the fact that they may not have too much longer to live and have accepted their mortality with dignity.

Recent efforts have been made to make dying a less painful experience. **Hospices,** or homelike places where dying persons spend their remaining days, have become common. At hospices, dying patients are treated with loving attention and compassion. The members of one's family are allowed to visit at any time. Personal belongings and even pets are sometimes permitted. The patients in

Hospices
homelike places where terminally ill patients spend their remaining days.

hospices are given the care they need but in an environment that resembles their own home.

LOSS OF A LOVED ONE

It would be a good idea to review the discussion of grief in Chapter 5. There will be further consideration here of how grief affects those who lose a loved one and how we can give some support to relatives or friends who are experiencing such a loss. It was noted in Chapter 5 that a person can experience grief because of several different losses. It doesn't necessarily have to relate to the death of a loved one. Our discussion here, however, relates primarily to a sense of loss due to a death.

Grief affects people differently because of the differences in their personalities, coping skills, and their relationships with the person who has died. A person may have ambivalent feelings, including anger, sorrow, relief, guilt, loneliness, or sadness. He or she will also experience the physiological effects of emotion and may have difficulty sleeping, eating, and generally taking care of oneself. A person may experience confusion and even have hallucinations of hearing or seeing the person who is no longer present. Some people resort to the use of coping mechanisms, which are psychological crutches that help us deal with situations when our regular coping skills are not adequate. It is important to know that experiences such as these are within the normal range of reactions to loss, but also to recognize that individual experiences vary in type, degree, and duration.

University of Chicago's Froma Walsh, in a *Psychology Today* interview, states,

> In healthy families and well-functioning families there is a sense that death is part of the life cycle and that it's inevitable. Healthier individuals and families tend to be more accepting of death as part of the life cycle. Given the life cycle, the most painful and unjust deaths are early death, untimely deaths. The death of a young adult or a kid is inherently unjust, doubly difficult because it reverses the life cycle (6).

SUPPORT TO OTHERS

It is natural to want to do something for our relatives or friends who are having difficulties—in this case, experiencing grief. Yet we often feel quite helpless in this type of situation. What can we do? What can we even say? Grief counselors Catherine Thompson and Barbara E. Moore in "Grief Is Not a Sign of Weakness," give the following suggestions:

- Stay in touch—don't expect the bereaved person to call you.
- Listen without giving advice, unless asked.
- Don't make blanket statements like, "You're young, you'll get married again," or "You can have another baby."
- Don't say, "I know how you feel"; grief is individual.
- Mention the dead person's name.
- Remember important occasions such as a wedding anniversary or the date of death.
- Don't say, "Don't cry"; rather, accept and share the tears.
- Don't expect the bereaved to be the same person again.
- Realize that the grief and pain never will be totally gone.
- Learn about grief and the grief process.
- Share your friend's or relative's bereavement (7).

What Would You Say? *Suppose you unexpectedly run into a person you know has recently experienced the loss of a loved one. What might you say to show the person you are aware of his or her grief and that you care?*

COPING MECHANISMS

Human beings attempt to protect themselves psychologically as well as physically. If someone harms you physically, you may want to fight back or you may try to protect yourself in some way. This reaction is an expression of your need for self-preservation.

Eugene Kennedy, in *The Pain of Being Human,* shares his understanding of this type of behavior in the following:

> Why do average persons turn to some form of defensive response in the course of everyday life? Ordinarily this occurs at a moment when we are caught off guard, or unprepared for a novel experience, or when we have not fully come to terms with some aspect of our personality (8).

Coping mechanism unconscious behavior patterns that help one maintain a favorable self-concept.

Attempts to protect yourself psychologically are expressions of the need for self-esteem. If necessary, you use **coping mechanisms,** or unconscious behavior patterns that help you maintain a favorable self-concept. Although coping mechanisms can be relatively immature ways of handling a situation, they serve as psychological crutches when an individual cannot handle a problem in a conscious, reasonable way. Since they are behavior patterns, or habits, regular reliance on certain coping mechanisms develops into personality traits of an individual.

Everyone uses coping mechanisms to some extent. None of us is so mature or so capable in all situations that he or she never has need of a psychological crutch. When you are using a coping mechanism, you are unaware of the real cause of your behavior in adjusting to an undesirable or threatening situation. However, the effects on you and others are real. The following are common coping mechanisms that people use to protect themselves psychologically.

DAYDREAMING

Daydreaming a simple form of unconscious mental activity during which one's mind flows freely.

Everyone daydreams; your mind is never completely inactive. **Daydreaming,** or fantasy, as it is also called, is the simplest form of unconscious mental activity. The mind wanders freely from one topic to another when you are daydreaming.

You may use daydreaming as an escape because reality is too uncomfortable, and changing reality can be too difficult. Another person may feel inadequate in social situations and have fantasies about being popular and more capable. Daydreaming often interferes with effective life, work, and self-improvement. It can also be harmful in other ways. If your mind wanders while you are driving a car, you may have a serious accident; if you are working with mechanical equipment, you may damage it or injure yourself.

Daydreaming, on the other hand, can lead to creative thinking. Thomas Edison was considered a daydreamer by his teachers, but he was a creative, constructive dreamer who patented more than 1,100 inventions in his lifetime. Daydreams can also give a vision of self that may motivate actual achievement.

Most daydreaming is harmless and can temporarily relieve frustration and provide mental relaxation. If you use daydreaming as an escape, however, you are employing a coping mechanism. The question is not, then, whether you daydream, but when, and to what extent, and why.

RATIONALIZATION

Rationalization
a coping mechanism in which one makes excuses for unacceptable behavior.

The expression "Don't kid yourself" is based on our tendency to rationalize. Some psychologists say our biggest task in life is to establish a satisfactory self-image and then to protect that image. **Rationalization** is one of the mental devices used to accomplish this. A student may not feel like studying for a test, so she rationalizes, "I probably wouldn't study the right things anyway." You may neglect to return an item borrowed from a friend by rationalizing, "He's probably glad to have it out of his way."

Two familiar types of rationalization are often called "sour grapes" and "sweet lemon." When a person fails to obtain something he wanted, he may say, "I really didn't want it, anyway." This would be like saying, "The grapes are sour, anyway." On the other hand, when one has to accept something he didn't want, he may rationalize by thinking or saying, "It's not so bad, after all." This is the "sweet lemon" reaction. This type of defense mechanism prevents us from being too disappointed by whatever happens to us.

When we rationalize, we do what we want to do and then interpret it as the best action or an acceptable action. Rationalization, or excuse making, stands in the way of honest evaluation of behavior. It can also interfere with our achievement by making us satisfied with inferior performance.

REGRESSION

Regression
a coping mechanism in which a person temporarily returns to an earlier form of behavior, a behavior that is often age-inappropriate.

A person who uses **regression** returns to an earlier form of behavior. A young man who suffers a decrease in income, becoming once again financially dependent on his parents, may return to the behavior of a child by relying on someone else to make his decisions for him. An adult who generally acts in a mature and responsible manner may regress to having a childish tantrum when a relationship with someone else doesn't go his or her way.

Other forms of regression are wanting to be pampered when ill or hurt, showing off to get attention, or pouting when not getting your way. The person who regresses is temporarily rejecting the "hard, cruel world" and seeking the greater security of childhood.

FIXATION

Fixation
a coping mechanism in which one develops psychologically to a certain point and then stays, or "fixes," there.

Fixation is a coping mechanism that resembles regression because the person is acting younger than his or her age. In regression there is a temporary turning back to earlier behavior. In **fixation** a person develops psychologically to a certain point and then stops or "fixes" personality development there. This can happen in late adolescence when an individual is breaking the last bonds of childhood dependence and becoming an independent adult. A person who has a shattering experience at that time, such as the breaking of an engagement or failure in some other important venture, may refuse to enter the final doorway to the adult world, preferring to remain dependent on others. Such a person never really grows up psychologically, even while continuing to grow older in years.

DISPLACEMENT

One of the most troublesome of the coping mechanisms is displacement. There is a three-part relationship in **displacement,** involving: (1) the person who is frustrated, (2) the person or thing that is the cause of the frustration, and (3) the innocent third party onto whom the frustrated person transfers or displaces the frustration. When something is bothering you and you don't know what you can do about it, you often displace your frustration onto someone else. If you have trouble with your car or do poorly on a test, for example, you may displace your frustration by being critical of a friend.

Anyone would readily admit that this is unreasonable behavior, yet everyone probably uses displacement to some degree at least occasionally. If you acquire an understanding of this kind of behavior, you will have a better chance of becoming aware of it in yourself and others. And recognition of a personal weakness is the first step in self-improvement. If you can recognize displacement in yourself, you can make a greater effort to determine the cause of your frustration and find a constructive, or at least harmless, method of releasing tension.

If you recognize the behavior of someone else toward you as displacement, you can control your reaction better and avoid further complications. Suppose your supervisor is worried and upset about a problem at home. Until the problem is solved, the supervisor may be tense and irritable, perhaps blaming the employees in your department for minor things that ordinarily would be taken in stride. If you are a victim of displacement and can recognize this type of behavior, you can try to be more tolerant and understanding; you may even try to help the frustrated person do something about the problem. It would be a mistake to assume that all anger and criticism are forms of displacement, however. To take the attitude "It can't be me; something else must be the problem" will block the path of effective problem solving and adjustment.

PROJECTION

In **projection** you defend yourself psychologically by accusing others of having the personality weakness that you yourself have. You may at some time have heard someone reprimand another person for being irresponsible, extravagant, or selfish, when it was obvious to you that the person was describing himself or herself. The person using projection, however, is unaware of why the reprimand or accusation is made. If you are quite certain that criticism of you is really only defensive behavior, you may ignore or tolerate it without becoming upset. As with displacement, however, you must be careful that you are not being defensive in assuming innocence.

REPRESSION

Repression should not be confused with suppression, which is not a coping mechanism. **Suppression** is a conscious control of one's behavior to avoid hurting

Displacement
a coping mechanism in which an individual transfers frustration from another source to an innocent third party.

Projection
a coping mechanism in which you defend yourself psychologically by accusing others of having your own personality weakness.

Suppression
conscious control of one's behavior to be accepted.

someone's feelings or causing a problem for oneself. Suppression is sometimes referred to as tact and is necessary for effective human relations. Repression, on the other hand, is unconscious and is a coping mechanism. **Repression** is pushing into your unconscious what is frightening, contrary to your moral standards, or unacceptable to you for some other reason. There are some ideas or desires that people cannot consciously tolerate, or the memory of an experience may be so frightening or disgusting that they "forget"; they are no longer conscious of the experience. These repressed ideas and memories in an emotionally disturbed person are sometimes revealed during therapy. It is believed that the unconscious mind influences our feelings and behavior, even though we are not aware of what is thus affecting us. Repressed ideas or feelings may also be activated in dreams, in which the dreamer has no conscious control.

Repression
a coping mechanism in which a person pushes back or buries in the unconscious that which is unacceptable.

DENIAL OF REALITY

Rather than facing a situation squarely and determining how to cope with it, some people resort to **denial,** a refusal to accept the situation as real. This way they can at least temporarily avoid the pain and fear of dealing with the actual circumstances. Thus, students may deny that they are failing a course and therefore not worry about it. When they do fail, they may deny that it is important. Some people deny that they have a drinking problem or that they are showing favoritism in their relationships with others. Denial, like many other coping mechanisms, is an unconscious attempt to live with oneself and a potentially threatening situation. People who use denial are deceiving themselves more than others. They are coping with the situation in a self-defeating, nonproductive way.

Denial
a coping mechanism in which one refuses to believe a hurtful or threatening event or circumstance.

IDENTIFICATION

Another common coping mechanism is a type of behavior called **identification.** In this coping mechanism, a person's identity is associated with that of another person who is greatly admired. Small children do this by pretending to be their current heroes. This type of behavior is also common in adolescence, when young people may be dissatisfied with themselves and may be striving to become something more than or different from what they are.

Identification
a coping mechanism in which a person's own identity is associated with that of an admired person.

Identification limits one's behavior. Parents sometimes attempt to relive their youth through the lives of their children, for example. This is disturbing to young people, who want to live their own lives. The parents are also depriving themselves of fully experiencing a stage of life that should be satisfying and complete in itself.

There are also variations of identification. In **imitation** a person acts like another person, because he or she feels inadequate or has low self-esteem. This behavior usually has undesirable effects because the imitator is playing a role and neglecting his or her development as a unique individual.

Imitation
process of acting like another person.

Such imitation is in contrast to **emulation,** which is a conscious attempt to improve oneself and is therefore not a defense mechanism. In emulation one admires characteristics of another person and attempts to develop similar characteristics in his or her own way. Behind every successful person there are probably several people who have influenced and inspired that person's self-actualization or self-development in this way.

Emulation
attempt to develop characteristics similar to those of an admired person.

COMPENSATION

Compensation
a coping mechanism in which a person who is prevented from doing something by a disability or circumstance substitutes another activity.

Nobody is perfect. Everyone has personal weaknesses in ability and self-development. If some circumstance or disability prevents a person from being successful at something she would like to do, she may compensate by trying something else that she knows she will be able to do. **Compensation** is a type of unconscious substitution that helps a person to experience success and have a good feeling about herself or himself. A person who would like to be an athlete, but lacks the ability, may compensate by becoming a referee, for example. We should not conclude from this, however, that all referees are thus compensating. Some of them have been successful athletes in the past, and others may never have wanted to be an athlete in the first place.

Conscious substitution of goals, as well as some coping mechanisms, can help us experience success in life. There have been many instances in which what was accepted as next best turned out to be the best for someone. A strong desire to do something is often related to one's having the potential to accomplish a goal. If physical disabilities or environmental circumstances stand in the way of developing potential, however, it is reasonable to substitute another objective or goal. For example, a young woman who would like to become a model, but isn't tall enough for most assignments, may choose a career in fashion design, instead.

EFFECTS OF COPING MECHANISMS

It can be concluded, after considering the preceding coping mechanisms, that some of them are relatively harmless unless carried to extremes. Daydreaming is an example. Other coping mechanisms can help one to make a better adjustment to oneself, to others, or to the situation or environment. Compensation is an example of this type. Displacement, on the other hand, is an example of a coping mechanism that indicates maladjustment and that can interfere with purposeful living and effective relationships with other human beings.

After learning about coping mechanisms, we must be careful not to interpret practically all behavior that we observe in others as the use of coping mechanisms. Certain types of behavior are coping mechanisms more because of *why* people act that way than because of *what* they do. And it is very easy to misinterpret why people do what they do.

The use of coping mechanisms is usually an immature, inadequate way of coping. But they do reduce anxiety that might otherwise cause more serious problems. They may be only temporary reactions, until a person learns how to solve problems or adjust more effectively. Ways of reacting become habits, however, which are not easy to change.

NEUROSIS

Maladjustment and excessive anxiety in one or more respects is known as **neurosis.** This difficulty in coping may be the result of conflicts and frequent frustrations or personal inadequacies. Persons with neuroses may have

Neurosis
maladjustment and excessive anxiety in one or more respects without serious mental illness.

repressed fears or aggressive feelings from childhood experiences that they are no longer aware of as such but that influence their present behavior.

There are identifiable symptoms of neurotic behavior. If an adult is neurotic about safety and has an excessive fear of the dark, for example, that behavior is immature and childish. Andrea is 35 years old but must have a light on in her room at night and carries a large flashlight in her handbag at all times "in case the lights go off."

Second, neurotic behavior is excessive as a reaction. Although there is always some possibility that lights will go off, Andrea takes more than ordinary precautions. Her reaction is out of proportion to the actual threat.

A third symptom of neurotic behavior is that it is persistent or typical of the person's usual way of reacting. Andrea has this excessive anxiety about the dark whether she is in her own home or in an environment where she could be confident that others would adequately take care of the situation if the lights went off. Andrea's excessive fear is a *phobia,* as discussed in Chapter 5. Unless a person receives some type of therapy, a phobia can be a lifetime maladjustment.

Another person may be excessively self-centered and neurotic about appearance. Alvin checks his apparel or hair every few minutes to see that everything is exactly as it should be. Physical appearance is important, but after normal attention to personal cleanliness and appearance, Alvin should be confident about his appearance and concentrate on what he is doing. If he fails to moderate his abnormal behavior, he will not be efficient on the job or even interesting as a person.

Fortunately, most neuroses are minor, and many people with neuroses manage to cope satisfactorily, even though it requires extra effort and may cause them some discomfort. Severe problems and psychological disorders will be discussed in Chapter 11.

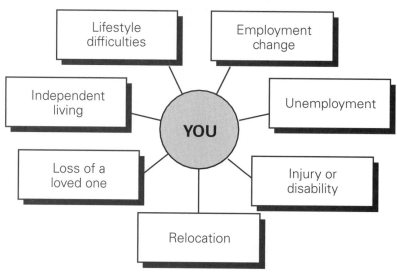

How Well Would You Cope?

INABILITY TO COPE

It is not so much what happens to a person, however, as how he or she reacts that determines the seriousness of the situation. One of the most tragic results of the inability to cope is suicide. People who commit suicide perceive their situation as being hopeless or intolerable. Some of the most common causes of suicide are depression, drug abuse, personal expectations that are unreasonably high, inability to live up to what one perceives as expectations of others, revenge toward members of one's family or another person, sense of loss or rejection, or even need for attention.

The inability either to solve a problem or to adjust to it leads some people to escape from life itself. Others may lead suicidal lives. They may drive recklessly or engage in other life-threatening behavior. The problems that cause some people to take their lives are no worse than the problems many other people have. The difference is in the individual's *reaction* to the problem.

A person who is thinking about ending his or her life needs help. Suicidal persons need to know that they can be accepted for who they are and that they can change themselves and develop ways to cope with their situations. It can also be helpful for others to be familiar with identified clues to possible suicides. These include previous attempts, threats to take one's own life, extreme depression, drastic changes in behavior or personal hygiene, or giving away valued possessions.

Those who loved the person who has taken his or her own life often experience lifelong grief and guilt about what they might have done to prevent the suicide. Mariette Hartley, whose father committed suicide, shares the following in an interview with Julia Lawlor in *USA Weekend*: "Suicide has a built-in core of stigma, blame, shame, what if, if only, why, I should have known. There are no other deaths like that" (9).

There are crisis and suicide prevention centers in most communities to which those who feel they need help can turn. There are also support groups for family members who have experienced the suicide of a loved one.

WAYS TO REDUCE STRESS

Although some stress is desirable in our lives, we also know that we can experience much undesirable stress or distress. We must not only be able to recognize such stress and be aware of its possible effects, we should have constructive ways of avoiding and reducing it. Consider the ways you can apply the following suggestions to yourself and your particular situations.

BECOME A BETTER PROBLEM SOLVER

You will recall from Chapter 7 that the ability to problem-solve is part of the definition of coping. Since the better we cope, the less stress we experience, it follows that we can prevent some stress and reduce other stress by improving our ability to problem-solve.

Quiz Yourself on Stress Symptoms

What are your stress symptoms? This scale measures the minor physical and emotional symptoms that indicate difficulty in dealing with everyday stress. During the past month, how much of the time were the following statements true for you? Place a checkmark in the appropriate column.

	Most of the Time	Some of the Time	Almost Never
1. I felt tense, nervous, anxious, or upset.	_____	_____	_____
2. I felt sad, depressed, down in the dumps, or hopeless.	_____	_____	_____
3. I was low in energy, exhausted, tired, or unable to get things done.	_____	_____	_____
4. I couldn't turn off my thoughts at night or on weekends long enough to feel relaxed and refreshed the next day.	_____	_____	_____
5. I had difficulty falling asleep and/or staying asleep and didn't feel rested when I awakened.	_____	_____	_____
6. I found myself unable to sit still and had to move around constantly.	_____	_____	_____
7. I felt discouraged, pessimistic, sad, self-critical, inadequate, or guilty.	_____	_____	_____
8. I was so upset that I felt I was losing control of my feelings.	_____	_____	_____
9. I have been preoccupied with a serious personal problem.	_____	_____	_____
10. I have been bothered by vague body aches and pains, nervous indigestion, or jitters.	_____	_____	_____
11. I have been in unpleasant situations that I felt helpless to do anything about.	_____	_____	_____
12. I felt tired in the morning, with no energy to get up or face daily activities.	_____	_____	_____

To score: Total your checkmarks in each column. Enter here: _____ _____ _____

Allow 2 points for Most of the Time
1 point for Some of the Time
0 points for Almost Never

Total Score _____

A total score of 10 or more indicates a need to take active steps to improve coping.

Source: Dennis T. Jaffe, *Healing from Within*, Knopf, New York, 1981. Used with permission of the publisher.

ACCEPT YOUR LIMITATIONS

It is important to understand ourselves as we really are, as discussed in Chapter 2. It is much easier to agree with this than to apply it, however, as with many other aspects of personal psychology. If we expect too much of ourselves or are perfectionists, we are bound to create undue stress for ourselves. We should know and accept our limitations, our humanness, and be able to handle disappointment in our own performance. This does not mean that we shouldn't strive to do our best and to improve, but it does mean that we should realize we are not perfect.

KNOW YOUR PRIORITIES

It is true that human beings have many needs and wants in common, but our individual values have an order of importance that is our own. Since we do not have the time or money or energy to do or have everything that may have some value for us, we have to be selective. If we try to do more than is reasonable for us, we will experience stress. Knowing your priorities, or the order of importance of what you want, will help you to avoid stress. Although we should consider the effect of our values on others, it is important for each of us to establish our own values and priorities. Continually trying to please others can be stressful.

ACCEPT THE REALITIES OF LIFE

This pertains not only to our own limitations, as discussed previously, but also to realities such as working for a living and experiencing difficulties in life. We should try to find the type of work that we can find satisfying, but it is unrealistic to resent the fact that we have to work at all. In fact, there is much evidence in our society that not working can be more stressful than working. Also, if we expect some difficulties and disappointments in our lives, as is true of everyone's life, we will be able to cope better with such experiences.

AVOID TOO MANY CHANGES IN YOUR LIFE AT ONE TIME

Too many changes in a given period of time, even though some of them are welcome, can create stress. Although we do not have control over everything that happens to us in life, we can selectively delay some changes if we have recently experienced a great many changes. We can give ourselves a chance to adjust and adapt to some changes before becoming voluntarily involved in others. Circumstances that may be very disturbing to us at first can become almost negligible after a while. We can become accustomed to situations that at first seem barely tolerable.

LEARN TO RELAX

We can avoid some stress and reduce what we cannot avoid by learning to relax. There are numerous ways we can do this. What may work best for one person may not be effective for another. Some people find "doing nothing" in the sun very relaxing, for example, although others may find it stressful. Some find relaxation in music; others prefer meditation, a form of relaxation achieved when they sit in a comfortable position, breathe slowly and deeply, and free their minds of other thoughts and concerns. Progressive relaxation, another type of relaxation,

This woman is taking time out for herself, relaxing with a cup of tea and her favorite book.

involves step-by-step relaxation of various muscles of the body. People may begin, for example, flexing their fingers and relaxing each hand. They then move to the arms, the shoulder, and so on, to the toes. Another technique useful to some people is **biofeedback.** With biofeedback, a person monitors her body functioning with the use of a machine until she learns what type of behavior modifies her blood pressure, heart rate, or other body functions. Everyone should be able to find an activity or nonactivity that promotes relaxation.

Biofeedback
a way to monitor your body functions with the use of a machine until you learn what type of behavior modifies your blood pressure, heart rate, or other body functions.

GIVE ATTENTION TO OTHERS

Too much attention to oneself and one's own concerns can cause stress. One of the best ways of avoiding or reducing stress, therefore, is to give attention to others. That is not the only reason for giving attention to others, of course. Regardless of one's reason, however, getting one's mind off one's own problems can be an effective technique for relieving stress. Tiredness from constructive activity and involvement with others is not nearly as stressful as fatigue caused by tension and stress.

LET GO OF PREJUDICES AND GRUDGES

Although prejudices and grudges are by definition directed at others, they often cause the greatest problem for those who carry them. If you can free yourself of unreasonable attitudes toward others and learn to forgive and forget, you will be doing yourself a greater favor than anyone else. Even if you think you are justified in not wanting to be associated with another person, do not cause yourself an additional problem by building a barrier between yourself and that person. Those who maintain, "She doesn't bother me; I don't have anything to do with her" are being bothered by maintaining that attitude more than they realize.

FOR BETTER or FOR WORSE

By Lynn Johnston

© Lynn Johnston Productions, Inc./Dist. by United Feature Syndicate, Inc.

BE ORGANIZED, YET FLEXIBLE

It can be stressful not to have some plan or structure to our activities. It can be reassuring and relatively relaxing, on the other hand, to have goals and a plan to achieve them. But it is also important to be flexible, to be able to adjust our plans if circumstances suggest. Those who feel they must follow through on an original plan even though it is no longer practical or even desirable are setting themselves up for a stress-related problem. Too much rigidity in our behavior can be as stressful as disorganization.

DON'T TRY TO CHANGE OTHERS

There is a difference between trying to influence others to change and trying to control them. Those who are involved in a stressful situation with others often ask, "How can I make him (or her) change?" If they are trying to do the impossible, they are only asking for stress. If we really believe that another person would be better off if she or he changed in some way, we should try to influence that person to want to change. We should recognize, at the same time, that everyone is entitled to and responsible for his or her own life. Therefore, people have a right to be the kind of persons they are as long as they are not interfering with the rights of others.

COMMUNICATE; TALK OUT YOUR STRESS

Some problems involving others can be avoided if we make our needs and situations known to them. We should also be aware that some problems are basically misunderstandings, which communication can rectify. Talking about how we feel can also give us insight into why we feel the way we do and help to reduce stress.

What Would You Do? *If you felt that you were under too much stress from a combination of studies, work, and personal responsibilities, what would you do?*

Physical exercise and activity offer positive ways to relieve tension, while aggressive reactions are negative ways of reacting to stress.

LEARN TO RECOGNIZE JOB BURNOUT

Burnout
a reaction to excessive stress over time, leading to feelings of helplessness and apathy and making one unproductive.

Although we can become "burned out" in any situation, one of the most serious problem areas is work. **Burnout** is generally thought of as a reaction to excessive stress over time, leading to feelings of helplessness and apathy and making one unproductive. To avoid burnout, it helps to know the reasons for what we are doing and to experience a sense of achievement. We also need some variety in our work as well as in the rest of our lives. We need vacations and ways of refreshing ourselves so that we do not become victims of this undesirable condition.

FIND WAYS TO RELEASE TENSION

It was suggested earlier that we should be realistic. It would be unrealistic to think that we can avoid all tension and undesirable stress. Tension, in this sense, refers to physiological stresses and strains. Physical exercise and activity help to release such tension. Some people resort to aggressive behavior in an unconscious effort to reduce tension. This alternative, of course, is not condoned. Others, who have better understanding of themselves and better control, find harmless or even constructive ways of getting rid of such tension. Participation in physical work or sports helps to reduce tension, for example.

LIVE ONE DAY AT A TIME

Can you live more than one day at a time? In spite of this obvious limitation, we can create unnecessary and undesirable stress for ourselves by worrying about problems that may never materialize. We should have goals and plans, but we also need to adjust those when circumstances warrant it. If we know our priorities and can adjust them when necessary, we will avoid much of the stress common in modern living. We will not only accomplish more, but we will also enjoy life more.

KEEP WELL

Wellness is the theme of the next chapter, and we will consider ways of maintaining wellness. It will be noted here, however, that exercise, adequate sleep, proper nutrition, and positive mental health attitudes help to avoid and reduce stress.

Summary

Stress is physiological disturbance and psychological frustration caused by physical conditions, unmet needs, and external pressures, real or perceived. Stress is the individual's reaction to stressors, or the sources of stress. The individual's inability to cope with these stressors causes stress. Hans Selye has referred to the body's reaction to stress as the general adaptation syndrome. This syndrome consists of the alarm, resistance, and exhaustion stages. Good stress, or eustress, makes life interesting and exciting.

Some experiences in life that often require major adjustments are school entry, adolescence, independent living, marriage, divorce, illness or disability, and retirement. Job-related adjustments involve the new employee, working hours, changes in supervision and procedures, job change, unemployment, and numerous other situations.

Death and dying and grief involve some of the most difficult adjustments in human life. Understanding the related experiences can be helpful. We can also learn to be supportive of others who are facing death or experiencing grief.

Coping mechanisms are unconscious psychological devices used to maintain self-esteem and to adjust to unpleasant realities in life. These include daydreaming, rationalization, regression, fixation, displacement, projection, repression, identification, denial of reality, and compensation. The results of the use of coping mechanisms can range from the relatively harmless to useful to the seriously harmful, depending on how the coping behavior affects those who use it and their relations with others.

Maladjustment and severe anxiety in one or more respects is known as neurosis. Identifiable symptoms of neurosis are behavior that is immature, excessive, and persistent.

Inability to cope effectively causes excessive tension and stress. A tragic result of inability to cope can be suicide.

PSYCHOLOGY IN PRACTICE

1. Write an autobiography including a description of the major adjustments you have had to make in your life. Include a final paragraph explaining what you have learned about coping that may help you to deal with situations in the future.

2. Ask three people you know who have recently started a job about their job-related adjustments. Attempt to identify people who have started on different kinds of jobs. Compare similarities and differences.

3. Brainstorming is a creative problem-solving technique discussed in Chapter 7. Set up a brainstorming session with other class members on how to reduce stress in the lives of students.

There are numerous ways to reduce stress in our lives. Understanding ourselves and stress symptoms can lead us to the most effective ways of managing stress and getting help in doing that.

A person who has learned to cope effectively has taken a basic step toward total wellness, the subject of the next chapter.

Key Terms

Adjust	Hospices	Repression
Coping	Coping mechanism	Denial
Stress	Daydreaming	Identification
Stressors	Rationalization	Imitation
Eustress	Regression	Emulation
General adaptation syndrome	Fixation	Compensation
Adolescent	Displacement	Neurosis
Puberty	Suppression	Biofeedback
Flextime	Projection	Burnout
Status quo		

Learning Activities

Turn to page LA-45 to complete the Learning Activities and Enrichment Activities for this chapter.

Endnotes

1. Hans Selye, *The Stress of Life,* rev. ed., McGraw-Hill Book Company, New York, 1976, p. 74.

2. Ibid. pp. 36–40.

3. Kevin Chappell, "Co-Parenting After Divorce, *Ebony,* March 1966, p. 62.

4. The NWNL Workplace Stress Test, Northwestern Life Insurance Company, copyright 1992, in Barry L. Puce and Rhonda Brandt, *Effective Human Relations in Organizations,* 5th ed., Houghton Mifflin Company, Boston, MA, 1993, pp. 511–514.

5. Elisabeth Kübler-Ross, *On Death and Dying,* The Macmillan Company, New York, 1969, Copyright 1969 by Elisabeth Kübler-Ross.

6. Froma Walsh, "Loss, Loss, Loss," *Psychology Today,* July/August 1992, p. 90.

7. Catherine Thompson and Barbara E. Moore, "Grief Is Not a Sign of Weakness," *USA Today,* July 1991, p. 93.

8. Eugene Kennedy, *The Pain of Being Human,* The Crossroad Publishing Company, New York, 1997, p. 44.

9. Julia Lawlor, interviewer, "Suicide: The Silent Epidemic," *USA Weekend,* June 28–30, 1996, p. 14.

Wellness

11

Your body was built to be exercised. If an owner's manual came with your body at birth, its basic instruction would be three words: Move it—regularly.

Art Turock

LEARNING OBJECTIVES

After completing this chapter, you should be able to do the following:

1. Identify nutrients needed for body functioning and describe the role of each.

2. Describe the four basic qualities associated with physical fitness.

3. Discuss major threats to wellness and suggest how they might be minimized.

4. List three "red flags" to watch for when choosing medical treatments.

5. Identify characteristics of a mentally healthy person.

6. Identify six different types of psychological disorders.

7. Explain the difference between biochemical therapy and psychotherapy in the treatment of persons with psychological disorders.

8. Identify types of assistance provided in an employee assistance program.

9. Give suggestions for breaking a habit that is detrimental to wellness.

10. Describe what is meant by "balances" in maintaining wellness.

What does it mean to be well? It has come to mean much more than not being sick. Wellness today emphasizes *total* wellness, with individuals assuming greater responsibility for every aspect of their well-being.

You may have heard the term *holistic health* in discussions on wellness. John and Muriel James give us an explanation of the origin of this approach to wellness in *Passion for Life*. They write,

> Vitality and an eagerness to live are best observed in people who are healthy. The word health comes from the Anglo Saxon root *hal,* which means both whole and holy. The word *holistic,* sometimes spelled wholistic, was first used in the 1930s by Jan Christiaan Smuts, former premier of South Africa. Today it has become increasingly popular in the fields of medicine and psychology. A healthy approach to life emphasizes the wholeness and health of body, mind, and spirit (1).

More specifically, holistic health involves a balance among the different components of well-being such as physical health and fitness, mental health, stress management, environmental safety, emotional stability, vocational competence, social effectiveness, and spiritual harmony. When an individual is experiencing a problem in one of these areas, it affects his or her total well-being.

Some aspects of wellness have already been discussed, and others will be discussed in further chapters.

Components of Holistic Health

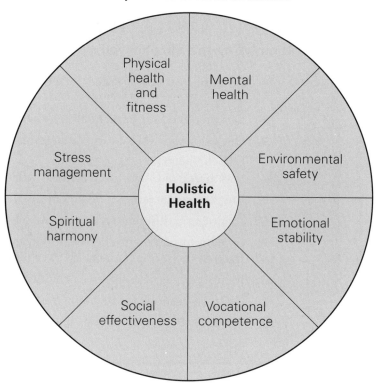

NUTRITION

What we eat, or don't eat, affects our total well-being. If we eat too much or eat too much of certain foods, we gain weight. If we don't eat a well-balanced diet, we become more susceptible to illness or certain diseases. Too much sugar or caffeine can have negative effects on how we feel. Insufficient amounts of certain vitamins can cause problems, and even disease. Overuse of vitamins can also have detrimental effects. As we become adults and are more responsible for our wellness than we have ever been before, it is not enough to eat just because we are hungry or because some things taste good. We should know and apply basic principles of nutrition. Eating well-balanced meals of nutritious foods is a major factor in our total wellness. Most of the foods that are good for you are common and relatively inexpensive. Poor eating habits are primarily due to eating what we like rather than what is best for our health.

Nutrition refers not only to the characteristics of food itself but also to how the body handles it. It includes the process of digestion and distribution of nourishment. Your body has basic needs that can be fulfilled by an adequate diet. Otherwise some kind of vitamin or mineral supplement may be required to maintain good health.

It is important to recognize that malnutrition can be caused by several factors. It is not just those people who don't have enough food to eat who have nutrition problems. In fact, millions of Americans who can afford to eat well suffer from malnutrition.

Nutrition
the characteristics of food and the impact of food on the body.

NUTRIENTS

Nutrients are substances required for body functioning. Proteins, carbohydrates, fats, vitamins, and minerals are such essentials. A minimum amount of each is needed for energy, growth, tissue maintenance and repair, and to keep the systems of the body functioning properly. While water and fiber are not nutrients in the strictest sense, they are also essential to physical well-being. The following descriptions of nutrients will give you a better understanding of nutrients and their roles in good health.

PROTEIN Protein forms the foundation of every living cell in your body. Since your body is constantly using protein, it must be replaced to maintain good health. Bones, muscles, skin, hair, and nails all need protein. Some body energy is also derived from protein. The best sources of this nutrient are meat, poultry, fish, cheese, milk, eggs, and beans.

CARBOHYDRATES Carbohydrates are the body's main source of energy. They are found in grain products, such as bread and cereal, sugar, honey, and starches. When the body does not have an adequate supply of carbohydrates, proteins and fats are used up. Carbohydrates are needed so that protein can be used to rebuild the body rather than to supply energy.

FATS Some people may believe that they should eliminate fats from the diet. This is not true. Stored fat can be used as an emergency energy supply. Fatty tissue helps retain body heat and protects the vital organs and other parts of the body from injury. We should avoid an excess of animal fat in the diet, however.

VITAMINS A regular intake of vitamins is essential to good health, and a well-balanced diet will supply the vitamins you need. Cereal, milk, and some other foods sometimes have vitamins added. Many people also choose to take care of possible deficiencies in their diets with a daily vitamin supplement. Even so, the diets of many people are deficient in vitamins they should have. A well-balanced diet is, in most cases, the best solution.

MINERALS A sensible daily diet can also provide needed minerals. All protein foods, for example, contain some minerals. Milk and milk products are rich in calcium. Sources of iron, an important ingredient of blood, are liver, green leafy vegetables, and raisins. In addition to calcium and iron, our bodies need phosphorus, iodine, magnesium, copper, zinc, and numerous other minerals. A daily vitamin supplement often also contains minerals.

FIBER Although fiber does not have nutrient value, it is important in the elimination of body waste. Common sources of fiber are whole-grain breads and cereals, popcorn, apples, peas, and broccoli.

WATER The human body is about 65 percent water. Constant replacement of this body water is essential. In fact, a person can live without food longer than without water. A week without water could prove fatal, but one can survive for weeks without food.

FUNKY WINKERBEAN

A BALANCED DIET

A balanced diet means that we obtain nourishment daily from combinations of different types of foods. The original four basic food groups you may have learned about in earlier education have been modified due to better understanding of body needs and more awareness of health factors related to our diets.

The federal Food and Drug Administration now requires food labeling containing nutrition facts on almost all food products. The new labeling is easier for

Food Guide Pyramid
A Guide to Daily Food Choices

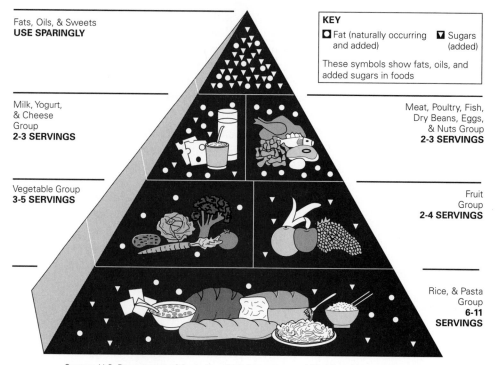

Source: U.S. Department of Agriculture/U.S. Department of Health and Human Services.

the ordinary consumer to understand than has been the case in the past. Also, to help us with our nutrition needs, the U.S. Department of Agriculture/U.S. Department of Health and Human Services now recommends a Food Guide Pyramid as a guide to daily food choices. The recommended amounts in each of the six categories are shown in the illustration of the pyramid.

THE CALORIE COUNT

As mentioned earlier, energy is supplied by proteins, carbohydrates, and fats. A **calorie** is a measure of the energy supplied by what we eat and drink. One pound of weight is equivalent to 3,500 calories. One of the ways often suggested for determining whether you are overweight is by what is called the pinch test. Pinch a fold of skin and fat at your waist or the underside of your upper arm. If you are pinching more than an inch, you are probably overweight.

To some extent you can vary the balance between the calories you eat and the calories you use. If you eat 500 extra calories today, you can eat a little less tomorrow and get a little more exercise. It's a good idea occasionally to look at a chart indicating the number of calories certain foods contain and the number of calories that are used by certain activities. A cup of string beans contains only 25 calories, whereas a cup of macaroni and cheese contains 350. Twenty potato chips contain about 150 calories—and that's without dip. On the other hand, walking briskly for a half hour uses up about 170 calories. Swimming and running burn up over twice that many. A combination of diet control and exercise is needed for weight reduction and the maintenance of wellness.

Weight loss medication should be used with caution. According to a Mayo Clinic Health Letter, "Medication should be used only if you weigh at least 30 percent above your ideal weight and you have a serious health condition related to your weight" (2). Among cautions given to would-be users of such medications, without a physician's approval, are that there could be health risks, that they may not work for some persons, and that long-term treatment may be necessary to keep weight off.

In our discussion of both nutrients and calories, we should also consider **nutrient density,** or the amount of nutrients contained in a food in proportion to the number of calories. A 12-ounce can of regular cola contains 150 calories, for example, but it has little or no nutritional value. An equal amount of skim milk, on the other hand, contains, protein, minerals, and vitamins and is only about 120 calories.

It's important to check food labels carefully if you are interested in maintaining a healthy diet.

Those who have become more conscious of nutrition are also reading food labels more carefully. We can now check nutrient content, calories per serving, various types of fat content, sodium, and other ingredients. Restaurants are also providing their customers with information on calories and fat content of various menu items.

Calorie
a unit of energy or the fuel value of food.

Nutrient density
the amount of nutrients contained in a food in proportion to the number of calories.

It can be confusing and sometimes deceiving to ordinary consumers, like most of us, to pay attention to what we are eating and drinking and their effects on our well-being. But no one should be expected to be more responsible for what we do to and for our bodies than ourselves. We must also remember that our physical conditions affect other aspects of holistic health.

SUGGESTIONS FOR HEALTHFUL EATING

Individual needs, lifestyles, and values vary, and they all affect our eating habits and wellness. The following guidelines should at least be considered in maintaining wellness, however. Doesn't everyone want to be well?

- Watch your eating habits. It is recommended that you eat only when seated at a table, lunch counter, or wherever for you is a regular place to eat.

- Do not eat just for something to do. Also avoid eating when you are angry or nervous but not really hungry.

- Take your time when you eat. We can often eat less but enjoy eating more. Give your attention to your enjoyment of your food, rather than eating while you are reading, watching television, or doing something else.

- Avoid too much caffeine, found in coffee, tea, cola, and chocolate. There are 100 milligrams (mg) of caffeine in a cup of regular coffee, and it is recommended that we do not exceed 200 to 300 milligrams a day.

- Avoid crash or fad diets. The basic idea is to have an understanding of nutrients, calories, and sensible eating habits. It is better to learn to live and eat differently than to try to lose a large amount of weight in a short time.

- Learn to shop wisely. We probably all watch prices, but we should also read labels. On a label, the first ingredient listed is present in a greater amount than any of the other ingredients.

- Avoid junk food. Don't even buy junk food. If you are in the habit of eating such food and snacks, cut down, at least.

- Learn to cook. One of the reasons why Americans eat so much junk food is that they don't know how to cook or don't bother to. Anybody who can read this book can learn to cook.

- Follow the basic guidelines in the Food Guide Pyramid, including a good supply of fiber.

- Avoid excessive salt, sugar, saturated fats, red meat, and preservatives such as nitrates in meats.

- Drink more water, including a glass of water before or with a meal. Six to eight glasses of water daily are recommended, in addition to water we consume in other drinks or foods.

Will there come a time when all of the nutrients we need will be available in pills? Can you imagine yourself so busy that you would prefer a handful of nutrient capsules as your daily diet? Would such a diet provide you with better health? Read what an article entitled "The New Scoop on Vitamins," in *Time* has to say on this subject:

> Call it the Jetson diet: a futuristic feast of prefab pellets containing all the nourishment any 21st century citizen would want. It makes for a nice cartoon fantasy, but could people really eat this way? Not a chance. Real food is here to stay.
> Multiple-vitamin pills do not contain the fiber, carbohydrates, and proteins necessary for maintaining the body and giving it energy. Such nutrients can be put into pills, but they would have to be taken in such large quantities that they would be impractical—not to mention tasteless—substitutes for real food (3).

Eating is a human experience that most people enjoy. We shouldn't just "live to eat," but on the other hand, most of us want more than to "eat to live," or to provide for our nutritional needs in the simplest way possible.

 What Will You Do? *What will you do to improve your eating habits as a result of the information, and reminders, discussed in the nutrition section of this chapter?*

PHYSICAL FITNESS

We would probably all like to be physically fit. Many of us look at others who appear to be physically fit and wonder whether they really had to do what we think we would have to do to *become* physically fit. Many of us ride nearly everywhere we go and take elevators or escalators instead of climbing the stairs in buildings. Work is more sedentary than it used to be, requiring less physical activity. Americans generally have become spectators rather than participants. Leisure hours are often spent watching television and walking to the kitchen for snacks. There are numerous benefits, however, to our becoming more physically fit, if we recognize that there is room for improvement.

Posture and physical fitness are related: One affects the other. Poor posture can cause cramping of internal organs, interfere with circulation, and produce muscle strain. Good posture, on the other hand, is easier and more natural when you have proper weight distribution and good muscle tone and coordination. When people are confident that they look good, they have a favorable self-concept and, consequently, feel better about the rest of the world, too. They are happier and easier to get along with wherever they may be.

WHAT IS PHYSICAL FITNESS?

Fitness Fundamentals, developed by the President's Council on Physical Fitness and Sports, states,

> Physical fitness is to the human body what fine tuning is to an engine. It enables us to perform up to our potential. Fitness can be described as a condition that helps us to look, feel, and do our best. More specifically, it is:
>
> > the ability to perform daily tasks vigorously and alertly, with energy left over for enjoying leisure-time activities and meeting emergency demands. It is the ability to endure, to bear up, to withstand stress, to carry on in circumstances where an unfit person could not continue, and is a major basis for good health and well-being.
> >
> > Physical fitness involves the performance of the heart and lungs, and the muscles of the body. And since what we do with our bodies also affects what we can do with our minds, fitness influences to some degree qualities such as mental alertness and emotional stability (4).

Four basic qualities are usually associated with physical fitness. They are flexibility, muscular strength, muscular endurance, and cardiorespiratory endurance.

Recreation and exercise are often combined and lead to healthy lifestyles.

Flexibility is the ability to move one's muscles freely, with a full range of motion. Muscular strength refers to the ability to apply force for a relatively brief time. Muscular endurance is the ability of a muscle, or a group of muscles, to continue applying force against a fixed object. Push-ups are often used, for example, to test endurance. Probably the most important component of fitness is cardiorespiratory endurance. This pertains to the ability of the circulatory system to supply adequate oxygen and nutrients to the body over a sustained time. The process involves taking oxygen into the lungs, distributing it to the muscles, and getting it back to the heart and then to the lungs to begin the cycle again.

Another term often associated with physical fitness is *motor fitness*. Motor fitness refers to the physical abilities dominated by the kinesthetic, or muscle sense, including balance, flexibility, agility, strength, power, and muscular endurance. Motor fitness plays an important part in the coordination necessary for playing games and sports, maintaining balance on slippery sidewalks, standing on a bus or subway, and moving with ease.

STARTING YOUR OWN PHYSICAL FITNESS PROGRAM

There are many physical fitness programs. An exercise program called aerobics, developed by U.S. Air Force doctor Kenneth H. Cooper, has become very popular. **Aerobics** is a physical fitness program of exercises that stimulate heart and lung functioning. A major objective of the program is to increase the supply of oxygen to all parts of the body to improve and maintain physical fitness. Numerous other aerobic exercise programs have been developed.

Aerobics
physical fitness program or exercises to stimulate functioning of the heart and lungs.

Anyone can develop a personal physical fitness program. Basically it is a plan for understanding your current state of wellness and physical fitness, setting realistic goals for the condition you would like to attain, and developing a schedule of activities that will help you to attain those goals.

Unless you know your current state of health and fitness, it is recommended that you have a checkup and approval of a physician before beginning a rigorous fitness program. When determining realistic goals, review existing fitness programs to get ideas about how often certain types of exercises or activities should be done and how long it takes to get results. In most cases, vigorous exercise for thirty minutes at a time three or four times a week is recommended. It is also recommended that one start with stretches of the muscles that are used most. Both a warm-up and a cool-down period are important each time you engage in your physical fitness activities.

One of the problems with most of us is that we want too much too soon in terms of results and are discouraged if we don't perceive the benefits of the program in a short time. Keeping a chart of your activities and progress helps to keep your fitness program organized and consistent. This is an important factor in achieving results. A progress chart also encourages you to continue toward your goal. Those who are physically fit at the present time should remember that it is easier to maintain good health and physical fitness than to attempt to regain them later in life. Some activities appropriate for a physical fitness program are discussed briefly in the following sections.

RUNNING Everybody—just about—is running. Some of those who aren't are talking about starting. It is an inexpensive, stimulating way for millions of people to relax and keep themselves in shape. Most people who run speak with favor of the psychological as well as physical benefits of running. It is not quite as easy as it looks, however. There are cautions about exposure to heat or cold or overexertion. Anyone thinking about becoming a serious runner should check with a reliable source for advice about how to run or jog safely.

WALKING Not to be overlooked is the value of the common and natural exercise of walking. It increases one's cardiorespiratory fitness and helps keep a person trim. Walking can be both relaxing and invigorating; it can also take us to some of the places we want to go. Although it is preferable to have comfortable shoes with good support, walking does not require special equipment. In addition to being a good basic physical fitness activity for all of us, walking has other advantages. Regular walking also can lower blood pressure, help lose weight, relieve back pain, and generally improve how a person thinks and feels.

SWIMMING Although swimming does require a place to swim, it is considered one of the best forms of exercise. It involves all of the major muscles of our arms, legs, and body trunk and contributes to total body development and well-being. If you are serious about swimming for physical fitness, you should swim in a facility that has lanes so that you can swim without interference. Your goal might be to swim continuously for twenty to thirty minutes. The crawl stroke is considered excellent, but a variety of strokes should be used. People of any age, and even people with disabilities, can swim and benefit from this activity. It is not necessary to belong to a health club to be able to swim during most of the year. Many schools and public facilities have indoor pools. To benefit from swimming as an exercise, one doesn't necessarily have to swim all year long. Other types of exercise can be substituted when swimming is not practical.

JUMPING ROPE Jumping rope used to be mainly a children's activity or a training exercise for boxers and athletes. In recent years, however, it has become a widely popular fitness exercise, included in many organized fitness programs. It is also good exercise for those who cannot leave their living quarters or do not care to. Its numerous forms can be tailored to suit the interests and stamina of the individual.

Since jumping rope can be very strenuous, someone with a health problem should not begin this exercise without a physician's recommendation. Even a person in good health should start working out gradually. Ten minutes of vigorous rope jumping can be equivalent to thirty minutes of jogging. As with all exercises, there should be three phases: a warm-up period, a workout, and a cooling-off phase.

SITTING For those who are involved in work that requires many hours of sitting, there are even exercises that can be done in a chair. Such exercises include "jogging in your chair" by first raising one heel as high as possible and then the other, at the same time raising your arms in a bent position and rocking rhythmically forward and back as in walking. Even a class could well begin with a moment of such jogging. This activity might jog our mental powers a bit, also.

Many people combine keeping physically fit with relaxation and enjoyment. Team sports, racketball, and cross-country skiing serve all these purposes for growing numbers of people. Regularity in an exercise program is important to keeping physically fit.

What Would You Suggest? *If a friend asked you, "How can I get more exercise when I just don't have the time for a fitness program?" What would you suggest?*

THREATS TO WELLNESS

In spite of a better-educated public and advances in medicine, threats to wellness are increasing. Some of the major threats are discussed in this section.

STRESS

The effects of undue stress and some ways to use a reasonable amount of stress were discussed in Chapter 10. We know that too much stress, particularly over time, can cause illness. This phenomenon shows how emotional, mental, social, and physical aspects of a person's life are interrelated.

Psychosomatic illness a physical disorder caused or aggravated by stress and unpleasant emotions.

Physical illness caused by or made worse by emotions and stress is called **psychosomatic illness.** This type of illness is not imaginary. It causes very real pain, and the person can become seriously ill. But the cause of the illness has been tension or another unpleasant emotional experience over time. The resulting stress can cause chronic headaches, backaches, muscular pains, circulatory problems, and ulcers. Some physicians believe that at least half the patients in their waiting rooms have health problems caused by stress. Dr. Hans Selye, referred to in Chapter 10, calls this type of stress "distress." Common signals of harmful effects of stress include pounding of the heart, feelings of overall exhaustion, inability to sleep well or to relax, and a general feeling of frustration. These, in turn, can lead to more serious physical problems. Persons experiencing such problems often seek relief in increased smoking or alcohol or drug abuse, which only worsens their difficulties.

DRUG ABUSE AND ADDICTION

You are no doubt aware of the importance of prescribed drugs to wellness. Not all drugs are bad for us; nor are all drugs good for us. Sometimes it is not the drug itself but abuse of the drug that has harmful effects. *Drug abuse* is the use of a drug for other than medicinal purposes. It includes the use of illegal drugs but also the overuse and misuse of prescription drugs. In addition to possible harmful physical effects, there can be a psychological dependence that interferes with a person's ability to function at school, at work, or as a member of a family. *Drug addiction* refers to a biochemical or physiological dependence on drugs or a particular drug. A person who is addicted to a drug usually needs help in breaking the dependence that is grossly interfering with his or her wellness and life. All such misuses of drugs can cause physical as well as mental, emotional, financial, and social problems.

Drugs can be classified in different ways. They are commonly classified broadly as depressants, stimulants, hallucinogens, narcotics, inhalants, and cannabis sativa. A brief description and some examples of each of these classifications follows.

DEPRESSANTS Drugs belonging to this classification are commonly referred to as "downers" because they slow the activity of the central nervous system. Barbiturates and tranquilizers are examples of depressants. Although depressants and antianxiety sedatives are legal and are often prescribed, they can become addictive. Overdose can result in coma or death.

STIMULANTS These drugs are essentially the opposite of depressants and are commonly referred to as "uppers." They tend to increase the activity of the central nervous system. Amphetamines, cocaine, and crack belong to this group. Crack, a smokable form of cocaine, delivers a much greater impact than "snorting" cocaine and can cause death from heart or respiratory failure. Caffeine is also a stimulant and is relatively harmless if used in moderation. Expectant mothers are advised not to use it, however, because of possible harmful effects on their unborn babies.

HALLUCINOGENS Lysergic acid diethylamide (LSD) belongs to this classification. Hallucinogens are so named because they cause perceptual distortions or hallucinations. Those who use them are usually seeking a sense of euphoria, but in some cases they cause frightening perceptual experiences or violent reactions that can lead to death.

NARCOTICS Opiates is another term for this classification of drugs because they are derived from the opium plant. Opium, morphine, codeine, and heroin are narcotics. Although some of these drugs do have legitimate medicinal purposes in relieving pain, they can become addictive, and overdose can also cause death.

INHALANTS Chemicals that are inhaled or "sniffed" to get the user high belong to this category. Such chemicals are found in paints, lighter fluids, glues, aerosols, and insecticides. These products are readily available, and adolescents are the largest users. Many users are simply after fun and adventure without realizing the dangers involved. Effects can include liver and kidney damage, brain damage, or even death by instant heart failure.

CANNABIS SATIVA Marijuana and hashish, which belong to this category, are derived from the hemp plant. Marijuana consists of crushed stems, leaves, and flowers of the plant, whereas hashish is its dried resin. Both are smoked. Among possible adverse effects are perceptual distortions, short-term memory loss, and interference with the reproductive system. Marijuana is sometimes classified as a hallucinogen.

According to the Department of Health and Human Services, "Contrary to many young people's beliefs, marijuana is a harmful drug, especially since the potency of marijuana now available has increased more than 275 percent over the last decade. For those who smoke marijuana now, the dangers are much more serious than they were in the 1960s" (5).

What Would You Suggest? *What are some additional ways drug abuse could be reduced in today's society?*

Alcohol and nicotine are also drugs that can be addictive and are discussed separately in the following sections. These drugs, in addition to marijuana, are sometimes referred to as "gateway drugs" because they are believed, in some cases, to lead to the use of drugs described above.

It is important to recognize that drugs do not affect all persons in the same way. In a publication entitled *A Guide to Commonly Abused Drugs*, the effect of any drug is related to the following factors:

- The expectations of the user
- The setting in which the use takes place
- The amount of the drug taken
- How often it is taken
- The user's personality
- The body weight of the user (6)

Drug abuse and addiction continue to be a major problem in the United States and throughout the world. It is important that we all learn about drugs and their effects. Education is not the only answer, however. Illegal drug traffic is a major concern, and more effective apprehension and prosecution of dealers is essential. Floyd E. Bloom, in an editorial in *Science,* states,

> Despite growing investment of federal and state funds in controlling the supply of illegal drugs (amounting to at least twice the total annual U.S. expenditure on biomedical research), all price indicators suggest that supplies have not been constrained. Estimates of illicit drug use suggest undiminished numbers of hardcore users and growing numbers of inexperienced youthful abusers, for whom even the tobacco and alcohol products used by adults are illegal (7).

More effective apprehension and prosecution of drug dealers is obviously needed. Continued educational efforts are also important. But the individual user is responsible too. The abuse of drugs is partly attitudinal. Many do not accept the reality that drugs can ruin their lives because they believe they can handle what they are doing. Evidence proves, however, that most cannot.

What Would You Do? *If you observed disturbing signs of poor health in a friend, what would you do?*

ALCOHOLISM

Alcohol is not only a drug: It is considered by many to be the most abused drug in the United States. One of the reasons is that, to some extent, it is socially acceptable to "drink." Many people use alcohol as a temporary escape from the problems and stresses of everyday life.

Alcoholism
compulsion to consume alcohol caused by physiological, psychological, and social factors.

There is a difference between problem drinking and **alcoholism,** which is an illness whereby a person has a compulsion to consume alcohol. There are millions of alcoholics in our society today, and each of them contributes to problems and suffering for many more.

The Alcoholism Council of Greater New York defines alcoholism as:

> A complex illness caused by a combination of physical, cultural, and psychological factors. Alcoholism can be identified whenever drinking consistently interferes with daily life: job, family, and health. Warning signals include

blackouts (amnesia), withdrawal symptoms (shaking, hallucinations), morning drinking, or gulping of drinks. At the levels consumed in chronic alcoholism, ethanol (alcohol) is toxic to most of the organs and systems in the body, including the brain, liver, kidneys, pancreas, blood and the respiratory and cardiovascular systems. Alcoholism's physical toll can lead to death—but alcoholism is treatable and the alcoholic can fully recover (8).

Alcoholism, like other illnesses, has some specific warning signals. Any one or more of the following signs may indicate a drinking problem:

- Family or social problems caused by drinking
- Job or financial difficulties related to drinking
- Loss of a consistent ability to control drinking
- "Blackouts," or the inability to remember what happened while drinking
- Distressing physical and/or psychological reactions if someone tries to stop drinking
- A need to drink increasing amounts of alcohol to get the desired effect
- Marked changes in behavior or personality when drinking
- Getting drunk frequently
- Injuring yourself—or someone else—while intoxicated
- Breaking the law while intoxicated
- Starting the day with a drink

If any of the above warning signals apply to you, you should seriously evaluate your drinking and your lifestyle. If others have been trying to convince you that you have a problem, it is time to start listening to them. One of the biggest difficulties in identifying one's own problem is the tendency to deny. Admitting that one is an alcoholic is the first step toward controlling the problem.

Alcoholics Anonymous (AA) has helped many persons solve their problem and change their lives. This organization consists of recovering alcoholics who admit their individual helplessness. They openly place their trust in a Higher Power and in support from one another. Al-Anon and Al-a-Teen groups are for family members of alcoholics. These groups help families to understand the alcoholic and to cope with their own situation.

The topic of drug abuse could be an extensive study in itself. Also, there is still much that is unknown of the long-term effects of several drugs. Extensive research is being conducted, and we can expect to know more about the effects of drugs in the future.

SMOKING

Is it possible for anyone not to know that smoking is a threat to health? Many people have learned to use denial—to ignore the warning on their packages of cigarettes, however. Most public places do not permit smoking. Others allow people to smoke only in designated areas. Some restaurants have moved from having smoking and nonsmoking sections to becoming totally nonsmoking establishments. This is intended primarily to protect the rights of nonsmokers. There is increasing evidence that "passive smoking," or breathing smoke-filled air, can also be a health hazard.

Even though nicotine in cigarettes is addictive, there is probably no one who could not quit smoking if he or she really wanted to. The critical factor is determining that you want better health for yourself and those who share your environment. Many people quit on their own—with varying degrees of difficulty and success. Some programs involve hypnosis; others advocate wearing nicotine patches. Those who wear such patches should be aware that there are additional health hazards if a person smokes while wearing them. In spite of everything, the motivation of the smoker is usually the determining factor. The smoker faces an approach-avoidance conflict. Does he or she want to quit smoking enough to endure what is entailed in becoming a nonsmoker?

Smokeless tobacco has been substituted for cigarette smoking by some people. However, that, too, can be hazardous. Its use can lead to oral cancer, which is painful, disfiguring, and disabling, and can be fatal.

SEXUALLY TRANSMITTED DISEASES

Sexually transmitted diseases (STDs) are diseases of the sex organs that eventually affect the whole body. Syphilis and gonorrhea were once the most common types, and they still affect millions of people every year. More recently, however, several new types of STDs have been identified. They are nongonococcal urethritis (NGU) and type 2 herpes simplex.

STDs are spread by direct sexual contact. They are found most frequently in an age group ranging from the early teens to the late twenties. There may be no early symptoms of the disease, and even when there are early signs of possible STD, they may disappear. This does not mean the disease is cured, however. In nearly all cases, an STD needs treatment to be cured. It is extremely important that STDs be recognized and treated properly. Minors can now be treated for STDs without parental knowledge or consent.

Health and medical personnel urge those who suspect they have an STD to contact a doctor, school nurse, or public health agency. They will not be punished or even embarrassed unnecessarily. It is also important to give the names and addresses of others with whom there has been sexual contact because these people must also be treated for the disease and prevented from spreading it further. Because people needlessly fear seeking medical help or hesitate to give the names of others involved, a disease that can be controlled has become an epidemic. Syphilis and gonorrhea can be cured with penicillin. Other antibiotics are effective in most cases of NGU. There is promising research being conducted for the treatment of type 2 herpes simplex.

All types of STDs should be given medical attention as soon as they are suspected. Untreated venereal disease can result in damage to the nervous system, mental illness, and sterility; it also can endanger unborn children. Because it takes so many lives, AIDS will be discussed separately in the next section.

AIDS

Acquired immune deficiency syndrome (AIDS) is caused by the human immunodeficiency virus (HIV). One can carry the virus for a long time without being aware of it because it takes an average of 10 years for AIDS to develop after someone is infected. AIDS results in a weakening and finally a destruction of the body's immune defenses. The immune system of our body defends us against disease. In later stages of AIDS, the individual is no longer able to combat even a mild illness or infection, and death results. Michel Thuriaux and Suzanne Cherney, in *World Health,* share the following opinion:

> AIDS is more than a personal or a social tragedy. In our minds, the infection is closely linked to aspects of life that are hard to talk about, such as sexuality (heterosexual or homosexual) and drug injecting. So to sickness and death must be added the burden of unspoken fears, isolation, social exclusion and the popular belief that "AIDS is other people." This very image of AIDS is part of the problem, and persists even though directly or indirectly, we are all confronted by the fact of AIDS with increasing frequency (9).

HOW IS AIDS ACQUIRED? The most common means of acquiring AIDS is through sexual intercourse with someone who has the HIV virus or by using drug-injection needles that have been contaminated by infected blood. Pregnant women who have HIV can also transmit the disease to their unborn babies. In the past, some hemophiliacs developed AIDS after receiving transfusions of blood containing the HIV virus. Since 1985, however, all blood has been screened before transfusions, so that this risk no longer exists. AIDS, it is widely agreed by medical authorities, is not transmitted through kissing, by shaking hands, by using public restrooms or swimming pools, from food handlers, or through casual contact with a person who has AIDS. Caution should be taken, however, in contacting a person who is bleeding.

WHAT ARE THE SYMPTOMS? It may be difficult to identify the symptoms of this disease. Some resemble symptoms of other ailments. For example, a person with swollen glands and a fever may be believed to have some other infectious illness. Other symptoms may include excessive tiredness, pink or purple blotches or bumps, sore throat, easy bruising, bleeding from any area of the body, or severe headaches. Some people who are HIV positive may not have any of these symptoms, at least not for many years. In the meantime they may be infecting others with the virus. Those who suspect that they may have been exposed to HIV should be clinically tested.

WHO ARE THE VICTIMS? According to the Center for Disease Control in Atlanta, the largest number of persons in the United States with AIDS have been homosexual or bisexual men and drug addicts who share needles. Of the newer cases, a growing number have been women involved in heterosexual relationships. Heterosexual individuals who have multiple sex partners are passing HIV to others. Married persons having extramarital sexual relations are infecting their spouses. And, as mentioned earlier, unborn babies may develop AIDS from their mothers. AIDS is becoming a disease that potentially could claim anyone as a victim.

There has been a decrease in the number of deaths annually due to AIDS because new treatments are allowing those with the disease to live longer. There is still no preventive vaccine or cure, however. Some are optimistic about still better treatments and a cure, but we must be realistic about the current dangers of this disease to individuals and to society.

Everyone should be knowledgeable about AIDS. School health services and public health departments can provide additional information about this life-threatening disease and preventive measures. A newsletter, P.R.I.D.E. (People Related Immune Deficiency Epidemic), is also available to those who have AIDS or others who are interested (10). Information and assistance available to those in the workplace will be discussed as part of employee assistance programs later in the chapter.

What Would You Say? *If a coworker confided to you, "I don't want any contact with a person who has AIDS," what would you say?*

EATING DISORDERS

For reasons that are not entirely understood, eating disorders have become a serious health hazard in today's society. The three most common disorders, anorexia nervosa, bulimia, and binging, will be described briefly here.

Anorexia nervosa is often referred to as the "starving disease." It is most common among adolescent girls and young women who take losing weight to a dangerous and sometimes fatal extreme. A key element in the disease is what is called "distorted body image." As strange as it may seem to others, victims of anorexia nervosa perceive themselves as undesirably fat, even when they are dangerously thin.

Bulimia nervosa is an eating disorder in which the individuals go on eating binges and then take laxatives, induce vomiting, or exercise excessively to rid themselves of the effects of the food they have consumed. As with anorexia nervosa, this disease is most common among adolescent girls and young women.

Binge eating is similar to bulimia in some ways but is considered a separate eating disorder. Those who binge, like bulimics, eat large amounts of food, but they do not attempt to purge, or get rid of, the food they have consumed. Most people with this disorder are understandably obese.

According to Beatrice T. Hunter of *Consumers' Research,*

> Eating disorders are complex and cannot be treated solely with dietary means. Individual cases may need to address fundamental psychological, familial, societal, and cultural aspects of the disorder. The development of an eating disorder is not necessarily triggered only by a desire to be thin. Although much has been written about the role of Hollywood, professional models, and the media in presenting unrealistic body images to young people, the main cause of eating disorders is not from trying to achieve the perfect body. . . . Depression, anxiety, loneliness, stress, anger, troubled relationships may all contribute to disordered eating patterns (11).

If you think you might have an eating disorder, talk to a counselor, nurse, or family doctor about it.

OTHER THREATS

Among the numerous other threats to wellness in today's world are various environmental hazards such as pollution of water, soil, and air. Asbestos is known to cause lung problems. Cholesterol is believed to cause heart disease. Food additives are suspected of causing cancer. There is also growing concern about overexposure to radiation. It is obviously impossible to avoid all threats to our total well-being. However, it seems sensible to avoid or counteract the factors that seem most dangerous or potentially harmful.

Anorexia nervosa
an eating disorder most common among young females; disease in which people believe they must continue to lose weight even after becoming dangerously thin.

Bulimia nervosa
an eating disorder in which individuals go on eating binges and then take laxatives, induce vomiting, or exercise excessively to rid themselves of the effects of the food they have consumed.

Binge eating
an eating disorder in which individuals eat large amounts of food at one sitting but do not attempt to purge what they've consumed.

What Do You Know? *Do you know of any serious threats to wellness that were not mentioned in this section? If so, how might they be avoided or counteracted?*

PROPER TREATMENT

Although we can do a lot to maintain our wellness, most of us are limited in our ability to test and treat ourselves. You may be familiar with some of the self-diagnostic devices for measuring blood pressure, blood sugar levels, and other conditions. These have their merit, but they should supplement, rather than substitute for, professional attention.

Alternative medicine is a term you may be hearing more often. Perhaps some form of alternative medicine or treatment such as the use of herbs, hypnosis, acupuncture, or biofeedback has been helpful to you. Isadore Rosenfeld, M.D., in *Dr. Rosenfeld's Guide to Alternative Medicine,* points out,

> [T]he gap between "conventional" and "unconventional" practitioners is narrowing, as more and more doctors (and patients) realize that the "other" medicine can no longer be ignored, that *any* rational and promising approach must be evaluated impartially and scientifically. One of the main reasons for this attitude, in addition to societal pressure, is that newer diagnostic techniques, and the appreciation of the tie between the brain (where emotion is generated) and the immune system (whose strength and integrity determine vulnerability and resistance to disease), have resulted in a better understanding of how some forms of alternative medicine may be effective (12).

"Before you examine me, promise me nothing's wrong."

Reprinted from The Saturday Evening Post.

We should keep in mind that there are still many unknowns with alternative medicines, however. Many unreliable or unethical sources attempt to take advantage of unwary individuals. Isadora B. Stehlin, in "An FDA Guide to Choosing Medical Treatments," offers the following "red flags" to watch out for in a section called "Tip-Offs to Rip-Offs":

- Claims the product works by a secret formula. (Legitimate scientists share their knowledge or their peers can review their data.)
- Publicity only in the back pages of magazines, over the phone, by direct mail, in newspaper ads in the format of news stories, or 30-minute commercials in talk show format. (Results of studies on bona fide treatments are generally reported first in medical journals.)
- Claims the product is an amazing or miraculous breakthrough. (Real medical breakthroughs are few and far between, and when they happen, they're not touted as "amazing" or "miraculous" by any responsible scientist or journalist.)
- Promises of easy weight loss. (For most people, the only way to lose weight is to eat less and exercise more.)
- Promises of a quick, painless, guaranteed cure.
- Testimonials from satisfied customers. (These people may never have had the disease the product is supposed to cure, may be paid representatives, or may simply not exist. Often they're identified only by initials or first name.) (13)

These warnings do not imply that alternative medicines and treatments are of no value. But they do suggest that we should be alert to possible frauds or exaggerations.

On a lighter side, humor is gaining recognition today as contributing to wellness. Although the value of humor in staying well and even as a supplement to medical treatment of illness is not new, there is growing interest in its therapeutic effects. The American Association for Therapeutic Humor is an example of a networking source for the application of humor in the caregiving professions.

All efforts to maintain wellness must be realistic. There are times when a person has an illness or disease that requires professional advice and treatment. Family practice is an area of care concerned with preventive care as well as the health problems of the individual. Most clinics also have specialists to diagnose and treat particular problems.

It is impossible to state clearly and easily what is proper treatment in all cases. If you

Stretching before exercising is important to keep the body flexible and free from injury before exercising.

have a medical problem, you should be aware of your choices and take personal responsibility for medical decisions.

MENTAL HEALTH

We should not take our mental health for granted any more than we should take our physical health for granted. Although mental health is not necessarily the same for everyone, there are some common characteristics. Individuals are usually considered mentally healthy if their behavior falls within a normal range and if they are reasonably well adjusted and happy. But what is normal?

Do you consider yourself normal? Most people do. But what is a normal condition and what is normal behavior? The answer can be important to each of us in evaluating our state of wellness. It can also be important to professional people in suggesting and applying treatment for types of abnormality. It should be kept in mind that the difference between normal and abnormal is largely a matter of degrees of certain types of behavior rather than completely different kinds of behavior. Some fear is normal, for example, but fear of being among people one does not know can be abnormal.

One way to determine what is normal is by comparing one's behavior with that of others. It is normal to make some mistakes in judgment and to have some apprehension about failure. It is normal to experience some anxiety about starting a new job. But it is also normal to look forward to a vacation after you have been working on your job for a year. A range of behavior can be expected of normal human beings.

Another way to evaluate the normality of behavior is to consider what is typical of a particular individual. What is usual for one person may be very unusual for another. A still further method of determining what is normal is first to identify or define what is abnormal. Anything else, then, can be accepted as normal. It is abnormal to feel tired all the time or to "see things" that aren't there. We must have an understanding of what is normal to detect what is abnormal. But since the range of normality contains so many variations and degrees, it is sometimes easier to recognize what is outside the range of normal behavior. Common characteristics of a mentally healthy individual include the following:

- Accepts oneself; has a positive, realistic self-concept
- Can cope with situations in one's life
- Gives reasonable attention to total wellness
- Can problem-solve and make decisions effectively
- Understands one's fears and apprehensions
- Expresses emotions in acceptable, constructive ways
- Is responsible toward others
- Is basically content but is motivated to become more self-actualized

PSYCHOLOGICAL DISORDERS

Psychosis as a term for mental illness is declining in use in today's society. It is being replaced by more specific terms referring to psychological disorders. Therefore, the term *psychological disorder* will be used in our discussion of

Psychological disorder
difficulty or inability to adapt to the realities of life, including behavior that is considered abnormal.

these types of problems. *Psychological disorders* refer to the difficulty or inability to adapt to the realities of life. They include behavior usually considered abnormal in society, such as thought disturbances and difficulty in understanding oneself and relating to others. The causes of these disorders are somewhat debatable but they are believed to be influenced by genetic, physiological, psychological, and social factors. Psychological disorders are usually identified as the following types: *anxiety disorders, somatoform disorders, dissociative disorders, mood disorders, schizophrenic disorders,* and *personality disorders.* David G. Myers, in *Exploring Psychology,* gives us the following explanation of the classifications:

> In both psychiatry and psychology, diagnostic classification ideally aims to describe a disorder, to predict its future course, to imply appropriate treatment, and to stimulate research into its causes. Indeed to study a disorder we must first name it and describe it. The current authoritative scheme for classifying psychological disorders is The American Psychiatric Association's *Diagnostic and Statistical Manual of Mental Disorders (Fourth Edition)* nicknamed DSM-IV (14).

ANXIETY DISORDER

Generalized anxiety disorder, panic disorder, phobic disorder, and *obsessive-compulsive disorder* are the primary types of anxiety disorders. Each is briefly described below.

Generalized anxiety disorder
a disorder in which a person experiences a chronic overwhelming feeling of anxiety.

GENERALIZED ANXIETY DISORDER A chronic overwhelming feeling of anxiety characterizes **generalized anxiety disorder.** It is sometimes referred to as "free-floating anxiety" because it is difficult to determine what might be causing feelings of persistent nervousness and discomfort, both emotional and physical. It includes the characteristics of anxiety discussed in Chapter 5.

Panic disorder
a disorder in which a person experiences severe physiological symptoms.

PANIC DISORDER A person with a **panic disorder** experiences severe physiological symptoms such as heart pounding, a sense of choking, and dizziness. The attack comes on suddenly and, although it may last only a few minutes, it can be terrifying. The cause is usually unknown, but it is believed that both hereditary and psychological factors can be involved.

Phobic disorder
a disorder in which a person has severe abnormal, illogical fears.

PHOBIC DISORDER Phobias were also discussed in Chapter 5, and were defined as abnormal, illogical fears. Phobias can be relatively mild and not too disturbing or they may be severe and extremely frightening. The more severe phobias would ordinarily be considered a **phobic disorder.** Common types of phobic disorders relate to ordinary things, such as fear of cats, water, people, and public places. This last type, fear of public places, is called agoraphobia, and is one of the more common types of phobic disorders.

Obsession
an irrational thought that a person is unable to dismiss from his or her mind.

Obsessive-compulsive disorder
a disorder in which a person has an irrational thought that he or she is unable to dismiss from his or her mind.

OBSESSIVE-COMPULSIVE DISORDER As is indicated by the name **obsessive-compulsive disorder,** it involves two subtypes. An **obsession** is an irrational thought that a person is "hung up on" and is unable to dismiss from his or her mind. Obsessive-compulsive disorders can be relatively harmless, such as continuing to think about a particular person for no apparent reason, or they can be extremely disturbing. It is common, for example, for obsessions to pertain to violence or unacceptable moral behavior.

Compulsion
irresistible impulse to
engage in a certain
activity.

Compulsions involve uncontrollable repetition of behavior or rituals. The behavior has no rational purpose, but the person seems to be unable to stop the behavior, nonetheless. A very common type of compulsion is an excessive washing of one's hands. The merit of having clean hands cannot be denied, but persons with a compulsive disorder go beyond what would be considered practical and can't seem to restrain themselves. Obsessive thoughts can lead to compulsive behavior in the sense that persons who are obsessed with cleanliness will relieve some of the related anxiety by compulsive washing of the hands.

SOMATOFORM DISORDER

Conversion
a disorder in which one
loses a physical ability,
although there is no
physiological cause; for-
merly called hysteria.

Common examples of this disorder are **conversion** and **hypochondria.** With conversion, once referred to as hysteria, a person loses a physical ability even though there is no physically related cause. The condition is caused by emotional stress and is not necessarily permanent, but the individual usually needs professional help to overcome the disorder.

Hypochondria
type of neurosis charac-
terized by imaginary
physical ailments.

You probably have heard the term *hypochondriac,* but it is not always used correctly. Persons with this disorder think they have serious physical problems even though they may be in relatively good health. They interpret any minor disturbance as related to an illness, often associated with something they have recently heard about or seen on a television program. Hypochondriacs have a tendency to disbelieve results of medical tests and professionals.

DISSOCIATIVE DISORDER

Amnesia
loss of memory and
identity, usually brought
on by stress.

Amnesia, sometimes referred to as psychogenic amnesia, is one type of dissociative disorder. A person who experiences amnesia may lose his or her identity to the extent that they do not know who they are or any of the details of their past experience or lives. Amnesia is usually considered to be a reaction from emotional stress to the point at which those afflicted psychologically escape from their identities and responsibilities. Amnesia has been an element in fictional writing, but in reality it is not common.

Multiple personality
a disorder in which an
individual has several
distinct personalities,
usually in sharp contrast
to each other.

Multiple personality is a second dissociative disorder that has been the subject of books and movies, often based on actual cases. Two such examples are *Sybil* and *The Three Faces of Eve.* As is implied by the name of the disorder, such persons have two or more distinct personalities. Usually these personalities are in sharp contrast to one another. One may be very shy and proper, for example, and the other may be nonconforming and bold. The personalities may be unaware of one another, but each may reveal itself without any particular warning or explanation.

MOOD DISORDER

Major depression
a disorder characterized
by an uncontrollable
sense of sadness and
fatigue, to the extent that
the individual afflicted
has difficulty performing
daily functions.

Major depression, often simply referred to as depression, and bipolar depression, are the most common types of mood disorder. Although it is normal to have moods—to feel much better psychologically at some times than others—persons who experience major depression have an uncontrollable sense of sadness and fatigue, have difficulty in performing ordinary daily activities, and have a general sense that life is not worth the effort. Sometimes this type of depression is brought on by a traumatic event such as a death in the family and is referred to as *reactive depression.* This type of depression usually passes with time, although counseling may help the individual make the adjustment required. In contrast, depression can also be "inner," without being related to any specific experience in the person's life. This type of depression is usually more severe and longer lasting than reactive depression.

Physiological problems are also usually present with depression, such as difficulty in sleeping and eating. There is still some debate about the causes of depression, as with many other psychological disorders, but it often has both a psychological and biochemical basis. Severe depression that is not recognized and treated can lead to suicide.

Bipolar, or **manic-depressive disorder,** consists of extreme mood swings from experiencing feelings of high enthusiasm and energy to the type of despair described above. These mood changes tend to run in cycles and are not directly related to what the person is doing or what is happening in his or her life. Bipolar disorders are relatively rare, but can cause extreme difficulty for a person attempting to function consistently and constructively.

Manic-depressive disorder
a disorder in which a person goes from periods of mania (extreme activity and excitement) to depression (extreme sadness and gloom).

SCHIZOPHRENIC DISORDER

Schizophrenic disorder
a disorder in which one has a "split" in thoughts and emotions; the individual may become disoriented, hallucinate, and have delusions.

Schizophrenia has sometimes been confused with multiple personality disorder because it involves a "split" in thought and emotions. The person becomes disoriented and may have delusions or false beliefs about his or her identity. Persons with this disorder may also have hallucinations, often hearing voices that give them orders or ridicule them. The major classifications of schizophrenia are *disorganized,* whereby behavior is incoherent, bizarre or silly, and generally inappropriate; *catatonic,* whereby behavior ranges from unresponsiveness to extreme hyperactivity; *paranoid,* whereby a person generally has delusions of persecution, but may also have delusions of grandeur; and *undifferentiated,* whereby behavior does not fit the other classifications. Approximately half of the people admitted to hospitals for psychiatric treatment have schizophrenic disorder, but treatment, including new drug therapy, is increasingly encouraging.

PERSONALITY DISORDER

Personality disorder
a disorder in which a person experiences difficulty adapting to life and to interactions with others.

With a **personality disorder,** persons experience difficulty adapting to their personal lives and interactions with others. They have difficulty coping with life in ways that are generally considered within a normal range of behavior. *Antisocial personality* is one of the most common types of this disorder. Antisocial, in this sense, does not mean avoiding social interaction with others, as one might suspect. Instead, it consists of behavior that is irresponsible, aggressive, and often in violation of the rights of others.

TREATMENT OF PSYCHOLOGICAL DISORDERS

Many people who receive treatment for mental or psychological disorders are able to return to normal productive lives. It is also encouraging to know that many functional disorders can be prevented. People can learn to accept themselves, to adjust to others and situations, and to face problems realistically. There is increased emphasis, therefore, on mental health and the prevention of disorders. Also, promising new drugs that are effective in helping to control psychological disorders have been developed in recent years.

Recovery depends on the nature and degree of the disorder, as well as on the patient's desire to return to normal functioning and good mental health. It also, of course, depends on the quality of the treatment and care the person receives. In addition to assistance available from local and state agencies, treatment facilities include hospitals, outpatient clinics, and halfway houses. Many communities also provide housing for relatively independent living that is supervised by a mental health agency. In spite of these opportunities, however, it is believed that thousands of persons with psychological disorders live in the streets, suffering physical deprivation as well as the effects of the disorder itself.

There are several proven methods of treating psychological disorders. Treatment usually begins with a physical examination, including gathering of background information about the individual, such as work, personal activities, and medical and family history. The examination may also include laboratory tests. Types of treatment may include **biochemical therapy** (the use of prescription drugs), **electroconvulsive therapy** (ECT or electric shock, which is controversial but is sometimes used for severe depression), or a number of types of **psychotherapy.** With psychotherapy, emphasis is placed on the psychological, rather than the physical or chemical, treatment of the disorder, although some medication may be prescribed to treat disturbing symptoms during the process. The therapist and patient develop a trusting, open relationship so that the patient feels comfortable expressing himself or herself freely. Together they develop ways for the individual to learn more realistic coping skills.

Group therapy is often used with other types of therapy. Individuals with common disorders have the opportunity to interact with others and come to discover that their problems are not unique. Group members feel relatively safe in sharing experiences and expressing themselves. Although there are various types of independent support groups, this type of treatment as therapy is under the guidance of professionals.

The type of treatment used depends on the diagnosis of the disorder, the particular specialization of the therapist, and the preference of the patient or guardian. Clinical psychologists and psychiatric nurses provide various types of therapy, but most treatment is administered under the direction of a psychiatrist.

Misunderstanding about what a psychiatrist is and does is common. A **psychiatrist** is a physician who has specialized in the branch of medicine that diagnoses and treats persons with mental or psychological disorders. Those who go to a psychiatrist should not be judged to have a severe psychological disorder any more than a person who goes to an internal medicine specialist should be judged to have a serious physical illness. There are many degrees of all types of disorders. Many people recognize that they need professional help to maintain or restore the kind of mental health that will contribute to making their lives less stressful and more meaningful as a whole.

GETTING HELP

Any problem involving one's general wellness can be handled more easily if attended to at an early stage. Many health problems result from negligence; ignoring problems only makes them worse. When you are in need of help or advice with regard to any health problem, do not hesitate to seek help. People you respect and trust can usually give you some direction. These might include family members, friends, teachers, clergy members, or counselors. Another person

Biochemical therapy
use of prescription drugs to treat psychological disorders.

Electroconvulsive therapy
a therapy that uses electric shock as a treatment.

Psychotherapy
a therapy that relies on the psychological treatment of a disorder.

Group therapy
interaction with others in a group situation, under the guidance of a professional, as treatment for psychological disorders.

Psychiatrist
a physician who specializes in treating persons with mental and psychological disorders.

can view your situation more objectively. He or she can help you make a wise decision and can also give you support. The final responsibility for your well-being is yours, of course.

It may help to know that the American Hospital Association has issued a leaflet entitled *A Patient's Bill of Rights*. These rights include the right to be told about an illness and its treatment, the right to refuse treatment within legal limits, and the right to receive proper care and information about costs. You have the right to care about what is happening to you. You have the right to expect others to care also. Most persons working in health professions are dedicated to their work. It is seldom necessary to insist on one's rights.

GIVING HELP

It is not always easy to give or suggest help to a person who seems to need it. Sometimes people refuse to admit that they have a problem, especially if the problem involves drug or alcohol abuse or mental health. The following suggestions may be helpful:

1. Suggest a change in routine. Perhaps the person needs a change of pace or a vacation. Some people may need more relaxation. Others may need more meaningful activity.
2. Remind the person that no one is perfect. Discuss the value of living one day at a time, without excessive concern about the past or future and without excessive demands of oneself.
3. Encourage the person to see a doctor, a clergy member, or some other professional person.

Be patient. Be a good listener. Your suggestions will be accepted only if they are offered in the right way at the right time. Avoid being too pushy in trying to help others. People often have fears that make action difficult, or they may not be quite ready to do what you think they should. Too much pressure at the wrong time can do more harm than good. Knowing that others care and are available to talk or to help out in other ways is often what a person needs.

It can be difficult to recognize the need for outside help. For one thing, an illness may develop gradually. Neither the ill person nor others may be aware of the degree of change. Behavior that is generally considered abnormal—such as experiencing hallucinations—requires attention, however. Also, a drastic change in what would be considered normal in the habits of a particular person may be a sign of an impending serious illness. No one has perfect mental health at any one time; maintaining such perfection is no more possible than experiencing perfect physical health at all times. There are various degrees of mental health. A person who has most of the characteristics of a normal person is mentally healthy. Lacking one or two characteristics may cause problems but does not make a person mentally ill.

YOUR JOB AND WELLNESS

Your wellness is not strictly your own business. Your wellness is of concern to many others, even if you don't have a communicable disease. You would expect someone selling you health or life insurance, for example, to be interested in your physical condition. But prospective employers are also concerned about the health of the people they hire. Because businesses cannot operate properly with a reduced number of employees, absenteeism due to illness is of major importance to employers. Sick leave and replacement training are also costly. Even employees on the job who don't feel well can hinder effective operation. For these reasons you will be asked to indicate the condition of your health on most job applications; you may even be required to have a physical examination, including tests for drug use, before you are hired. You will also be required to follow safety regulations in your job environment and to report illness and injury. And there are government regulations pertaining to health and safety measures.

Hazards on the job also include unsanitary working conditions and noxious fumes or waste particles in the air. Injuries to the back and hands are also common. Hazards to the eyes and ears were discussed in Chapter 4, and are often associated with one's work. Stress, discussed in Chapter 10 and also earlier in this chapter, is considered a major factor in wellness related to one's work. Paul J. Rosch, in an article entitled "Job Stress: America's Leading Adult Health Problem," in *USA Today Magazine,* has the following to offer:

> The nature of job stress varies with different occupations, but affects workers at all levels. Some of the major sources that have been identified are:
>
> - Inadequate time to complete a job to one's satisfaction
> - Lack of clear job description or chain of command
> - Little recognition or reward for good job performance
> - Inability or lack of opportunity to voice complaints
> - Lots of responsibility, but little authority
> - Inability to work with superiors, coworkers, or subordinates because of basic differences in goals and values
> - Lack of control or pride over the finished product
> - Insecurity caused by pressures from within or without due to the possibility of takeover or merger
> - Prejudice because of age, gender, race, or religion
> - Unpleasant environmental conditions (smoky or polluted air, crowding, noise, fear of exposure to toxic chemicals or carcinogens)
> - Chronic commuting difficulties
> - Concerns related to responsibilities for employees
> - Not being able to utilize personal talents and abilities effectively or to full potential
> - Fear, uncertainty, and doubt (15)

EMPLOYEE ASSISTANCE PROGRAMS

The number of companies offering employee assistance programs (EAP) has increased in recent years. Both the organizations offering these programs and the employees have benefited. Business and industry have benefited from these programs as a result of less absenteeism and fewer worker compensation claims, for example. Employees are offered assistance with an array of concerns that may pertain to family problems, personal finances, alcohol and drug abuse, smoking, diet and exercise, safety, and stress management. Assistance with stress management helps to avoid *burnout,* discussed in Chapter 10.

The EAP program offered by the Wausau Hospital in Wisconsin is an example of a comprehensive program valuable to the organization and its employees and members of their families. It offers the following:

- Eight short-term counseling sessions, with referrals to community resources if recommended and desired by the employee.
- 24-hour toll-free helpline to employees and their family members.
- Supervisory training and consults to help supervisors recognize employee problems and to ask for assistance in dealing with problematic situations.
- Back to work "contracts" for disciplined employees.
- Case management for special service coordination on request or recommendation.
- Employee orientation to familiarize new employees with the EAP benefits and procedures.
- Quarterly newsletter covering various health and wellness issues.
- Topic brochures and presentations on wellness issues or timely subjects.
- Tailored services to meet special needs (16).

Important characteristics of this program, as well as similar programs, include commitment of management and participators, flexibility in meeting needs, and most important, confidentiality.

One of the most challenging approaches to wellness in the workplace pertains to employees with AIDS. The Americans with Disabilities Act (ADA), passed in 1990, requires employers to make reasonable accommodations to allow employees with AIDS or HIV to contribute as long as they are physically able. Many employees would be willing to do this without the legal requirement. In spite of the requirement, however, there are claims of firings, changes in insurance benefits, and harassment. It is important not only that those with AIDS be given job protection, but that other employees are informed about contact and relationships with workers with this disease. There are many myths about the disease and how it is transmitted (or not transmitted) that should be dispelled. Polaroid and Levi Strauss are examples of companies who have provided education and resources to both workers with AIDS and their coworkers. Better understanding will lead to more realistic attitudes and behavior.

The interest in employee wellness is not for the exclusive benefit of the company; there is obvious growing interest in employees as human beings with personal lives and responsibilities. The Family and Medical Leave Act, passed in 1993, recognizes such responsibilities. It provides for eligible employees to receive up to 12 weeks of unpaid leave per year following birth or adoption of a child or to care for a seriously ill child, spouse, or parent. All 12 weeks need not be taken at once. Most companies can make accomodations for their employees to take advantage of this act as needed.

HABITS

Habit
a pattern of behavior that has been repeated until it becomes automatic.

Although we may admit that we are creatures of habit, it isn't likely that we even know what all our habits are. A **habit** is a pattern of behavior that has been repeated until it becomes automatic. If a habit is something we do without thinking, it is understandable that we may not be aware of all our habits.

You hear about good and bad habits. It is more correct, however, to consider how a habit affects a particular person. What may be good for you may be harmful to someone else. Vigorous exercise is good for a healthy person. It may be fatal for someone with a heart problem.

BREAKING HABITS

To break a habit, one must first be aware of it and be motivated to change the behavior pattern. Even then, people who want to break a habit may have to make several attempts until they discover or work out the method that will be effective for them. They will also probably receive much advice. Some successful habit breakers advise, "Don't taper off unless this is recommended by medical authorities because of physiological effects. Decide you are going to quit a particular habit and do it. Don't allow yourself to 'one more time' your undesirable habit. Begin and don't make exceptions."

Sometimes outside help is needed or at least is beneficial in breaking habits. Doctors attempt to help people who seriously want to give up smoking. People meet in groups, are shown films of the harmful effects of smoking, and are then advised on how to break the habit. The degree of commitment to breaking a habit can be a deciding factor. Once individuals announce, so to speak, that they are going to do something, they suffer lack of self-esteem if they don't live up to that claim.

Others may advise, "Take your habit breaking one day at a time." This is one of the successful techniques used by Alcoholics Anonymous. The recovering alcoholic resolves not to take a drink today and makes the same resolution again tomorrow and the next day.

Breaking a habit as part of a group who has the same objective has proved successful for many. This is one of the methods used by weight-loss groups. Members have the common habit of eating too much or eating the wrong foods. By working at their common problem together, they make a commitment they feel obliged to fulfill. They also give one another moral support and encouragement.

As with all human behavior, habits are complex. The real reason for certain types of habitual behavior may have to be identified and dealt with before the habit can be changed successfully. Esther has a habit of eating too much too often, not because she is hungry but because she is lonely and frustrated. Habit analysis can determine such motives.

Several stimuli or related activities are involved in a habit. Smoking, for example, involves taking out a cigarette, lighting it up, inhaling, blowing smoke, tapping ashes, and perhaps making miscellaneous gestures with the cigarette. All of these are part of the habit. So a person not only has to overcome a craving for the cigarette, but in a sense must also substitute another activity for the smoking routine.

Since many habits are a sequence of activities, one of the ways to break a habit is to avoid the first step that triggers the sequence into motion. Understanding how habits were formed in the first place helps one to understand how a situation may be changed or a stimulus removed to promote the breaking of a habit.

FORMING NEW HABITS

More attention is usually given to habit breaking than to new habit formation. An undesirable habit such as biting fingernails can be quite conspicuous. It takes more careful analysis to determine what new habits could be beneficial.

Sometimes breaking an undesirable habit and forming a desirable habit can be accomplished together. A desirable habit can be substituted for an undesirable one. Eating raw vegetables can be substituted for eating sweets, for example. Substitution is useful in habit breaking because, as already mentioned, related activity is an integral part of the habit. But unless you substitute a harmless or beneficial activity, you may discover you have just substituted one undesirable habit for another.

If you want to form a new habit, you should begin immediately or as soon as possible. If you prolong the time between deciding to do something and doing it, you often begin to make excuses for yourself. You may rationalize that this really isn't important anyway. But remember—the formation of new habits takes special effort at first; after a while, new habits can become as easy to follow as the old, poor habits were.

What Do You Think? *In your opinion, why do people continue habits that they know are hazardous to their health?*

BALANCES

The need for balance in our personal lives and in society was discussed in Chapter 1. Keeping well requires a number of balances. We need a balanced diet. We need a balance of activity and rest. We need some stress to function at our best, although too much stress can make us ill. You may have heard, "All things in moderation; nothing in excess." This saying applies to wellness in many respects.

A realistic attitude is a balance between what we would like to be and what is reasonably possible. Self-image, too, can help us become and stay healthier. Those who think of themselves as being the kind of person they want to be are more likely to take care of themselves.

Summary

Wellness, or holistic health, involves a complex interrelationship among physical health and fitness, mental health, stress management, environmental safety, emotional stability, vocational competence, social effectiveness, and spiritual harmony.

We can keep ourselves well in several ways. It is important that our diets include appropriate amounts of the following nutrients: protein, carbohydrates, fats, vitamins, and minerals. Water is essential to life itself and fiber is important to healthy body functioning. The Food Guide Pyramid suggests daily food choices for a well-balanced, healthful diet. There should also be a balance between calorie intake and energy use to maintain desired weight.

Physical fitness can improve our wellness in many ways. The four basic qualities of fitness are flexibility, muscular strength, muscular endurance, and cardiovascular endurance. Any reasonably healthy person should be able to keep physically fit through various activities. Popular activities are sports, exercise programs, running, walking, and swimming. There is also emphasis today on aerobics to stimulate heart and lung functioning. Many combine exercise and recreation. Improved appearance is also a result of weight control and physical fitness.

Among the major threats to wellness in today's society are stress, drug abuse and addiction, alcoholism, smoking, sexually transmitted diseases, AIDS, and eating disorders. Improper treatment can also be a threat to maintaining or regaining wellness.

The FDA offers a number of "red flags" to watch for in making treatment decisions. The warnings suggest that we should be alert to possible frauds and exaggerations.

Mental health is a vital component to holistic health. If the behavior of individuals falls within a normal range of behavior and if they are well adjusted and happy, they are usually considered mentally healthy. Mental health varies with

PSYCHOLOGY IN PRACTICE

1. Develop a physical fitness program that you believe would be realistic for you. Use a physical fitness book or guide as a reference. Do not follow the plan, however, unless you are confident that you can do so without risk.

2. Present some information to the class about a wellness hazard not discussed in the chapter. Public health officials or other agencies may be able to give you pamphlets or display materials.

3. Investigate organizations or agencies within your area that offer wellness services and materials to the public. Obtain available pamphlets and information from one of them and, with a fellow student, present your findings to the class.

4. Find out what you can about types of treatment for mental illness and psychological disorders in your area. To the best of your ability, determine some of the problems in helping those with such disorders become mentally healthy and functioning members of the community.

individuals, but there are some common characteristics related to this aspect of wellness.

Psychological disorders refer to difficulty in adapting or inability to adapt to the realities of life. They are commonly classified as anxiety disorder, somatoform disorder, dissociative disorder, mood disorder, schizophrenic disorder, and personality disorder. Treatment of psychological disorders includes biochemical therapy, electroconvulsive therapy, and many types of psychotherapy, including both individualized and group therapy. Many people with psychological disorders are treated as outpatients rather than being institutionalized, as in the past.

Business and industry are becoming increasingly concerned about the wellness of their employees. This concern is to their benefit because it reduces costly absenteeism and replacement training. But there is also evidence of sincere interest in wellness among employees as human beings with personal lives and responsibilities. Increasing numbers of businesses and organizations have extensive employee assistance programs, providing for the needs of employees and their families. The Family Leave and Medical Act of 1993 has also made it possible for employees to take time off to provide for the needs of family members.

We should all be interested in maintaining a high level of total wellness. To some extent, total wellness requires breaking bad habits and developing desirable ones. We also need balances in diet, exercise, and other activities.

You will notice that several topics discussed in previous chapters will relate to topics in the next chapter.

Answers to Quiz Yourself on page 256

1. c	**6.** a	**11.** b
2. a	**7.** c	**12.** a
3. a	**8.** c	**13.** b
4. b	**9.** b	**14.** c
5. c	**10.** a	

Key Terms

Nutrition
Calorie
Nutrient density
Aerobics
Psychosomatic illness
Alcoholism
Anorexia nervosa
Bulimia nervosa
Binge eating

Psychological disorder
Generalized anxiety disorder
Panic disorder
Phobic disorder
Obsession
Obsessive-compulsive disorder
Compulsion
Conversion
Hypochondria

Multiple personality	Amnesia
Major depression	Electroconvulsive therapy
Manic depressive disorder	Psychotherapy
Schizophrenic disorder	Group therapy
Personality disorder	Psychiatrist
Biochemical therapy	Habit

Learning Activities

Turn to page LA-49 to complete the Learning Activities and Enrichment Activities for this chapter.

Endnotes

1. John and Muriel James, *Passions for Life: Psychology and the Human Spirit*, A Dutton Book, Penguin Books USA Inc., New York, 1991, p. 70.

2. Mayo Clinic Health Letter, Mayo Clinic, Rochester, MN, October 1997, p. 6.

3. Janice M. Horowitz, Elaine Lafferty, and Dick Thompson, "The New Scoop on Vitamins," *Time*, April 6, 1992, p. 56.

4. *Fitness Fundamentals: Guidelines for Personal Exercise Programs*, developed by the President's Council on Physical Fitness and Sports, Department of Health and Human Services, Washington, D.C., (no date), p. 2.

5. *Turning Awareness into Action*, U.S. Department of Health and Human Services, Public Health Service, Washington, D.C., rev. 1991, p. 56.

6. *A Guide to Commonly Abused Drugs*, Winters Communications, Inc., Tampa, FL, 1989, p. 2.

7. Floyd E. Bloom, editorial, "The Science of Substance Abuse," *Science*, October 3, 1997, p. 15.

8. *A Health and Fitness Guide to Alcohol*, Alcoholism Council of Greater New York, NY (no date, no page).

9. Michel Thuriaux and Suzanne Cherney, "AIDS Affects Us All, *World Health*, January–February 1997, p. 20.

10. Lee Berry, ed., "On the Road Again," *P.R.I.D.E. Newsletter*, Project PRIDE, P.O. Box 1551, Rogue River, OR, September 5, 1996. Available on the Internet: http://id.mind.net/community/pride/newspr2.htm (October 16, 1997).

11. Beatrice T. Hunter, *Consumers' Research*, September 1997, p. 13.

12. Isadore, Rosenfeld, M.D., *Dr. Rosenfeld's Guide to Alternative Medicine*, Random House, New York, 1996, p. xviii.

13. Isadora B. Stehlin, "An FDA Guide to Choosing Medical Treatments," a reprint from *FDA Consumer Magazine*, Food and Drug Administration, U.S. Government Printing Office, July 1995, no page.

14. David G. Myers, *Exploring Psychology,* 3rd ed., Worth Publishers, New York, 1996, p. 417.

15. Paul J. Rosch, "Job Stress: America's Leading Adult Health Problem," *USA Today Magazine,* May 1991, pp. 43–44.

16. *Wausau Hospital Employee Assistance Programs,* Wausau Hospital, Wausau, WI, October, 1997.

Valuing Diversity

12

You cannot shake hands with a clenched fist.

Golda Meir

LEARNING OBJECTIVES

After completing this chapter, you should be able to do the following:

1. Give reasons for valuing diversity.

2. Describe or illustrate the steps toward valuing diversity.

3. Identify the dimensions of diversity.

4. Give examples of personal examination questions concerning the dimensions of diversity.

5. Describe ways in which communities have been involved in valuing diversity.

6. Describe how valuing diversity is promoted and practiced in education.

7. Give examples of the benefits of diversity in the workplace.

8. Identify potential problems related to diversity and growth in valuing diversity.

9. Give guidelines for valuing diversity.

Diversity
differences among
people.

What does the word *diversity* bring to your mind? You may think of all the different kinds of people in the society in which you live and in the world. **Diversity** refers to differences among people or ways in which they are unlike one another. In this chapter, we will also look at groups of people and how they differ from other groups. We should remember, however, that we are part of that diversity. Each of us belongs in some way to each of the dimensions of diversity that will be discussed. In spite of these differences, we have much in common with other human beings. For example, we have the same basic needs and we have many similar emotional experiences.

Much of what we studied in previous chapters will relate to this chapter. Certainly *self-concept* from Chapter 2 is closely related, as are *values* from Chapter 3 and *attitudes* from Chapter 6. References to other earlier chapters will be made as we proceed toward learning more about understanding and valuing diversity.

WHY VALUE DIVERSITY?

What is meant by valuing diversity? Although the meaning of terms often seems obvious to us, it can be surprising how differently they can be interpreted. Therefore, some clarification on what is intended will be helpful in working through this chapter. We *value* what is important to us. Our values are not limited to just what we believe is important for ourselves, however. In addition to having personal values, we value many issues and relationships in our society that we believe to be beneficial to others and to society as a whole. A person may value quality child care, for example, even if he or she does not have any children.

Before we consider some reasons why we might value diversity, the dimensions of diversity that we will be considering in this chapter should be identified. Those dimensions are gender, race, ethnicity, abilities/disabilities, sexual/affectational orientation, lifestyle, age, religion, education, socioeconomic status, and occupation. Each will be discussed later. Now let's consider some reasons why we might value diversity pertaining to these dimensions.

REASONS FOR VALUING DIVERSITY

There are many reasons for valuing diversity. Consider the following:

- Diversity is a reality. We live in a global society and interact with others who have different characteristics. To a large extent, we are interdependent.
- Conflicts among human beings resulting in psychological pain and even violence could be avoided or reduced.
- Pleasurable experiences in life would be increased as we broaden our horizons, open ourselves to others, and seek to value them.
- Tension in our daily interactions with others would be reduced.
- Businesses and other organizations could direct energy and other resources toward achieving goals.

 What Would You Suggest? *What would you suggest as another reason for valuing diversity?*

STEPS TOWARD VALUING DIVERSITY

There are progressive steps toward valuing diversity. These steps begin with *awareness* of differences, and proceed to *knowledge, tolerance, understanding, acceptance* and finally *valuing* persons who have characteristics different from our own. The illustration shows this progression toward valuing diversity.

For many people, valuing diversity follows the progression through the steps illustrated. Because we are all unique, however, there are many variations of ways to achieve the valuing of diversity. Awareness of differences may lead a person to seek more knowledge about those with different characteristics but could also result in intolerance toward the person or persons. Even if some persons didn't actively seek more knowledge, they might incidentally become more knowledgeable over time if they were not intolerant. Some persons may skip the tolerance step and move from knowledge to understanding. Certainly this progression is not so simple that a person would experience awareness and then consciously try to determine what the next step or steps should be.

Steps to Valuing Diversity

Valuing
Acceptance
Understanding
Tolerance
Knowledge
Awareness

The steps are meant to give us an understanding of the way many people learn to value diversity. It is unrealistic to assume that everyone will learn to value diversity in the same way or to the same degree. There are also differences in the degree to which individuals may value the different dimensions. For example, an individual may have no difficulty valuing gender differences but have more difficulty with differences in one of the other dimensions.

CHARACTERISTICS OF THOSE WHO VALUE DIVERSITY

What are characteristics common to persons who value diversity? It seems as if they would have a curiosity about life in general and an interest in other people. Such persons would likely have a broad perspective of life and welcome new experiences. Differences intrigue rather than repel them. They have a favorable self-concept and self-esteem. They value themselves and the characteristics that make them unique.

THE WAY IT WAS . . .

As noted at the beginning of this chapter, no dimension of diversity is new. There is, however, a new emphasis on valuing diversity. Before we consider the dimensions of diversity and why there is new emphasis, let's look at some of the historical factors and events that have led to our current focus on diversity.

Diversity in this country did not begin with the pilgrims coming from England on the Mayflower and other early migrations. Diversity already existed in America among the Native Americans themselves. There were many different tribes, each with its own language and customs, and there was a great deal of rivalry among them. The immigration of Europeans, of course, added to this diversity, and there was diversity among the new immigrants themselves. Although most of the first immigrants were from the British Isles, there were also early immigrants from other countries in Europe. They were not always welcomed by groups that had come earlier. Most of the early immigrants stayed together, giving them a continued sense of identity in their religion, language, and customs.

Melting pot
a description of American life whereby those of different backgrounds were expected to give up their heritage and blend into American culture.

In the earlier days of this country's history, immigrants were expected to become part of the **melting pot,** whereby those of different backgrounds were expected to give up their ethnic heritage and become part of American culture. This concept has now been replaced by what has been called a **mosaic,** whereby each culture retains its identity and cherished customs while still becoming part of the multicultural whole.

In time, some restrictions to immigration were developed. In 1921, following World War I, Congress passed the first quota law, which limited the number of immigrants from any country to 3 percent of those of that nationality already living in the United States.

Mosaic
a concept of immigration in which cultures retain their identity within American culture.

After World War II, under the Displaced Persons Acts of 1948 and 1950 more than 400,000 persons from Europe entered the United States. More recently, in the years from 1960 to 1990, for example, the total white population of the United States dropped and minority groups, particularly Hispanics, Asians, and Pacific Islanders, increased in number.

In 1965, an amendment to the Immigration and Nationality Act did away with the national origins quota system. For example, it limited the number of immigrants from Western Hemisphere countries to 120,000 a year, regardless of the country of origin. It limited immigration from countries in the Eastern

Hemisphere to 170,000, with a limit of 20,000 from any one nation. There have been over 16 million immigrants since 1965. In addition, many undocumented immigrants cross borders.

Students and visitors who stay in the United States after their original visas have expired also account for a large number of immigrants. In the mid 1970s, most immigrants came from Mexico and the West Indies. During the last generation, there has been an influx of immigrants from Asian countries. A special issue of *Time* noted that 1 million immigrants, mostly from Asia and Latin America, arrive each year (1).

No one should ever forget the hundreds of thousands of Africans who were forcibly brought to the United States as slaves. It seems incredible to many that we still have racial problems more than 100 years after the Civil War. In 1964 the Civil Rights Act was established but has been less than perfect in its effects. Additional legislation has been passed, but human rights are still violated in the United States today.

More than legislation is needed. Human beings caring about one other can do more than laws. Rosa Parks may have considered herself an ordinary black person asserting her right when she refused to give up her seat to a white person on a Montgomery, Alabama, bus in 1955, but she has gone down in history as a champion of human rights. Martin Luther King, who now has a national holiday in his memory, is respected and appreciated for literally giving his life for the cause of human rights.

Dimensions of Diversity

DIMENSIONS OF DIVERSITY

There are dozens of dimensions of diversity, depending on how we choose to note differences. The dimensions we will consider in this chapter are those that seem to have the greatest impact on our lives and our relationships with others. As noted earlier, these dimensions are gender, race, ethnicity, abilities/disabilities, sexual/affectational orientation, lifestyle, age, religion, education, socioeconomic status, and occupation. See the accompanying illustration.

Naturally, each person has some characteristics that would be considered different by some others. Also, the degree to which a particular characteristic affects an individual may be different from how the same characteristic affects another person. For example, a disability may affect one person much differently from the way a similar disability will affect another person. While reading this chapter, it will be important to keep in mind that we are all not only individuals, but that the characteristics we have affect ourselves and others in different ways. Valuing diversity pertains to all of the dimensions of diversity mentioned above. Some dimensions will be discussed in more detail here and in other sections of this chapter, but that does not mean that they should be valued more than others.

GENDER

Gender
identification of human beings as either male or female.

Sexuality
state or sense of being male or female.

Gender is a dimension of diversity found throughout the world, identifying human beings as either male or female. The term *gender* is preferable to *sex* because sex is primarily biological, whereas gender includes the roles males and females play in their lives. The term **sexuality,** as defined in Chapter 2, includes what it means to an individual to be male or female and is related to gender.

How each gender is looked upon and how each fits into a particular society or culture varies greatly. As we interact more with people of different cultures wherever we live, it is important to be familiar with customs, expectations, and even taboos of other groups related to gender. Some of these are related to potential problems discussed later in this chapter. One example pertains to American females, who often prefer the term *woman,* to *lady, girl,* or even *female.* Other terms, now falling out of use, are obviously unacceptable. Terms of endearment to a new or casual acquaintance should also be avoided.

Sexual harassment of women in the military and in military academies has been a problem in recent years. Sexual harassment, which is not necessarily confined to women, was discussed in Chapter 9. Gender differences in approaches to thinking and problem solving were discussed in Chapter 7, and differences in communications styles were discussed in Chapter 8. You may want to review these sections at this time.

RACE

Race is a significant aspect of the identity of an individual, both to oneself and to others. Katharine Esty, Richard Griffin, and Marcie Schorr Hirsch, in *Workplace Diversity,* define race as follows:

> Traditionally it was believed that there were three major races, each with its own blood type and physical characteristics. That view has been discredited. Today it is not that simple. The Census Bureau has used four official racial categories: American Indian or Alaskan Native, Asian or Pacific Islander, Black, and White. In the 1990 census those who did not fit one of those four categories were asked to check 'other' (2).

The Census Bureau now has revised the number of categories to six for the 2000 census: American Indian or Alaskan Native, Asian, Black or African American, Hispanic or Latino, Native Hawaiian or Other Pacific Islander, and White.

There has always been some controversy about what the people of a particular race prefer to be called. "People of color" has been used in the 1990s to refer to people who are nonwhite, but some do not like that designation. The use of the term *minorities* is objected to by Asians, who point out that they are the majority group on earth. If we choose to respect others, we should be sensitive to how they want to be identified.

Racism
the belief that one race is inherently superior to another.

Race is a heated issue in today's society. Its roots, of course, run deep. African Americans, dehumanized by slavery from early Colonial days to the 1800s, have continued to be discriminated against, and this has fueled deep feelings of resentment. This is compounded by **racism,** the belief that one race is inherently superior to another. Racism causes more than just discrimination. It can spawn atrocious hate crimes, cause riots, and result in real violence and death. Racism is not just about whites hating and discriminating against blacks. It can be blacks against whites, or any race who discriminates against another.

The growing number of interracial marriages has lessened racial tensions to some extent. According to an article entitled "In Living Colors" in *Newsweek,* "interracial marriages have risen dramatically since the 1960's and in the U.S. now comprise more than 2 percent of all marriages" (3). But there are mixed reactions by society to this also—even among members of the races that have been involved. The goal would be for each person to take pride in his or her race, or combination of races, and to be treated with respect by all others. This is still somewhat idealistic but there is definitely progress in that direction. In support of this view, Kathlyn Gay, in her book *I Am Who I Am,* shares part of a personal interview with Andra Johnson from Indiana, whose father is of German heritage and whose mother is of Cherokee and black ancestry. The author quotes Andra as saying,

> When people ask about my background I always tell them I'm mixed, even though they want to label me "black." I'm not ashamed that I am part black, but I am also not ashamed that I am part white. . . . I refuse to pick sides for anyone. . . . I am who I am, and until people decide to change their narrow-minded view of the world, I am just going to have to continue to remind them (4).

The example of Tiger Woods, who became a popular professional golfer in the 1990s, has also done much to encourage the valuing of mixed racial heritage. He has stated that he takes pride in the fact that he is one-quarter black, one-quarter Chinese, one-quarter Thai, one-eighth White and one-eighth American Indian. Because of his achievements and popularity, each of these groups might like to claim him as its own. Many consider him black because he "looks" black. He makes it clear, however, that he does not want to deny any of his heritage. In fact not denying his heritage but actually taking pride in it is what he seems to be about (5). Many others of multiracial and ethnic backgrounds, especially the young, look to him as a role model. Some persons with a multiracial background prefer to identify themselves with one race. Each person's preferences should be honored.

ETHNICITY

Ethnicity
national origins that identify persons as belonging to particular groups and connecting them with certain values and customs.

Ethnicity is defined in different ways and some definitions include race, but most definitions of ethnicity consider race as a separate dimension, as it was discussed in this chapter. **Ethnicity** refers to national origins that identify persons as belonging to particular groups and connecting them with certain values and customs. An **ethnic group,** therefore, is a group with similar culture, customs, and language. Ethnic traits are cultural and therefore learned or acquired. The term **ethnocentrism** is the belief that one's ethnic group is superior to others. This belief obviously does not lead to valuing diversity.

Ethnic group
a group with similar culture, customs, and language.

Ethnocentrism
the belief that one's ethnic group is superior to others.

Culture
values, beliefs, customs, and lifestyles that characterize members of a group with a common ancestry or national origin.

Extended family
a lifestyle that includes immediate family and other relatives, including grandparents.

Other definitions used in Chapter 1 should be helpful in understanding this chapter. *Cultural diversity,* also called *multiculturism,* was defined as differences identified with cultures within a larger group. Multiculturism includes a mix of cultural groups within a larger group. We have cultural diversity in the United States, for example. What was defined as **culture** in that chapter is included in our discussion of ethnicity in this chapter. There is often little distinction between the two terms.

A few of the differences among ethnic groups are listed below with reference to topics that affect our lives and activities.

TIME Members of some cultures are generally more time-conscious than those of other cultures. It is common among some groups to be more flexible.

FORMALITY As a group, White Americans are more casual in human relationships. They may use first names with new acquaintances, supervisors, and instructors, for example. Asians, on the other hand, are more formal, especially with new acquaintances. This formality is common of some other cultures as well.

FAMILY Members of ethnic groups such as American Indians, Hispanics, and Asians are more likely to have **extended family** lifestyles, with parents, grandparents, and even uncles and aunts living in the same household and caring for one another. White Americans are less likely to live with their extended families (6).

Tiger Woods, a young professional golfer of mixed racial heritage, has attracted many new golf fans of all ages.

The above are just a sampling of examples, and surely there are exceptions to what is stated here for any particular group. It is helpful to know the values common to a particular group and to individuals within that group if we are to appreciate their diversity and value them as persons.

What Would You Say? *If someone told you a joke that had an ethnic punch line, what would you say?*

ABILITIES/DISABILITIES

Exceptional
those with special differences: talents, disabilities, or psychological problems.

People with all degrees of abilities or disabilities are part of total diversity. The term **exceptional** has been used to include people with disabilities or psychological problems as well as those who have special abilities or talents. The gifted and talented are exceptional, for example, as are those with a wide range of disabilities. People with special abilities are usually offered educational opportunities to learn according to their abilities and interests. One of the concerns of those promoting the valuing of diversity is that many people of racial, ethnic, or other types of diversity have been overlooked and have not had opportunities to develop their potential. This omission is not only a loss to the individual but to society as a whole. It is not that people with disabilities are actively discriminated against; it is more often the case that they are ignored or rejected.

At first it would seem that giftedness may be the one area of abilities that does not have problems associated with it. For the gifted and talented, finding a job may not be a problem, but finding employment that is adequately challenging can be. Additional problems associated with talented people can include being very critical of others and oneself, and resisting direction and pressure to conform. Also, because of their need for success, the gifted and talented may become frustrated easily.

Qualitative approach
regarding a person with a disability as a different kind of person.

Quantitative approach
a view of a person based on her or his degree of an ability.

In the past, the **qualitative approach,** whereby a person with a disability was regarded as a different *kind* of person, was common. Most recently, the **quantitative approach** has been used to indicate that a person has a different *degree* of an ability. This degree of difference does not make him or her a different kind of person. We should not say *deaf person,* for example, but should refer to a person who is deaf or who is hard of hearing.

An example of how people with disabilities object to how they are perceived by society in general was evident in their reaction to the memorial for Franklin D. Roosevelt in 1997. The memorial showed FDR, who was disabled by polio, without his wheelchair. Those with disabilities, especially those who used wheelchairs, objected. They maintained that omitting the wheelchair suggested that a disability was something to be hidden or ashamed of and referred to the memorial as a hypocrisy in that respect.

It is also important to differentiate between what is known as a *disability* and a *handicap*. This distinction is explained by D. P. Hallahan and J. M. Kauffman, in a book on exceptionality:

> [D]isability is an inability to do something, a diminished capacity to perform in a specific way. A handicap, on the other hand, is a disadvantage imposed on

an individual. A disability may not be a handicap, depending on the circumstances. Likewise a handicap may or may not be caused by a disability. For example, blindness is a disability that can be anything but a handicap in the dark. In fact, in the dark the person who has sight is the one who is handicapped. Being in a wheelchair may be a handicap in certain social situations, but the disadvantage may be the result of other peoples' reactions, not the inability to walk. Other people can handicap a person who is different from themselves (in color, size, appearance, language, and so on) by stereotyping them or not giving them the opportunity to do the things they are able to do (7).

Disabilities themselves are sometimes handicaps but handicaps can also be imposed by others, often because others don't give the exceptional person the opportunity to participate or to develop or use his or her abilities. Required educational opportunities for individuals with disabilities will be discussed in the section on Education and the American Disabilities Act will be discussed in the section on Diversity in the workplace.

SEXUAL/AFFECTATIONAL ORIENTATION

Sexual/Affectational orientation
one's sexual preference; whether one is homosexual, heterosexual, or bisexual.

Diversity related to sexual/affectational orientation is one of the most controversial today and one in which individuals claim great misunderstanding, rejection, and discrimination. **Sexual/affectational orientation** refers to whether a person is heterosexual, homosexual, or bisexual.

Much public reaction to sexual/affectational orientation in recent years concerns rights to serve in the military, rights to marry, social acceptance, and coverage for health and other benefits for those in homosexual relationships. No federal law protects known homosexuals in the workplace. There are some large companies with policies against discrimination on the basis of sexual discrimination, however. Examples are Xerox, Procter & Gamble, and AT&T.

Those who value diversity of whatever type in society discourage criticism and jokes about those who have a sexual/affectational orientation different from theirs. Those who do not value others in this respect may at least be able to move to the steps of tolerance and understanding. This is a minimal goal promoted by those who are working toward increased valuing of diversity of every dimension. An editorial entitled "Sexuality Shouldn't Be an Issue," in a Wisconsin daily paper stated,

> The debate over whether homosexuality is a lifestyle or an orientation, a choice or a biological destiny, nurture or nature, is irrelevant. Homosexuality simply is, just as heterosexuality is. . . . There is much cruelty and hate in our world—murders, rapes, assaults, drive-by shootings, wars, genocide—should we affirm love, wherever it exists, rather than condemning those who love? It is a thought to consider (8).

LIFESTYLE

Lifestyle
how one lives and with whom.

Lifestyle refers to how one lives and with whom. One's lifestyle also includes ones values, habits, and relationships with others. Your lifestyle may change several times during your lifetime, depending on your needs or desire for dependence, independence, or interdependence. For the most part, one is able to choose his or her lifestyle.

There are numerous variations in lifestyles today: the traditional family, consisting of a mother and father and their children; married couples with no children; single parents; remarried couples; stepparents and step- or blended families; two-career couples; stay-at-home dads; single persons who have never married; group living; divorced persons; cohabitants; widows and widowers; homosexual couples; and perhaps others. People today seem to be more accepting of all these lifestyles than in the past. There is more of a "live and let live" attitude toward the lifestyles of others. According to Joseph F. Coates in "What's Ahead for Families: Five Major Forces of Change," in a *World Future Society* publication, "The greatest changes in families have to do less with the family structure and more with economics. The change richest in implications is the rise of the two-income household" (9). Unless those involved in a particular lifestyle are causing problems for others, diverse lifestyles are generally accepted.

AGE

If you live long enough, you will become old. While that is not a profound statement, it is a reminder of reality. There is a difference between getting old and aging, however. Everyone gets older every day and age is marked by the number of years one has lived. **Aging** is a process pertaining to the *effects* of growing older. The effects of aging differ from individual to individual. Although some physical and mental abilities generally decline as one grows older, many individuals in their seventies, eighties, and even in their nineties are physically active, mentally alert, and productive.

Aging
process pertaining to the effects of growing older.

Older persons should be valued, not only for the contributions they made when they were younger but for the contributions they continue to make. They spend many hours in volunteer work, share their wisdom at living and their vast work experience with others, and offer loving services to their families. Older persons will be discussed later in this chapter with our consideration of diversity in the workplace and also as a section of the next chapter. We want to recognize here, however, that *age* is a dimension of diversity.

The population of the United States is also changing with respect to age. *Time* notes that Baby Boomers are becoming fifty years old at the rate of about one in eight seconds. They state, "That means that by 2020, more than a third of all Americans will be 50 or older. And by 2050, those 65 or older could outnumber kids 14 and younger for the first time in U.S. history" (10).

Although most of the discrimination pertaining to age has been directed toward older persons, all ages should be valued. Life-span development (the subject of the next chapter) discusses common characteristics of age groups, but some points pertaining to valuing life are appropriate here. For example, there is evidence that children are not always properly cared for or protected from abuse. Laws protect children, but the media almost daily reports serious problems of abuse. There are also reports of children in other parts of the world who are exploited in child labor.

Another age group that is not always valued consists of teenagers. Adolescence can involve difficult types of adjustment for teenagers themselves and trying times for some parents, but they need acceptance and valuing, perhaps more than at any other time of their lives.

RELIGION

Beliefs related to religion are part of our diversity. Major world religions include Christianity, Islam, Hinduism, Buddhism, Confucianism, Shinto, Taoism, Judaism, among others. Although it is possible that some people may be insincere

Reprinted from The Saturday Evening Post.

about their religious practices, for whatever reason, one cannot be insincere about what he or she believes. There is no attempt in this discussion to encourage valuing one religion, denomination, or sect more than another. Also, it is recognized that the beliefs opposed to religion and religious practices must be respected. The extent to which references to religious beliefs or allowance for religious practices can be allowed in public education or in public education facilities has been controversial. There has been growing respect for diversity in religious beliefs in both education and the workplace in recent years, however. Many students and employees of diverse religions, for example, are given time off to celebrate their respective religious holidays. Diversity of beliefs should be recognized and respect for beliefs must be honored. This respect is not only everyone's right, but it is consistent with valuing the diversity that forms our society.

EDUCATION

Diversity in education has not posed the problems that some of the other dimensions of diversity have. Although it is an academic practice to measure education by years of schooling and degrees, there are those who have essentially educated themselves through reading, life experience, and various informal educational experiences. These types of educational experiences are being recognized by educational institutions and by business and industry, even though they are much more difficult to measure. If we are to value education and value the diversity among individuals in this respect, we must look at all aspects of becoming educated. Valuing the education of an individual does not mean that the *person* is of more value. Her or his services may be of more value to business and industry, but equality of individuals is inherent and is protected by the U.S. Constitution. It is obvious, however, that this is not always recognized.

Placing value on education requires that educational opportunities should be available to all. Public Law 94-142, passed in 1975, declares that education must

Students from different countries enjoy time together between classes.

be available to all handicapped persons, up to 21 years of age. In addition, education for those with disabilities must be made available in what the law calls "the least restrictive environment." Efforts should be made to give them the assistance they need without unduly isolating them or interfering with other aspects of their education. For many reasons related to other types of diversity, such as race and ethnicity, educational opportunities have not been equal. Progress in valuing all types of diversity would improve educational opportunities for all.

SOCIOECONOMIC STATUS

Socioeconomic status societal position that involves both social and economic factors.

Since we live in a capitalistic, free-enterprise society, we have diversity in socioeconomic status. These socioeconomic levels are generally referred to as *upper class, middle class,* and *lower class.* Many other terms are used in referring to each class. **Socioeconomic status** is a societal position that pertains to factors that are both social and economic. These two factors affect one another. Our economic status, for example, affects our lifestyles, which are part of our social identification.

There is not as much actual starvation but recent reports suggest that there is just as much malnutrition in the United States as there is in other countries. We also have many citizens live in poverty, lacking what are generally considered essentials in life. Countless programs at all levels of government assist those who cannot work or can no longer work. Numerous organizations and agencies assist individuals and families. Exactly how much should be done and by whom is controversial, however. The value of socioeconomic diversity is also evident in the tax systems of the national and state and local governments. Everyone does not agree with the system, but most would agree that the amount of taxation should be related to one's ability to pay.

According to social ladders, who you are also makes a difference in where one can live, what clubs one can join, and to what extent one is shown respect in a community. These groups do not determine one's value as a person, however. And they do not enhance their own value by excluding others. Some of these clubs or organizations automatically exclude some because of high dues or other qualifications. Socioeconomic factors are not the only factors involved, of course. Race, gender, and sexual orientation are among other factors that exclude some members of society. In recent years, however, laws and policies have lifted some restrictions on club memberships, entrance into schools, and other organizations.

OCCUPATION

Diversity was discussed in Chapter 1 as an aspect of the global society in which we live and as a growing characteristic of the workplace. There were also references to diversity in Chapter 9. An upcoming section of this chapter is entitled Diversity in the Workplace.

Which one is different?
cw

According to *Occupational Outlook Handbook,* 1996, "The labor force will become increasingly diverse. The number of Hispanics and Asians and other races will increase much faster than blacks and whites. Non-Hispanic Blacks will increase faster than White non-Hispanics" (11). The kinds of work persons do also factors into diversity. Service-producing industries, especially in the business and health industries, will account for the most new jobs. This publication also reports that jobs requiring the least education will provide the most openings but offer the lowest pay. Women will continue to make up an increasing share of the workforce, from 46 to 48 percent by 2005.

Legislation also has affected the composition of the workforce. Federal laws, executive orders, and some federal grant programs bar discrimination in employment based on race, color, religion, sex, national origin, age, and disability. Additional information on employment will be found in an upcoming section on workplace diversity.

A PERSONAL APPROACH

The self-understanding you gained in Chapter 2 will be helpful in valuing diversity. You may have identified yourself in the various categories of the self-portrait in Learning Activity 7 for that chapter. Some of those categories will also apply in your developing a personal portrait in terms of diversity. Think of yourself in terms of all the different dimensions of diversity discussed earlier. Remember that, at the beginning of this chapter, it was noted that each of us is different—you and me—as well as everyone else. Your responses to the following questions related to each of the dimensions of diversity will help you develop this personal portrait.

Gender
How do I feel about being either male or female? Do I feel that my gender is an advantage to me personally or in the workplace? Have I ever felt discriminated against because of my gender? Do I have any prejudices against the opposite sex?

Race

Am I of one race or mixed? If I have a mixed racial background, do I have approximate knowledge of what the mix is? Do I identify with one race of my mixed background? How do I feel about my racial identity? Why do I feel the way I do? How do I feel about people of other races?

Ethnicity

What nationality do I know or believe myself to be? Do I know what nationalities make up my heritage? How do I feel about being the nationality or nationalities that I am? Why do I feel the way I do? What cultural customs, traditions, and beliefs do I have that are related to my ethnic background? How important are these to me? How do I practice and express them? Do I hesitate to practice ethnic customs and express my beliefs because of fear of ridicule? How do I feel about people with different ethnic backgrounds?

Abilities/Disabilities

How would I describe my abilities? Do I believe I have special abilities? If I have special abilities, do I consider them natural talents or learned? In what ways do I use and/or share my special abilities? Do I have any disabilities? If so, were these inborn or acquired through illness or accident? How do I feel about having a disability? Am I making the most of my life and abilities in spite of a disability? How do I relate to people with special abilities or disabilities?

Sexual/Affectational Orientation

What is my sexual/affectational orientation? Am I heterosexual, homosexual, or bisexual? How do I feel about being what I am? Do I believe that it is natural to be what I am? If I am homosexual or bisexual, how do I deal with the critical attitudes and behaviors of others with a different sexual orientation? Do I believe that one's sexual/affectational orientation is her or his personal right? How do I relate to people with sexual/affectational orientations different from mine?

Lifestyle

What is my lifestyle at this time? With whom do I live or would I prefer to live with in the future? What is my opinion of homosexual lifestyles? What is my opinion of interracial marriages? Are there any lifestyles of which I disapprove? How do I feel about single parents and stepfamilies? What is my idea of a caring, nurturing family or relationship?

Age

What is my age? How do I feel about the age I am now in life? Is there a particular age or time in life that I consider ideal? Can I identify advantages to being at any time in one's life? How do I feel about people who are older than I am? How do I feel about people who are younger than I am?

Religion

What are my religious beliefs? How were they acquired? Do I freely acknowledge what my beliefs are? Do I think that it is necessary or important? Why or why not? Do I believe anyone has the right to criticize others because of what they believe or don't believe?

Education

How would I describe my education up to now? What do I believe the values of education to be? What advantages do I believe a person with education has in the world of work? What is my attitude toward those who have less formal education than I have? What is my attitude toward those who have more formal education than I have?

Socioeconomic Status

How would I describe my socioeconomic status? Do I believe people are personally responsible for the class to which they belong? Do I believe the poor could find more ways to help themselves? Do I believe the wealthy have an obligation toward society? Do I think people in one class are basically happier than those in another class?

Occupation

Am I now involved in the type of work I have chosen for my career or am I in the process of preparing for that career? Do I respect people in all types of work? Is there some type of work I would consider degrading? What benefits do I believe my work should contribute to my life?

These are just a sampling of the questions that can be considered in determining who you are in the diverse society in which we live. Were you offended by any of the questions? If so, do you know why? You may be justified in believing some important questions were omitted. They were not omitted for any particular reason, however. The questions presented in each of the categories were intended for you to gain a better understanding of yourself, your own characteristics, and your beliefs and reactions toward others who are different from you. A Psychology in Practice activity at the end of the chapter will give you an opportunity to revise this self-examination. Keep in mind that the purpose of the self-examination is to gain understanding rather than to pass judgment on yourself or others. Guidelines for valuing diversity, found later in the chapter, will relate to some of the question topics.

You may have experienced some personal difficulties related to one or several of the types of diversity. Every human being should have the freedom and encouragement to recognize and value whatever dimensions of diversity he or she possesses and who she or he is as an individual. If we all value ourselves and others, the evils and suffering associated with diversity would disappear.

WHAT COMMUNITIES ARE DOING

What is happening in our communities with regard to valuing diversity? No matter where you live, you have some contact and relationship with others in the society in which you live. The area where you live may be part of a large city, a small community, or rural area; you also reside in a state or other such division of the country. It was noted in Chapter 1 that we also live in a global community. This sense of community at whatever level has made us not only more interdependent but has put us in contact with others that are different from us in some ways—as we are from them. Every individual is not in contact with others who have all the diverse characteristics discussed earlier, but we are influenced by this diversity, nonetheless. Those in business and marketing, education, and government are among those who may regularly engage in business and activities that require understanding and valuing of others.

Everyone in a community, of any size, has responsibilities and opportunities to show that they value diversity and to encourage others to do so. They are learning that differences should not be resented or ignored but should be appreciated and used to everyone's advantage. Every group has members with talents and skills that can be useful in problem solving and achieving community goals. Some are active in government and other civic groups; others participate in educational or religious groups. Others are involved in cultural or recreational groups. There are endless possibilities. If we have already been active participants, we can be open and supportive of others who are also anxious to participate. And others who could contribute, but are hesitant for fear of rejection or lack of confidence, can be encouraged to become active members of their communities.

Carla J. Stoffle and Patricia A. Tarin, in an article entitled "No Place for Neutrality: The Case for Multiculturism," say, "A multicultural organization is built on the understanding that each person makes a unique and positive contribution to society and does so because of, not in spite of, his or her differences" (12). Everyone can learn from one another. Can't we all get along? Can we do better than just getting along?

What Can You Do? *What can you do to contribute to valuing diversity in the community or area in which you live?*

WHAT EDUCATION IS DOING

Educational institutions, on all levels, have a serious responsibility and many opportunities to encourage and contribute to valuing diversity. Educational programs and educators provide knowledge and promote understanding and valuing of all the diverse groups in society. Recall from Chapter 6 that an attitude is a combination of what we think and how we feel and that behavior results from attitudes. Attitudes develop from experiences, also discussed in Chapter 6. While it is not the purpose of education to teach people how to think and feel, it is generally agreed that prejudice, an attitude, is undesirable, and efforts should be made to reduce or eliminate it.

Education consists of much more than giving people factual knowledge. Even facts and statistics can be distorted, intentionally or unintentionally. But even if accurate, facts and statistics are only a small part of what it is to learn. Educators can give lectures and show videos on valuing diversity, but it takes

In many communities, multicultural celebrations include costumes, food, and customs from different eras.

actual experience to make a difference. One of the most valuable resources is the diverse nature of all student bodies today. To begin with, that diversity is part of their educational experience. Diversity is even more evident at the postsecondary level of education. Obviously, there are more differences in age and in sexual/affectational orientation, for example, than there would be in the lower levels.

Activities must provide experience in getting to know others and their values, and to share cultural customs and concerns. Students must also have the opportunity to work together in diverse groups, as in a forum. Deliberate efforts must sometimes be made to encourage those who have a tendency to sit together, eat together, and study together because of some ethnic similarity or other common characteristic to reach out to others.

Extracurricular activities can, and usually do, provide a wealth of opportunities to become familiar with diversity and related characteristics. These activities include sports, drama, music, art, literature, social studies, guest speakers, and others. Career days can be of particular value to students who may not be aware of the opportunities in the world of work.

Many educators know that students learn from role models and associate with their students in informal non-academic activities. They are also aware that educational objectives must be consistent over time and often go beyond the formal medium for learning. They realize that learning involves changing attitudes and behavior and takes time and interaction by the learner with others.

This chapter section will not explain the curriculums that promote understanding and valuing diversity, but we can be assured that this is an objective throughout education today. If everyone participates in activities with an open mind and an "unclenched fist," experiences can be pleasurable as well as educational.

DIVERSITY IN THE WORKPLACE

Valuing diversity is of vital importance in the workplace. Although the workplace has always reflected diversity, today's workplace is more diverse than ever. Also, reactions to this diversity in the workplace, as well as the rest of society, are changing. Katharine Esty, Richard Griffin, and Marie Schoor, in *Workplace Diversity*, give us the following description of the workplace of the past:

> In the typical workplace of the nineteenth and early twentieth centuries, managers saw themselves as helping in the melting down process of diminishing differences. It was a common assumption that assimilation was the goal—i.e., assisting those who were different to become more like the people already in the workplace, or more exactly, more like the people in power. For years, this goal of assimilation was taken for granted. Expressing differences through dress, language, perspective, customs, practices, or values was discouraged. People responded by Americanizing their names, shedding their ethnic dress, attending night school to learn English, and working hard to become part of the American dream (13).

This approach was referred to earlier as the "melting pot."

THE CHANGING WORKFORCE

Let's consider the changing composition of the workforce and the factors that brought this change about. Part of it is simply the result of living in a more global community—a more interactive world, as discussed earlier in the chapter. Not only are more immigrants coming to the United States, but more companies are establishing businesses and branches of their businesses in other countries. They have found that a diverse workforce can improve productivity and customer relations. Also, more businesses deal with international markets. Another reason is that an increasing number of women have joined the workforce. Also, as many people's eligibility for welfare expires, they are finding their way into the job market. The Americans with Disabilities Act has made it possible for many people with disabilities to become part of the workplace. Passed in 1990 and in effect in 1992, the act prohibits discrimination against qualified individuals with disabilities. It requires that employers make reasonable accommodations for employees as long as the employee is able to perform the essential functions of the job and the accommodation causes no undue hardship to the company. As explained in *Ability: The Bridge to the Future*, by the President's Committee on Employment of People with Disabilities,

> Reasonable accommodations are adjustments or modifications which range from making the physical work environment accessible to restructuring a job, providing assistive equipment, providing certain types of personal assistants (e.g., a reader for a person who is blind, an interpreter for a person who is

deaf), transferring an employee to a different job or location, or providing flexible scheduling (14).

A growing number of people over 55 and even over 65 are remaining in the workplace or are re-entering. They may re-enter because of disillusionment with retirement or because they have found their financial situation is inadequate. Still further changes in the composition of the workplace has been contributed by part-time, flextime, and temporary employees, who would not have been able, or did not want, to be full-time employees. These are just some of the major changes in the composition of the workforce today.

BENEFITS OF DIVERSITY IN THE WORKPLACE

Why is valuing diversity in the workplace so vital today? Consider the following benefits:

- When persons are aware that they are accepted, appreciated, and valued, they feel better about themselves, others, and their companies and are motivated to do better work.
- When people are motivated to do a higher quality of work, productivity is also increased and business prospers. Jobs are saved and often new jobs are created.
- Business with steady customers is maintained. Some companies and individuals quit doing business with companies if they are known to have poor relations with various members of their diverse workforce.
- New customers and business transactions are obtained. A diverse workforce whose input is valued in product development and marketing can help expand markets.
- When the diverse perspectives and talents of persons are valued, a business can be more innovative. The business can then expand and compete with other companies.

Pepper . . . and Salt

THE WALL STREET JOURNAL

"Gentlemen, there's been some criticism from some quarters about the supposed lack of diversity in the top ranks of this company."

© Cartoon Features Syndicate.

- A business that values diversity attracts people of talent from all groups because they know they will be valued and given opportunities to use their abilities and to grow.
- Improved decision making and problem solving results from a diversity of input. Different backgrounds and ways of analyzing and evaluating a situation can produce better results.
- Fewer grievances and lawsuits, which often result in high costs and unfavorable reputation, are found in companies that value diversity.

POTENTIAL PROBLEMS

Although there are benefits to diversity in the workplace, there are also potential problems. Some of these are the result of stereotypes that are difficult to change but that can interfere with efforts to accept and value diversity. A **stereotype,** as defined in Chapter 6, is the assumption that all members of a particular group conform to the same pattern and react in the same way. Stereotyped thinking becomes a habit and is therefore difficult to examine and modify. Since stereotypes can lead to prejudice and discrimination, they can keep us from being fair with others and from valuing diversity.

Stereotype
the assumption that all members of a particular group conform to the same pattern and react in the same way.

Misunderstandings also interfere with harmonious relationships and can cause communication problems related to gender, ethnicity, education, work experience, or other dimensions of diversity. When a person suspects that he or she misunderstands another person, that person can make an effort to correct it. But many misunderstandings are not recognized as such. When we think we understand but do not, the problem is compounded.

Emotions such as fear resulting from either real or perceived threats can interfere with a harmonious environment and relaxed relationships that promote valuing one another. Jealousies can also be detrimental. Distrust between genders or races, for example, can stem from these emotions and cause problems with acceptance and working together.

If the company itself does not make the effort to change the workplace to accommodate diversity, problems can result. For example, some people may not have the strength or stature to work in certain environments. Others may have disabilities that require accommodation and still others may be older and have problems with dexterity, vision, or fatigue.

Another potential problem is related to promoting programs for valuing diversity verbally but doing nothing in actual practice. Unless management personnel, as well as employees, are sincerely interested in valuing diversity, efforts can be superficial and can actually do more harm than good.

What Do You Think? *What do you think is the biggest obstacle to valuing diversity in the workplace?*

MANAGING DIVERSITY

It takes more than putting people together to get them working smoothly and effectively together. It takes more than talking about valuing diversity to get people to actually value diversity. In fact, the process of realizing the benefits of diversity in the workplace and anywhere else takes time. More harm than good can be done by trying to force people to value anything and to change their attitudes and behavior. Companies themselves are taking positive steps toward promoting diversity.

Some companies are making special efforts to place women and minorities in management positions. According to Linda Himelstein and Stephanie A. Forest in an article entitled "Breaking Through," Motorola is setting goals for diversity in management it aims to reach by 2000. They report, "Top execs are required to name the woman or minority best suited to succeed them: Those people are targeted for career development" (15).

Because much time and effort must be put into making the most of diversity in the workplace, a great deal of emphasis has been on managing diversity (as well as educational programs and activities that would contribute to desired results). Some of the training programs are seminars and workshops, and others are ongoing management programs. They stress getting to know coworkers, recognizing similarities as well as differences, and treating all people with dignity and respect. Emphasis is placed on withholding assumptions about what people can't do and giving everyone opportunities to develop and use skills. Training is also related to cultural sensitivity, disability awareness, and communication. The active participation of all employees is important in training programs to encourage valuing diversity. Role playing can be an effective technique to understand others but has be to done skillfully and tactfully not to offend others.

Management must also be knowledgeable about the numerous laws that affect diversity in the workplace. Some are federal laws but there are also state and local laws. Among the major pieces of legislation are the Civil Rights Act of 1964; the Age Discrimination Employment Act of 1967; the 1987 amendment that banned compulsory retirement for most workers; the Equal Pay for Equal Work Act of 1963; the Civil Rights Act of 1991, which gave a person the right to a trial by jury and the right to recover punitive and compensatory damages; laws that make it illegal to offer different retirement packages such as 401(k) plans to employees, even though other benefits may vary; the American Disabilities Act that went into effect in 1992, and Affirmative Action laws and requirements still in force in many places. Some larger cities have laws protecting the rights of those of homosexual orientation. In 1993, the Equal Employment Opportunity Commission (EEOC) amended the "hostile environment" requirement to include bias against race, disability, age, religion, color, and national origin.

According to Larry Reibstein in *Newsweek,* 75 percent of large companies use diversity training in addition to observing legal requirements (16). An essential aspect of these programs must be the commitment of the entire organization. Managers themselves must be dedicated to valuing diversity in action, not just laying out plans for others to get along and value one another.

As with other objectives and goals of some organizations, policies are written and distributed but are not put into practice. Such "programs" can only highlight potential difficulties and even intensify existing problems. Everyone must be sincerely interested in achieving the benefits of a harmonious workforce, participating in activities, giving recognition to one another, and helping one another in whatever way possible. This is a tall order, but at least serious attempts can be made to maintain a thriving program.

Conflict resolution must be an essential part of a valuing diversity program in the workplace. Skills in this area are important in any workplace situation, as discussed in Chapter 9, but they are crucial to resolving conflicts when dimensions of diversity are involved. Conflicts may arise between management and employees, between employees and customers, or between employees themselves.

Training and experience in working effectively as team members can be valuable. If all team members feel that they are respected as individuals and valued as members of the team, results can be impressive. Team members with diverse dimensions can stimulate one another and add perspectives that would be lacking in a group where all members had similar characteristics. They have a wider range of knowledge, abilities, and experience and can contribute to the achievement of team goals. Other areas of training programs should relate to topics such as understanding customs and ethnic values, communication styles, work ethics, common concerns among diverse groups, and how to obtain information and assistance when needed or desired.

Managers themselves should be well versed on what types of questions are legal and appropriate to ask in job interviews. These questions cannot pertain to age, personal and family status, and disabilities. For example, a middle-aged person cannot be asked how many more years he or she plans to work before retiring. A female cannot be asked whether she intends to have children. Neither a male nor female can be asked how his or her spouse feels about a particular job. No one can be asked whether she or he has a disability that would interfere with job performance.

GUIDELINES FOR VALUING DIVERSITY

Consider the following guidelines, which can be helpful in determining individual approaches to valuing diversity:

- Treat each person with respect as a unique individual.
- Recognize communication differences and possible misunderstandings. Ask questions tactfully for clarification.
- Be perceptive to values different from your own.
- Show genuine interest in the person rather than simple curiosity about differences.
- Avoid being judgmental.
- Let people know what you admire about them.
- Avoid stereotyping. Treat each person as an individual.
- Use empathy. Try to see others as they see themselves and their situations.
- Be honest. Be willing to share how you feel.
- Try to see yourself as the other person sees you. You are different too.
- Be open to new acquaintances and new experiences.
- Avoid using labels and terms that offend others.
- Refer to a person's race or ethnic background according to his or her preferences.
- Become familiar with customs and possible taboos of cultures other than your own.

- Remember that we all have more in common as human beings than we have differences.
- Remember that everyone has feelings. Everyone needs acceptance and love.
- Remember that a smile is a natural, universal expression of pleasure and goodwill.
- Remember that most people would like to be as independent and responsible as their circumstances allow.

PROGRESS CONTINUES

We cannot expect that everyone is willing and ready to learn how to become better at valuing diversity. You may be among those who value others but feel you are not equally valued in return. Prejudice, perhaps in your immediate environment, may stand in the way of valuing diversity. A major objective in valuing diversity would be to lessen such prejudice. Negative reactions to diversity include ignoring others, denying them rights and opportunities, and even suppression and violence. Individuals can still continue to work toward understanding and accepting others and valuing differences. Everyone can benefit from each measure of success.

In a speech to the Diversity Network Calgary in Canada, Holger Kluge shared his views:

> Diversity is a state of mind. It's a mentality that automatically values the contributions that different nationalities, races, genders, ages and even different styles and experiences can bring to an organization. It's a mentality that not only acknowledges differences but accepts them. It's a mentality that recognizes similarities because diverse individuals often share common goals, experiences, and attributes (17).

This chapter has taken a positive, optimistic approach to diversity and to valuing diversity. It was not intended to deny obstacles or to evade problems. The road to valuing diversity may be a long, difficult one, with many barriers still to overcome, but there is encouraging evidence that progress continues.

Summary

Diversity refers to differences among people or ways they are unlike one another. Reasons for valuing diversity in today's society include the reality of diversity, conflict avoidance or reduction, increase of pleasurable experiences, reduction of tension in daily living, and more successful experiences in business and other organizations.

Progress toward valuing diversity commonly includes the following steps: awareness, knowledge, tolerance, understanding, acceptance, and finally valuing. Not everyone progresses toward valuing in the same way or to the same degree.

Major dimensions of diversity include gender, race, ethnicity, abilities/disabilities, sexual/affectational orientation, lifestyle, age, religion, education, socioeconomic status, and occupation. Responding to questions pertaining to each of the dimensions of diversity can be helpful in developing a personal portrait in terms of valuing diversity.

Among community activities that encourage valuing diversity are participation in government, educational, religious, and other civic groups. Cultural and recreational activities also offer experiences in valuing diversity. There are endless possibilities. Education promotes valuing diversity through activities such as lectures, videos, art, music and drama programs, forums, guest speakers, and career days.

Diversity in the workplace has expanded in recent years due to legislation, global markets, and other factors. Some of the numerous benefits to valuing diversity in the workplace are increased motivation and productivity, higher quality of work, improved business relations, more innovative problem solving, fuller use of talents, and fewer grievances and lawsuits.

There are also potential problems related to diversity in the workplace. Stereotypes still lead to prejudice and discrimination; misunderstandings related

PSYCHOLOGY IN PRACTICE

1. Pick a particular dimension of diversity and write a description of where you believe you are in relationship to the steps toward valuing diversity. Explain how you believe you could advance to the next step.

2. With two other persons whose dimensions of diversity are different from yours (for example, different gender, race, age, or ability/disability), develop two additional guidelines for valuing diversity pertaining to those dimensions.

3. Compare your responses to the personal examination questions with two other persons. Discuss what you believe to be the reasons for any differences. Change or add questions to make the examination more appropriate to yourself.

to gender, ethnicity, education, work experience, or other dimensions of diversity arise; and emotions such as fear and jealousy, with resulting distrust, can be detrimental. Still further problems can result from a workplace that has not adapted to a diverse workforce.

Full commitment by management in company programs to increase valuing of diversity is crucial. Any attempts to force changes in attitudes and behavior can be detrimental. Active employee participation in various well-planned activities is essential to improving harmonious and productive relationships.

Guidelines can be helpful in determining individual approaches to valuing diversity. Such guidelines pertain to better understanding ourselves and to making progress in valuing others. In spite of remaining problems in our society and in the workplace, progress in valuing diversity has been made and is expected to continue.

The next chapter will also contribute to your gaining better understanding of yourself and others.

Key Terms

Diversity	Extended family
Melting pot	Exceptional
Mosaic	Qualitative approach
Gender	Quantitative approach
Sexuality	Sexual/Affectational orientation
Racism	Lifestyle
Ethnic group	Aging
Ethnocentrism	Socioeconomic status
Culture	Stereotype

Learning Activities

Turn to page LA-53 to complete the Learning Activities and Enrichment Activities for this chapter.

Endnotes

1. The Editors, "America's Immigrant Challenge," *Time*, Special Issue, Fall 1993, p. 3.

2. Katharine Esty, Richard Griffin, and Marcie Schorr Hirsch, *Workplace Diversity*, Adams Publishing, Holbrook, MA, 1995, p. 34.

3. John Leland and Gregory Beals, "In Living Colors," *Newsweek*, May 5, 1997, p. 60.

4. Kathryn Gay, *I Am Who I Am: Speaking Out About Multiracial Identity*, Franklin Watts, New York, 1995, p. 57.

5. Hugh B. Price, "Black America and Tiger's Dilemma," *Ebony*, July 1997, p. 32.

6. *Appreciating Diversity*, a tool for building bridges, AARP Minority Affairs, American Association of Retired Persons, Washington, DC, 1996, p. 35.

7. Daniel P. Hallahan and James M. Kauffman, *Exceptional Children*, 5th ed., Prentice-Hall, Englewood Cliffs, NJ, 1991, p. 6.

8. "Sexuality Shouldn't Be An Issue," *Wausau Daily Herald*, editorial, May 1, 1997, p. 8A.

9. Joseph F. Coates, "What's Ahead for Families: Five Major Forces of Change," *World Future Society*, 1996, p. 3.

10. John Greenwald reported by Susan Agrest and Emily Mitchell, with Bureau Reports: "Age Is No Barrier. Post—50 Americans Are Far from Over the Hill," *Time*, September 22, 1997, pp. M7+.

11. *Occupational Outlook Handbook*, 1996–1997, JIST Works, Inc., Indianapolis, IN, 1996, p. 6.

12. Carla J. Stoffle and Patricia Tarin, "No Place for Neutrality: The Case for Multiculturalism," *Library Journal*, July 1994, p. 49.

13. Katharine Esty, Richard Griffin, and Marie Schoor Hirsch, *Workplace Diversity*, Adams Publishing, Holbrook, MA. 1995, p. xv.

14. *Ability: The Bridge to the Future*, Education Kit, President's Committee on Employment of People with Disabilities, Washington, DC, 1997, p. 11.

15. Linda Himelstein and Stephanie A. Forest, "Breaking Through," *Business Week*, February 17, 1997, p. 67.

16. Larry Reibstein, with Anne Underwood, Vern E. Smith, and Annetta Miller, "Managing Diversity," *Newsweek*, November 25, 1996, p. 50.

17. Holger Kluge, "Reflections on Diversity," *Vital Speeches of the Day*, January 1, 1997, p. 172.

Life-Span Development

13

Perhaps the most valuable result of all education is the ability to make yourself do the thing you have to do when it ought to be done, whether you like it or not.

Thomas Huxley

LEARNING OBJECTIVES

After completing this chapter, you should be able to do the following:

1. Describe two different ways that life-span development can be studied.

2. Trace three types of development from early childhood through childhood.

3. Compare the influence of peers with the influence of parents during adolescent development.

4. Describe important challenges and decisions associated with young adulthood.

5. Explain the life-span dependence/interdependence curve and describe your place on such a curve.

6. Identify the eight stages of psychosocial development according to Erikson and describe the contrasting characteristics of each stage.

7. List the six stages of moral development according to Kohlberg.

8. Give the characteristics of four different types of maturity.

Development
a type of growth.

How many birthdays can you remember? How many birthdays have you had? The answers to these questions are only a small part of the more obvious ways in which you have developed, learned, grown, or matured since the day you were born. Several types of development will be discussed in this chapter.

If we think of **development** as a type of growth, we have to acknowledge that not all types of growth are desirable. Although we are concerned when an infant or child does not gain weight in a normal way, we also know that it is possible to gain too much weight. We also know that other types of growth or learning can be unfavorable, as in the learning of bad habits. Another type of growth that is threatening is cancer.

For the most part, however, this chapter is concerned with the types of development and maturity that are desirable. Some of these are natural or automatic. For example, physical growth takes care of itself under favorable conditions. Other types of development, such as cognitive or mental development, occur quite naturally under favorable conditions. Still other types of desired development require effort throughout life.

The main types of life-span development considered in this unit are physical, mental, moral, and what Erikson calls psychosocial. Emotional, social, intellectual, and vocational maturity will also be discussed, primarily as they relate to adults. You should be able to apply each of these to yourself in terms of past, present, and future development. You may note that all the terms—development, growth, maturity, learning—are ways of describing types of life-span development. For that reason there will be references to both earlier chapters and the last chapter. **Life-span development** is not only continuous but it also involves every aspect of a person's being and functioning.

Life-span development
continuous growth over one's life that involves every aspect of a person's being and functioning.

YOUR LIFETIME AND LIFE SPAN

A family photograph album may contain pictures of you engaged in activities at different times of your life. You probably have also heard your parents or other relatives talk about their lives before you were born. You may have read history books about events that occurred hundreds, or even thousands, of years before your life began. In spite of all this knowledge, however, it is difficult to think of yourself as not existing, isn't it?

You probably have observed that elderly people do not move as fast as you do and are often unsteady. They were once young and agile, and you yourself will

Three generations welcome this infant into the family.

likely live to be their age or older. Some of you reading this textbook will live to be 100 years old or more. Others will live to their eighties and nineties. It isn't likely that you are giving much thought to aging at this time in your life, of course. You are no doubt busy with the present and making plans for your more immediate future, as it should be. It does make sense, however, to have long-range goals and to understand the totality of life-span development. It also helps us to understand others, younger and older, in our personal lives and in society.

Life-span development has been studied in different ways. Some researchers have observed all the different types of development taking place at a particular time of life, such as in childhood or adolescence. Others have focused on a particular type of development across the life span. Discussion in this chapter will pertain to both approaches to understanding life-span development. We will consider several types of development during childhood, adolescence, and young adulthood, for example. Then there will be discussion of types of development, such as moral development and psychosocial development, across the life span to see how various stages relate to one another. Any repetition you notice should be helpful in understanding the interrelatedness of the types of life-span development.

LIFE-SPAN STAGES

D an Levinson, a noted psychologist on the subject of life-span development, divided the adult life span into eleven stages according to age ranges and what he called "life structures"—or the dominant tasks and transitions associated with a particular decade or period of one's life. Levinson divided Early Adulthood into four stages: the first stage, Early Adult Transition, covers the years from 17 to 22; the second stage, Entering the Adult World, covers the years from 22 to 28; the third stage, Age 30 Transition, covers the years 28 to 33; and the final stage of early adulthood, Settling Down, covers the years from 33 to 40. He describes a **transition** as a "change in life structure. Either a moderate change, or more often, a severe and stressful crisis"(1). All of these stages, for those interested, can be found in Levinson's book, *The Seasons of a Man's Life.* It is obvious from the title of his book that he was studying the life-span development of men at this time. Later in his life and studies, he conducted a similar study involving women and "found that he could divide the life cycle of women into similar periods to those of men"(2).

Another approach to understanding the stages of adult development is what Robert Havighurst calls "developmental tasks." He states:

> A developmental task is a task which arises at or about a certain period in the life of the individual, successful achievement of which leads to his happiness and to success with later tasks, while failure leads to unhappiness in the individual, disapproval by the society, and difficulty with later tasks (3).

He identifies what he considers developmental tasks for six different periods in a person's life ranging from infancy to old age. Developmental tasks for Young Adulthood, for example, include such tasks as selecting a mate, learning to live with a partner, becoming a parent, beginning a career, assuming appropriate civic responsibilities, and establishing a social network.

Times and events in an individual's life are sometimes described in terms of one's biological clock, psychological clock, and social clock. One's **social clock** is the time, according to the culture in which one lives, when one is expected to marry, have children, establish one's lifestyle, pursue a career, and retire. There are obviously many more variations in these expectations than in previous generations.

This chapter will discuss the following stages of life-span development: early childhood, childhood, adolescence, young adulthood, middle adulthood, and later adulthood.

Transition
change in the dominant tasks associated with a period of one's life.

Social clock
the socially expected schedule; the socially prescribed time for life's milestones: marriage, parenthood, retirement, etc.

EARLY CHILDHOOD

The life of newborns may seem relatively simple. Some of their behavior is unlearned and automatic. They suck, cry, and react to discomfort. They have startled reactions to loud noises and to sensations of falling.

There is new evidence, however, that the brain of the newborn is much more complex than previously thought. According to Madeleine Nash in a Special Report in *Time,*

> Of all the discoveries that have poured out of neuroscience labs in recent years, the finding that the electrical activity of brain cells changes the physical structure of the brain is perhaps the most breathtaking. For the rhythmic firing of neurons is no longer assumed to be a by-product of building the brain but essential to the process, and it begins, scientists have established, well before birth. A brain is not a computer. Nature does not cobble it together, then turn it on. No, the brain begins working long before it is finished. And the same processes that wire the brain before birth, neuroscientists are finding, also drive the explosion of learning that occurs immediately afterward (4).

This young child will soon be exploring her world on her own.

This special report describes the development of perception, emotions, language, and motor abilities and suggests what parents can do to enhance further brain development and abilities.

It is also important for parents and others caring for infants to recognize that human beings need tender physical handling and love. From birth on, children need to feel secure and have their physical needs satisfied. Psychologist Erik Erikson claims that in the first year of life a baby develops a sense of either trust or mistrust toward others, which will affect later development. Erikson has also identified other stages in development, and we will consider those later in this chapter.

Babies begin to smile at about six weeks of age. They may make responsive sounds in the early months, but they do not usually say words until after a year or so. The use of short, simple sentences is normal around the age of two years. Experts in the study of language development discourage the use of baby talk in communicating with children. Children learn to talk primarily by imitation; therefore, adults should use proper speech for children to imitate.

Maturation refers to development of the nervous system and physical development of the body. The development of physical abilities is particularly apparent in infants and young children.

There are average ages at which children develop physical abilities. For example, most children crawl at about eight months and walk at about one year. However, in reality, children crawl or walk when they are ready, and attempts by eager parents to get them to do so earlier do not make much difference. There seem to be family patterns both in language development and in the rate of physical development in children.

Maturation
development of the nervous system and physical development of the body.

The abilities of children develop rapidly during the first few years of life. This can be a very exciting time for both the children and their parents. Two-year-olds can walk, run, and climb. They recognize a number of people, animals, and things, and they learn new words every day. Between the ages of two and three, children quickly absorb the countless new experiences in their lives.

Young children also develop in other ways during the first two years of life. They learn that people and things do not cease to exist just because they are out of sight. They also develop ways of reacting to others. Infants do not react to strangers in the same way, for example. Some of them are fearful of strangers; others are not. Some youngsters are content to play with toys by themselves for long periods; others cry when they cannot see a familiar person. This is the beginning of **social development,** or individual ways of interacting with others. This early social development contributes to the formation of what we called personality in Chapter 2.

Social development growth in interacting with others.

The arrival of a new little brother or sister may have varying effects, especially on the first child. A child who is included in the waiting and preparation for the new baby will feel a part of the event and is not likely to feel threatened. On the other hand, children who have been the focus of the parents' attention may suddenly feel that the new baby is taking their place. It is natural that children would resent this and would consider the newcomer a rival. Young children in this frustrating position may return to earlier forms of behavior such as thumb sucking or wetting their clothing. If children are given some exclusive attention and are allowed to enter into what is happening, such behavior is usually short-lived. The children make an adjustment, as discussed in Chapter 10. Good adjustments in these situations help children make better adjustments later.

What Do You Recall? *To what extent can you recall your own early childhood years? Can you think of any particular person or event that affected your development?*

These young children are learning skills through firsthand experience—making cookies!

CHILDHOOD

It is not necessary for us to follow all the types of development from year to year. However, some childhood developmental experiences are discussed here. In addition to continued physical growth, children become better coordinated in physical activities. They develop better control over the use of their bodies. It is also desirable that preschool children learn to control their behavior to some extent.

They must learn to do some tasks for themselves and to share items and experiences with others. Language development should continue. Some children have problems in learning to talk properly, and it is also common for preschoolers to have difficulty with certain sounds. Some young children may lisp or stutter. Undue alarm of parents can make the problem worse. Many such early language difficulties are outgrown. Obvious abnormalities, of course, will probably be noticed and should get attention. Children with serious language difficulties may also have a hearing problem, for example.

Intellectual development was discussed in Chapter 7. You will recall, or can review in that chapter, the stages of cognitive, or mental, development identified by Piaget. This development is a very important aspect of life-span development, including the beginning of the ability to reason, around seven years of age. Cognitive development is involved in our education and in career choice and success.

Childhood is a special time in an individual's life. This point is emphasized by David Elkind, the child psychologist, in his book *The Hurried Child*. He says:

> No matter what philosophy of life we espouse, it is important to see childhood as a stage of life, not just as the anteroom to life. Hurrying children into adulthood violates the sanctity of life by giving one period priority over another. But if we really value human life, we will value each period equally and give unto each stage of life what is appropriate to that stage.
>
> Valuing childhood does not mean seeing it as a happy, innocent period, but rather, as an important period of life to which children are entitled. It is children's right to be children, to enjoy the pleasures, and to suffer the pains of a childhood that is infringed by hurrying. In the end, a childhood is the most basic human right of children (5).

"I don't understand, gramps. If they didn't have computers when you were a kid, what did you run your software on?"

Reprinted by permission. The American Legion Magazine © January 1996.

ADOLESCENCE

Adolescence is a time of transformation from child to young adult. It is a period of physical and psychological growth or transformation during which a person achieves a new degree of independence and competence as an individual. Another term for adolescent is teenager. The teen years, particularly those from 13 to 17, are generally considered the period of adolescence.

TRANSITION: CHILD TO ADULT

Sexual development, making the young person capable of reproduction, is known as **puberty.** Production of the hormone estrogen in females and the hormone testosterone in males stimulates the development of sexual characteristics.

Physical growth for both sexes during the years of puberty may be erratic. One part of the body may grow faster than another. It is not unusual for a teenager to have feet that are temporarily too big for the rest of the body. Adolescents develop a new consciousness of their bodies and physical appearance. The 15-year-old who disliked cleaning up may now spend hours on personal hygiene and hair care, for example.

Girls tend to mature earlier than boys in terms of physical development. This difference in physical maturity is noticeable in any group of first-year high school students. Girls experience a spurt of physical growth and development, on the average, between the ages of 11 and 13. Boys, on the other hand, experience this spurt several years later. This difference in the rate of growth can be awkward for both sexes. The girls, for example, are generally taller than the boys for a few years. By the end of the senior year, most of the boys will be taller than the girls, as is characteristic of adults.

Social acceptance and experiences are an important part of adolescent development. John W. Santrock says in *Life-Span Development,*

Crowd
a large group of people; the largest and least personal of all adolescent groups.

> Most peer group relationships in adolescence can be categorized in one of three ways: the crowd, the clique, or individual friendships. The **crowd** *is the largest and least personal of adolescent groups.* Members of a crowd meet because of their mutual interest in activities, not because they are mutually attracted to each other. **Cliques** *are smaller, involve greater intimacy among members, and have more group cohesion than crowds* (6).

Cliques
small, intimate, often exclusionary groups.

Members of the student body of a school attending an athletic event would be part of the crowd. Most high school students could identify the cliques in their grade level, whether they are part of one themselves or not. Many young people prefer to be open to friendship with individuals rather than being part of a clique.

Adolescence usually marks the beginning of sexual/affectational relationships and dating. This period can be a very exciting time of life for young people, and lasting relationships may be formed. It is important that they learn to understand themselves as persons with awareness of their sexual capabilities and values.

The fact that young people mature physically and are capable of reproduction, or becoming parents, before they become emotionally and socially mature and are economically independent can cause problems, both for themselves and for society. Yet many do their best to be responsible. According to Diane E. Papalia, Sally W. Olds, and Ruth D. Feldman in *Human Development,*

> About half of the 1 in 10 teenage girls who become pregnant each year have and keep their babies, often drastically limiting the mother's career opportunities. Talking with a sympathetic, knowledgeable school counselor may help a prospective teenage mother sort out her options (7).

INFLUENCE OF PEERS

Social customs, particularly what others who are one's own age, or **peers,** are doing, are important factors in teenage relationships. Adolescents are influenced to a great extent by what others of their peer group think of them and by what they think the others think of them. Some of their apprehensions are imaginary.

Adolescents are at an age when they are developing into socially mature, independent people and are psychologically in need of approval from other young people with whom they identify. Adolescents express their admiration of leaders in their school, class, or other groups, for example, by imitating their behavior. Whatever a recognized leader is doing, some others have a tendency to do also. In more recent times, however, there has been a turn toward independent thinking and saying no to drugs, sex, or whatever a teenager believes is wrong for him or her. This independent thinking is related to moral development, which will be discussed later in this chapter.

INFLUENCE OF PARENTS

Accelerated growing up is sometimes encouraged indirectly by parents. These parents may be seeking a sense of security or social status for themselves by having achieving, popular offspring. Or they may want their children to have things they couldn't have or to do the things they couldn't do, which may prove to be too much too soon. Dr. Bruce A. Baldwin, a practicing psychologist, refers to the dangers of giving one's children too much in "Positive Parenting: How to Avoid Raising Cornucopia Kids." He defines them as young people who are self-centered, avoid responsibilities, and want only to have a good time. Even after they leave home, according to Baldwin, they expect someone else to foot the bills. In his article, Baldwin says:

> Cornucopia Kids simply don't deal well with the "real world" because they have never been exposed to it. They are children who learn through years of direct experience in the home that the good life will always be available for the asking, without personal accountability or achievement motivation. These indulged children have lived their lives in an artificial environment created by naive and compliant parents. Life is always easy. They've never had to struggle; nor are they expected to give back in return for what they've been given. The real world, when at last they confront it, finds them unprepared and overwhelmed (8).

TRIALS AND TRIUMPHS

Adolescents experience many ups and downs, triumphs and trials. Many think there has been too much emphasis on the negative aspects of adolescence. There is always more emphasis on problems in any subject area because problems are obvious and disturbing. But many young people, and others who admire them, have objected to the publicity given to juvenile delinquency and other problems that involve a small percentage of their age group.

Young people during these years are more apt to take risks, often defying the possibility that they can be seriously harmed. Some psychologists have referred to this attitude as the "personal fable." Such attitudes include, "I can handle this drug," "I won't have an automobile or motorcycle accident," "I won't get pregnant," "I can take care of myself," or a similar kind of statement about whatever the particular risk happens to be.

Adolescence offers the developing individual new opportunities but also requires more decisions. Young people during these years may become confused about their ambitions and may feel pressured by parents, instructors in school, and others in the fast-moving, demanding world. Some become troubled enough so that they need professional help; they have problems that they will not simply outgrow.

Adolescence is a time of mixed feelings and reactions for young people. Their lives are a combination of situations calling for both childhood dependence and adult independence, a subject that will be discussed later in this chapter. No one can deny that adolescence is a turning point in life and can be trying to young people who are not certain which way they should, or even want to, go. Although, as indicated earlier, adolescence is usually associated with the teen years, some psychologists include early years of the twenties as part of adolescent experience.

In spite of the perplexities, contradictions, and trials of this time of life, adolescence can be rewarding for young people, their parents, and others who are part of their lives. Life at this time is promising and challenging in ways it has never been before.

 What Would You Say? *How would you respond to someone who says, "I can't understand why teenagers can't just be kids until they get to be adults"?*

YOUNG ADULTHOOD

Age can be confusing in studying stages of development. What a person can do and is doing is more important than age. Look around you. You see young adults acting in different ways, don't you? That is why deciding whether the legal age for various types of activities and responsibilities has created some problems. Some young people are mature enough for new responsibilities. Others are not. Some are adult in many ways even before they are 18. For the most part, we should be thinking of the young adult, during this discussion, as ranging from 18 through the early thirties. There is considerable difference between the maturity and perceptions of those at the beginning and end of this age range, but they nevertheless have a great deal in common.

Young adulthood involves a number of important challenges and decisions. Most people during this time of their lives complete the major phase of their formal education, decide on an initial career, and decide whether they want to marry or be single. There may be some conflict between giving up some independence to establish meaningful interdependence in marriage or other relationships.

This time of one's life also involves new relationships with one's parents and any siblings. There can be a sharing of oneself and ideas and experiences that is not possible at a younger or less mature level. The author of an article in *Psychology Today* has this to say about adult sibling relationships:

Rivalry forged in childhood and carried into early and middle adulthood becomes less and less important with time. What matters more is that as constants in our lives, siblings provide a reference against which to judge and measure ourselves. They know us in a unique way during childhood and share a history that can bring understanding and a sense of perspective to adulthood. Friends and neighbors move away, former coworkers are forgotten, marriages break up, parents die, but our brothers and sisters remain our brothers and sisters. As we age and begin to sense our own mortality, many siblings rediscover the values and strengths of family (9).

Have you found this to be true in your life?

Young adults have many more options, and decisions, related to family responsibilities than their parents or grandparents had. Some married couples decide not to have children. Others choose to have smaller families. Some adopt children; others experience parental roles by caring for foster children. Still others become stepparents. It is apparent that "the children" may live in a number of parent-child relationships. Relationships in all these types of families can be equally close and rewarding. And, unfortunately, with every type of family there can also be conflict and even abuse.

The total parent-child relationship in a family has the utmost significance in the lives of all family members. Again, such relationships have changed greatly in recent times. For example, fathers are more involved now in caring for young children. Children themselves notice less difference in the roles of their mothers and fathers.

Part of the role of parents is to guide and sometimes correct the behavior of their children. Children need discipline that is neither too strict nor too permissive. They need the assurance that their parents love them enough to care what they do and don't do. They need discipline that is relatively consistent but that is reasonable in view of circumstances.

A parent should ask, What result do I want? Do I want my children to suffer in some way? Do I want to release my own frustrations by using my children as whipping posts? Do I want my children to learn and to improve their behavior? Consideration of these questions will help the parent to react more rationally and to use methods of discipline that have favorable results. A parent should keep in mind the purposes of discipline: to teach children respect for others and the rights of others, to prevent harm to the children themselves, and to teach children self-control or discipline, which they will use throughout life. Lack of discipline in childhood is blamed for some of the insecurity in the lives of young people today.

Responsible adults—whether raising their natural children or adopted children or temporarily caring for foster children—are concerned with their present and future behavior. Rules and guidelines are necessary and even give the children a sense of security, but the ultimate goal should be self-discipline.

DEPENDENCE OR INTERDEPENDENCE?

Before we continue to look at later stages of life-span development, consideration of the life-span dependence/interdependence curve can give us some insight into our own past and future development. Although we started our lives

Life-Span Dependence/Interdependence Curve

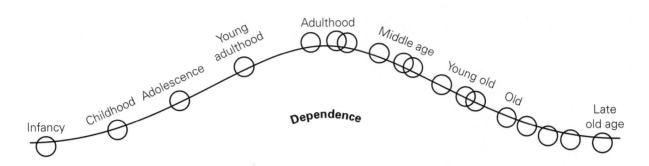

almost totally dependent on others, there is a natural striving for independence that becomes evident very early in life.

The goal of a young adult is usually to be "on my own," or as independent as possible. This goal is understandable and is encouraged by society. Total independence is seldom achieved, or even desired, in today's society, however. We live in a complex, specialized world where a degree of dependence on one another is part of normal living. We may derive satisfaction from doing things for ourselves, but in most lifestyles we are more **interdependent,** or dependent on one another, than we realize.

Besides the increase in daily dependence on one another to satisfy our physical needs, there is voluntary interdependence, which can enrich living. This type of dependence is different from earlier dependence on one's parents or others. It is only possible as long as persons involved are able to be independent in some respects. Interdependence of this type is related to emotional and other psychological needs, as well as to physical needs. In voluntary interdependence, a person must be able and willing both to give and to receive love and support of various kinds. It involves risks in allowing ourselves to be dependent on others when it is not necessary to do so. However, the most rewarding of human relationships cannot be achieved without such voluntary interdependence and risks. A successful marriage is an example of voluntary interdependence.

The accompanying figure illustrates the extent to which a person can be dependent, independent, or voluntarily interdependent at various times during his or her life span. The life-span dependence/interdependence curve combines life-span development with variations in dependence, independence, or interdependence. It also shows how these might apply to different lifestyles during one's adult life. The curve itself represents the life span from infancy to possible late old age. The area below the curve represents dependence; the area above the curve represents independence. The interlocking of circles represents voluntary interdependence. Persons who share a degree of voluntary interdependence still maintain a large measure of independence in their lives. Positions of the circles above or below the line show the degree to which a person is (or may be) dependent or independent at various times of life. Note that at adolescence, for example, the circle is halfway above and halfway below the line. Also note that human beings are almost totally dependent at birth and some may

Interdependent dependence of people on one another.

Life-Span Development **323**

These adults—still young at heart—are off on a ride through the woods.

become so again if they live to be very old and become unable to care for themselves. Although this will not happen to most of us, it is realistic to recognize there are many aged adults in nursing homes today who are almost totally dependent on others. Although it is not represented on the curve, we also know that, at any time during the life span, persons can become dependent because of accidents or illness.

The life span is represented as a curve to show that during young adulthood, adulthood, and the middle-age years, persons have greater choice in their lifestyles. They are also more likely to have an interdependent relationship or lifestyle, which is more complicated in many ways than independence. But it may be more desirable.

Most human beings in today's society move from the dependency of infancy, through the blend of dependence/independence of adolescence, to the independence of young adulthood. From there to the possible dependency of old age, there can be a variety of independent or voluntarily interdependent lifestyles.

It can be of value to sketch one's own dependence/interdependence curve up to one's present lifestyle and to project one's anticipated lifestyles in the future. Although we cannot always foresee what we might do in the future, the changing of our lifestyles and relationships with other people should not be haphazard. The better we understand ourselves, our goals, and our relationships with other people, the more satisfying and rewarding our lives will be.

MIDDLE ADULTHOOD

As with other life-span development stages, there are different ways of describing middle age. For many, it is the first personal awareness of "getting old." Many persons just entering this stage actually feel older, for this reason, than they may feel ten years later in their life span. Others react with a new sense of freedom and challenge. Many see this as a "now or never" turning point in their lives when they decide whether to further their education, change careers, or make some other significant change in their lives. Others may come to the realization that they are on the "right track" in their lives in terms of self-understanding, work, family relationships, and progress toward fulfillment of goals.

Many middle-aged adults are involved in activities for which there might not have been time in earlier years. This time of life has been referred to as "the empty nest," with reference to the fact that one's children have been raised and have left home to be on their own. Another expression, "overcrowded nest," however, has been coined to refer to a relatively common experience today, in which adult sons and daughters return home to live with parents, at least temporarily. This return home may be due to illness, loss of job, or relocation that involves housing delays. A definition of family and home that would apply here is: "Home is where, when you have no place to go, they take you in." Although that may not always be the case, it has worked out for many on a short-term basis.

Roger Gould, who has done extensive research on adult development, believes that individuals typically give up a number of false assumptions or myths as they go through the stages of adult development. According to Gould, these "false childhood assumptions that we must lose" are:

> We'll always live with our parents and be their children.
> Our parents will always be there to help us out.
> Our parents' version of reality is correct.
> There is no real death or evil (10).

In terms of how these myths have applied to you, it should be pointed out that there is a difference between "knowing" something intellectually and understanding it and accepting it in terms of your own experience. It is very possible, for example, to know something "in your head" such as "people die" and yet not apply the truth or reality of it to yourself and those you love until you are confronted with the experience or repeated evidence that affects your life. When we have learned to cope with such realities, we have become adults in the full sense of the word. This acceptance of reality can be at any age of adulthood, or it may never happen at all. Frequently, it happens during middle adulthood.

Retirement can be a time to relax, enjoy hobbies, and spend time with grandchildren.

LATER ADULTHOOD

Exactly what the term *later adulthood* means could depend on the entire life span of the individual. There is an obvious effort in today's society to avoid referring to people who have lived a long time as "old." Instead they are called "seniors," "senior citizens," or "the elderly." They may also be spoken of as in their "golden years" or "harvest years."

There is a definite physical decline in many respects in one's later years. Sight and hearing usually weaken, and older people may have difficulty walking or using their hands. Part of this may result from arthritis, a common ailment in later adulthood. There is no doubt that many abilities decline with age. Some people experience memory problems and may remember what they did long ago better than they can recall what happened recently. However, the common belief in intellectual decline in age is largely a myth. In actual practice, society provides older citizens with limited opportunities to remain mentally active. Since intellectual abilities are affected by boredom and lack of motivation, in addition to other causes, the decline in mental alertness results partly from the absence of challenge and stimulation. There are many examples of old people who live full, productive lives characterized by energy and alertness.

To some extent, age represents an attitude rather than the number of years a person has lived. Many older persons continue to learn, to be socially active, and to have new experiences. You probably know older people who continue to work toward new goals and lead meaningful lives.

STAGES OF PSYCHOSOCIAL DEVELOPMENT

So far we have dealt with several types of development taking place at various times from early childhood to later adulthood. *Psychosocial* pertains to the development of feelings about oneself and attitudes toward others. According to Erik Erikson, there are eight stages of psychosocial development, with the type of development taking place at each stage having some influence on development at later stages. These eight stages and the approximate time in life they normally occur are shown in the accompanying figure (11).

During infancy, or the first year of life, an individual develops a sense of either trust or mistrust toward others. Since infants spend most of their time with their parents or some other primary caretaker, the type of care they receive largely determines whether they develop trust or mistrust. This doesn't mean that children lie in a crib or sit in a playpen and think, "If he doesn't come with some food pretty soon, I won't trust him." Obviously, infants are not capable of this type of thinking. But if they receive care and loving attention, trust is likely to develop. If they are neglected and live in an environment full of discord and tension, distrust is likely to develop. In the first year of life, therefore, the basis for either favorable or unfavorable psychosocial development is formed.

As you look at the figure shown on page 327, you will notice that the first term of each one of the stages could be considered positive, or desirable, and the term following *vs.* could be considered negative, or undesirable. It would be generally agreed, for example, that it would be better to develop a sense of trust

Erikson's Eight Stages of Psychosocial Development

							Ego integrity vs. despair	Later adult
						Genera- tivity vs. stagnation		Middle adult
					Intimacy vs. isolation			Young adult
				Identity vs. role confusion				Adolescent
			Industry vs. inferiority					Elementary school child
		Initiative vs. guilt						Preschool child
	Autonomy vs. shame, doubt							Toddler
Basic trust vs. mistrust								Infancy

Adapted from *Childhood and Society*, Second Edition, Revised, by Erik H. Erikson, with the permission of W. W. Norton & Company, Inc. Copyright 1950, © 1963 by W. W. Norton & Company, Inc.

toward others than a feeling of mistrust. This doesn't mean that a person should develop trust toward others without exception or limitations. The basic idea is that trust is the foundation of meaningful relationships with others.

What Do You Think? *If a person does not develop trust during his or her first year of life, does that mean that the rest of that person's psychosocial development will be negative? Think about this as you read about psychosocial development.*

Autonomy independence; compe- tence.

When children are two or three years old, or toddlers, they develop either autonomy or shame and doubt. If they have developed trust during infancy, it is more likely that they will develop autonomy during these years. The term **autonomy** refers to a sense of independence or competence. Now, obviously a toddler cannot be very independent. But if you know any two- or three-year-olds, you are aware that they like to do things for themselves. They want to pour their own juice or dress themselves, even if a few things get on backward. If Mandy is not allowed to "help" or do some things for herself, she is not likely to develop a sense of autonomy. If she is constantly scolded for doing things wrong, making a mess, or getting in the way, she is likely to develop a sense of shame or doubt.

Initiative
an interest in trying new things.

The next two childhood stages of psychosocial development follow essentially the same lines. **Initiative** at age 4 or 5 refers primarily to interest in trying new things, in going ahead with responsibilities and activities of interest. At this age, responsibilities may be as simple as putting clothes or possessions away. This leads to a sense of worth and achievement, however, that is important to the child and leads to further positive development. On the other hand, if William's behavior receives a negative response, he is likely to develop a sense of guilt. The guilt of a preschool child is likely to lead to a sense of inferiority in the elementary school child, and a feeling of inferiority is not likely to lead to activity that is challenging and constructive in the child's development.

If you were to visit any of the grade schools in your area and observe the children's behavior, you would see some who are hesitant to go ahead with assignments and activities or are timid about either asking the teacher for help or reciting in class. This reflects both children's feelings about themselves, or self-concept, and their attitudes toward others. They are not willing to become involved if they feel unsure of themselves, are afraid to make mistakes, and do not trust others.

Identity
an understanding of one-self as an individual.

Role confusion
values and behavior that change frequently.

You could conclude correctly that such children will have still further problems at the next stage or adolescence. This is the stage where they begin to develop identity as an individual or experience role confusion. **Identity** refers to understanding yourself as an individual with personal values and goals. **Role confusion,** on the other hand, refers to values and behavior that frequently change, often being influenced by one's companions at the time. If Sarah doesn't feel good about herself, she will have difficulty making independent decisions and determining some goals for her future. She is more subject to peer influence, relying on identity with others or with a group, rather than establishing her own identity as an individual. She is experiencing role confusion.

Before we consider the last three stages of psychosocial development, let's consider the question asked earlier: "If a person does not develop trust during his or her first year of life, does that mean that the rest of that person's psychosocial development will be negative?" The answer is, "Not necessarily so, although it is more likely to be negative than positive." It will take some special influence or particular effort by the individual to counteract an unfavorable psychosocial beginning. Fortunately for the child, and for society, this is possible. When children start school and become involved in other activities, they have contact with different people and environments. Often a scout leader, coach, older brother or sister, teacher, or some other person with whom the child feels comfortable can have a positive effect on the child's development. The child may begin to feel better about himself or herself, develop more self-confidence, and be willing to try more things. Essentially he or she has to develop a sense of trust and then progress through the positive aspects of the other stages of psychosocial development. This progress takes time but it can and does happen.

Intimacy
any close, personal, loving, and open relationship.

If you are a young adult, you should be able to recognize yourself as having some degree of intimacy or isolation. It is important to keep in mind that there are degrees of psychosocial characteristics as well as different stages. **Intimacy** refers to a close, sharing relationship with at least one other person. This could be a boyfriend or girlfriend, spouse, best friend, or some other special person or persons. You are not likely to share your feelings, your dreams and disappointments, or the person you really are with someone you do not trust. Trust in this sense, quite obviously, does not refer to our money or possessions. We are more likely to risk those than we are to risk being ridiculed and rejected.

A person can be married and still not experience intimacy in this sense. It is also possible to have a great deal of interaction with other people and yet have a personal sense of **isolation,** or aloneness. The person who is afraid to become psychologically close to others probably has had unfavorable psychosocial development. It is not realistic for us as adults to blame someone else for the person we are today, however. We can learn to understand ourselves and to make changes in ourselves and in our lives. It helps to have support, and we can give support to others, but psychosocial disadvantages can be overcome with self-understanding, determination, and time.

The middle adult stage in this type of development pertains to what happens to a person after some of life's major challenges have been met (or avoided). **Generativity** means reaching out and becoming involved in what is happening outside one's immediate sphere of life. After their own family has been raised, many middle-aged people become interested and involved in other activities that benefit youth or the community and keep themselves active and stimulated in the process. Others experience **stagnation,** or a lack of meaningful activity and sense of purpose. For many of these people, life was always more frustrating than challenging and stimulating, and it is easier to fall back into a passive existence.

By the time a person reaches later adulthood, or what we commonly think of as old age, he or she has developed either **ego integrity** or *despair*. If persons at that stage in life feel good about themselves, are satisfied with what they have done with their lives, and have rewarding relationships with others, they have acquired ego integrity. On the other hand, if they feel dissatisfied with themselves and their accomplishments (or the lack of them) and are disgruntled with their families and others with whom they have contact, they are experiencing despair. If you have contact with some older persons, you can probably recognize the difference. Persons experiencing despair are telling us that they have had frustrating, relatively meaningless lives.

This discussion of psychosocial development should have been helpful in understanding yourself and others. Remember that, as adults, we can change ourselves and our situations. We can also be supportive to others who seem to lack trust or other positive characteristics of this type of development. Having had some psychosocial disadvantages is no reason to miss out on present and future stimulating experiences and challenges.

Isolation
aloneness; a feeling of being "outside."

Generativity
an interest in others, including those outside one's family.

Stagnation
lack of meaningful activity and sense of purpose.

Ego integrity
satisfaction with one's life and relationships.

MORAL DEVELOPMENT

We were not born with a sense of right and wrong, yet all of us today believe that some types of behavior are right and others are wrong. It is unlikely, however, that all of us would agree on what kinds of behavior belong in each category.

What do we mean by moral development, and how is it acquired? **Moral development** essentially means acquiring a standard of what we believe to be right and wrong. Since this type of development is learned, a natural question to ask

Moral development
acquiring a standard of what one believes to be right and wrong.

would be, How is moral development learned? To begin with, what we *must* do or *can't* do was learned from those with whom we lived or from those with whom we spent considerable time in the early years of our lives. In today's society that would most likely be parents, or personnel in day-care centers. As one progresses through life, moral development is influenced by many others and becomes more complicated. Eventually we become responsible for our own moral standard.

One of the best known theories of moral development is that of Lawrence Kohlberg. He describes moral development in terms of six stages that motivate one's behavior. The following is a simplified explanation of why people act the way they do at each stage, according to Kohlberg's theory.

The Six Moral Stages

Reasons for Doing "Right"

Stage 1   Fear of punishment.

Stage 2   Concern with meeting one's own needs; expects others to do the same.

Stage 3   Belief in the golden rule; it is important to treat others right; they will then also treat you right.

Stage 4   Belief that society and other groups need rules to function properly; therefore, I must obey the rules; respect for authority.

Stage 5   Belief in democratic approach; since everyone does not want the same things, what is best for the majority is right.

Stage 6   Belief in universal moral principles and one's personal commitment to them.

---

(12)

Notice that the first stage is related to fear of punishment and the last stage is based on a personal commitment to what one believes is right or wrong. Although stages in moral development seem to follow the order outlined by Kohlberg, individuals may function at different stages for different reasons. A person may not speed when driving, for example, for fear of paying a fine. That same person would not steal a car because he or she believes it is wrong to take the possessions of other people. Also, there are some people in society who may never function at the higher stages of moral development. In fact, some individuals may never progress much beyond Stage 1, which would mean that there isn't anything that they wouldn't do if they thought they wouldn't be punished or suffer undesired consequences. If this were common, we would not have a civilized society.

In fact it is questioned whether Stage 6 should be included because few people, if any, reach that stage in their moral development. According to Laura E. Berk in *Infants, Children, and Adolescents,*

> A striking finding is that moral development is very slow and gradual. Stages 1 and 2 decrease in adolescence, while Stage 3 increases through midadolescence and then declines. Stage 4 rises over the teenage years until, by early adulthood, is the typical response. Few people move beyond it to stage 5. In fact, postconventional morality (Stages 5 and 6) is so rare that there is no clear evidence that Kohlberg's Stage 6 actually follows Stage 5. The highest stage of moral development is still a matter of speculation (13).

Berk defines the postconventional level as the level "in which individuals define morality in terms of abstract principles and values that apply to all situations and societies." The two levels preceding the postconventional level (Stages 5 and 6) are identified by Kohlberg as the preconventional level (Stages 1 and 2) and the conventional level (Stages 3 and 4). We must remember that many factors, such as culture, learning, influence of others, and personal choices, influence moral development, so that it is difficult to predict how an individual will react in a particular situation. We can conclude from reviewing the stages, however, that moral development begins with fear of punishment, before a child is capable of making rational choices. From there it can move to the recognition that society needs rules and laws and a respect for what is best for the majority.

 What Would You Say? *How would you respond to someone who says, "Laws are to be broken, as long as you don't get caught"?*

Situational ethics
a system of ethics by which acts are judged within their contexts instead of by categorical principles.

In the determination of right and wrong, many people maintain that the situation must be considered. Those who believe in **situational ethics** consider the total situation rather than just the behavior itself in determining whether an act is right or wrong. Judd may believe it is wrong to steal, for example, but he may believe it would be acceptable for a person to steal food for her starving family. Problems arise in legal matters in this respect because situations can be interpreted and evaluated differently.

MATURE BEHAVIOR

So far we have dealt with several types of development throughout the life span. We must keep in mind that not all types of maturity occur as stages in a process. Some require conscious effort by the individual. In addition to moral development, such types of maturity include emotional, social, intellectual, and vocational development. All these aspects of maturity deserve the attention of young adults. James W. Vander Zanden in *Human Development* gives us the following definition of maturity:

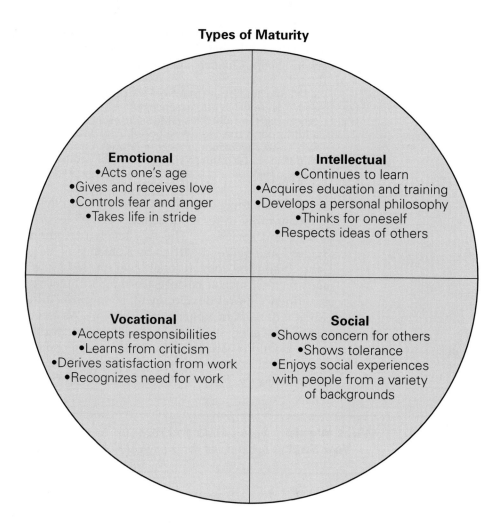

Types of Maturity

Emotional
- Acts one's age
- Gives and receives love
- Controls fear and anger
- Takes life in stride

Intellectual
- Continues to learn
- Acquires education and training
- Develops a personal philosophy
- Thinks for oneself
- Respects ideas of others

Vocational
- Accepts responsibilities
- Learns from criticism
- Derives satisfaction from work
- Recognizes need for work

Social
- Shows concern for others
- Shows tolerance
- Enjoys social experiences with people from a variety of backgrounds

Maturity is the capacity of individuals to undergo continual change in order to adapt successfully and cope flexibly with the demands and responsibilities of life. Maturity is not some sort of plateau or final state but a lifetime process of becoming. It is a never-ending search for a meaningful and comfortable fit between ourselves and the world—a struggle to "get it all together" (14).

EMOTIONAL MATURITY

Reference to mature behavior usually means what is here identified as emotional maturity. Probably the reason for this is that emotional immaturity can be conspicuous and troublesome. Emotionally mature people have learned to control and use their emotions sensibly and for the greater enjoyment of life.

Paul J. Gelinas, in his book entitled *Coping with Your Emotions,* shares his ideas on emotional maturity in saying,

> If you are realistic, you'll face the truth even when it hurts your feelings. Many disturbing situations affect your life and those of your loved ones, and this fact must be anticipated if you are to achieve emotional strength. As the years go

by you will encounter severe disappointments, sorrows, and shocks. You may develop a stoic philosophy, becoming hardened to possible disasters, shutting off your emotions in resignation. However, such an outlook on life not only saves you from being hurt, but it also robs you of love and many other emotions that make life worthwhile. Accordingly, you should accept difficulties as challenges to be used as a means of further emotional growth. Courage will be your helpmate, preparing you to fight firmly when hardship strikes. Either you must struggle to avert tragedy or seek to change defeat into success (15).

Emotions can create difficulties and cause pain or can make life more satisfying and exciting.

Mature people experience love, fear, anger, and other emotions, but they do not let their responses become harmful to themselves or to others. Mature people may even occasionally act in an irrational, or emotional, way. They may not have perfect emotional control at times or always act with complete emotional stability, but they usually make better responses than others under an existing set of circumstances. Mature people also are able to recognize immature behavior.

ACT YOUR AGE What might be acceptable behavior at one age may not be acceptable at another. If at 10 years of age you had a disagreement with your teammates during a game and walked away and went home, you were acting your age; you had not yet learned that dropping what you are doing and stalking away do not settle differences. However, an 18-year-old would be expected to use more self-control, even though some people that age and even older may act like balky 10-year-olds.

GIVE AND RECEIVE LOVE Mature people know that you may love in different ways. A woman does not love her spouse in the same ways as she loves her brother, for example. Mature people have an unselfish interest in and are concerned with the welfare and happiness of other people. This is an essential characteristic of love.

CONTROL FEAR AND ANGER Even though it is normal to have some fears, mature people do not let these interfere with their normal activities. They recognize that it is sensible to fear things and situations that pose a threat to them. But mature people know what their fears are and know what to do about them. They can maintain emotional control in emergency situations without their fears turning into panic.

Anger is a basic human emotional response. Even very young children show behavior that can be interpreted as anger. But they express such feelings with no attempt at control or consideration for others. Adults who lose their temper at the least provocation are acting like children in an emotional sense. Justifiable anger of mature adults is expressed in a nondestructive way. Many of life's problems would not be solved if people did not become disturbed enough to try to solve them. The question is to determine what is worth fighting for or against. Then you can act in socially acceptable, effective ways.

TAKE LIFE IN STRIDE Mature people respond calmly to most disappointing situations. They understand that some things just aren't worth getting worked up about. Angelina, a graphics student, was not assigned the particular task she preferred on Tuesday morning, but she was able to accept another assignment and did her best work on it. If, because of the time schedule, she cannot take a particular class she needs to complete her program, on the other hand, she has reason to be disturbed. She should still be able to solve the problem in a mature, rational manner, however. It is better for all concerned to approach most of life with a calm interest and rational concern and to save emotional involvement for issues that really matter.

Mature people recognize the relative importance of what happens to them and what they do. They have learned to laugh at themselves, at their human limitations, which sometimes get them into predicaments. They can be amused by their occasional stupidity and the harmless but ridiculous consequences of some of the things they do. On the other hand, they should not react with a laugh-it-off response to all mistakes and problems. Mature people can distinguish between the harmless mistake and the serious error. A sense of humor includes recognizing such differences.

SOCIAL MATURITY

Social maturity can be defined as having mutually satisfying experiences with both sexes, people of different ages, and individuals from various backgrounds. Socially mature people relate well to people of different races, religions, and occupations. They do not live in their own little world. They share experiences with friends and with many others, at home and at work. They are also dependable in obligations and promises. Some of the characteristics of this type of maturity are discussed in the following sections.

SHOW CONCERN FOR OTHERS Concern for other people is a characteristic of social maturity that must be learned and often takes effort and self-denial. Human beings by nature, and therefore from birth, are self-centered. The satisfaction that people get from doing things for others, however, can be greater than the pleasure they get from thinking only of themselves. It is an ironic, or unexpected, twist in life that the more people give of themselves to others, the more content they themselves will be.

Everyone is familiar with the golden rule, "Do unto others as you would have them do unto you." An interpretation of this rule, "Do unto others as they would have you do unto them," is based on the principle that each human being is different. Perhaps other people don't want to be treated the same way you would like to have them treat you. You should try to understand other people, to use empathy, and to act accordingly. The golden rule can also be interpreted to mean "Do not do unto others as you would not have them do unto you." In other words, some types of behavior should be avoided—for example, insult, distrust, neglect, or deliberate harm.

In an old legend, Jupiter, ruler of gods and mortals in Roman mythology, is persuaded by Juno, his wife, to help out a man in his problems with other human beings. Jupiter teaches the man to take advantage of the principle of reciprocal behavior. The point is to treat others with consideration and respect so that they will react the same way toward you and make your life easier and happier.

Mature people are interested in others for their sake rather than for personal benefit. One finds that when mature people treat others with consideration, they benefit too. Whether people are concerned with others from a selfish or unselfish motive, they find themselves better off. A comparison of two young home appliance demonstrators in their sales work is an example. Larry is attentive and helpful in explaining and demonstrating appliances to customers because he knows that it will help him sell more appliances and increase his commission. This is a selfish motive, but it is effective in sales nevertheless. Karen also shows interest in customers and is helpful, but primarily because she is interested in people and gains satisfaction from helping them make the wisest selection and use of appliances. Both people have similar sales records, but it is apparent that Karen is more socially mature and, therefore, experiences more complete satisfaction in her work.

SHOW TOLERANCE Another characteristic of social maturity is tolerance. Tolerance is readily accepted as desirable but can be extremely difficult to practice. The familiar saying, "It is easier said than done," applies to tolerance as well as to many other characteristics of maturity. Tolerance includes allowing others to be what they are as long as they are not interfering with the rights of others. It is the recognition and acceptance of different backgrounds with different values and customs. It also includes being open-minded about differences in personal appearance and lifestyle within one's own culture. Mature people strive to see such differences from other points of view. Tolerance does not mean understanding or agreeing, however. Even when we "can't imagine why . . . ," we can at least be tolerant of others when we and others are not adversely affected.

ENJOY SOCIAL EXPERIENCES The definition of social maturity includes the idea of having mutually satisfying experiences with people with different characteristics. If Mark goes to a family reunion, for example, he talks to the old people, aunts and uncles, and even children. He may spend most of his time with relatives his own age, it is true, but it can be a good experience for both him and others to move about and become more actively involved. In another type of situation, if Carole goes to a reception and knows only one person there, she still introduces herself to others. She does not confine herself to being with just that one guest. A socially mature person can adapt to several different situations and make them enjoyable experiences.

INTELLECTUAL MATURITY

Learning, thinking, and interpreting are classified as *intellectual* behavior and development. Human beings begin to learn at birth, and they have new experiences throughout life. The ability to understand various concepts, for example language and mathematics, is largely developmental. Children have only a vague notion of the length of a week, or a month, or a year, partly because they have had less experience in living. You may recall, or can review, Piaget's stages of cognitive development discussed in Chapter 7. When a person has reached the formal operations stage (usually around 12 years of age or during the teen years) he or she is capable of abstract thinking. The individual can evaluate ideas and can think more critically. This is one of the reasons adolescents often challenge the thinking and values of their parents. They are using intellectual ability they haven't had before, even though they are characteristically overconfident about being right.

CONTINUE TO LEARN Mature people know how to make learning more efficient, interesting, and lasting. They recognize that learning is a lifelong process, which can continue to make life stimulating and challenging. In addition to taking classes, some of the ways people continue to learn are by reading, general observation, association, and experience. Mature people seek new experiences and exposure to different ideas. They change and continue to expand their interests as they grow in years and experience.

ACQUIRE EDUCATION AND TRAINING People not only must develop their learning abilities but must take advantage of educational and training opportunities. Intellectually mature people know that mental and manual competencies are valuable attributes in today's technological world but that they are not acquired easily and quickly.

How adults learn changes somewhat as a person ages, however. Older persons do not respond as quickly as they did when they were younger. It takes them longer to learn. Older people also seem to relate what they are learning to their experiences and ideas more than younger people do. It might be said that a younger person is sharper mentally, whereas an older person is wiser.

DEVELOP A PERSONAL PHILOSOPHY How and what people think is much more than automatic mental development, however. In fact, *how* the mind functions and *what* one thinks are actually two different topics. People in the process of growing up must seek answers to **philosophical questions.** These pertain to the meaning of life and to the significance of one's particular existence.

Philosophical questions concerns about the meaning of life.

Intellectually mature people have established a set of beliefs or principles that give direction to their lives. These beliefs and principles are usually not written;

Frank and Ernest

© 1989 Used with permission of Bob Thaves.

in fact many people are not aware of them on a day-to-day basis. If you asked some people what their philosophy of life is they might respond: "What are you talking about?" Nevertheless, everyone does have a formal or informal philosophy of life that directs personal behavior.

What one believes and values includes some code of morality and a sense of right and wrong. This may be based on religious belief, social approval, or personal standards. One's behavior and relationships with others are affected by these convictions and values. This type of maturity is thus related to the levels of moral development discussed earlier.

THINK FOR YOURSELF Intellectual independence is part of intellectual maturity. People who are maturing are learning to think for themselves and to make their own decisions. They evaluate new ideas objectively for what they are worth, rather than blindly accepting or rejecting them. They develop thoughtful self-discipline and assume responsibility for their own behavior. To do what individuals themselves think they should do, whether they are required by others to do it or not, is considered by many to be an essential feature of mature character. Their behavior is neither completely imitative nor purely automatic. They are conformists in many aspects of living, but they know what they are doing and why.

RESPECT IDEAS OF OTHERS Mature people are willing to listen to and consider the ideas and advice of others. They are also pleased when someone else asks them for their opinion or advice. But they are not offended if the person decides not to follow their suggestions. Experience in living gives one wisdom, but no one ever reaches the point in life of having all the answers. Mature individuals have respect for authority. Everyone has a supervisor—if not the boss, at least others who require accountability in some way. Most people at some time in their lives also have some degree of authority over others. Mature people do not misuse this authority to bolster their self-esteem or to show they have power. Remember that many people have authority only because it is given to them by others. Mature people recognize the need for rules and regulations in an orderly society and do not expect special privileges. This also involves some aspects of social maturity, as just discussed.

VOCATIONAL MATURITY

Even in a person's early years, today, much attention is given to career education. *Career* is a broader term than *job*. A person may be preparing for a marketing career, for example. This, in turn, would include several different jobs. You are probably now enrolled in some specific program of education, preparing yourself for a particular type of career. Finding the right job will be a task deserving your full attention when you finish. What is right for someone else may not be right for you. At that time it would be to your advantage to consider the approach-avoidance conflicts discussed in Chapter 3.

As important as it is to choose a career, prepare for it, and find a job, these events are only preliminary to vocational maturity. Some of the other characteristics of vocational maturity are discussed next.

RECOGNIZE THE NEED TO WORK Most members of a society must be productive. In fact, many people consider themselves fortunate to have a job and to be able to do it. Maturity, in a sense, is doing what you are expected to do, even when you might enjoy doing something else more.

There are very few people who do not need to work—in their homes, for themselves, or for others. Some people are not expected to hold full-time jobs in the world of work, of course. These would include the very young, the very old, and those with severe disabilities. And, of course, there are still people in our society who are able to work and—if all facts were known—would be expected to be in the workforce, but they are not. They are being supported by those who do work. This is not a reference to the unemployed who want work but rather to those who take undue advantage of social programs and entitlements. This situation is becoming less of a problem for everyone because of various assistance programs that require persons to receive some kind of job training and to become financially independent over time. In reality, this is what many people who are receiving temporary assistance want.

A vocationally mature person accepts work as a reality of life and tries to find work that he or she is suited for, rather then resenting the fact that work is necessary. Some persons face this reality most of their lives, every morning when their alarm goes off, but have never accepted the fact with a constructive attitude.

A young person who has given careful thought to the choice of a career and is preparing for a career through education and training has a sound beginning in vocational maturity. Since we spend so much of our lives on our jobs, vocational maturity is one of the most important types of maturity we can develop.

DERIVE SATISFACTION FROM WORK It is common for young people starting out in their careers to experience "reality shock." Young people typically have confidence in themselves and have high expectations of what they can do and what the world of work will offer. Although such qualities can be favorable, they are not always realistic. Aspects of most jobs are not enjoyable or particularly satisfying, but which must be accepted and performed as well as one can. Over the years, work becomes a part of one's identity as a person. The answer to "What kind of work do you do?" is a significant factor in how we perceive ourselves.

When people can accept the need to work and the realities of the world of work, they can learn to gain satisfaction from work. This can be done in several ways. First, satisfaction comes from doing your best no matter what the job is. Another kind of satisfaction comes from increasing your skills. There are very few things a person can't learn to do better. Some improvement comes with experience, but attention and an effort to learn also make a difference. It is largely through work that most of us achieve esteem and move toward self-actualization as well as satisfy the lower-level needs on Maslow's hierarchy. We can continue to develop our work potential whether we advance on a job, change jobs, or become more skilled at the job we now have.

Some satisfaction can also come when the quality of our work is recognized by others. Additional satisfaction can be measured in material rewards—raises, bonuses, and the like. People who gain satisfaction from their work do not need as much extrinsic motivation as those who work only for a living. Some find their work so satisfying that they would continue it even if they did not need the pay.

Maturity Self-Evaluation?

The purpose of this exercise is to give you a better understanding of yourself and some direction for self-improvement rather than to provide an accurate analysis of your behavior. Check your response to each question. Possible answers are listed on page 343.

Behavior	Yes	Somewhat	No
a. Do I catch myself acting silly or juvenile when I feel awkward or lack confidence in a situation?	____	____	____
b. Do I admit mistakes that I make and accept the consequences of what I do or don't do?	____	____	____
c. When I don't get my own way with another person or in a group, do I try to cooperate and to make the experience worthwhile anyway?	____	____	____
d. Can I accept disappointment and frustration without becoming depressed or difficult to get along with?	____	____	____
e. Do I show consideration for others by following ordinary rules of courtesy?	____	____	____
f. Am I concerned about problems that others have and do I make some attempt to help them or help eliminate the problems?	____	____	____
g. Am I both a contributor and a receiver as a member of an interdependent society?	____	____	____
h. Do I make up my own mind on issues and decisions after availing myself of information and advice?	____	____	____
i. Am I tolerant of others, even though I may not like them personally or agree with their ideas?	____	____	____
j. Do I say or do things when I am angry that I regret later?	____	____	____
k. Do I have a sense of responsibility and belongingness toward other members of my family?	____	____	____
l. Are there at least a few people toward whom I feel deep affection and from whom I can accept affection?	____	____	____
m. Do I recognize unfounded fears and try to overcome them?	____	____	____
n. Am I unsure of my goals in life and of what my real values are?	____	____	____
o. Am I interested in becoming better educated and in keeping well informed on current events?	____	____	____
p. Do I gain satisfaction from work?	____	____	____
Totals	____	____	____

LEARN FROM CRITICISM Mature people realize they have weaknesses and will always have much to learn, especially in our rapidly changing world. There is always the possibility that we may not be doing our work the best way or that we have made a mistake. Mature persons are willing to accept and attempt to profit from criticism, without holding grudges. Although criticism may not always be given in a constructive manner, we should "keep our cool," think about it, and decide what we can learn from it. This subject will be discussed further in Chapter 14.

ACCEPT RESPONSIBILITIES Any type of maturity requires responsibility. This responsibility might be thought of as fulfilling reasonable expectations without undue supervision. Vocationally mature people follow through with what is expected of them on the job. They are on time, take care of equipment, use sick leave wisely, help out as needed, follow company policies, and, of course, do the expected work. They are also reasonable in what they expect from their employer in terms of wages, fringe benefits, and other job conditions. They realize employers must make a profit to be able to continue in business.

Even people who are self-employed have responsibilities to others. They are a link in the total chain of the workforce. If they are weak or broken links, other parts of the workforce are affected. They are also responsible to their customers if their work involves a product or service.

All members of a group in a democratic society are expected to carry their share. This is true within a family or within society as a whole. It pertains to people who work but do not necessarily receive wages. Anyone can give fuller meaning and satisfaction to his or her life through work. Most people spend a large share of their lives on their jobs. They may change jobs numerous times in life. But work constantly offers people a chance for meaningful activity, a sense of achievement and self-development that cannot be found any other way.

In the preceding pages, a few characteristics have been described for different types of maturity. It is no doubt evident that some of the characteristics pertain to more than one type of maturity. Accepting responsibility applies to our relations with others in our personal lives as well as on the job. We can learn to react calmly and constructively to criticism in many different situations. We cannot entirely separate types of maturity.

SIGNS OF IMMATURITY

It is easier to recognize signs of immaturity than of maturity. These are always more obvious, just as a dirty shirt is more obvious than a clean one. Common examples of immature behavior are blaming others, making excuses, breaking appointments and promises, and satisfying only immediate wants. Others are continual tardiness, panic in a crisis, unfinished business, abuse of others, and revenge.

It is easier to recognize immature behavior in others than in ourselves. You may recall from Chapter 10 that both neurotic behavior and use of coping mechanisms are basically immature. Although immature behavior in others may be disturbing to us, it is more important to recognize such behavior in ourselves.

Summary

There are many ways of determining stages of life-span development. Levinson refers to different times and related tasks in a person's adult life as life structures. Havighurst uses the term *developmental tasks* in referring to life-span stages. Times and experiences can also be measured by "clocks": biological, psychological, and social.

The approach in this chapter was to consider developmental characteristics and experiences at the following times in an individual's life span: early childhood, childhood, adolescence, young adulthood, middle adulthood, and later adulthood.

Human development, which begins before birth, can continue, at least in some respects, until death. The first years of a child's life involve great physical growth and also the beginnings of emotional, mental, and social development. How children learn to feel about themselves and others also begins at an early age.

Adolescence is a time of great physical and psychological change. Young people are struggling to become independent but are still dependent in several ways. They may experience several trials and triumphs during these years. They may be influenced more by their peers than by their parents or other adults, but they are also on their way to becoming more independent in their thinking and in making decisions.

Young adulthood involves a number of important challenges and decisions. Some of these pertain to continuing education; deciding on a career; and deciding whether to marry, have a family, or follow another lifestyle.

A person reaches a peak of both physical and mental development in the early twenties. Ability to learn continues into late adulthood, but older persons usually respond more slowly in a learning situation. Sight, hearing, and other physical abilities also decline in later years.

PSYCHOLOGY IN PRACTICE

1. Observe a child less than six years old for at least half an hour. Write a description of the child's behavior and development as you interpret it. Observe as many types of development as you can.

2. With one or two other students, create two scenarios of immature behavior. Your scenarios may be based on real experiences, observations, or hypothetical situations. Role play them for the class and ask class members to suggest more mature behavior.

3. Visit an assisted living facility for the elderly or a nursing home. Ask one of the residents to tell you about her or his life as a young, independent person. Ask the person to share with you a favorite memory.

One's development and options throughout life can be understood in another respect—through the dependence/interdependence curve. There are times during the life span when a person can make choices about relationships with others in this respect.

Erikson has identified eight stages of psychosocial development that begin in the first year of life and continue into later adulthood. Each stage develops in either a positive or negative way in relation to stages preceding it.

The theory of moral development by Kohlberg has become widely accepted, with some reservations. Kohlberg's original six stages of moral development might be modified to eliminate the last stage, because some believe that few if any people ever reached that stage of development.

Young adults, especially, should be concerned about the development of four basic types of maturity: emotional, social, intellectual, and vocational. The development of these types of maturity is not automatic. We can evaluate our present state of maturity in each of these respects and work at acquiring related characteristics.

It is relatively easy to become familiar with what maturity is in its various forms, and even to recognize immaturity in others. However, it seems more difficult to recognize immaturity in ourselves—and even more difficult to overcome problems of immaturity. Growing as a person requires conscious, constant effort.

The maturity of individuals also affects goal achievement, the subject of the next chapter.

Answers to "Maturity Self-Evaluation"

The answers to questions *a, j,* and *n* should be *no.* The remaining questions are best answered *yes.* A *somewhat* answer is not the best response to any of the questions, even though you are likely to have several such answers. Although there is no precise measure of maturity, mature young adults should respond as indicated to twelve or more of the questions. Fewer than eight such answers signal a degree of immaturity that might cause a person serious problems.

Key Terms

Development
Life-span development
Transition
Social clock
Maturation
Social development
Crowd
Cliques
Interdependent
Autonomy
Initiative

Identity
Role confusion
Intimacy
Isolation
Generativity
Stagnation
Ego integrity
Moral development
Situational ethics
Philosophical questions

Learning Activities

Turn to page LA-59 to complete the Learning Activities and Enrichment Activities for this chapter.

Endnotes

1. D. J. Levinson, *The Seasons of a Man's Life,* Alfred A. Knopf, New York, 1978. Reference from Kathleen S. Berger, *The Developing Person Through the Life Span,* 2nd ed., Worth Publishers, Inc., New York, 1988, p. 432.

2. Philip Rice, *Human Development,* 3rd ed., Prentice-Hall, Upper Saddle River, NJ, 1998, p. 445.

3. Robert Havighurst, *Developmental Tasks and Education,* 3rd ed., David McKay, New York, 1972. Reference from Guy Lefrancois, *The Lifespan,* 4th ed., Wadsworth Publishing Company, Belmont, CA, 1993, pp. 48 and 49.

4. Madeleine Nash, "Special Report: Fertile Minds," *Time,* February 3, 1997, p. 50.

5. David Elkind, *The Hurried Child,* rev. ed., Addison-Wesley Publishing Company, Inc., Reading, MA, 1988, p. 202.

6. John W. Santrock, *Life-Span Development,* 6th ed., Brown & Benchmark, Madison, WI, 1997, p. 390.

7. Diane E. Papalia, Sally W. Olds, and Ruth D. Feldman, *Human Development,* 7th ed., McGraw-Hill, New York, 1998, pp. 380–381.

8. Bruce A. Baldwin, "Positive Parenting: How to Avoid Raising Cornucopia Kids," *PACE Magazine,* November 1988, p. 16.

9. Jane M. Leder, "Adult Sibling Rivalry," *Psychology Today,* January/February 1993, p. 93.

10. Roger Gould, *Transformations: Growth and Change in Adult Life,* Simon & Schuster, New York, 1978, p. 39.

11. Erik H. Erikson, *Childhood and Society,* 2nd ed., W. W. Norton & Company, Inc., New York, 1963, p. 273.

12. Lawrence Kohlberg, "Moral Stages and Moralization: The Cognitive Developmental Approach," in T. Lickona (ed.), *Moral Development and Behavior: Theory, Research and Social Issues,* Holt, Rinehart and Winston, New York, 1976, pp. 34 and 35.

13. Laura E. Berk, *Infants, Children and Adolescents,* Allyn & Bacon, Boston, 1993, p. 582.

14. James W. Vander Zanden, *Human Development,* 4th ed., Alfred A. Knopf, New York, 1989, p. 493.

15. Paul J. Gelinas, *Coping with Your Emotions,* The Rosen Publishing Group, Inc., New York, 1989, p. 10.

Goal Achievement

14

Don't be afraid to take a big step if one is indicated. You can't cross a chasm in two small jumps.

David Lloyd George

LEARNING OBJECTIVES

After completing this chapter, you should be able to do the following:

1. Describe and give an example of a primary purpose in life.
2. Identify factors that contribute to goal achievement.
3. Identify primary causes of failure.
4. Define procrastination and explain how it interferes with goal achievement.
5. Describe factors that contribute to attaining career goals and advancement.
6. Identify characteristics possessed by a leader and describe three common leadership styles.
7. Explain what is meant by "putting it all together" in terms of goal achievement.

Everybody wants to be successful. But what does being successful mean? Certainly there are many variations to the answer. Is it possible that some of those who want to be successful really do not know what it would take for them to feel that way? If so, it is possible that they do not have goals. And unless we know what our destination is, on a trip or in life, it isn't very likely that we will reach where we might have wanted to be.

For our lives to be meaningful, we need to have goals. We also need to have some idea of how we will attain them. Our goals should be specific and should be stated in positive terms. In other words, think about what you want rather than what you don't want. It also helps to write goals down so you can review them periodically.

Stating your goals doesn't mean that you should never modify them or even develop new ones. But it does mean that at any particular time in your life you should have a clear idea of your personal and career objectives and how you might be successful in achieving them.

Some persons who consider themselves successful state that their efforts and experiences in working toward their goals were as stimulating and satisfying as the achievement of the goals themselves. You probably recognize this as intrinsic motivation, which was discussed in Chapter 3. There will be other references to this chapter and other earlier chapters as we discuss goal achievement because all the subjects we have studied contribute to success in life and work.

WHAT ARE YOUR GOALS?

Goal setting begins with self-understanding. Remember that there is no other human being exactly like you. You have the right to determine what is important to you and what you want out of life and your working career. The better you understand yourself as an individual, the easier it will be to determine goals. Some of the questions each of us should think about are: What do I enjoy? What subjects have I liked best in school? Who is the person I most admire and what do I admire about that person? Do I consider myself an introvert, extrovert, or ambivert? Am I a "morning lark" or a "night owl" in terms of what time of day I am at my best? How important have my relationships with others been in the past? What kind of relationships would I like with others in the future? How do I best like to spend my free time? How important are material possessions to me? Let's consider some of the major factors that should be taken into consideration in determining our goals.

WHAT IS YOUR PRIMARY PURPOSE?

It is desirable not only to determine the purpose of life in a universal sense but also to work out the primary purpose of your individual life. It is not necessary that you interpret the meaning of life in the same way as someone else, but it is important that your life have meaning and purpose. Determination of your life's primary purpose will affect all your other goals. Often a person's primary purpose is closely related to one's religious beliefs or a basic belief in the origin of life.

MONEY—WHAT DOES IT MEAN?

Most of us have to work for a living, and perhaps none of us will ever have to worry about having too much money. There can be a wide range of differences, however, as to what extent money relates to our goals. The following are some examples:

- I'll do whatever pays the best.
- It has no value in itself. It's simply a means of exchange.
- Money may not buy happiness, but it can sure buy comfort.
- There is too much emphasis on money in today's society.
- Who doesn't want to be rich? Isn't it everyone's dream?
- There are probably as many happy poor people as happy rich people.
- I need it so I work to get it; if I didn't need it, I wouldn't work.
- The best things in life are free; that makes us all rich.
- I want all I can get. It's easier to spend or give it away than it is to get it.

 What Would You Say? *How would you respond to a person who asks, "How important is making a lot of money to you?" (Assume the person is in a position to have the right to ask.)*

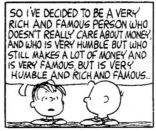

PEANUTS reprinted by permission of UFS, Inc.

HOW IMPORTANT IS WORK?

Have you determined a goal pertaining to the career you are preparing to enter? Even though your first thought may be "to get a job and make some money," it is important that you think about the kind of job you want, and what you would like to be doing five, ten, or even twenty years from now. A prospective employer might ask what your long-range goals are. If so, it wouldn't be advisable to say, "I don't have any. I just want to get a job and make some money." *Occupational Outlook Quarterly*/Fall 1992 states:

> Choosing a career is one of the hardest jobs you will ever have. You should devote extensive time, energy, and thought to make a decision with which you will be happy. Even though undertaking this task means hard work, view a career as an opportunity to do something you enjoy, not simply as a necessity or as a means of earning a living. Taking the time to thoroughly explore career opportunities can mean the difference between finding a stimulating and fulfilling career or hopping from one job to the next in search of the right job. Finding the best occupation for you also is important because work influences many aspects of your life—from your choice of friends and recreational activities to where you live. (1)

No doubt you have given consideration to the kind of work you will find satisfying if you are enrolled in a particular educational or training program. You may also know people who have changed programs or jobs because they didn't think the work was appropriate for them. You may have done this yourself. Some say that persons who do this don't know what they want. In reality, they may be giving more thought to what they want than persons who stay in jobs they find boring and unrewarding.

Be aware here that dissatisfaction is not always due to the job; it may be a person's attitude toward work itself. Some people think of work solely as a means of making money to satisfy other needs. A few think of it merely as something to do. Others recognize these purposes but view their work as an opportunity to lead a challenging, productive life. They are involved in developing their potential, in becoming more self-actualized. With almost everyone, work enters into the concept of success. This is true even for people who say, "If I were rich, I wouldn't work." For most of us, then, it is practical to consider how work-related goals fit into our broader goals in life.

Special training and education don't always guarantee that you will make more money. But they usually allow a person to find work that is satisfying and rewarding in numerous ways.

WHERE DO OTHERS COME IN?

Each of us has his or her own life to live, but our lives are interwoven with the lives of others. Probably all of us have personal goals that involve our relationships with others. For some of us, establishing and maintaining mutually satisfying human relationships is the most important goal in our lives. It is not wise, however, for our total well-being and happiness to depend on a relationship with another person.

For the most part, we can determine our own values in life, but we must keep in mind that how we attempt to live according to those values affects the lives of others. If you have a family or another type of interdependent lifestyle, for example, what you want to do with time, money, and other resources also affects others. You will recall from Chapter 3 that our values affect everything we do. It is common for persons who value human relationships to take them for granted.

Another type of involvement with others is not so personal but can be an integral part of what we want to do with our lives. This involvement includes service to others, which for many people is a primary goal. It can be related to one's career or it can be voluntary service outside one's work. Dr. Albert Schweitzer, the multitalented humanitarian and physician, spent much of his life treating those in need at a hospital he established in Africa. Mother Teresa of India is another example of someone who devoted her life to helping the "poorest of the poor." There are many more such examples.

HOW IMPORTANT IS FREEDOM?

You may not have thought of freedom as a goal you would like to achieve. If you haven't, it could very well be because at this time you already have all the freedom you want. Freedom is an intangible value that many of us take for granted. This value is evident in the problems of adjustment that arise when one loses a degree of freedom.

Real or perceived restrictions in our life and work can also affect our sense of freedom. Several individuals can be in the same basic situation and evaluate their circumstances differently, for example. Do you remember our comparison of influence and control in Chapter 3? Some individuals experience and enjoy almost complete freedom in their lives. Others in similar situations believe they have little freedom and often feel restricted and frustrated. For them, a goal may be to have greater freedom; however, they may already have more than they recognize or appreciate. One's sense of freedom is not always determined by the situation itself, but rather in how he or she interprets the situation.

A sense of freedom is considered by many to be a deciding factor in determining both personal and career-related goals. Of course, voluntarily giving up some freedom for an interdependent relationship or a particular type of work situation is more acceptable than being denied freedom by outside forces.

FACTORS THAT CONTRIBUTE TO GOAL ACHIEVEMENT

ndividuals who have achieved goals or have already experienced considerable progress toward achievement of their goals frequently refer to the following contributing factors: unified purpose, money management, time management, flexibility, recognition of opportunity, self-confidence, interpersonal skills, perseverance, and constructive reaction to criticism. Each of these factors will be discussed in further detail on the following pages.

UNIFIED PURPOSE

Individuals have numerous wants and may even have conflicting motives, but to be successful they must establish priorities and make choices. Successful people know what they want as well as what they want to be and do, and they are willing to pay the price in time and effort. Whatever the guidelines, the successful person has both short- and long-range goals. One's primary purpose in life can be thought of as one's personal philosophy, as discussed in Chapter 13. Life lived on a daily basis and over the years consists of numerous ambitions and goals, however. We may have long-range goals, for example, related to savings or material possessions, career achievements, interpersonal relationships, or service to others. Each long-range goal can be broken down into short-range goals, which are what we work at on a day-to-day basis. We find, then, that achieving a series of subgoals helps us to reach a long-range goal.

It is important that all these goals be related, in the sense that achieving one goal makes it easier to achieve others. Those who do not determine goals might develop one habit or activity that is in conflict with something else they want. Although we can expect to have conflicts, we should learn to recognize and resolve them so that we don't defeat our own purposes.

People with clear goals live one day at a time, but they know what they are trying to accomplish and why. They have a primary purpose and related goals and subgoals. Each day, therefore, has meaning and purpose.

MONEY MANAGEMENT

We must not only have an adequate income, but we must manage our money to meet our needs and have some left over for recreation and savings. This money management is especially necessary in a society that offers liberal credit.

TIME MANAGEMENT

Time is often considered our most valuable resource. We must have time to work and to enjoy leisure. The length of our lifetimes will vary but each day that we live has the same amount of time. Perceptions of time vary, however. Do any of the following statements describe your perception of time?

- I never have enough time.
- I waste too much time.
- I'd rather have some of your time than a gift.
- I don't know what to do with my leisure time.
- I wish I could make better use of my time.
- I'm looking forward to some future time.

You can't find more time, but you can learn to use your time more effectively. Effective time management is one of the key reasons some people accomplish more than others or are more satisfied with their lives. They do not have more time.

Many people rationalize about not having a budget. Either they "don't have enough money to budget" or they "have enough money so that I don't need a budget." But many money problems and financial crises can be avoided by setting at least some general guidelines about how much money is coming in and where it is going. People can also acquire possessions related to long-range goals by using foresight and saving for those goals.

The way one's income is spent depends on short-term and long-term goals as well as one's underlying concept of success. Some people want more costly vacations; others value travel; still others may be more interested in security. Some spend less money on food or clothing so they can spend more on education and other types of self-improvement.

In setting up a budget you must consider both fixed and variable expenses. *Fixed expenses* may include items such as house payments or rent, real estate taxes, insurance, church support, and installment payments. The word *fixed* does not necessarily mean that the amounts of these expenses do not change. For example, your rent or your real estate taxes may go up. Rather, fixed expenses are fairly stable from month to month in a year's budget plan. In contrast, *variable expenses* include items such as clothing, utility bills, medical care, recreation, and gifts. These expenses are usually not the same from month to month, and an estimated percentage of one's income is set aside for them.

Many successful people report that they always save a percentage of their income regardless of variable expenses, unexpected situations, or immediate wants. Although this may not be easy, one young adult reports that voluntarily deducting savings from her paycheck had become as automatic as payroll deductions for income tax or health insurance. Even a small amount adds up as time passes. Once the habit of saving has been established and some long-range goals have been set, you can pay more attention to your immediate concerns and short-range goals. You also gain satisfaction from seeing regular progress toward long-range goals.

Once we make certain decisions, we do not have control over all of our time. We agree to take a job where we are expected to work so many hours a day. If we drive an automobile, we spend time sitting at red lights. If we decide to see a doctor about our swollen glands, we spend some time in the waiting room. And you also spend time waiting in various lines, don't you? We cannot easily eliminate these experiences from our lives, but we can learn to use time in waiting rooms and standing in line to do some creative thinking, work on a small project we carry with us, or even to relax, instead of getting frustrated and wasting time.

During the time you can call your own—that during which you can plan what you will do—setting priorities should be your first step. That doesn't mean that the top priority should be related to accomplishment of a task; one's top priority may be exercising, or talking to one's spouse, or playing with one's children. It means deciding what is most important to you. A top priority doesn't necessarily have to be the first thing that you do. It only means that it is more important than other things that you decide to do and therefore you plan time for it in your day's activities.

Richard Carlson, in his book *Don't Sweat the Small Stuff . . .* , reminds us, "If you regularly take a minute to check in with yourself, to ask yourself, 'What's really important?' you may find that some of the choices you are making are in conflict with your own stated goals. This strategy can help you align your actions with your goals and encourage you to make more conscious, loving decisions" (2). You have a right to your own priorities, but you should know what they are and do yourself the kindness of living by them.

To make use of our time, we should identify time wasters in our lives. Out of habit, we do many things that are relatively unimportant to us. Do you watch television programs that you really aren't interested in? Do you wander around aimlessly before you decide what you will do? Do you take a nap even when you don't need the sleep? We all should be able to identify some time wasters or actions we do that have such low priority for us that we really should not use our time for them. When we do, we are neglecting something that has higher priority, because we have only so much time. Knowing your priorities and your time-wasting habits is essential to using time more effectively to accomplish our short-range goals and to progress toward long-range goals.

What Would You Do? *Is there something you would like to do that you don't seem to have time for? What can you do to use your time more efficiently and thus include this activity?*

FLEXIBILITY

To change your behavior with purpose is to have flexibility. It takes continual evaluation and decision making, and often courage, to be flexible, but it is a common factor in goal achievement. It is easier to react according to habit or established rules, and many do, especially those who wonder why they are not more successful. Achievers are doers, but they constantly take related factors into consideration in charting or changing their course of action toward their destinations. They are not afraid to say they were wrong and to try something new. They may have many failures, or setbacks, but they also have more successes than those unwilling to modify their goals or take new risks.

RECOGNITION OF OPPORTUNITY

Factors often associated with timely recognition of opportunity are insight, intuition, pull, or luck. But the better you as an individual understand yourself, your priorities, your strengths, and your limitations, the more readily you will recognize and react to opportunities for goal achievement that others may miss. Those who achieve their goals seldom make it completely on their own, but they recognize the who, what, where, and when of opportunity.

Networking
using all possible human contacts to find ways to achieve a goal.

A strategy for goal achievement used increasingly today is called **networking.** A person who networks is using all possible human contacts to find ways to achieve a goal. Networking is often related to finding a job but it can also be helpful in accomplishing other purposes. Individuals with the need or purpose inquire of coworkers, neighbors, relatives, and everyone they have contact with for leads on achieving their goal. Those who do not know what you need or want may have valuable information that you will never know about.

Networking is not intended to take advantage of anyone or to ask for unreasonable favors. It is not luck or pull, but an accepted strategy today for getting results.

SELF-CONFIDENCE

Self-confidence results from a positive, realistic self-concept as discussed in Chapter 2. It is bolstered by knowing what you want and recognizing your capabilities. It can be the determining factor in what you achieve. Henry Ford, the pioneer automaker, once said, "Whether a person believes he can do a thing or not, he is right."

Those who have overcome problems of inadequate self-confidence frequently state that the key was getting their minds off themselves. If people are concerned with others and what they want to accomplish, they don't have time to dwell on inadequacies, which are often imaginary or exaggerated. This suggestion has also been given for overcoming shyness, which is often related to lack of self-confidence.

People gain more self-confidence as they establish realistic goals and begin to see that they are making some progress toward attaining those goals. If they see that they are lacking a skill, they can do something about it, such as taking a class to learn the skill. As they overcome their deficiency, they begin to see themselves as more competent individuals and justifiably gain more self-confidence.

INTERPERSONAL SKILLS

Even if we are very competent and self-confident, it usually takes interpersonal skills to achieve our goals. Our goals themselves may include relationships with others. It was noted in Chapter 2 that understanding ourselves and having positive self-concepts help us to understand and accept others. Chapters 5, 8, 9, and 12 also relate to interpersonal skills.

We develop interdependent relationships with others that lead to our supporting one another in achieving our goals. We don't always assist others in the same ways that they may be helpful to us, but interpersonal relationships seem to work out as beneficial to all over time. We not only appreciate advice, encouragement, and occasional assistance, but the achievement of goals is usually more meaningful when we can share our successes with others.

PERSEVERANCE

Perseverance
continuing efforts to reach a goal, in spite of barriers and setbacks; a determination to succeed.

Perseverance is continuing efforts to reach a goal, overcoming barriers and setbacks with determination to succeed. It has been called stick-to-itiveness by some and stubbornness by others. (Could it be that when we don't give up, we think of it as perseverance; when others don't give up, we think of it as stubbornness?)

Many successful people could tell you about the importance of working long and hard, of not giving up when you believe in yourself and what you are doing. The path to success is often uphill, progress is not always assured, the next milestone is not always in sight, and it is natural to slacken in motivation and become discouraged. Persevering people work toward their goals when encouraged and work harder when discouraged.

Daniel L. Ruettiger is an example of a person who achieved his goal after his family and friends tried to convince him it was unrealistic. Ruettiger, better known as "Rudy," wanted desperately to go to Notre Dame University and play on their football team. An obstacle in Rudy's way was his dyslexia, a learning disability that made reading very difficult. After much determination and hard work, he was accepted at Notre Dame, but his chances of making the football team were slight. He made the team, even though he didn't actually get to play until near the end of the last game of his senior year. When he finally got in the game, he sacked the quarterback of the opposing team and was carried off the field by his admiring teammates. A movie called *Rudy* has been made of Ruettiger's struggles and goal achievement. He is now a motivational speaker and has written a book, with Mike Celizic, called *Rudy's Rules.*

In his book, Rudy challenges others to follow their dreams and achieve their goals, in saying,

> Don't ever, ever quit. That's the key that holds it all together. If you quit, you go right back with the whiners and complainers; with the people who live their lives in bitterness because of what they woulda, coulda, and shoulda done. Recognize that stopping now, regrouping to try a new approach isn't quitting. And as long as there is one shred of anything that you can still do— one phone call, one trip to the library, one letter—you have to do it. If you quit, you'll regret it forever.
> Finally, be ready to reach your goal, and when you do, have another one waiting to take its place. Getting what you want is only a problem if you have nowhere to go next. Dreaming is a lifetime occupation (3).

We should be able to recognize the characteristic of self-discipline in what Rudy is saying. Success lies in following through with whatever is needed to

Rudy Ruettiger inspires a young man to be successful in pursuing his goals in spite of a learning disability they share—dyslexia.

achieve one's goal. Many people want something, but they don't want it badly enough to make the required effort.

CONSTRUCTIVE REACTION TO CRITICISM

Another characteristic of many successful people is the ability to accept criticism and profit from it. This isn't easy, because it is more natural to resent criticism, to defend yourself from an attack on your self-esteem. You must give yourself a chance to calm down, therefore, before evaluating criticism. Then you should examine the qualifications of critics to determine whether they know what they are talking about and have valid reasons for criticism. Secondhand criticisms should be treated lightly because they are likely to be inaccurate.

A person who pays attention to criticism should remember that it is impossible to please everybody. No matter what you do or how you do it, you are a target for a certain amount of criticism. If you expect occasional criticism, it will lessen the blow to your pride and be easier to cope with. Probably the best approach is to develop habits of self-evaluation and criticism. Constructive self-criticism can be an important step toward self-improvement.

Factors That Contribute to Goal Achievement

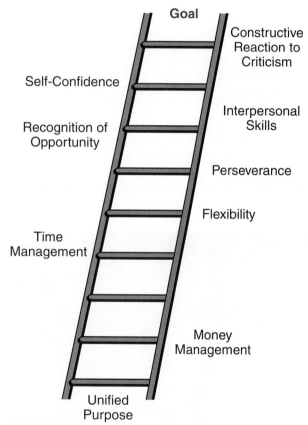

WHEN YOU FAIL

The heading of this section is *When* You Fail rather than *If* You Fail. Each of us can think of examples of when we have fallen short of what we have attempted. There is a big difference, however, between the verb *fail* and the noun *failure.* It has been said, "No one need think of himself as a failure unless he gives up on a goal he would still like to achieve." Even then there can be reasons why one should not be considered a failure. If one fails to achieve a particular goal, he or she can set a new goal and likely experience success. Ordinarily, people do not deliberately fail. All people want to be successful when they begin working toward a goal they have set for themselves.

There are characteristics common to people who frequently fail just as there are characteristics common to people who reach most of their goals. And since success and failure are opposites, some of these characteristics are opposites. Common characteristics of failure are discussed in the following section.

TRYING TO GET SOMETHING FOR NOTHING

Somebody is paying for everything that is "free." Most of the time you are paying for it yourself, but the costs are hidden. Very seldom is the person or the company offering free items or services covering the actual cost. Sooner or later most people learn that achieving goals is seldom easy and that rewards must be earned one way or another. Those who expect to achieve goals by following the path of least resistance often wonder why they are not happy or successful.

POOR MONEY MANAGEMENT

"What a waste of money" can be heard almost any day. You may even think or say to yourself, "I certainly wasted that money." When we come to the conclusion that we have wasted money ourselves we often link it to lack of knowledge or poor judgment. When someone evaluates the use of money by others (even when it's none of his or her business) the main issue is one of different values.

Some of our conclusions about waste might also be due to conflicts. We may decide to spend a month's earnings on a two-day vacation, but when it's over we may decide it was a waste of money. We wanted the vacation, but we evidently didn't want to pay the price. Some ways in which we may be wasting money or at least spending it unwisely are discussed next. Keep in mind that what is wasteful for one person may not be so for another. Also notice that some of the ways we waste money are the opposite of how we manage money, discussed earlier.

- **Impulse Buying** Many people buy things they don't need and don't even really want. Remember, advertisers and merchants want to profit from your impulses. *You* should be the judge of how you want to spend your money.
- **Fad Buying** "It's the newest thing" is sometimes the reason for making a purchase. Fad purchases seldom are useful and soon lose their appeal.
- **Wasteful Living** Wasting food, power, fuel, and other supplies is like throwing money away.
- **Overpaying** Try to avoid paying more for products than you need to pay. Shop around for major purchases. Watch for sales.
- **Excessive Risk-Taking** Be aware of risks. Know the extent of the risk and whether you can afford to take it. This pertains to various types of gambling, but it also refers to making major purchases without carefully checking their condition and value.
- **Buying Carelessly** Take your time and shop around for important purchases. For example, people sometimes buy the wrong kind of insurance for their situation. The type of insurance one needs is highly individualized. It should not be purchased hastily or carelessly.
- **Overbuying on Installments** This kind of expense may pertain to credit card purchases as well as to payments on a home. It is often the total amount of installment payments that causes financial problems. If your home payments put a strain on your budget, avoid buying other items on an installment plan or credit.

OUTDATED IDEAS AND USELESS HABITS

Modern men and women live in a rapidly changing world, as we discussed in Chapter 1. Unless they can accept new ideas and change old habits, they will be left behind and will not experience personal progress or success. If they reject examination and evaluation of the new, they may be setting themselves up to fail. The world of success is a world of change. Those who fail may not have developed the important trait of regularly examining habits of thinking and behavior.

Developing constructive habits, on the other hand, can free your attention from the numerous details of daily living. With freedom to concentrate on more interesting, challenging activities, you will be more productive and will have time to pursue your personal goals.

Habits pertaining to well-being and personal care can help you look better and feel better with little effort. They can be major factors in goal achievement.

UNFAVORABLE PERSONALITY CHARACTERISTICS

A single dominant negative personality characteristic can cause failure. Or several minor irritating personality weaknesses can do the same. Unfavorable personality characteristics cause more failures than any other factor. People who are intolerant, inconsiderate, or hard to get along with, for example, lose jobs, friends, and chances for success in life. They are their own worst enemies and, therefore, cannot escape failure.

FEAR

Ironically, fear of failure can be the very cause of failure. "The only thing we have to fear is fear itself," Franklin Delano Roosevelt told the nation in his first inaugural address in March 1933, during the Great Depression. Fear has been a major cause of failure before and since. It can cripple or smother initiative and potential success. It may cause a person to take the wrong course of action or may prevent her or him from doing anything at all—which can be worse than trying and failing.

Without realizing it, some people are even afraid of success itself. They experience a conflict between the advantages of attaining their goals and the responsibilities or risks involved with their success. Such fear may relate to possible rejection by family and friends if one's situation changes as a result of achievement. This rejection need not happen. Reaching our goals should not make us different as persons, and success need not change our relationships with others.

Success and efforts toward success often involve risk-taking, however. It's excessive risk-taking that should be avoided. We must be willing to assume the additional challenges that go with attaining our goals. Successful persons know what risk is and know what they will do if they lose in a particular risk. They also know what they are not willing to risk. They are not overcome, therefore, by the fear of failure.

NOT PROFITING FROM SETBACKS

Every area of success includes winners who, at some time in their struggle toward their goals, experienced disappointment and temporary setbacks. The important word in this statement is *temporary*. For some people a setback means failure and giving up. For them it *is* failure, but only because they allow it to be. A disappointment or setback only means a person has failed *this* time or in a particular way.

Thomas Edison conducted thousands of unsuccessful experiments before he succeeded with his electric light bulb. Those who do not profit from setbacks have difficulty experiencing success. On the other hand, repeated setbacks do not guarantee success. A person must not only be able to accept a temporary hindrance or setback but must also be able to use it as a stepping-stone to success.

A temporary setback can even be a learning experience. The following realizations can help you see such disappointments as positive experiences:

- People are not perfect. You are human, and no human being is perfect.
- People learn from mistakes. Disappointment or failure can help you to reassess your abilities and opportunities.
- It builds personal character to experience occasional setbacks.
- You can try again, or you can try something different.
- Family and friends accept you for yourself, not for what you accomplish or don't accomplish.
- Setbacks can release tensions and give you a temporary rest and a chance to rebuild your strength, resources, and spirit for another try.

MAKING TOO MANY MISTAKES

Different kinds of mistakes might be classified as careless, reasonable, and innocent. Let's consider how some of these types of mistakes are made and how some of them might be avoided.

We make *careless* mistakes when we are not paying enough attention to what we are doing or are in too much of a hurry. A person in a hurry, for example, may neglect to turn off a machine or lock a door. Careless mistakes can also occur when one is doing repetitious work that does not require much thought. We can avoid careless mistakes by having a routine that includes essential tasks or by paying more attention to activities when we know that mistakes could be costly.

A *reasonable* mistake might be misplacing correspondence in the file of a person by the same name. In this type of error, a person can explain to those inconvenienced and make every effort to see that there is no delay in satisfying the customer or otherwise correcting the problem.

Innocent mistakes are made by inexperienced employees who haven't as yet learned exactly how something should be done. An effective training program or job orientation will reduce the number of such mistakes. Nevertheless, they do happen. Although we can learn by all mistakes, this is the "experience is a good teacher" type of mistake. Someone appropriately remarked, "Considering what it can cost, experience should be the best teacher."

If you make too many mistakes, your employer may justifiably decide that keeping you is too costly. Let's remember that we are not perfect, but we can avoid many mistakes, we can correct some of those we make, and we can learn from all of them.

PROCRASTINATION

Procrastination
the habit of putting off tasks without having a logical reason for doing so.

If you have ever said, "I'll do it tomorrow", does that make you a procrastinator? Hardly. But a person who has said it might be a procrastinator. Merely putting something off to another time might be a logical thing to do. If you're painting a house and the weather is bad, it would be logical to put off completing the job until another time. **Procrastination,** on the other hand, is a habit of putting things off without having a logical, sensible reason for doing so. Oh, we use the coping mechanism of rationalization to convince ourselves that we have a good reason, but it would not hold up under close, objective examination.

CHARACTERISTICS OF PROCRASTINATION

In addition to procrastination becoming a habit, it has other characteristics that interfere with goal achievement. It puts us behind schedule. If we put off a job today, we probably are already in the habit of doing so. That means we started out the day with things put off from yesterday. Tomorrow we start out with the carryover from today.

We not only get behind, but we get discouraged, and lessen our motivation and enthusiasm for each day's activities. Short-term goals give us direction and a sense of achievement as we move toward long-term goals. Procrastinators are functioning with a feeling of futility much of the time.

Putting off tasks also upsets priorities. It is usually the unpleasant chores that are put off and lessen our motivation for getting started tomorrow. The answer provided by some individuals is to do unpleasant tasks first in each day's schedule. That can be a good idea, but only if the tasks are necessary, do not take too much time, and it doesn't make any difference when they are done. Otherwise, we may be neglecting tasks that should have higher priority. It is possible that we put off doing some things that don't need doing in the first place. In that case, we are only burdening ourselves with an empty carton. Although our priorities for a day, as well as for life, should be flexible, to accommodate unforeseen complications and interruptions, we should always know what our priorities are and why.

Procrastination can produce feelings of anxiety about having too much to do tomorrow and a feeling of guilt for not doing what we at least unconsciously know should have been done today. Although it was recognized earlier that procrastinators rationalize, we are not always that good at kidding ourselves. These unpleasant emotions can reduce our energy and self-confidence.

WHY DO WE PROCRASTINATE?

We know from our study of human behavior thus far that individuals do similar things for different reasons. Let's consider some of the common reasons for procrastination. Perhaps you will identify reasons why you procrastinate among them.

Procrastination becomes a personality characteristic. If we get in the habit of responding to situations in a certain way, we continue that type of behavior without giving it much thought. If you ever ask someone to write a job recommendation for you, you wouldn't want that person to say you were a procrastinator, would you? Now is the time, not to procrastinate about when you will break the habit, but to do something constructive about it.

Another reason for procrastination is lack of clear goals. An individual is unsure of the value of the activity itself or of how it relates to long-range goal achievement. If we don't know the purpose of what we are doing, we often aren't motivated to get it completed. Although we have been talking primarily about work-related tasks, we don't want to lose sight of recreational or leisure activities as worthwhile activities. But we aren't as likely to put those off, are we?

Individuals also procrastinate because their goals may be unrealistic and they are unsure of their ability to do or complete a particular task. None of us want to be embarrassed, to feel incompetent, or to fail. Lack of self-confidence, therefore, can cause us to procrastinate.

Difficulty of the task is another common reason for putting off a task. This can be related to being unsure of oneself, but it can also be for other reasons. If a task is very demanding of both our mental and physical abilities, even though we can do it, we may avoid the related stress by putting it off.

There are additional reasons for procrastination. Maybe you can add a few yourself.

What Would You Do? *If you became aware that you have a habit of procrastinating, what would you do to break the habit?*

CAREER GOALS AND ADVANCEMENT

Much of this book has been directed toward career goals and success at work. Review, for example, Chapters 2, 5, 6, 8, and 9. Many other topics in other chapters and earlier in this chapter can be applied to our work goals. It is recognized that success at work is an integral part of our lives. A few additional suggestions for advancing at work follow.

CONTINUE TO LEARN

Continuing to learn is characteristic of the intellectually mature person, as discussed in Chapter 13. People who increase their knowledge and broaden their learning are likely to advance in their jobs. One-time training is an impossibility in the rapidly changing workplace of today and tomorrow.

Fortunately, continuing to learn is a principal factor in maintaining interest in work. Those training for jobs today don't have to be concerned about doing "the same old thing" for the rest of their working lives. Those who not only accept change but are active in their vocational fields, determining what some of the inevitable changes will be, are the ones who will advance in the future.

Cliff Hakim, in his book *We Are All Self-Employed,* states as one of his attitudes, "I will commit myself to continuous learning, personal growth, and gaining new perspectives. My career is a lifetime endeavor. My mistakes and successes lead to expanded thinking and further contribution" (4). There are many ways to continue learning. We can take classes, go to seminars and workshops, study on our own, learn from others, or learn from experience on the job. It is especially critical that we continue to learn about our work, which will continue to change and challenge us.

KNOW YOUR COMPANY

It was suggested earlier that you show knowledge of and interest in a company when applying for a job. This step is only the beginning, however. The more you know about the company and how it functions and what all its products and services are, the more valuable you will be to that company. People who want to advance in an organization ensure that someone else knows how to do their job and that they become familiar with the work of those above them in the work hierarchy. In this way, they can quite easily be replaced and can make a relatively easy transition to a job at a higher level. Aside from this, people who are eager to give their best to their work can be assured that the organization will be interested in receiving the best contribution they have to make.

KNOW YOUR COMPETITION

Knowing the competition is especially important for those in management and decision-making positions, but it is also useful for the employee interested in advancement. Successful businesses can be assured of competition, and unless a company can meet competition, it is in jeopardy. Ambitious people are interested not only in their jobs and the company for which they work but also in the entire career field of their employment. They may even decide at some point in their careers that they would rather work for a competitor than for the company of their original employment. This kind of change keeps people focused on their place in the total occupational scene and is advantageous to a free-enterprise economy.

BE RECEPTIVE TO CHANGE

Many people do not advance in their company or line of work simply because they are satisfied with where they are and what they are doing. It cannot be denied that these people are successful if they have accomplished their goal and are not motivated by what others call further vocational advancement. Those who seek advancement, on the other hand, must be willing to accept changes in responsibilities, human relationships, and environment.

DO A LITTLE EXTRA

Most of what we do at work is "our job." We are expected to perform certain tasks with an acceptable degree of competence. We may also have some responsibilities in our work situation. What we do beyond these expectations may be a small percentage of our total effort and may take only a few extra minutes. But it shows that we care about the company, take pride in our work, and take personal satisfaction in our performance.

There are always some who criticize such efforts and others who actually heckle an ambitious, dedicated employee—a form of defensive behavior that is a cover-up for their own inadequacy. You can learn not to let this type of behavior bother you. A positive attitude can apply to a total outlook on life, including one's work. Decide what you want to do and how you want to do it. Then, don't let negative reactions of others prevent you from pursuing your goal. Extra effort is usually recognized in some way. Measure the rewards—including personal satisfaction and inner peace—against the immature reactions of a few people whose effort is poor.

WHO BECOMES A LEADER?

Every company and organization needs people in leadership positions. Who will be these leaders? Why do some people become leaders? One response to the latter question is that some people want to be leaders and others do not. Or an individual may be a leader in one group but not in another.

If you were to make a study of effective leaders in different types of groups or even various groups of the same type, one of the conclusions you would soon draw is that not all leaders are alike. Individuals have distinctive personalities, and there are different leadership styles. Three of the most common leadership styles are authoritarian, democratic, and laissez-faire. The **authoritarian style leader** uses a great deal of control. He or she makes many of the decisions and delegates the work. A group with this type of leader, if they accept their leader, may complete a large quantity of work. Leaders who follow the **democratic style** involve group members in discussing alternatives and making choices. The leader gives direction but is not as dominant as the authoritarian leader. Quality and originality are characteristics of this type of group's activities. The **laissez-faire style** is to let others do their work without interference. Some groups seem to have this type of leadership when they have an inexperienced leader with no particular leadership approach. Other leaders use the laissez-faire style because they believe it is the best approach to have individuals work together to achieve a common goal. As you might expect, a group with this type of leadership often has the lowest productivity. Perhaps too much time is spent deciding what will be done and who will do what.

Effective leaders, regardless of their particular style, usually have certain characteristics, described next.

Authoritarian style leader
leadership style whereby a leader uses a great deal of control; the leader is "boss."

Democratic style
leadership style whereby the leader involves others in discussing alternatives and making decisions.

Laissez-faire style
a leadership style whereby the leader interferes as little as possible.

PERSONAL EFFECTIVENESS

To be an effective leader of others, a person must be effective as an individual. You must have control over yourself before you can expect to influence others. This ability to handle yourself and your own affairs promotes a sense of self-confidence that inspires support from others. You deserve and receive admiration and trust.

ORGANIZATION

Leaders use various available resources, including time and money, as well as opportunities to use special equipment and to consult others. What may appear to others to be luck—such as being in the right place at the right time—is often the result of careful planning with an element of risk-taking.

Organization requires setting priorities. Progress toward some goals requires a definite order of effort and activity. There is a step-by-step pathway to achieving many goals. In other situations, the main factors may be total time and effort.

ABILITY TO COMMUNICATE

You cannot get very much accomplished by your club, team, or other type of organization unless you can make yourself understood. The messages you deliver must be honest and straightforward, yet be received without offense. This ability requires a diplomacy developed from an understanding of human nature and an interest in individuals.

ENERGY AND ENTHUSIASM

Leaders know how to organize and develop a plan of action, but they are also enthusiastic workers. They motivate and inspire others by their own eagerness to get a job done well and their willingness to work at least as hard as anyone else. They make group members feel they are working with them rather than for them.

COURAGE AND INTEGRITY

Courage involves taking risks. We may ordinarily think of courage as risking one's life in some heroic way, but there are other ways to act courageously. For example, it requires courage to take a stand in support of an unpopular issue.

Integrity is related to courage in the sense that one's beliefs and behavior are consistent, even though other actions might be easier. Integrity includes basic honesty and responsibility. Leaders with integrity can be trusted.

Group members respect leaders who don't back down when problems arise or when opposition becomes a threat. Effective leaders believe in themselves and the purpose of the group. They encourage active participation by members, but they are also willing to carry their own responsibilities.

FAIRNESS

If a leader expects others to work together constructively, they must feel that their leader is not playing favorites. Favoritism can be a problem in some situations because individuals do not always perceive what is happening accurately. Nevertheless, a person in a leadership position must try to be impartial and fair.

APPRECIATION

"You did a great job on that project, Andrew." Words can have tremendous power, especially when we know that they express honest appreciation. A leader

Service to others—helping and mentoring other people—can enhance one's life and one's self-esteem.

must organize, assign responsibilities, and communicate what is to be done, but he or she is also aware of what has been done and who has contributed to the achievement. Effective leaders observe, listen, and express appreciation. They also acknowledge efforts and achievements to the entire group, when appropriate. They are more concerned with achieving goals than with looking good personally or with receiving credit. But, of course, when their group does well, they do look good.

TEAMWORK

We considered team functioning in Chapter 9. Even people in leadership positions, or those who seek to attain leadership positions, should know how to function as a member of a team. Consultants Donna C. L. Prestwood and Paul A. Schumann, Jr., in writing about leadership principles, advise,

> We must become a member of the team and utilize our abilities—joining in the shared purpose—to help the team achieve its maximum potential. There are always three choices—lead, follow, or get out of the way. The wisdom of leadership in the Age of Interaction is to know which action to choose for each situation (5).

PUTTING IT ALL TOGETHER

Looking back at each of the chapters, learning objectives, learning activities, and related materials, you should be able to see numerous interrelationships that can contribute toward achieving your goals.

Learning about psychology, the scientific study of human behavior, will help you to describe, understand, predict, and control or influence your own behavior

By Tom Wilson

Universal Press Syndicate, Inc.

and the behavior of others. Recognizing that we live in a rapidly changing world will help us to prepare for the future, to control or influence to some degree what is happening to us and our environment, to prevent undesirable occurrences, and to promote desired changes or to make things happen.

Self-concept and personality were discussed in Chapter 2, but they are also related to numerous other subjects. How we perceive ourselves is probably the most important factor in what we do and what we are willing to attempt to do. Our personality characteristics affect our relations with others and many facets of our work.

Becoming a well-adjusted, integrated person must be a lifelong process. It is sometimes referred to as "getting it together." But we must be motivated to work at "keeping it together," or we will miss out on much of what life can offer.

To a certain extent each of us lives in his or her own world. Although we may have similar experiences through our senses, it is our interpretation of these experiences that makes a difference. Understanding factors that affect perception will help us understand our own world and, to some extent, the worlds of others.

Your emotions make you human, but your emotions can either help you or hinder you, and you are free to make the choice. Uncontrolled emotions can cause endless difficulty and unhappiness, but you can learn to be the master of your feelings and behavior in ways that will contribute excitement and joy to your life.

Your attitudes, or how you think and how you feel, affect your behavior. We may be prejudiced toward people or groups; that prejudice in turn can lead to discrimination. Positive, constructive attitudes lead to behavior that is also positive and constructive. It can be beneficial to all of us, therefore, to examine our attitudes periodically. If we can become better problem solvers, our lives will be less stressful and we are more likely to achieve our goals. There are several approaches to problem solving, including various methods of creative thinking. We often think of problems as disturbing, which they can be, but problems can also be stimulating and challenging.

The ability to communicate effectively in different situations cannot be underestimated. An essential aspect of communication is listening. There can be serious consequences to poor listening. In addition to practicing positive communication skills, we must be aware of and make efforts to decrease or eliminate barriers to communication.

Human relations at work have become increasingly important in recent years. We should also keep in mind that some distinctions must be made in our relations with coworkers, customers or clients, and management. The person who has job-related skills in addition to effective human relations skills has a combination that will contribute greatly to achieving career-related goals.

Most people experience stress in their lives and work. We should be able to recognize stressors, or causes of stress, and have effective ways of dealing with them. The better adjusted we are, the less likely we are to resort to coping mechanisms in dealing with stress-producing situations. It helps to know how to change what we can and how to adjust to or accept what we cannot change.

Our total wellness affects all areas of our lives. There are physical, emotional, mental, and other aspects of total wellness. We have a tendency to take our wellness for granted, but maintaining it requires understanding and effort.

We are increasingly aware of the different dimensions of diversity in the world in which we live. We can learn to value this diversity and thereby enrich our personal lives and reduce tension and conflict in society. The progressive steps toward valuing diversity are awareness, knowledge, tolerance, understanding, acceptance, and valuing.

Life-span development includes different types of development, including emotional, social, intellectual, and vocational maturity. To mature is to grow, and that is what we must do to achieve our long-range goals in our personal lives and in our careers.

Only a few of the key points of Chapters 1 through 13 have been reviewed here to show their interrelatedness in meaningful living and in achieving our personal and career goals. Reviewing the summaries of each chapter will give you a wider overview. The summary of this chapter, which follows, also incorporates earlier chapters. It all fits together.

Summary

A person who wants a meaningful life has goals. In deciding on goals in life, one should consider the following questions: What is my primary purpose in life? How important is money to me? How important is work? What kind of relationships do I want with others? How important is freedom? It is vital that you determine priorities since you do not have the time, energy, or other resources for everything.

Factors that contribute to goal achievement are unified purpose, money management, time management, flexibility, recognition of opportunity, self-confidence, interpersonal skills, perseverance, and constructive reaction to criticism. The effects of these factors must be considered continuously in our efforts to attain our goals. Although it is important to keep our focus on reaching our goals, the experience of working toward goals should also give us satisfaction.

Common causes of failure are trying to get something for nothing, poor money management, outdated ideas and useless habits, unfavorable personality characteristics, not profiting from setbacks, and making too many mistakes. Some setbacks should be expected in life. Instead of thinking of them as failures, however, they can be opportunities to evaluate our priorities and to learn from our mistakes.

Procrastination is a habit that not only lessens what we achieve but also interferes with an ongoing sense of achievement. When we are always trying to catch up or are faced with yesterday's unpleasant tasks, we deprive ourselves of some of the daily joy of life and achievement.

Suggestions for achieving career goals and advancement include continuing to learn, knowing your company, knowing your competition, being receptive to change, and doing a little extra.

Who becomes a leader? Common characteristics of leaders are personal effectiveness, organization, ability to communicate, energy and enthusiasm, courage

PSYCHOLOGY IN PRACTICE

1. Ask three persons employed in different types of jobs, "How important is your work in your life?" Also ask at least one retired person, "How important has your work been in your life?" Compare their answers and relate them to your own ideas about the importance of work in a person's life.

2. With two other persons (not necessarily class members) share a mistake each of you has made, discuss possible causes of the mistakes, and what was learned or could have been learned by each mistake.

3. Make a list of tasks you plan to do on a particular day on which you expect to be very busy. List the items in order of priority and check them off as they are completed. Determine whether the list helped you to be more organized and accomplish more.

and integrity, fairness, appreciation, and interest in company goals. These are admirable traits for anyone, but they are especially valuable to those who aspire to be leaders.

Not every leader has the same style of working with others. Three of the most common leadership styles are authoritarian, democratic, and laissez-faire.

As you become an established part of the world of work and develop new relationships with others, you will become more aware of how all the elements of goal achievement interact. Better understanding of yourself and others will enrich your life and help you to achieve your personal and career goals.

Key Terms

Networking

Perseverance

Procrastination

Authoritarian style

Demoncratic style

Laissez-faire style

Learning Activities

Turn to page LA-65 to complete the Learning Activities and Enrichment Activities for this chapter.

Endnotes

1. *Occupational Outlook Quarterly,* Fall 1992, p. 3.

2. Richard Carlson, Ph.D., *Don't Sweat the Small Stuff . . . and it's all small stuff,* Hyperion, New York, 1997, p. 234.

3. Rudy Ruettiger and Mike Celizic, *Rudy's Rules,* WRS Publishing, A Divison of WRS Group, Inc., Waco, TX, 1995, pp. 151–152.

4. Cliff Hakim, *We Are All Self-Employed,* Berrett-Koehler Publishers, San Francisco, CA, 1994, p. 135.

5. Donna C. L. Prestwood and Paul A. Schumann, Jr., "Future View," *The Futurist,* January–February, 1997, p. 68.

Glossary

A

absolute threshold   Smallest amount of stimuli that one can detect about half of the time.

abstractions   Ideas that are not directly related to specific objects.

acoustics   Scientific control of sound.

ad hoc committee   Committee set up to perform a particular task and dissolved when the task is completed.

adjust   Changing oneself in response to an unchanging situation.

adolescence   Teen years of life.

aerobics   Physical fitness program or exercises to stimulate functioning of the heart and lungs.

affirmative action   Government guidelines that require businesses receiving government contracts to hire representative numbers of minorities.

aggressiveness   Asserting your rights in a way that takes advantage of others.

aging   Process pertaining to the effects of growing older.

agora   Greek for "marketplace."

agoraphobia   Fear of crowded places.

alcoholism   Compulsion to consume alcohol caused by physiological, psychological, and social factors.

amnesia   Loss of memory and identity, usually brought on by stress.

amygdala   Almond-shaped portion of the brain that becomes activated when a person responds to a stimulus.

anorexia nervosa   Eating disorder, most common among young females, in which people believe they must continue to lose weight even after becoming dangerously thin.

apathy   Lacking interest; lack of concern about events or circumstances.

appraisal interview   Interview that occurs after a prescribed amount of time on the job (6–12 months) to review an employee's performance to date.

arbitration   Hearing in which both cases present opposing viewpoints along with supporting facts and evidence.

artificial intelligence   Ability of computers to solve problems.

assertiveness   Protecting your rights in a situation without harming others or abusing their rights.

associate   Person with whom one crosses paths because of common experience, such as work.

association   Relating of something new with what is already accepted.

attitude   Disposition, or readiness to act, involving both thinking and emotions.

auditory learner   Someone who acquires knowledge most effectively by hearing information.

auditory sense   Commonly called hearing, responds to a world of sound that affects us in various ways.

authoritarian style   Leadership style whereby a leader uses a great deal of control; the leader is "boss."

autonomy   Independence; competence.

B

Baby Boomer   Person born during the time period from 1946 to 1964.

behavior   Activity; what a person does.

behavior chain   Sequence of stimuli and responses, whereby a response becomes a stimulus for the next response.

behavior modification   Approach to improving behavior through a system of rewards or withholding of rewards.

behavioristic theory   Motivation theory that emphasizes the influence of the environment and learning on behavior.

belongingness   Feeling included and involved.

binge eating   Eating disorder in which individuals eat large amounts of food at one sitting but do not attempt to purge what they've consumed.

biochemical therapy   Use of prescription drugs to treat psychological disorders.

biofeedback   Way to monitor your body functions with the use of a machine until you learn what type of behavior modifies your blood pressure, heart rate, or other body functions.

bipolar depression   Manic-depressive disorder that consists of extreme mood swings.

bisexual   Sexually attracted to both sexes.

blind spot   Place where the nerves of the eye come together to form the optic nerve.

brainstorming   Group creative thinking involving a period of wild, uncritical generation of ideas.

brainwashing   Attempt to change a person's thinking and feelings completely, causing him or her to reject former loyalties and adopt new beliefs.

bulimia nervosa   Eating disorder in which individuals go on eating binges and then take laxatives, induce vomiting, or exercise excessively to rid themselves of the effects of the food they have consumed.

C

calorie   A unit of energy or the fuel value of food.

camouflage   Principle of perception involved when articles blend into their surroundings.

cardiorespiratory endurance   Ability of the circulatory system to supply adequate oxygen and nutrients to the body over a sustained period of time.

cerebral cortex   Portion of the forebrain that gives us the ability to speak, think, solve problems, learn, and remember.

channel   Means of communication.

circular team   Creative, open, democratic team functioning; team leader directs and facilitates activities.

clairvoyance   Type of extrasensory perception whereby one is aware of the location of objects without the normal use of the senses.

claustrophobia   Fear of confined places.

cliques   Small, intimate, often exclusionary groups.

closure   Principle of perception involved in a closing of gaps in what is perceived.

cognitive   Characteristics related to mental development.

color coding   Use of color to convey messages or meaning.

committee   Group of people working for a common goal or toward a common end.

common sense   Approach to problem solving involving reason and use of what has been learned in the past to solve new, similar problems.

comparative methodology   Method used to compare observations of behavior to identify similarities and differences.

compensation   Coping mechanism in which a person who is prevented from doing something by a disability or circumstance substitutes another activity.

compulsion   Irresistible impulse to engage in a certain activity.

conditioning   The association of a secondary stimulus with a primary stimulus so that one eventually reacts to the secondary stimulus alone.

conflicts   Opposing motives or goals.

constancy   Principle of perception involved when established perceptual concepts or images are maintained.

control group   In an experimental study, the group that does not receive a change, or independent variable.

conversion   Disorder in which one loses a physical ability, although there is no physiological cause; formerly called hysteria.

coping   Solving problems or adjusting to what cannot be changed.

coping mechanism   Unconscious behavior patterns that help one maintain a favorable self-concept.

corpus callosum   Connection of network fibers in the brain that allows the hemispheres to interact.

correlational methodology   Method that looks for a pattern of relationships in a set of observations.

counseling interview   Interview that occurs when an employee has a problem.

covert behavior   Activity of an individual, usually mental or emotional, that is not observable to others.

credibility   Believability; having others believe your message.

crowd   Large group of people; the largest and least personal of all adolescent groups.

cultural diversity or **multiculturalism**   Differences identified with cultures within a larger group.

culture   Values, beliefs, customs, and lifestyles that characterize members of a group with a common ancestry or national origin.

cutaneous sense   Sense of touch.

D

daydreaming   Simple form of unconscious mental activity during which one's mind flows freely.

democratic style   Leadership style whereby the leader involves others in discussing alternatives and making decisions.

denial of reality   Coping mechanism in which one refuses to believe a hurtful or threatening event or circumstance.

dependent variable   Original condition of both groups in a study using the experimental method.

depressant   Substance that slows down the activity of the central nervous system; "downers."

desire   Intense want for something.

development   Type of growth.

developmental task   According to Havighurst, a task which arises at or about a certain period in an individual's life.

disability   Inability to do something; diminished capacity to perceive or act in a certain way.

discretion   Good judgment.

discrimination   Behavior that is usually unfair and harmful toward an individual because he or she belongs to a particular group.

displacement   Coping mechanism in which an individual transfers frustration from another source to an innocent third party.

diversity   Differences among people.

downsizing   Reducing the number of employees, usually to lower costs.

drive   Urge resulting from a physiological imbalance that causes a person to seek satisfaction of a specific need.

drug abuse   Use of a drug for other than medicinal purposes.

drug addiction   Physiological dependence on drugs or a particular drug.

E

ego   According to Freud, the kind of person you are and what you do, as a result of the interaction of the id and superego.

ego integrity   Satisfaction with one's life and relationships.

egoism   Self-centeredness, with excessive self-love and boastful behavior.

egotist   One who is excessively concerned with him- or herself.

electroconvulsive therapy   Therapy that uses electric shock as a treatment.

emotion   Complex feeling that begins with some type of mental experience that, in turn, leads to physiological changes and a possible change in behavior.

emotional intelligence   According to Daniel Goleman, ability to know and manage one's emotions, to motivate oneself, to recognize emotions in others, and to handle relationships.

emulation   Attempt to develop characteristics similar to those of an admired person.

envy   Wishing you could have what someone else has or be what someone else is.

episodic memory   Memory of personal experiences or observations.

ergonomics   Human factor engineering; design of machines and the working environment to accommodate the worker.

esteem   Self-assurance; feeling of personal worth.

ethics   Standards of right and wrong behavior.

ethnic group Group with similar culture, customs, and language.

ethnicity National origins that identify persons as belonging to particular groups and connecting them with certain values and customs.

ethnocentrism Belief that one's ethnic group is superior to others.

eustress Positive stress resulting from excitement, enthusiasm, or anticipation of a desired event.

exceptional Those with special differences: talents, disabilities, or psychological problems.

exit interview Interview that occurs when an employee leaves a job or company.

expectancy theory Motivational theory based on the assumption that individuals believe in their ability to do work and that the rewards are forthcoming and worthwhile.

experimental group Group that receives a change or the independent variable in an experimental study.

experimental methods Methods that involve studying two groups of individuals: an experimental group and a control group.

extended family Lifestyle that includes immediate family and other relatives, including grandparents.

exterior senses Sight, hearing, touch, taste, and smell; senses that give us information about the outside world.

extinction Elimination of a behavior that is not positively reinforced.

extrasensory perception (ESP) Awareness that does not arise from the ordinary use of the exterior senses.

extraversion Personality preference for activities involving other people.

extravert Person who enjoys being with other people and likes to be involved.

extrinsic motivation Causes a person to do something for external reward.

F

family love Personal caring toward and among family members.

figure-ground Principle of perception involved when objects stand out from their surroundings.

fixation Coping mechanism in which one develops psychologically to a certain point and then stays or "fixes" there.

flextime A practice in which employees choose the hours they work.

forebrain Part of the brain primarily involved in thinking and problem solving.

formal channels Channels of communication that are well-defined and travel either vertically or horizontally.

foundation skills According to SCANS Report, basic skills, thinking skills, and personal qualities, needed by competent workers in today's high-performance workplace.

friendship Relationship with another characterized by a bond of mutual understanding, sharing, and affection.

G

gender Identification of human beings as either male or female.

general adaptation syndrome According to Hans Selye, a three-stage process of reacting to stress: alarm, resistance, and exhaustion.

generalized anxiety disorder A disorder in which a person experiences a chronic overwhelming feeling of anxiety.

Generation X Those born between 1965 and 1977.

generativity Interest in others, including those outside one's family.

grapevine Informal, usually verbal, communication that frequently becomes distorted.

group therapy Interaction with others in a group situation, under the guidance of a professional, as treatment for psychological disorders.

groupthink Situation that results when members of the group suspend their own better judgment to achieve agreement.

gustatory sense Sense of taste.

H

habit Pattern of behavior that has been repeated until it becomes automatic.

handicap Disadvantage imposed on an individual, which may or not be related to a disability.

hate   Intense dislike.

hearing   How we physically experience sound.

hemo   Latin word for "blood."

hemophobia   Fear of blood.

heterosexual   Quality of being attracted to persons of the opposite sex.

hierarchy   Grouping persons or items by order of importance.

holistic health   Total wellness; a balance among the different components of well-being.

holography   Laser technology that allows an image to be re-created.

homosexual   Quality of being attracted to persons of one's own sex.

horizontal channels   Channels used for messages between department heads or other employees at the same level of the organizational structure.

hospices   Homelike places where terminally ill patients spend their remaining days.

hostile environment   Type of sexual harassment in which an employee is placed in a threatening environment because of his or her gender.

human factor engineering or **ergonomics** Design of machines and the working environment to accommodate the worker.

humanistic theory   Theory of psychology that recognizes some environmental and unconscious influence but emphasizes personal control and responsibility.

humanitarian love   Concern for other human beings.

hygiene factors   Factors pertaining to avoiding and eliminating conditions that cause workers to be dissatisfied with their jobs.

hypochondria   Type of neurosis characterized by imaginary physical ailments.

I

id   According to Freud, a person's most basic urges.

identification   Coping mechanism in which a person's own identity is associated with that of an admired person.

identity   Understanding of oneself as an individual.

illusion   Misinterpretation of stimuli received by the senses.

imitation   Process of acting like another person.

independent variable   Change received by the experimental group in an experimental study.

induced motion   Sensation of moving when one is not, caused by movement of an adjacent vehicle or object.

initiative   Interest in trying new things.

insight   Judgment based on knowledge and experience.

instinct   Inborn, unlearned behavior, shared by all members of a species.

instrumental value   Desirable modes of conduct such as honesty and independence.

intangible   Having no material or perceivable characteristics.

integrity   Underlying honesty or dependability of an individual.

intelligence quotient   Score on an intelligence test.

interdependent   Dependence of people on one another.

interior senses   Senses that give us the sensations of hunger, fatigue, and muscle tension.

intimacy   Any close, personal, loving, and open relationship.

intrinsic motivation   Causes a person to do something for the experience itself.

introvert   Person who enjoys solitary activity, often an imaginative person and one interested in art and nature.

intuition   Immediate understanding without conscious attention or reasoning.

isolation   Aloneness; a feeling of being "outside."

J

job interview   Face-to-face question-and-answer session to determine a person's suitability for a job.

job sharing   Working part-time by sharing a job with another person.

K

kinesthesis   Sense of body movement.

L

laissez-faire style   Leadership style whereby the leader interferes as little as possible.

learning   Acquisition of knowledge, the understanding of facts and principles, the development of skills, or the shaping of attitudes and values.

learning disability   Learning problem that inhibits a person's ability to interpret or link information.

learning style   Sensory style that maximizes an individual's learning.

left-brained   Dominance by the hemisphere of the brain involved in reasoning, language, and mathematical ability.

life expectancy   Average number of years a person of a given population can expect to live beyond his or her present age.

life-span development   Continuous growth over one's life that involves every aspect of a person's being and functioning.

lifestyle   How one lives and with whom.

LIFEType   Combination of preferences in a personality evaluation in the Myers-Briggs test.

linear teams   Team in which members operate *on* a team rather than *as* a team.

linguistic intelligence   Ability to understand and use language.

listening   Voluntary action that involves paying attention and interpreting sound.

long-term memory   Ability to recall information on demand.

love   Intense emotional attraction that involves caring and respect.

love of God or a higher power   Recognition of and commitment to a higher power.

loyalty   Standing up for and behind your company and your coworkers.

M

major depression   Disorder characterized by an uncontrollable sense of sadness and fatigue, so much so that the individual afflicted has difficulty performing daily functions.

manic depressive disorder   Disorder in which a person goes from periods of mania (extreme activity and excitement) to depression (extreme sadness and gloom).

maturation   Development of the nervous system and physical development of the body.

mediation   Effort by management and union employees to reach an agreement by requesting assistance from an unbiased third party.

mediator   Unbiased third party that helps parties resolve differences.

melting pot   Society in which immigrants were expected to give up their ethnic culture and become part of that society.

memory   Retention and holding of knowledge and the ability to retrieve it.

mnemonic device   Memory aid relying on association such as letter recognition.

moral development   Acquiring a standard of what one believes to be right and wrong.

mosaic   Concept of immigration in which cultures retain their identity within American culture.

motivation   Combination of the forces causing a person to act in a particular way.

motivation factors   Factors related to outcomes that increase job satisfaction.

multiculturism   Cultural diversity or differences identified with cultures within a larger group.

multiple personality   Disorder in which an individual has several distinct personalities, usually in sharp contrast to each other.

muscular endurance   Ability of a muscle, or a group of muscles, to continue to apply force against a fixed object.

myths   Mistaken beliefs.

N

nAch   Need for achievement; need for challenge in accomplishment.

negative reinforcement   Action that causes an undesirable experience to stop.

networking   Using all possible human contacts.

neurosis   Maladjustment and excessive anxiety in one or more respects without serious mental illness.

neuroticism   State or condition of being emotionally unstable.

nonshared environment   Influences that operate in different ways among children in the same family.

nontraditional career   Career that in the past was considered appropriate only for males or appropriate only for females.

nutrient density   Amount of nutrients contained in a food in proportion to the number of calories.

nutrition   Characteristics of food and the impact of food on the body.

O

obsession   Irrational thought that a person is unable to dismiss from his or her mind.

obsessive-compulsive disorder   A disorder in which a person has an irrational thought that he or she is unable to dismiss from his or her mind.

olfactory fatigue   Adaptation to an odor so that one is less aware of it.

olfactory sense   Sense of smell.

open-door policy   Company or organizational policy that allows employees to freely enter a manager's office to discuss problems or concerns or make a suggestion.

optimist   Person who habitually displays positive attitudes toward life in general and toward particular events.

Ouchi's Theory Z   Workplace motivational theory that involves employees in group decision-making and long-term employment built on loyalty and trust.

overlearning   Reviewing mentally or orally what is already known for greater retention.

overt behavior   Activity of an individual that is observable to others.

P

panic disorder   Psychological disorder in which a person experiences severe physiological symptoms.

parallel team   Team in which members contribute their unique special skills toward a particular project or market.

parapsychology   Psychological term for extrasensory perception.

participatory management   Management style that allows employees to have input into decision making.

peer   Member of one's own age group with similar characteristics.

perception   Awareness through the senses and one's personal interpretation.

perseverance   Continuing efforts to reach a goal, in spite of barriers and setbacks; a determination to succeed.

personality   Person's total habitual social behavior or social self; personal identity as perceived by others.

personality disorder   Disorder in which a person experiences difficulty adapting to life and to interactions with others.

pessimist   Person who habitually displays negative attitudes toward life in general and toward specific events.

phi phenomenon   Illusion in which alternating lights appear to be moving.

philosophical questions   Concerns about the meaning of life.

phobia   Abnormal fear; a fear out of proportion to the situation.

phobic disorder   Disorder in which a person has severe abnormal, illogical fears.

phobos   Greek word meaning "fear."

physiological   Pertaining to the functioning of the human biological system.

physiological needs   Basic requirements for human survival.

psychological wants   Experiences a person desires for comfort and happiness.

platonic   Nonsexual in nature.

positive reinforcement   Favorable response to behavior; reward.

precognition   Type of extrasensory perception that involves the ability to know in advance that something will happen.

prejudice   Prejudgment made without adequate information.

principle   Statement incorporating a generally accepted theory that applies to most cases and situations.

problem   Situation that offers a choice of actions and requires a decision.

procedural memory   Memory pertaining to skills one has learned.

procrastination   Habit of putting off tasks without having a logical reason for doing so.

projection   Coping mechanism in which you defend yourself psychologically by accusing others of having your own personality weakness.

proxemics   Spatial distance between people.

psychiatrist   Physician who specializes in treating persons with mental and psychological disorders.

psychoanalytic theory   Motivation theory that emphasizes unconscious influence on behavior.

psychodynamic theory   Theory or belief that stresses unconscious motivation in personality and motivation.

psychological   Attribute pertaining to behavior resulting from human needs and wants.

psychological disorder   Difficulty or inability to adapt to the realities of life, including behavior that is considered abnormal.

psychological wants   Experiences a person wants for comfort and happiness, some of which are necessary for survival.

psychology   Scientific study of human behavior.

psychosis   Mental illness; the term psychological disorder is now used to refer to similar disorders.

psychosomatic illness   Physical disorder caused or aggravated by stress and unpleasant emotions.

psychotherapy   Therapy that relies on the psychological treatment of a disorder.

puberty   Physical development during adolescence that makes one capable of reproduction.

punishment   Receiving an undesirable reaction to behavior.

Q

qualitative approach   Regarding a person with a disability as a different kind of person.

quality circle   Problem-solving group in which employees and managers in the same work area share ideas to improve quality and production and solve work-related problems.

quantitative approach   View of a person based on her or his degree of an ability.

quid pro quo harassment   Form of sexual harassment in which sexual activity is made a condition of employment or advancement.

R

racism   Belief that one's race is inherently superior to another.

rational   Quality of being reasonable or logical.

rationalization   Coping mechanism in which one makes excuses for unacceptable behavior.

reactive depression   Depression caused by reaction to a traumatic event, such as a death in the family.

recall   To retrieve information from memory.

recognize   To remember information with the aid of a sensory cue.

regression   Coping mechanism in which a person temporarily returns to an earlier form of behavior, a behavior that is often age inappropriate.

relearning   To relearn material previously retained in memory.

reliability   Accuracy or consistency of results.

repression   Coping mechanism in which a person pushes back or buries in the unconscious that which is unacceptable.

response   Reaction; behavior that results from a specific stimulus.

reverse discrimination   Preferences given to minorities, thereby discriminating against the majority race and gender.

right-brained   Dominance by the hemisphere of the brain involved in creative abilities.

robot   Computer-controlled machine capable of doing work.

role   Activity of a person in a particular situation involving personality characteristics that may not be dominant in another situation.

role confusion   Values and behavior that change frequently.

role model   Older person whom one emulates.

romantic love   Deep and committed caring and sharing involving sexual attraction.

rote learning   Word for word memorization.

rumor   Informal means of communication based on little or no fact, often negative in nature.

S

schizophrenic disorder   Disorder in which one has a "split" in thoughts and emotions; the individual may become disoriented, hallucinate, and have delusions.

security or **safety needs**   Items or experiences that give us a sense of security.

self-actualization   Development of one's abilities and potentials.

self-concept   How individuals perceive themselves and how they feel toward themselves.

self-disclosure   Allowing others to get to know the person one really is.

self-esteem   Sense of self-worth.

self-love   Positive, realistic self-concept and favorable self-esteem.

semantic memory   Memory of learned information.

sensory register   Stage of memory during which we are aware of something.

set   Predisposition to act a certain way.

sexual/affectational orientation   One's sexual preference; whether one is homosexual, heterosexual, or bisexual.

sexual harassment   Unwelcome advances or sexually motivated conduct.

sexuality   State or sense of being male or female.

shared environment   Influences that tend to make family members similar.

short-term memory   Retention that lasts less than a minute; also called working memory.

situational ethics   System of ethnics by which acts are judged within their contexts instead of by categorical principles.

social clock   Socially expected schedule; the socially prescribed time for life's milestones: marriage, parenthood, retirement, etc.

social-cognitive theory   Personality theory that emphasizes learning and experience.

social development   Growth in interacting with others.

social facilitation   Liking your coworkers.

socioeconomic status   Societal position that involves both social and economic factors.

sound   Sensation perceived through the hearing mechanism and caused by vibrations in the air.

stage   Recognizable type of behavior that is characteristic of a fixed period in a process of development.

stagnation   Lack of meaningful activity and sense of purpose.

standing committee   Committee that has a permanent status and several functions, although membership may change over time.

status quo   Existing conditions or environment at a certain time.

stereotype   Assumption that all members of a particular group conform to the same pattern and react in the same way.

stereotyping   Attitude that assumes all members of a particular group are alike.

stimulus   Anything that excites a need or want within a person, producing a reaction or response.

stress   Physiological disturbance and psychological frustration resulting from a person's reaction to physical conditions, unmet needs, or external pressures.

stressors   Sources of stress.

stroboscopic motion   Illusion in which a series of images on film appear as continuous motion.

superego   According to Freud, judicial force within a person that prevents the id from ruling behavior.

superstition   Illogical belief based on ignorance, sometimes related to good or bad luck.

suppression   Conscious control of one's behavior to be accepted.

survey   Method of studying psychology that seeks information and opinions through interviews and questionnaires.

T

tactile learner   Someone who learns best by doing or practicing a procedure.

tangible   Real, material, or perceptible.

task force   Members of an ad hoc committee, coming from different backgrounds, with some special interests or experience related to the task.

telepathy   Type of extrasensory perception in which ideas are transmitted from one person to another without any ordinary means of communication.

temperament   Predetermined ways of reacting to the environment.

terminal values   Desirable endstates of existence, such as equality or inner harmony.

theory   Belief based on present knowledge and thinking concerning human behavior.

Theory Y   Theory based on one's assumption and natural interest in work as a satisfying experience.

threshold of audibility   Point at which one hears sounds.

totality   Gestalt principle of perception whereby parts of a perceptual experience are organized into a meaningful whole or unit.

traits   Personality characteristics.

trait theory   Theory that focuses on both inherited and learned personality characteristics.

transition   Change in the dominant tasks associated with a period of one's life.

trophy syndrome   Practice of excessive use of prizes and awards to the point where they lose their meaning.

trust   Faith, placing reliability upon.

U

ultrasound   Sound waves at vibrations too high to be heard by human beings.

unisex   Characteristic appropriate for either sex.

V

validity   Degree to which a measuring device actually measures what it is intended to measure.

value   Worth of something to an individual or a group.

values clarification   Attempt to understand one's values and their relative importance to oneself.

vertical channels   Channels of communication in which messages are carried from top management to employees.

visual learner   Someone who learns best through watching and looking.

vocational maturity   Type of development related to work that includes recognizing the need to work, deriving satisfaction from work, learning from criticism, and accepting responsibility.

W

willpower   Determination to establish and observe priorities in situations involving motivational conflicts.

working memory   Temporary storage of information.

Index

A

Abilities, diversity and, 292–293
Absolute threshold, 77
Acceptance of realities, 243
Acceptance stage of dying, 233
Accidents, visual hazards and, 78
Achievement, need for, 195–196
Acoustics, 82
Acquaintances, 184
Acquired immune deficiency syndrome (AIDS), 265–267, 277
Active listening skills, 175–176
Addiction to drugs, 261–265
Ad hoc committees, 161
Adjustments, 223
    to death and dying, 232–235
    job-related. See Job-related adjustments
    major, in life, 224–228
Adolescence
    adjustments during, 226
    development during, 318–321, 328
    fears during, 102
    parental influences during, 320
    peer influences during, 320
    trials and triumphs during, 320–321
Adulthood
    later, development during, 326, 329
    middle, development during, 324–325, 329
    transition to, 319
    young. See Young adulthood
Aerobics, 259
Affectational orientation, diversity and, 293
Affirmative action, 127–128
Age. See also specific age groups
    diversity and, 294
Age Discrimination in Employment Act of 1967, 305

Aggression, 105–106
Aggressiveness, 186
Aging, 294
Agora, 102
Agoraphobia, 102
Agreeableness, 29
AIDS (acquired immune deficiency syndrome), 265–267, 277
Al-Anon, 264
Alarm stage of general adaptation syndrome, 224
Al-a-Teen, 264
Alcohol, accidents related to, 78
Alcohol abuse/addiction, 263–264
Alcoholics Anonymous (AA), 264, 278
Allen, William B., 128
Alternative medicine, 268–269
Ambition, job success and, 40
American Association for Therapeutic Humor, 269
Americans with Disabilities Act (ADA), 277, 302, 305
Amnesia, 272
Amygdala, emotions and, 96
Anger, 104–106
    controlling and using, 104–106, 333
    physiological effects of, 99
    in workplace, 197–198
Anger stage of dying, 233
Anorexia nervosa, 267
Antisocial personality, 273
Anxiety
    adolescent and adult, 102
    fear compared with, 100–101
Anxiety disorder, 271–272
Apathy, 119
Appearance, nonverbal communication and, 177–178
Appraisal interviews, 199
Appreciation, leadership and, 364–365

Approach-approach conflicts, 49–50
Approach-avoidance conflicts, 50
Arbitration, 202
Aristotle, 4
Armstrong, Thomas, 148–149
Artificial intelligence, 146–147
Asbestos, 267
Assertiveness, 186–187
Associates, 184
Association
    attitude change and, 136
    learning and memory and, 152
AT&T, 293
Attention
    learning and memory and, 152
    to others, 244
    perception and, 76
Attitude change, 133–136
    behavior and, 134, 135
    drastic experiences and, 136
    outside influences on, 136
    personality and, 134–135
    time-related, 134
Attitudes, 119–140
    behavior and, 122–123
    of creative thinkers, 158
    discrimination and, 127–128
    expression of, 136–137
    influences on, 120–122
    positive and negative, 123–125
    prejudice and, 125–126
    sources of, 130
    work-related, 128–133
Attitude surveys, 124–125
Auditory learners, 87
Auditory sense. See Hearing
Authoritarian leaders, 363
Autonomy versus shame and doubt stage, 327
Avoidance-avoidance conflicts, 50

B

Baby Boomers, 294
Background, perception and, 74
Baddeley, Alan, 149
Bakke, Allan, 127
Balance, sense of, 88
Balances, 17, 279
Baldwin, Bruce A., 320
Bargaining stage of dying, 233
Baron, Robert A., 194
Barriers to communication, 170, 173, 188–189
Behavior, 47–50
    attitudes and, 122–123, 134, 135
    cause and effect and, 48
    conflicts and, 48–50
    mature. *See* Mature behavior
    overt, 48
    theories of, 50–53
Behavioristic theory, 51–52
Behavior modification, 51
Beliefs, perception and, 76
Bell, James D., 58
Belongingness need, 54, 56
Bem, Daryl J., 89
Benton, D., 202
Berk, Laura E., 331
Berry, Lilly M., 195
Binge eating, 267
Biochemical therapy, 274
Biofeedback, 244
Blindness, 72
Blind spot, 77
Bloom, Floyd E., 263
Body language, 178
Bone, Diane, 176–177
Bonica, John J., 83
Brain
    cognition and, 144–147
    computers compared with, 146–147
    emotions and, 96
    functioning of, 144
    gender differences in, 146
    hemispheres of, 144–146
    sexual orientation and, 35
Brainstorming, 159
Brainwashing, 136
Brazelton, T. Berry, 25
Brown, Tom, 111
Brownlee, Sharon, 77
Bulimia nervosa, 267
Bullies, 106
Burnout, recognizing, 245
Burns, Robert, 27–28
Burroughs, Marilyn S., 209

C

Calories, 255–256
Caminiti, Susan, 213
Camouflage, 86
Cannabis sativa, 262
Carbohydrates, 253
Career advancement, 361–363
Careless mistakes, 359
Caring, in workplace, 197
Carlson, Richard, 352–353
Carter-Scott, Cherie, 123
Caspi, Avshalom, 134
Catatonic schizophrenia, 273
Cause and effect, 48
Celizic, Mike, 355
Cerebral cortex, 144
Challenges, 6–7
Changes
    in others, trying to make, 245
    perception and, 76
    receptiveness to, 362
    reducing number of, 243
Channels of communication, 170, 173, 189
Chapman, Elwood, 129
Chappell, Kevin, 228
Cherney, Suzanne, 266
Childhood
    adjustment to experiences during, 225
    attitude development during, 120
    development during, 315–317, 318, 327, 328
    fears during, 101–102
    transition to adulthood from, 319
Cholesterol, 267
Circular teams, 210
Civil Rights Act of 1964, 216, 288, 305
Civil Rights Act of 1991, 305
Clairvoyance, 88–89
Claustrophobia, 102
Client relations, 204–205
Cliques, 319
Cloke, Kenneth, 59
Closure principle, 86
Coates, Joseph F., 294
Cognition, 143. *See also* Creativity; Intelligence; Learning; Memory; Problem solving
    brain and, 144–147
Cognitive consistency, 134
Cognitive development, 147–148
Cognitive dissonance, 135
Cold, numbness due to, 73
Color, vision and, 78–79
Color blindness, 72
Color coding, 79
Committees, 161
Communication, 169–191
    barriers to, 170, 173, 188–189
    components of, 170–173
    formal channels of, 214
    horizontal and vertical channels of, 214
    informal channels of, 214–215
    interpersonal. *See* Interpersonal communication
    in job seeking, 179–182
    leadership and, 364
    listening and. *See* Listening
    nonverbal, 177–179
    for stress reduction, 245
    at work, 213–215
Community
    approaches to diversity, 299–300
    global, 7–9
Company, knowing, 362
Comparative methodology, 4
Compensation as coping mechanism, 239
Competition
    knowledge of, 362
    in workplace, 207
Complaint handling, 204–205
Compulsions, 272
Computers, brain compared with, 146–147
Concentration, by creative thinkers, 158
Concern for others, 334–335
Concrete operations stage, 147
Conditioning, 102
    perception and, 86
Cones, 78
Conflicts, 48–50
    approach-approach, 49–50
    approach-avoidance, 50
    avoidance-avoidance, 50
    double approach-avoidance, 50
    in workplace, 206–207
Conscientiousness, 29
Consistency, cognitive, 134
Constancy, 85

Contract negotiations, 201–203
Contrast, perception and, 76
Control
    of anger, 104–106, 333
    of behavior, 61
    of fear, 102–103, 333
    of sound, 82
Conversion, 272
Cooper, Kenneth H., 259
Cooperation in workplace, 207–208
Copeland, Douglas, 63
Coping with stress, 223, 235–241
    coping mechanisms and, 235–239
    effects of coping mechanisms and, 239
    inability to cope and, 241
    neurosis and, 239–240
Cornish, Edward, 13–14
Corpus callosum, 144
Correlational methodology, 4
Costa, Paul T., Jr., 29, 34
Counseling interviews, 199
Courage, leadership and, 364
Coworker relations, 203–204
Creativity, 157–160
    brainstorming and, 159
    characteristics of creative thinkers and, 158–159
    lateral and vertical thinking and, 159–160
    in teams, 210
Credibility, 171
Criticism
    constructive reaction to, 356
    learning from, 340
Crowds, 319
Cultural diversity, 8, 291
Culture, 291
    attitudes and, 122
Customer relations, 204–205
Cutaneous sense, 82–83

D

Darwin, Charles, 32
David, Lester, 110
Dawis, R. V., 196
Daydreaming as coping mechanism, 235–236
Deafness, 72
Death and dying, adjustment to, 232–235
de Bono, Edward, 159–160
Deming, William E., 161
Democratic leadership style, 363

Denial as coping mechanism, 238
Denial stage of dying, 233
Dentistry, painless, 82
Dependence/interdependence curve, 322–324
Depressants, 262
Depression, 272–273
Depression stage of dying, 233
Depth, sense of, 88
Despair, 329
Development, 313. See also Life-span development
    moral, 329–331
    of personality, 32–35
    psychosocial, stages of, 326–329
    of self-concept, 24–25
    social, 317
Dickerson, Jeff, 128
Direction, sense of, 88
Disabilities
    adjustment to, 228
    Americans with Disabilities Act and, 277, 302, 305
    diversity and, 292–293
    handicaps compared with, 292–293
Discretion, 187
Discrimination, 127–128
Dislikes, perception and, 74
Disorganized schizophrenia, 273
Displaced Persons Acts of 1948 and 1950, 287
Displacement as coping mechanism, 237
Dissociative disorder, 272
Distractions as communication barrier, 188
Diversity, 285–309
    abilities and disabilities and, 292–293
    age and, 294
    community approaches to, 299–300
    cultural, 8
    education about, 300–302
    education and, 295–296
    ethnicity and, 290–292
    gender and, 289
    lifestyle and, 293–294
    occupation and, 297
    race and, 289–290
    religion and, 294–295
    self-understanding and, 297–299
    sexual/affectational orientation and, 293

    socioeconomic status and, 296–297
    valuing, 285–288, 306–307
    in workplace. See Workplace diversity
Divorce, adjustment to, 227–228
Double approach-avoidance conflicts, 50
Dreams, 51
Drives, 53
Drug abuse/addiction, 261–265
DuBrin, A. J., 214

E

Early childhood, development during, 315–317, 327
Eating disorders, 267
Edison, Thomas, 359
Education
    about diversity, 300–302
    diversity and, 295–296
    lifelong learning and, 13–15
    of older people, 336
Ego, 36, 37
Ego integrity, 329
Ego integrity versus despair stage, 329
Egotists, 106
Ekman, Paul, 97–98
Electroconvulsive therapy (ECT), 274
Elkind, David, 318
Emotional intelligence, 111–112
Emotional maturity, 332–334
Emotional stability, 29
    job success and, 41
Emotions, 95–115. See also specific emotions
    classification of, 97–98
    development of, 96–97
    enrichment provided by, 112–113
    managing, 112
    physiological effects of, 98–100
    recognizing in others, 112
    in workplace, 110–111, 197–199
Employee Assistance Programs (EAPs), 276–277
Employee associations, 202
Employee Polygraph Protection Act, 100
Employer-employee relations, 199–203
    interviews and, 199
    labor unions and management and, 201–203
    loyalty and trust and, 200–201
    management structure and, 199–200

Emulation, 238
Energy, leadership and, 364
Enthusiasm, leadership and, 364
Environment
    communication and, 172
    hostile, in workplace, 216
    perception and, 73–74
    personality and, 33, 34
Envy, 108
Episodic memory, 150
Equal Employment Opportunity
    Commission (EEOC), 305
Equal Pay for Equal Work Act of
    1963, 305
Equilibrium, sense of, 88
Ergonomics, 13
Erikson, Erik, 316, 326
Esty, Katharine, 289, 302
Ethics
    situational, 331
    standards of, 205–206
Ethnic groups, 290
Ethnicity, diversity and, 290–292
Ethnocentrism, 290
Eustress, 224
Evolution, 32
Exceptional people, 292
Exhaustion stage of general adapta-
    tion syndrome, 224
Exit interviews, 199
Expectancy theory, 195
Expectations, perception and, 76
Expenses, fixed and variable, 352
Experience
    attitudes and, 121, 136
    early, adjusting to, 225
    perception and, 74–75
    sharing in workplace, 213–214
Experimental methods, 4
Extended family, 291
Exterior senses, 77. See also Hearing;
    Vision
    smell, 84
    taste, 83–84
    touch, 82–83
Extinction, 51–52
Extrasensory perception (ESP), 88
Extraversion, 29
Extrinsic motivation, 52
Extraverts, 30

F

Facial expressions, 178
Failure, 356–359

excessive mistakes and, 359
fear and, 358
outdated ideas and useless habits
    and, 357–358
personality and, 358
poor money management and,
    357
setbacks and, 358–359
trying to get something for noth-
    ing and, 356–357
Fairness, leadership and, 364
Familiarity, perception and, 74–75
Family
    attitudes and, 120
    ethnic diversity and, 291
    extended, 291
Family love, 107
Fats, 253
Fear, 100–104
    adolescent and adult, 102
    anxiety compared with, 100–101
    childhood, 101–102
    controlling and using, 102–103,
        333
    failure due to, 357–358
    phobias, 103–104
    physiological effects of, 99
    in workplace, 198
Feedback, communication and, 173
Feldman, Ruth D., 319
Fiber, dietary, 253
Figure-ground principle, 85
Fixation as coping mechanism,
    236–237
Fixed expenses, 352
Flexibility
    of creative thinkers, 158
    goal achievement and, 353,
        357–358
    stress reduction and, 245
Flextime, 11–12
Fog, vision and, 73
Food Guide Pyramid, 254
Forebrain, 144
Forest, Stephanie A., 305
Formal channels of communication,
    214
Formality, ethnic diversity and, 291
Formal operations stage, 148
Freedom, importance of, 350
Frequency of sound waves, 80
Freud, Sigmund, 36, 51
Friendships, 107, 184, 216–217
Fruehling, R. T., 196

Frustration, reacting to, 105
Future, 5–6

G

Gardner, Howard, 148
Gay, Kathlyn, 290
Gelinas, Paul J., 332–333
Gender
    brain and, 146
    communication and, 184–185
    diversity and, 289
    of workforce, 10
General adaptation syndrome, 224
Generalized anxiety disorder,
    271–272
Generational differences in values,
    63–64
Generation X, 63–64
Generativity, 329
Generativity versus stagnation stage,
    329
Gestalt principle, 85, 154–155
Glare, vision and, 73
Global community, 7–9
Goal achievement, 347–369
    career advancement and, 361–363
    failure and. See Failure
    flexibility and, 353
    goal setting and, 348–350
    interpersonal skills and, 354
    leadership and, 363–365
    money management and, 351
    perseverance and, 354–356
    procrastination and, 360–361
    reaction to criticism and, 356
    recognizing opportunity and,
        353–354
    self-confidence and, 354
    time management and, 351–352
    unified purpose and, 351
God, love of, 107
Goldsmith, Joan, 59
Goleman, Daniel, 111–112
Gould, Roger, 325
Grapevine, 214–215
Gray, John, 184
Gregory, Sophronia Scott, 16
Grief, 110, 234
Griffin, Richard, 289, 302
Group participation, 182–183
Group problem solving, 160–162
Group therapy, 274
Groupthink, 161
Grudges, letting go of, 244

Guilt, 110
Gunn, Ronald A., 209
Gustatory sense, 83–84

H

Habits, 277–279
Hallahan, D. P., 292–293
Halloran, J., 202
Hallucinogens, 262
Hammerschlag, Paul, 80–81
Hammurabi, 157
Handicaps, disabilities compared with, 292–293
Hartley, Mariette, 241
Hashish, 262
Hate, 107–108
Havighurst, Robert, 315
Hearing, 79–82, 173–174. *See also* Listening
    auditory learners and, 87
    noise and, 80–82
    sound and, 79–80
    sound control and use and, 82
Hearing impairment, 72
Heerman, Max, 216
Hemispheres, cerebral, 144–146
Hemo, 102
Hemophobia, 102
Heredity, personality and, 33–34
Heterosexual, 35
Hierarchy of needs, 54–56, 196
Hillis, Danny, 146–147
Himelstein, Linda, 305
Hirsch, Marcie Schorr, 289
Hirsh, Sandra, 30–31
Holistic health, 251
Holmes, Oliver Wendell, 37
Holography, 173
Homosexual, 35–36
Honesty, job success and, 40
Horizontal channels of communication, 214
Hornblower, Margot, 63–64
Hospices, 233–234
Hostile environment in workplace, 216
Houston, John P., 195
Human contact, 83
Human factor engineering, 13
Humanistic theory
    of motivation, 52–53
    of personality, 29
Humanitarian love, 106–107
Human relations, 193–219. *See also*

Employer-employee relations
    communication and, 213–215
    competition and, 207
    conflict and, 206–207
    cooperation and, 207–208
    coworker relations and, 203–204
    customer relations and, 204–205
    emotions and, 197–199
    ethics and, 205–206
    friendships and, 216–217
    job enrichment and, 196–197
    motivation to work and, 194–196
    sexual harassment and, 215–216
    teams and. *See* Teams
Humor, wellness and, 269
Hunter, Beatrice T, 267
Hygiene factors, 194
Hypochondria, 272
Hypothalamus, sexual orientation and, 35

I

Id, 36, 37
Identification as coping mechanism, 238
Identity versus role confusion stage, 328
Illness
    adjustment to, 228
    perception and, 72–73
    psychosomatic, 261
Illusions, 88
Image, job success and, 40
Imitation as coping mechanism, 238
Immaturity, signs of, 341
Immigration, 287–288
Immigration and Nationality Act, 287–288
Immune system, stress and, 224
Incompatible personalities, 32
Independent living, adjusting to, 226–227
Induced movement, 88
Industry versus inferiority stage, 328
Infancy, psychosocial development during, 326–327
Informal channels of communication, 214–215
Ingham, Harrington, 185
Inhalants, 262
Initiative, 328
Initiative versus guilt stage, 328
"Inner" depression, 273
Innocent mistakes, 359

Insight, 162
Instincts, 48
Instrumental values, 63
Intangible values, 63
Integrity, 171, 364
Intellectual independence, 337
Intellectual maturity, 335–337
Intelligence, 148–149
    artificial, 146–147
    emotional, 111–112
Intelligence quotient (IQ), 148
Intensity, perception and, 76
Interdependence, 322–324
Interior senses, 77, 87–88
Interpersonal communication, 183–187
    assertiveness and, 186–187
    gender differences in, 184–185
    Johari window and, 185–186
    types of relationships and, 184
Interpersonal skills
    goal achievement and, 354
    job success and, 40
Interracial marriage, 290
Interviews
    appraisal, 199
    counseling, 199
    exit, 199
    for jobs, 180–182
Intimacy, 184, 328–329
Intimacy versus isolation stage, 328–329
Intrinsic motivation, 52
Introverts, 30
Intuition, 162
IQ (intelligence quotient), 148
Iris, 78
Isolation, 329

J

James, John, 251
James, Muriel, 251
James, William, 48
Jealousy, 108–109, 198–199
Job burnout, recognizing, 245
Job enrichment, 196–197
Job interviews, 180–182
Job-related adjustments, 228–232
    to changes in supervision and procedures, 230
    to job change, 230–231
    by new employees, 229
    to retirement, 232
    to unemployment, 231–232
    to working hours, 229–230

Job seeking, 179–182
Job sharing, 12
Johari window, 185–186
Johnson, Andra, 290
Johnson, David W., 209
Jumping rope, 260
Juno, 334
Jupiter, 334

K

Kauffman, J. M., 292–293
Kennedy, Eugene, 235
Kidder, Rushworth M., 65
Kildahl, John P., 124
Kimura, Doreen, 146
Kinesthesis, 88
King, Martin Luther, 288
Kluge, Holger, 307
Knowledge, sharing in workplace, 213–214
Kohlberg, Lawrence, 330
Kolb, D. A., 87
Krannich, C. R., 181
Krannich, R. L., 181
Kübler-Ross, Elisabeth, 233
Kummerow, Jean, 30–31

L

Labor unions, 201–203
Laissez-faire leadership style, 363
Language problems as communication barrier, 188–189
Lapp, Danielle, 151
Later adulthood, development during, 326, 329
Lateral thinking, 159–160
Lawlor, Julia, 241
Leadership, 363–365
Learning, 149
    continuous, 361–362
    contributors to, 151–153
    from criticism, 340
    by mature people, 336
    memory and, 150–151
Learning disabilities, 87
Learning styles, 86–87
Left-brained people, 144–146
Lerner, Janet, 87
Levinson, Dan, 314
Levi Strauss, 277
Lie detector, 99–100
Life expectancy, 16
Lifelong learning, 13–15

Life-span development, 313–343
    during adolescence, 318–321
    during childhood, 318
    dependence/interdependence curve and, 322–324
    during early childhood, 315–317
    immaturity and, signs of, 341
    during later adulthood, 326
    mature behavior and. See Mature behavior
    during middle adulthood, 324–325
    moral, 329–331
    psychosocial, 326–329
    stages of, 314–315
    during young adulthood, 321–322
Lifestyle, diversity and, 293–294
LIFETypes, 30–31
Lighting, vision and, 73
Likes, perception and, 74
Limitations, accepting, 243
Linear teams, 209–210
Lippert, John, 130–131
Listening, 173–177
    checklist of skills for, 175–176
    improving, 176–177
    poor, consequences of, 176
    reasons for, 174–175
Logical thinking, 160
Long-term memory, 150
Lose-lose conflict resolution, 207
Loudness of sound, 80
Love, 106–107
    giving and receiving, 333
    kinds of, 107
Loyalty to company, 131–132
    in employer-employee relations, 200–201
    job success and, 40
Luft, Joseph, 185

M

McClelland, David, 195
McCrae, R. R., 29
McCrae, Robert E., 34
McGregor, Douglas, 53
MacKay-Lassonde, Claudette, 64
Major depression, 272
Management. See also Employer-employee relations
    participatory, 200
Manic-depressive disorder, 273
Marano, Hara E., 106
Marijuana, 262
Marriage

adjusting to, 227
    divorce and, adjusting to, 227–228
    interracial, 290
Martorano, Joseph T., 124
Maslow, Abraham, 25, 54
Maturation, 316
Mature behavior, 331–340
    emotional, 332–334
    intellectual, 335–337
    social, 334–335
    vocational, 337–338, 340
Mayer, John D., 111
Mayer, Richard E., 143
Meaningfulness, learning and memory and, 151–152
Mediation, 202
Mediators, 202
Medical treatment, 268–269
Melting pot, 287
Memory, 149–150
    contributors to, 151–153
    learning and, 150–151
Mental health, 270. See also Psychological disorders
Message in communication, 170
Middle adulthood, development during, 324–325, 329
Minerals, 253
Minorities, 289
Mistakes, 359
Mnemonic devices, 152
Money, goals and, 348
Money management, goal achievement and, 351, 357
Mood disorder, 272–273
Moore, Barbara E., 234
Moral development, 329–331
Mosaic, 287
Mother Teresa, 350
Motivation, 47, 57–61
    control versus influence and, 61
    extrinsic, 52
    intrinsic, 52
    learning and memory and, 151
    of others, 57–59
    of self, 59–61, 112
    to work, 194–196
Motivation factors, 194, 195
Movement, induced, 88
Multiculturalism, 8, 291. See also Diversity
Multiple personality, 272
Myers, David G., 30
Myers-Briggs test, 30

N

Narcotics, 262
Nash, Melanie, 315
Nearness, sense of, 88
Needs, 53–56
 for achievement, 195–196
 hierarchy of, 54–56, 196
 perception and, 75–76
 physiological, 53, 54, 55
 to work, recognizing, 338
Neff, Walter, 40
Negaholism, 123
Negative attitudes, 123–124
 in workplace, 129–130
Negative reinforcement, 51
Nelson, P. E., 186
Nelton, Sharon, 111
Neurosis, 239–240
Neuroticism, 29
Newborn infants, emotions of, 96
Ng, Lorenz K. Y., 83
Nicotine, 263, 264–265
Noise
 distracting, 73–74
 hazards of, 80–82
Nonverbal communication, 177–179
 appearance and, 177–178
 body language and, 178
 facial expressions and, 178
 proxemics and, 178–179
Novelty, perception and, 76
Numbness, 73
Nutrient density, 255
Nutrition, 252–257
 balanced diet and, 254–255
 calories and, 255–256
 healthful eating and, 256–257
 nutrients and, 253

O

Obsessive-compulsive disorder, 271–272
Occupation, diversity and, 297
Occupational Safety and Health Act (OSHA), 81
O'Hara, Maureen, 34
Oldham, N. B., 196
Olds, Sally W., 319
Olfactory fatigue, 84
Olfactory sense, 84
Open-door policy in workplace, 214
Openness, 29
Opportunity, recognizing, 353–354

Optimists, 123, 124
Oral presentations, 182–183
Organization
 leadership and, 364
 stress reduction and, 245
Osborn, Alex, 159
Ouchi, William, 53
Overlearning, 152–153
Overman, Stephanie, 13
Overt behavior, 48

P

Pain, 83
Pain clinics, 83
Painless dentistry, 82
Panic disorder, 271–272
Papalia, Diane E., 319
Parallel teams, 210
Paranoid schizophrenia, 273
Parapsychology, 88–89
Parents
 adjusting to becoming, 227
 adolescents and, 320
 separation from, 225
Parks, Rosa, 288
Participatory management, 200
"Passive smoking," 264
Past experience. *See* Experience
A Patient's Bill of Rights, 274
Paulus, Paul B., 194
Pearson, J. C., 186
Peers
 during adolescence, 320
 attitudes and, 120–121
Perception, 71–76, 84–86
 attention factors affecting, 76
 camouflage and, 86
 closure and, 86
 conditioning and, 86
 constancy and, 85
 differences in, as communication barrier, 188
 enlarging, 89
 environmental effects on, 73–74
 extrasensory, 88
 figure-ground principle and, 85
 gestalt (totality) principle and, 85
 past experience and, 74–75
 physical abilities and limitations affecting, 72–73
 set and, 75–76
Performance, advancement at work and, 362–363

Perseverance, goal achievement and, 354–356
Persistence of creative thinkers, 158–159
Personal effectiveness, leadership and, 363
Personality, 23, 27–32
 attitudes and, 134–135
 big five factors in, 29–30
 goal achievement and, 357–358
 incompatibility of, 32
 job success and, 40–41
 others' perceptions of, 28–29
 self and, 36–37
 tests of, 30–31
 theories of, 29
Personality change, 38–40
 resistance to, 38
 self-analysis and, 38–39
 understanding others and, 39–40
Personality development, 32–35
 evolution and, 32
 heredity and environment and, 33–34
 stages in, 34–35
Personality disorder, 273
Personal philosophies, 336–337
Persuasion, 136
Pessimists, 123–124
Philosophical questions, 336–337
"Phi phenomenon," 88
Phobias, 103–104, 240
Phobic disorder, 271–272
Phobos, 102
Physical fitness, 257–261
Physiological conditions, as communication barrier, 188
Physiological needs, 53, 54, 55
Physiological responses to emotions, 98–100
Piaget, Jean, 147, 318
Pitch of sound, 80
Platonic relationships, 107
Polaroid, 277
Polygraph, 99–100
Positive attitudes, 123, 124
 toward change, 132–133
 in workplace, 129–130, 132–133
Positive reinforcement, 51
Powell, John, 39
Precognition, 89
Prejudice, 125–126
 causes of, 126
 letting go of, 244
 perception and, 76

Preoperational stage, 147
Prestwood, Donna C. L., 365
Principles, 5
Priorities, knowing, 243
Problems, 144
Problem solving
    in daily life, 163
    in groups, 160–162
    insight and, 162
    intuition and, 162
    steps in, 154–157
    stress reduction and, 241
Procedural memory, 150
Procedures, adjustment to changes
        in, 230
Procrastination, 360–361
    characteristics of, 360
    reasons for, 360–361
Procter & Gamble, 293
Projection as coping mechanism, 237
Promises, 7
Protein, 253
Proxemics, 178–179
Psychiatrists, 274, 306–307
Psychoanalytic theory, 51
Psychodynamic theory, 29
Psychokinesis, 89
Psychological disorders, 270–275
    anxiety disorder, 271–272
    dissociative disorder, 272
    mood disorder, 272–273
    personality disorder, 273
    schizophrenic disorder, 273
    somatoform disorder, 272
    treatment of, 273–275
Psychological factors as communica-
        tion barrier, 188
Psychological wants, 54
Psychology, reasons to study, 4
Psychosis, 270
Psychosocial development, 326–329
Psychosomatic illness, 261
Psychotherapy, 274
Puberty, 226, 319
Public Law 94-142, 295–296
Punishment, 51
Pupils, 78
Purpose of communication, 172

Q

Qualitative approach, 292
Quality circles, 160–161
Quality of life, 16
Quality of sound, 80

Quantitative approach, 292
Questions, responding to, during
        presentations, 183
Quid pro quo harassment, 216

R

Race, diversity and, 289–290
Racism, 290
Rapham, Melissa, 216
Rational, definition of, 119
Rationalization as coping mecha-
        nism, 236
Reactive depression, 272
Realities, accepting, 243
Reasonable mistakes, 359
Recall, 150
Receiver in communication, 170–171
Recognition, 150
    perception and, 74–75
Regression as coping mechanism, 236
Reibstein, Larry, 305
Reinforcement, 51
Relationships. *See also* Interpersonal
        entries
    goals and, 350
    handling, 112
Relaxation to reduce stress, 243–244
Relearning, 150
Reliability, 4
Religion, diversity and, 294–295
Repetition
    learning and memory and,
        152–153
    perception and, 76
Repression as coping mechanism,
        237–238
Resistance stage of general adapta-
        tion syndrome, 224
Respect for others
    assertiveness and, 187
    for ideas, 337
    in workplace, 132
Responses, 51
Responsibility
    accepting, 340
    job success and, 40
Résumés, 179–180
Retina, 78
Retirement, adjustment to, 232
Reverse discrimination, 127
Rhythm, sense of, 88
Right-brained people, 144–146
Robotics, 12–13
Rockefeller, John D., 193

Rods, 78
Rokeach, Milton, 63
Role confusion, 328
Role models, attitudes and, 121
Roles, 28–29
Romantic love, 107
Roosevelt, Franklin Delano, 292, 358
Rosch, Paul J., 276
Rosenfeld, Isadore, 268
Ruettiger, Daniel L., 355
Running, 259–260

S

Safety needs, 54, 55–56
Salovey, Peter, 111
Samuelson, Robert J., 196
Santrock, John W., 319
Satisfaction, from work, 338
Scanzoni, Letha, 35
Schizophrenia, 273
Schizophrenic disorder, 273
School, adjusting to, 225
Schoor, Marie, 302
Schumann, Paul A., Jr., 365
Schweitzer, Albert, 350
Security needs, 54, 55–56
Self, personality and, 36–37
Self-actualization
    characteristics associated with, 56
    need for, 54–55, 56
Self-awareness, 111
Self-concept, 23–25
Self-confidence
    of creative thinkers, 158
    goal achievement and, 354
Self-development. *See* Personality
        development
Self-esteem, 25–27
    need for, 54
    negative attitudes and, 123–124
Self-love, 106
Self-motivation, 59–61
Seligman, Martin E. P., 124
Selye, Hans, 224, 261
Semantic memory, 150
Sena, J., 203
Sender in communication, 170–171
Senses
    external. *See* Exterior senses;
        Hearing; Vision
    interior, 77, 87–88
Sensitivity to stimuli, 73
Sensorimotor stage, 147
Sensory adaptation to smells, 84

Sensory register, 149
Set, perception and, 75
Setbacks, 358–359
Setting, perception and, 74
Sexual harassment, 215–216
Sexuality, 35–36, 289
Sexually transmitted diseases (STDs), 265
Sexual orientation, diversity and, 293
Short-term memory, 149
Sibson, Robert E., 58
Sight. *See* Vision
Sitting, 260
Situation, communication and, 172
Situational ethics, 331
Skills for workplace, 15–16
Smell, 84
Smoke, vision and, 73
Smokeless tobacco, 265
Smoking, 263, 264–265
Social clock, 315
Social-cognitive theory of personality, 29
Social development, 317
Social experiences, enjoying, 335
Social facilitation, 203–204
Social maturity, 334–335
Socioeconomic status, diversity and, 296–297
Somatoform disorder, 272
Sound, 79–80
Sound waves, 79–80
Spatial distance, communication and, 178–179
Stages, 34
    of psychosocial development, 326–329
    in self-development, 34–35
Stagnation, 329
Standing committees, 161
Status quo, 230
Stehlin, Isadora B., 269
Stereotypes, 304
Stereotyping, 126
Stimulants, 262
Stimuli, 51
    sensitivity to, 73
Stoffle, Carla J., 300
Storms, vision and, 73
Strasser, S., 203
Stress, 223–249
    adjusting to. *See* Adjustments
    coping with. *See* Coping with stress

definition of, 224
    illness due to, 261
    reduction of, 241–247
Stressors, 224
Strikes, 202
Stroboscopic motion, 88
Substance abuse, 261–265
Suicide, 241
Superego, 36, 37
Superstition, 48
Supervision, adjustment to changes in, 230
Support for grieving, 234
Swimming, 260

T

Tactile learners, 87
Tangible values, 62
Tarin, Patricia A., 300
Task forces, 161
Taste, 83–84
Teams, 208–213
    advantages of, 210–211
    leadership and, 365
    members of, 212–213
    problems with, 211–212
    purposes and structures of, 209–210
Telepathy, 88
Temperament, 34
Tension, releasing, 245–246
Terminal values, 63
Tests of personality, 30–31
Theories, 5. *See also specific theories*
Theory X, 53
Theory Y, 53
Theory Z, 53
Thinking
    creative. *See* Creativity
    lateral and vertical, 159–160
Thompson, Catherine, 234
Thornburgh, Richard, 64
Threats, 6
Threshold of audibility, 80
Thuriaux, Michel, 266
Time
    ethnic diversity and, 291
    sense of, 88
Time management, goal achievement and, 351–352
Tobacco use, 263, 264–265
Tolerance, 335
Totality principle, 85, 154–155
Touch, 82–83, 87
Training of older people, 336

Traits, 29
Trait theory of personality, 29
Trust in employer-employee relations, 201, 202–203
Trust versus mistrust stage, 326–327
Twain, Mark, 134
Twin studies of personality, 33–34
Two-factor theory of motivation, 194–195

U

Unconscious, 51
Undifferentiated schizophrenia, 273
Unemployment, adjustment to, 231–232
Unions, 201–203
Unisex, definition of, 35
United Nations, 8–9
Universal human values, 65

V

Validity, 4
Values, 61–65
    influences on, 63–65
    perception and, 76
    tangible and intangible, 62–63
    terminal and instrumental, 63
    universal, 65
    valuing diversity and, 285–288
Values clarification, 62
Vander Zanden, James W., 331
Vaness, Margaret H., 78–79
Variable expenses, 352
Vertical channels of communication, 214
Vertical thinking, 160
Vision, 77–79
    color and, 78–79
    environmental effects on, 73
    light and, 78
    visual hazards and, 78
Visual impairment, 72
Visual learners, 87
Vitamins, 253
Vocational maturity, 337–338, 340

W

Waitley, Denis, 60
Walking, 260
Walsh, Froma, 234
Wants
    perception and, 76
    psychological, 54

Water in diet, 253
Wausau Hospital, 277
Weaver, Richard L., II, 131
Wellness, 251–281
    balances and, 279
    habits and, 277–279
    humor and, 269
    medical treatment and, 268–269
    mental health and, 270
    nutrition and. *See* Nutrition
    physical fitness and, 257–261
    psychological disorders and. *See*
        Psychological disorders
    for stress reduction, 246
    threats to, 261–267
    work and, 275–277
Willingness to learn, 132
Willingness to work, 132
Willingness to work with others, 132
Willpower, 60–61
Win-lose conflict resolution, 207
Win-win conflict resolution, 207
Wood, E. G., 34
Wood, S. E., 34
Woods, Tiger, 290, 291
Work
    deriving satisfaction from, 338
    importance of, 349
    recognizing need for, 338

Work attitudes, 128–133
Workforce composition, 10
Working hours, adjustment to,
    229–230
Working memory, 149
Work motivation, 194–196
Workplace. *See also* Human relations
    advancement in, 361–363
    communication in, 213–215
    current status of, 9
    diversity in, 10
    emotions in, 110–111, 197–199
    employer-employee relations and.
        See Employer-employee rela-
        tions
    future of, 9–10
    personality and job success and,
        40–41
    skills needed for, 15–16
    stress in. *See* Job-related adjust-
        ments
    vocational maturity and, 337–338,
        340
    wellness and, 275–277

Workplace diversity, 10, 302–306
    benefits of, 303–304
    changing workforce and, 302–303
    managing, 304–306
    problems related to, 304
Wundt, Wilhelm, 4, 84

X

Xerox, 293

Y

Young adulthood
    adjustment to independent living
        during, 226–227
    development during, 321–322,
        328–329

Z

Zajonc, Robert, 95
Zeuschner, Raymond, 174–175

Name _____ Date_____

 **Psychology in Our Changing World**

Learning Activities

1. Prediction is one of the purposes of psychology. Although predictions aren't always accurate, predict how technological change might affect the type of work for which you are preparing. Explain how you believe such predictions could be useful to you in your work.

   Type of work for which I am preparing:

   My prediction pertaining to technological change:

   How I believe my prediction could be useful to me in my work:

2. Reasons for interest in or concern about the future are contained in the following incomplete statements. Complete the statements by expressing your particular interest in or concern about the future. Make your statements as specific as possible.

   a. I am curious about

   b. I would like to prepare for

   c. I am interested in controlling or influencing

   d. Something I would like to have part in preventing is

   e. A possible change that I would like to promote is

Name _____ Date_____

3. Contrast yourself with a person of another culture in terms of any two cultural characteristics identified in the chapter. Also identify two characteristics you and this person have in common.

Contrasting Cultural
Characteristic   Myself   Person of
                                                                        Another Culture

a.

b.

Similar Cultural
Characteristic   Myself   Person of
                                                                        Another Culture

a.

b.

4. Identify two ways you can continue learning after you complete the program in which you are now enrolled. To what extent do you believe lifelong learning to be a personal responsibility?

Ways in which I can continue learning after I complete the program in which I am now enrolled:

a.

b.

The extent to which I believe lifelong learning is a personal responsibility:

5. There is an increase in the number of people working in their own homes, either as self-employed workers or as contractors for other businesses. List what you believe to be both advantages and disadvantages of using one's home as a workplace.

    a. Advantages:

    b. Disadvantages:

6. How would you evaluate yourself in terms of SCANS competencies? List them. Where do you need training? How will you get it?

Competencies	Training Needed	How to Get Training

7. Describe what you consider an appropriate balance between dependence and independence in your life at this time. Explain why you consider this balance appropriate.

My Dependence

My Independence

Why I consider this balance appropriate for me at this time in my life:

Enrichment Activities

1. Determine what you believe to be the advantages and disadvantages of life today compared to life when your grandparents were young adults.

2. With two other members of the class, check the Internet for courses or training available in your course of study. Each of you can use a different search engine. Compare your findings.

3. Describe what you consider the ingredients of a high quality of life and evaluate your life in terms of your description. What can you do to move closer to the quality of life you desire?

4. Interview a person who is employed in the area of work for which you are preparing. Ask him or her how the type of work has changed and how it might be expected to change in the future.

5. Talk to one of your program instructors about how he or she keeps up with the changing world of work for which he or she is preparing students. Ask for advice on how you might keep abreast of such changes when you enter or re-enter the world of work.

Self-Concept and Personality

Learning Activities

1. Explain how your self-concept and personality are interrelated. Also describe an incident showing how one's self-concept might have influenced his or her actions toward another person.

Interrelationship between self-concept and personality:

Incident showing how self-concept might have influenced actions toward another person:

2. Review Kevin's experience in starting his new job on page 26. Which attitudes and actions indicate he had appropriate self-esteem? Which do you believe would be the most challenging for you on a new job. Explain why.

Attitudes and actions I would find most challenging:

I believe these would be most challenging for me for the following reasons:

3. Describe yourself, to the best of your ability, in terms of the Big Five personality factors. Check the descriptions of these factors in the chapter.

Personality Factor   **Description of Myself**

a. Emotional stability

b. Extraversion

Personality Factor *(cont.)*   **Description of Myself** *(cont.)*

c. Openness

d. Agreeableness

e. Conscientiousness

· ·

4. According to Sigmund Freud, there are three main forces influencing each person's behavior: id, ego, and superego. Compare the relationship between the id and the superego and explain the effect they have on the ego or the person you *are*.

· ·

5. Define the terms *heredity* and *environment* and identify a personality trait of yours that you believe may have been influenced by each.

Definition of heredity:

Personality trait of mine that I believe may have been influenced by heredity:

Definition of environment:

Personality trait of mine that I believe may have been influenced by environment:

6. Explain the differences among John's John, the real John, and Thomas's John, according to O. W. Holmes.

John's John:

The real John:

Thomas's John:

7. The following self-portrait can give you insight into who you are. It is designed to give you a more objective understanding of self-identity characteristics, personality strengths and weaknesses, abilities, habits, ideas, and ambitions. For each of the following categories, describe yourself as completely and accurately as possible. If change is possible, describe the changes you would like to make. This self-portrait is for your use and is not to be handed in.

Category	Change Desired	Category	Change Desired
Marital status		Outlook on life	
Health		Optimistic or pessimistic	
Present occupation		Conformist or individualist	
Political affiliation		Most valued possession	
Religion			
Financial status		Hobbies	
Income		Sports	
Savings		Habits	
Debts		Relaxation	
Experience		Sleeping	
Work		Eating	
Travel		Physical exercise	
Education		Personal hygiene	
Group activity		Studying	
Emotional stability		Worst habit	
Love		Best habit	
Control of temper		Driving record	
Jealousy		Honors and awards	
Fears		Failures or setbacks	
Anxieties		Dependency	
Phobias			
Frustrations			

Category	Change Desired	Category	Change Desired
Responsibilities		Social relationships	
		Family	
Ideas about		Friends	
Dating		Neighbors	
Marriage		Coworkers	
Population			
control		Ambitions	
Nuclear power		Career	
Natural		Marriage and	
resources		family	
Religion		Continued	
National defense		education	
Abortion		Talent	
Freedom		development	
Politics		Vacations	
Purpose of life		Travel	
Education		Cultural	
Morality		experiences	
		Retirement	
Entertainment			

Enrichment Activities

1. Using a search engine such as the Web Crawler or Lycos on the Internet, find additional information on the use of personality tests in employment situations. One approach is to use "personality tests + employment" as your search subject. Compare your findings with several other members of your class working on this activity or find reviews of tests and how they are used.

2. Find out the personality traits of a famous person you admire. Determine how you think the traits have contributed to his or her success. Form a group with four other class members working on this activity and compare your findings and ideas.

3. Think about six different people you know well. Select people who are different in age, background, and occupation. Number them 1 through 6. List at least four personality traits of each. Compare these traits with the Big Five descriptions.

4. Describe yourself in terms of at least six outstanding traits you believe you have. What combination of hereditary and environmental factors do you think have contributed to making you the person you are today? To what extent do you believe a trait is one you have chosen to develop?

Name _____ Date_____

 Motives and Values

1. Identify the type of motivational conflict involved in each of the following situations as approach-approach, approach-avoidance, double approach-avoidance, or avoidance-avoidance. Also explain values you would consider in making similar choices.

    a. Francesca wants to begin a marketing career in the local branch of a national chain. But she does not want to begin a training session in the month of July.

    b. Megan and Barry are planning to buy a house and have been looking at houses in their price range in the part of town where they would like to live. After looking at houses for several months, they have found two that they like equally well and are having difficulty making a decision.

    c. Rick has been informed that, because of a special order at the shop where he works, everyone will be expected to work late three nights next week or work all day on Saturday. He doesn't like working overtime during the week. He has already made other plans for Saturday, yet he is supposed to inform his supervisor by 4 P.M. today when he will do his share of the extra work.

    d. Tricia has an opportunity to live with three other women in an apartment. This idea appeals to her, but the apartment is unfurnished, and she has no furniture to contribute and no money she can spare toward purchasing furniture. She also has a chance to rent a room close to school. The room has a kitchenette area, but she doesn't like the idea of living alone. The other women in the apartment want to know her decision as soon as possible so they can consider someone else if she decides not to live with them. She is considering all factors in both situations but still hasn't made up her mind.

2. The psychoanalytic, behavioristic, and humanistic theories are three of the major motivational theories. Briefly describe each.

Psychoanalytic theory:

Behavioristic theory:

Humanistic theory:

3. Characteristics common to self-actualizers are listed below. Evaluate yourself as a self-actualizer with respect to these characteristics.

They are realistic.
They are aware of their strengths and weaknesses.
They are concerned with problems outside themselves.
They recognize and use opportunities.
They enjoy a certain amount of privacy.
They appreciate the ordinary things of life.
Evaluation of myself:

4. A challenging problem in business and industry is the motivation of employees to do their best work. Indicate the type of job you will be prepared for immediately after completing your present education. Suggest three ways in which you might be motivated to do your best work.

Type of work I am preparing for:

Ways in which I might be motivated to do my best work:

a.

b.

c.

5. Some parents, teachers, political leaders, clergy, and law enforcement personnel claim to have control over the behavior of others. Determine whether you believe control or influence is being used in each of the following situations, and then write a brief justification for each of your decisions.

a. A father tells his teenage daughter to vacuum the living room after school. When the father comes home in the evening, he sees that the room has been vacuumed.

b. An instructor tells a student he must have his report turned in by the end of the week. On Thursday, the student turns in his report.

c. A member of the clergy informs the congregation that every adult member must contribute to the debt-reduction campaign. The following week, Brad Barrot, who had not contributed until then, contributed $400.

d. A person charged with causing an accident while under the influence of alcohol was ordered to attend a group dynamics class on the effects of alcohol. The following Tuesday this person was present for the first session of the class.

6. Analyze the nature of the following values and determine whether each is primarily tangible or intangible. Circle *T* if the value is primarily *tangible* and *I* if the value is primarily *intangible*. Add a tangible and an intangible value of your own. Explain why each is of value to you.

a. Motorcycle	**a.** T	I
b. Friendship	**b.** T	I
c. Set of books	**c.** T	I
d. Ring	**d.** T	I
e. Compact disc player	**e.** T	I
f. Photographs	**f.** T	I
g. Safety plaque	**g.** T	I
h. Television	**h.** T	I
i. Uniform	**i.** T	I
j. Computer	**j.** T	I
k. _____	**k.** T	I
l. _____	**l.** T	I

7. Terms from the chapter are listed below. Definitions of some of them are found in the glossary. Use a dictionary, if necessary, for the others. Select four of the terms and write the sentence or clause from the text in which the term is defined. Rewrite it, substituting a synonym or synonymous phrase for the term. Underline the term in the first sentence and the synonym or synonymous phrase in the second sentence. An example is given after the list of terms.

Conflict	Illogical	Principles	Response
Drive	Intrinsic	Priority	Stimulus
Extrinsic	Overt	Physiological needs	Theory

Example: Strictly speaking, a person has <u>physiological</u> *needs* for survival as well as psychological wants for comfort and happiness.

Rewritten: Strictly speaking, a person has <u>bodily</u> *needs* for survival as well as psychological wants for comfort and happiness.

Enrichment Activities

1. Find out more about behavior modification and how it is applied today. Talk to two parents or elementary or preschool teachers about their use of positive reinforcement as a means of changing children's behavior. Then form your own evaluation of behavior modification.

2. Make a list of your own needs and wants. Compare your list with those of at least two people. (They could be two other students carrying out the same activity.) Try to determine reasons why the lists differ.

3. Describe or illustrate a situation in which a person would have conflicting motives. Indicate what considerations affect decision making in the various types of conflict situations: approach-approach, approach-avoidance, double approach-avoidance, avoidance-avoidance.

4. Make a list of ten things that you value. Then number them in the order of their importance to you. Observe your activities for several weeks and evaluate whether you are giving adequate attention to what you have listed as high on your values list.

5. Make a list of what you believe to be your motivations for work. Research additional information on work incentives. Compare your findings with what you identified as your motivations for work. Determine whether you want to modify your own list of motivations as a result of your research.

Name _____ Date_____

 Senses and Perception

Learning Activities

1. Select a television commercial and a magazine advertisement to use as examples of how such commercials and advertisements are designed to appeal to the senses. Describe or give the script of the television commercial, and describe or attach a copy of the magazine advertisement. Indicate the sense or senses to which each advertisement appeals.

2. We are constantly exposed to loud sounds and noise. Referring to the following situations, suggest two ways the individuals involved might protect themselves from the hazards of sound.

    a. A music enthusiast has a CD player at home and plays CD's of favorite groups several times a day. This person also frequently attends concerts on weekends.

    b. A young married couple has an apartment close to the downtown area in a city of 200,000. They live on one of the busiest streets leading into the downtown business district. There are commuter train and construction noises during the day and sirens blowing throughout the night.

3. Give an example of your current learning through each of visual, auditory, and tactile means. Explain which style you believe to be most effective for you and how you might increase your learning in the future with this style.

Learning Style   **Example of My Current Learning**

    a. Visual

    b. Auditory

Learning Style *(cont.)*

c. Tactile (practicing a procedure)

Example of My Current Learning Style *(cont.)*

The style I believe to be most effective for me is:

I might increase my learning in the future using this style by:

....

4. Some of the factors that affect perception are listed next. Give an example of how each factor has affected *your* perception.

a. Physical ability or limitation:

b. Environmental condition:

c. Past experience:

d. Set—needs and wants:

e. Attention factors:

....

5. Using the principle of perception listed below, identify the principle of perception involved in each of the following experiences. Write the name of the principle in the space below each incident.

Principles of Perception

Constancy
Figure-ground
Totality, or gestalt
Camouflage
Closure
Conditioning

a. Sherry recently purchased new tinted designer eyeglasses. She could hardly wait for her friend Pam to see them; yet Pam didn't even notice them until Sherry brought them to her attention.

b. Lance grew up in a quiet small town. His first job after graduation took him to a city with a population of 150,000. The first week of living there he woke up several times a night because of sirens and other night sounds of large cities. After the first week, however, he slept soundly and didn't seem to notice them.

c. Beth and Jon went shopping for a cart for their microwave. They saw just what they wanted on display in a department store. They discovered that it came unassembled and they would have to put it together. Because the cart came with a shelf, a sliding door, and a drawer, its box contained a number of pieces. After carefully studying the enclosed instructions and diagram, they figured out how to put it together.

d. Dennis saw a police squad car stop across the street and the officer get out and approach the house. He immediately assumed that the woman who lived there was the driver of a hit-and-run accident. He remembered seeing some damage to the front of her car last week.

e. Mark lives in a northern state where snowbanks often reach six feet in winter. He was in the market for a new car. "I definitely do not want a white one," he commented to a dealer, "because it would be too difficult to see against the snow."

....

6. Describe how you can widen your world through three of the five exterior senses.

Sense   **How I Can Widen My World**

a.

b.

c.

Enrichment Activities

1. Find two additional examples of illusions. Prepare a sketch or demonstration to show to the class. Give an explanation for the illusions.

2. Play excerpts from classical, folk, jazz, and rock music from tapes or CDs for your class. Ask students to identify which they like best and ask them whether they know why they prefer one kind of music to the other. Give your own explanation of how likes and dislikes are acquired. Be sure to plan the activity within the time limit allowed by the instructor.

3. Spend a leisurely half-hour in a park, shopping center, library, or any other place of your choice. Notice sounds, colors, shapes, odors, and other stimuli that you ordinarily miss. Describe this experience in a small group including others who have also carried out this activity. You may also want to share your experience with the class.

4. Use several search engines on the Internet to gain more information on extrasensory perception. Take a position for or against extrasensory perception and explain it to your class or a small group.

5 Emotions

Learning Activities

1. The description of the physiological effects of fear experienced by Pam in the following incident is partially erroneous. To the right of each effect, circle C when the effect is *typical* of a fear response and *I* when the effect is *incorrect.* Next to each incorrect description, restate the effect to make it typical of a fear response.

> Mia had arrived earlier in the day in a large city to begin her first full-time job after her graduation from a community college. Since this was her first night in her apartment, she was a little uneasy. At four o'clock in the morning she heard what she thought was someone trying to open her door. She became frightened and didn't know what to do.

a. Her heart beat faster.   **a.** C   I

b. Her mouth felt dry.   **b.** C   I

c. She felt extremely hungry.   **c.** C   I

d. Her hands perspired.   **d.** C   I

e. Her muscles became limp.   **e.** C   I

f. Her breathing became
   very slow.   **f.** C   I

2. Propose one method by which each of the people in the following case studies might lessen or overcome his or her fear or anxiety.

   a. A 12-year-old boy is afraid to ride in a car after dark. Six months earlier, he was riding in a car with his brother when they ran out of gas on a lightly traveled stretch of road late at night. The youngster sat in the car alone for two hours while his brother went for help. Since that experience, the 12-year-old will stay at home rather than go somewhere in a car after dark.

   b. A mature woman is afraid of thunder and lightning. She remembers that as a child she would sit in a closet until a thunderstorm passed. Although too old for that type of escape now, she will sit terrified in a dark room during a storm.

3. We recognize now that emotions are a normal part of the workplace. Give an example of a positive effect or result of an emotion in the workplace. Your example can be from your own experience, or it can be hypothetical but realistic.

Emotion Expressed   Positive Effect or Result

4. Following is a description of a situation involving reasonable anger and a constructive reaction to it. Give another example from your own experience or observation that involved justifiable or reasonable anger and explain what you believe would be a constructive reaction to the incident.

   Marilyn has worked for the You-Name-It Packaging Company for four years. She has taken two night classes in management and sales and has had the impression that she would be made a department manager in the near future. Last Friday during a coffee break the personnel manager of the company introduced a person no one had ever seen before as the head of the sales department. Marilyn's first reactions were shock and disappointment. As she thought about it during the day, she became angry that she had not been offered the job. She believed herself to be better qualified and to be deserving of recognition for her record with the company in the past four years. She made an appointment with the personnel manager to discuss the situation and the possibility of her advancement in the future.

   Example from your own experience or observation:

   Constructive reaction or result:

5. The domains of emotional intelligence are listed below. Write a brief descriptive evaluation of your own emotional intelligence as related to each of the domains.

Domain   **Evaluation of My E.Q.**

Knowing one's emotions

Managing emotions

Motivating oneself

Recognizing emotions in others

Handling relationships

Name _____ Date _____

Enrichment Activities

1. Make a bulletin board, collage, or other display showing different types of emotions being expressed. Be as original as possible.

2. Get together with a group of friends and talk about your fears. Compare common fears and discuss how some childhood fears have been overcome. Report (in writing or orally) whether this experience was of value to you.

3. Select several poems on the subject of love and read them to the class. (A collection of poetry from a library would probably have many from which to choose.) Ask the class for their comments.

4. Research the subject of grief using Infotrac, electronic libraries, or the Internet. Develop your own guidelines for coping with grief or supporting others who are experiencing grief.

Attitudes

Learning Activities

1. Match the following numbered definitions with the terms given. Place the letter of the term in the answer blank to the right of the definition. More terms than definitions are given.

a. Apathy	**e.** Discrimination	**i.** Revengeful
b. Belligerent	**f.** Humane	**j.** Stereotype
c. Contradiction	**g.** Peer	**k.** Tolerance
d. Pessimist	**h.** Prejudice	**l.** Unrealistic

1. A person belonging to one's age group

1. _____

2. Behavior that is the opposite to previous behavior

2. _____

3. Readiness to argue and fight

3. _____

4. Lack of interest in events and circumstances

4. _____

5. Not seeing things as they really are

5. _____

6. A person who habitually holds negative attitudes

6. _____

7. Acceptance of others as they are, without ill feeling

7. _____

8. Prejudgment without adequate information or reason

8. _____

9. To assume that all members of a particular group have the same characteristic

9. _____

10. Trying to get even with another person

10. _____

2. The development of attitudes is influenced by family, peers, role models, experience, and culture. Identify two attitudes you have and state what you believe to have been the main influence in the development of each.

    a. Attitude:

        Main influence:

    b. Attitude:

        Main influence:

3. Attitudes may change with time as one has new experiences and changes some values. Describe a possible difference in attitude, between a teenager and a parent, pertaining to the use of money.

    Attitude of Teenager   Attitude of Parent

4. An example of reasonable prejudgment is given below. Explain how this type of prejudgment differs from prejudice.

    Trish ordered a sweater from a catalog because it came in the style and color she has been looking for. When she received the sweater, she found that it was defective and returned it. She was sent a new sweater but found that this one was also poorly made. She mentioned this to her friend Andrea, who said she had also bought a sweater of that brand and was dissatisfied with the quality. Soon after, another friend mentioned to Trish that a local store had this particular brand of sweater on sale and wanted to know whether she was interested in going along to look at them. Trish told her, "No, I will not spend my money on that brand of sweater."

    Explanation:

5. Causes of prejudice were identified in the chapter. Describe an incident of behavior resulting from prejudice and list possible causes of the prejudice.

Description of behavior resulting from prejudice:

Possible causes of the prejudice:

6. Using the example of the Reliable Construction Company described under "Discrimination" in the chapter, compare prejudice and discrimination by defining each. Then compare the effects of prejudice and discrimination on yourself and on others.

Definition of prejudice:

Definition of discrimination:

Comparison of the effects of prejudice and discrimination on myself and on others:

7. Work-related attitudes from the chapter are listed below. Name an additional attitude and explain why you consider it important.

a. Loyalty to the company
b. Willingness to work
c. Willingness to learn
d. Willingness to work with others

   e. Respect for supervisors, coworkers, customers, and clients
   f. Positive attitudes toward change

   g. _____

....

8. If your attitudes and behavior are not in harmony, you become uncomfortable. Give an example of such disharmony other than the examples in the chapter. Explain whether you think the attitude or the behavior should be changed, and why.

Example of attitude or behavior disharmony:

Which should be changed and why?

Enrichment Activities

1. Keep track of your reactions resulting in negative or positive attitudes within a two-week period. Then try to determine how you developed each of these attitudes. Also, decide whether you should make an effort to change the attitudes, the related behavior, or both.

2. Visit an employment office and ask an appropriate person there for information about discrimination and affirmative action. Determine your own ideas about affirmative action and reverse discrimination. Check with two other students to see to what extent their ideas agree with or differ from yours.

3. Ask several employers you know what work-related attitudes they consider important in people they hire. Also ask them whether they have any way of detecting these attitudes in interviews with employment applicants.

Name _____ Date _____

7 Thinking and Problem Solving

Learning Activities

1. The following incidents involve the use of either recognition or recall. Determine the type of memory involved in each incident, and write either *recognition* or *recall* in the space provided.

  a. A student knows that another student belongs to the Student Governing Board by the emblem on the jacket he is wearing. _____

  b. Allyson knows the answer to the question, "What is the meaning of overlearning?" _____

  c. Bart lost his list of supplies to buy at the bookstore, but he remembered them anyway. _____

  d. Lainie forgot the house number of a classmate she agreed to pick up but drove down the street and knew the house when she saw it. _____

2. In the blank above each age range given on the left, write the appropriate stage of cognitive development, according to Piaget. In parentheses before each stage, write the letter of the mental ability characteristic of each stage.

Cognitive Stage	**Characteristic**
( ) _____ Birth to 2 years	**a.** Can look forward to his or her birthday
( ) _____ 2 to 7 years	**b.** Knows that soda in a tall, slender glass is the same amount when poured into a short, wide glass

Cognitive Stage *(cont.)*	**Characteristic** *(cont.)*

( ) ——————————————————————
                7 to 11 years

c. Knows that when a ball rolls under the sofa, it still exists

( ) ——————————————————————
                12 years and up

d. Can think about the idea of heaviness without relating it to a certain heavy object

. . . .

3. Identify a skill related to your major area of study (such as information processing if you are a business student). Write this skill in the blank. Then describe how each of the listed factors that contribute to learning and memory can be applied to learning this skill.

Skill: _____

a. Motivation

b. Meaningfulness of material

c. Concentration

d. Association

e. Repetition

4. Describe a problem or situation that requires immediate action and explain how the given components of common-sense problem solving can be considered or used to handle it.

Problem or Situation

   a. Identify possible danger to life

   b. Identify possible hazards to equipment

   c. Consider probabilities in cause and effect

   d. Engage available human resources

   e. Make appropriate use of available tools and materials—improvising, if necessary

5. Define an actual or hypothetical problem, and explain how each of the following problem-solving guidelines might be used to solve it.

   a. Definition of the problem

   b. The total situation

   c. Problems within the major problem

d. Possible causes

e. Possible solutions

f. Plus and minus factors of two of the solutions

Solution   Plus Factors   Minus Factors

(1)

(2)

g. Possible sources of advice and assistance

h. Solution decided upon

i. First action step to be taken

j. How effectiveness of solution will be evaluated

6. Getting from one place to another presents problems of different magnitude depending on the situation or time in a person's life. The following are hypothetical transportation problems for you to analyze. In the space provided after each problem, suggest two possible sources of advice or assistance.

    a. *Past problem:* When you were 12 years old, you wanted to go to a circus 15 miles away but had no means of transportation.

    b. *Present problem:* You need a daily ride to school, which is 8 miles from where you live; you don't have a car, and there is no public transportation.

    c. *Future problem:* You would like to take a 1,000-mile trip, but you aren't sure about the best route or means of transportation.

7. Problems faced by Tony and Margo Lombardi, a young married couple, are described below. Suggest two possible solutions for the problems, and circle the number of the solution you believe to be the better one. Give a reason or reasons for your choice.

    Tony's working hours have been cut back from forty to thirty hours a week. Tony and Margo are making house and car payments and are living on a tight budget. They can foresee a problem in making the payments with Tony's smaller paycheck.

(1)

(2)

Reason or reasons:

Enrichment Activities

1. Make a poster or collage, using newspaper headlines, magazine articles and pictures, and material from other sources, that gives evidence of a modern social problem that has not yet been solved. On the basis of what you have learned in this course in previous chapters, explain the poster or collage in writing or orally to the class. Explain why problems involving people are often more difficult to solve than problems involving equipment or materials.

2. Research artificial intelligence on the Infotrac or some other periodical reference in your college or public library, or use a search engine on the Internet to find recent information on the development of artificial intelligence. Summarize your findings and determine your opinion on the future development and uses of artificial intelligence.

3. Reviewing and overlearning can be interesting and rewarding if done in teams or small groups, with an exchange of questions and answers. Try overlearning material you now know to retain it for later use. Also review material and procedures for a test in another class with someone else taking the same class. Report on the results.

Name _____ Date _____

8 Communicating Effectively

Learning Activities

1. Give a specific example, preferably from your own experience as a sender, of each of the purposes of communication.

Purpose   **Example**

a. To inform

b. To instruct

c. To persuade

d. To support

e. To be social

f. To entertain

2. Explain the difference between hearing and listening by defining each. Give a specific example of your listening to understand in a program-related class in which you are enrolled.

Definition of hearing:

Definition of listening:

Example of my listening *to understand* in a program-related class:

3. Identify a job you might apply for in the future. State three questions you might be asked in an interview for that job. Also state your likely responses.

Type of job applying for:

a. Question:

Response:

b. Question:

Response:

c. Question:

Response:

4. Identify and give an example of four types of nonverbal communication. Explain what you believe can be negative effects of one of the types.

Type   Example

a.

b.

c.

d.

Possible negative effects of a, b, c, or d:

5. The open area of the Johari Window represents what is known to both oneself and others. Identify two ways a person might enlarge the open area, and explain why this could be desirable.

a. Ways to enlarge open area:

(1)

(2)

b. Why enlarging the open area could be desirable:

6. Explain how an interpersonal relationship might develop from *acquaintance* to *intimacy*. Describe what a person might do and say in each type of relationship.

How an interpersonal relationship might develop:

What a person might do and say in the following types of relationships.

a. Acquaintance

b. Associate

c. Friend

d. Intimate

7. Give an example of each of the following barriers to communication. Try to give examples from your own experience. Suggest how the example related to *channel characteristics* can be overcome or minimized.

Type of Barrier   **Example**

a. Distraction

b. Physiological condition

c. Psychological factor

d. Perceptual difference

e. Language problem

f. Channel characteristics

How the barriers related to channel characteristics can be overcome or minimized:

Name _____ Date _____

1. With two classmates, ask three owners of small businesses or department managers of larger businesses how they handle complaints. Ask them how they handle a situation where the complainer continues to be dissatisfied. Prepare a group report and present it to the class.

2. Develop a dialogue involving a misunderstanding between two people in a type of work situation with which you are familiar. Explain how communication and human relations are interrelated. Suggest how the misunderstanding may have been prevented.

3. Role-play a job interview with another student. Conduct the interview twice, changing roles as employer and applicant. One of the mock interviews could contain examples of poor interview practice. Present this to your class and ask students to evaluate the examples, identifying the poor practices and suggesting improvements.

Name _____ Date _____

Human Relations at Work

Learning Activities

1. Distinguish between hygiene factors and motivation factors, according to Herzberg. Identify a company that makes a certain product or sells a certain service and give an example of how you believe a factor of each type affects its employees.

Explanation of hygiene factor:

Explanation of motivation factor:

Company (real or hypothetical):

How I believe a hygiene factor affects employees:

How I believe a motivation factor affects employees:

2. Using the expectancy theory of motivation, give an example of a work-related goal an employee might have, explain why the employee believes the goal is attainable, and describe the activity of the employee that might make the goal attainable. Your example may be hypothetical, but it should be realistic.

Goal an employee might have:

Why the employee believes the goal is attainable:

Activity of the employee that might make the goal attainable:

3. Explain how you would respond to a customer who is angry because a product he or she purchased from you didn't work. Give specific applications of at least three suggestions for handling customer complaints.

Product that customer says didn't work:

Applications of suggestions for handling the customer's complaint:

a.

b.

c.

4. Interpersonal relations can involve conflict, competition, or cooperation. Compare these by describing a work-related experience involving each. The experience you describe should be a work situation related to your program but may be real or hypothetical.

Work experiences involving:

a. Conflict

b. Competition

c. Cooperation

5. Describe two advantages of a work team that would include the following types of members: (1) president of the company or owner, (2) production or service manager, (3) secretary to service department, (4) production or service employee, and (5) maintenance employee.

Advantages of team composed of members described above:

a.

b.

6. Select one of the possible problems of team functioning and suggest a possible solution to the problem.

Possible problem of team functioning:

Possible solution to the problem:

7. Explain what is meant by an open-door policy within an organization. Explain your attitude toward such a policy and give an example supporting your attitude.

Explanation of open-door policy:

My attitude toward an open-door policy:

Example (real or hypothetical) supporting my attitude:

8. Define sexual harassment in your own words. Explain why, in your opinion, some cases of sexual harassment might not be reported.

My definition of sexual harassment:

Why, in my opinion, some cases of sexual harassment might not be reported:

Name _____ Date _____

1. Look up information on the charges of sexual harassment by Anita Hill against Clarence Thomas in 1991. Draw your conclusion about the charges and give an explanation for your conclusion.

2. Research ethics in the workplace using the Electric Library, an Internet search engine, Infotrac, or some other library research tool. With another student who has done the same research, role-play the handling of a hypothetical ethics dilemma for your class. One of you should be an employee involved in the questionable behavior, and the other should play a coworker who disagrees with the employee's way of handling the dilemma.

3. Find out from an instructor in your major area of study how you might expect to be involved in team functioning in your future work. Ask this instructor about his or her opinion of teams in the workplace and about his or her related experience.

Name _____ Date_____

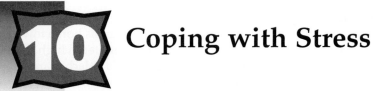

Coping with Stress

Learning Activities

1. Some of life's experiences require major adjustments. Give a specific example of how a person might adjust to adolescence, independent living, marriage, illness or disability, grief, or retirement. Relate your example to an experience you have had or know about.

2. Cheryl is beginning a new job as a salesperson in the electronics department of a large chain department store. Suggest five types of information or orientation experience that would be helpful to her in becoming competent in her new job.

3. Job-related situations are given below. Listed below them are aspects of life affected by job situations. Determine which aspects of life are affected by each job situation. Write the numbers of the situations in the blank space. Use numbers more than once, or use more than one number for an aspect of life if more than one applies.

Job-Related Situations
1. First full-time job
2. Rotating shifts
3. New department supervisor

4. Promotion within company
5. Transfer to branch plant
6. Employment layoff

Aspects of Life

a. Family schedules

b. Work procedures

c. Residence

d. Finances

e. Social relationships

a. _____

b. _____

c. _____

d. _____

e. _____

4. An apparel manufacturing company decided to cut back on its line of clothing, causing a reduction in the number of employees. Jack had been working for the company, which is in his home town, for 14 years when he received his layoff notice. Jack has a family, with a son and daughter in high school; his wife Marie works part-time at the post office. Jack's elderly father and Marie's elderly parents live in their own homes, but Jack and Marie are available to assist them when needed. Add one additional factor to their situation. Explain how the family might cope with this change in their total situation.

Additional factor:

How the family might cope with their total situation:

5. The five stages of coping with the approach of one's own death, according to Dr. Kübler-Ross, are (1) denial, (2) anger, (3) bargaining, (4) depression, and (5) acceptance. Explain why you believe or don't believe a person experiences these stages in this particular order.

6. Common coping mechanisms are listed below. Identify the coping mechanism used in each of the incidents described and write the name of the coping mechanism in the blank space following the description.

Coping Mechanisms

Daydreaming	Displacement	Repression
Rationalization	Projection	Compensation
Regression	Denial of reality	Fixation

a. A bookstore employee has difficulty paying attention to her work. She frequently stands around and imagines she is a fashion designer and has visions of models parading before her in her creations.

Her coping mechanism is ————————————.

b. A 34-year-old man had a hard day at his auto supplies sales and service store. His assistant was on sick leave, so his work was constantly interrupted by having to answer the phone and talk to customers. One of the customers had complained, "I specifically told you . . . and now why isn't it done?" although no one had any record or recollection of his requests. He worked 45 minutes overtime and had a headache by 5:45. When he got home, he became angry at his kids for having the television too loud and at his wife because his dinner wasn't hot enough.

He was obviously using ————————————.

c. A mechanical-drafting student is supposed to graduate from college in two weeks but has fallen far behind in his drawings. He just never seems to get around to them—for various reasons. One day he feels as if he might be coming down with a cold and decides he really should get some rest so he can accomplish more the next day. On Thursday afternoon, "everybody else" (two of his classmates who are caught up with their work) goes home early, so he decides he wouldn't get much done anyway and puts his unfinished work away and follows. He doesn't have his work done, but he has very good excuses, at least excuses that are acceptable to him at the time.

This student is using ———————————————.

d. A woman wanted to be a model, but an evaluation of career opportunities determined that she wasn't tall enough to qualify for the type of assignments that would interest her. So she decided she would rather become a clothes designer and is specializing in clothes that make short girls appear taller.

The coping mechanism used is ———————————————.

e. A 22-year-old man has had an excellent record as an automobile salesperson. He really gets a thrill out of selling someone a new car and works hard at making a sale. Those who work with him, however, say he regularly throws a tantrum if he thinks he has a deal just about closed and it doesn't go through. He has even been known to dent a car with his fist in his furious disappointment.

The coping mechanism used is ———————————————.

f. After three years of marriage and the birth of two children, Harry still finds it difficult to give up his independence and nights out with his friends. Each week he gives his wife what he considers adequate money to run the house and pay for the children's needs and keeps the rest of his check for his "expenses." Harry's wife barely manages on her allotment, yet he constantly accuses her of spending money foolishly.

He is unconsciously using the coping mechanism known as ———————————————.

....

7. Rebecca has enrolled in an information processing course at a community college 70 miles from her parents' home. She has saved $600 toward her living expenses and also intends to get a part-time job. She rented an unfurnished apartment within walking distance of the school. This is the first time she has been on her own. Give two suggestions that she might use in learning to live independently.

Enrichment Activities

1. Visit a rehabilitation center, if there is one in your vicinity, and ask for information on how the disabled are helped to adjust to their disabilities.

2. What adjustments would a person who worked for a company ten or twelve years and was transferred to another state have to make? Compare hypothetical old and new situations.

3. Visit several retired people you know. (They will probably welcome the company.) Ask them about their adjustments to retirement. Listen carefully. Ask them whether the transition to their retirement could have been made easier in any way.

Wellness

Learning Activities

1. Plan a day's menu for yourself and include recommended amounts from each of the six categories of the Food Guide Pyramid. Plan three meals, but include any combination of foods you prefer in each meal as long as they add up to the recommendations for a day. You need not include items from each of the categories for breakfast, for example. Then evaluate how close your eating for a typical day is to the day's menu you planned.

Breakfast:

Lunch:

Supper or Dinner:

Comparison of my eating in a typical day to the menu (circle the appropriate response):

Right on   Very close   Not bad   Way off

2. Describe a way in which you are not as physically fit as you might be. Indicate two types of activity that would be realistic ways for you to improve that condition. Then explain why you intend (or do not intend) to follow through with the activity to become more physically fit. If you are as physically fit as you might be, explain in the following spaces how you achieved that state of fitness.

I believe I would be more physically fit if I _____

_____

Activities that would be realistic for me to improve the condition:

a.

b.

Why I intend, or do not intend, to follow through to become more physically fit (circle either *intend* or *do not intend* and complete the statement):

....

3. Explain the difference between drug abuse and drug addiction and give an example of each.

Explanation of difference:

Example of drug abuse:

Example of drug addiction:

....

4. Explain the difference between an obsession and compulsion as components of obsessive-compulsive disorder and give what you believe to be an example of each (other than the examples given in the chapter).

Difference between an obsession and compulsion:

What I believe to be an example of an obsession:

What I believe to be an example of a compulsion:

5. Identify a habit you would consider desirable for your wellness. Then devise a plan for forming this new habit. State whether you expect to follow this plan and be successful in acquiring this habit, and give reasons for your decision.

Habit:

Plan for forming the habit:

Expectation for following the plan:

6. Identify a habit you have now that you consider detrimental to your wellness and set up a plan for breaking this habit. State whether you expect to follow this plan and be successful in breaking this undesirable habit, and give reasons for your decision.

Habit:

Plan for breaking the habit:

Expectation for following the plan:

Enrichment Activities

1. Contact the personnel office of two different businesses or organizations in your community or vicinity and ask them about their Employee Assistance Program. Compare the two programs.

2. Check on the training practices of professional athletes. Give a report on a particular athlete you admire.

3. After discussing it with your instructor, arrange for an authority on alcoholism to talk or present a program to the class. Most communities have people qualified and willing to do this. Take the responsibility of program chairperson and introduce the speaker to the class.

4. Make a collage showing characteristics of good mental health. You may want to contact your local mental health organization for some materials.

Valuing Diversity

Learning Activities

1. Sketch the steps to valuing diversity. Identify what you believe to be the most difficult step and explain why.

   The step I consider most difficult is:

   The reason I consider this step most difficult is:

2. List four reasons for valuing diversity. Identify the one you consider most important and explain why.

   Reasons for valuing diversity:

   a.

   b.

   c.

   d.

   I believe _____ is most important because:

3. List the dimensions of diversity and give a defining statement about each.

    a.

    b.

    c.

    d.

    e.

    f.

    g.

    h.

    i.

    j.

    k.

....

4. Select any three dimensions of diversity for which questions are offered in the personal self-examination. Write one additional question that could be considered for each of the dimensions you selected.

    a. Dimension:

        Question:

    b. Dimension:

        Question:

    c. Dimension:

        Question:

5. Describe a community activity that contributes to valuing diversity and explain how you believe it contributes. You may describe an activity that is not included in the chapter.

Description of a community activity:

How I believe it contributes to valuing diversity:

6. Describe an activity or program offered by education to promote valuing diversity and suggest one additional activity that could promote valuing diversity. The additional activity you suggest may be an original idea.

Activity or program offered by education:

Additional activity or program that could promote valuing diversity:

7. Identify two potential problems related to workforce diversity and suggest how they can be solved or minimized.

    a. Potential problem related to workforce diversity:

    How it might be solved or minimized:

    b. Potential problem related to workforce diversity:

    How it might be solved or minimized:

8. Identify the three guidelines for valuing diversity that you consider the most important and suggest how you can personally participate in following each.

    a. Guideline:

    How I can personally participate in following it:

    b. Guideline:

    How I can personally participate in following it:

    c. Guideline:

    How I can personally participate in following it:

Enrichment Activities

1. Visit an area business and inquire about company policies and practices for valuing diversity. Ask for copies of written policies or programs and report back to the class.

2. Ask a person from Student Activities in your school or college to talk to the class about the school's efforts to promote valuing diversity and how members of your class can participate.

3. With several other persons (possibly other members of the class), attend a community activity or program related to ethnic customs. It might be a food fair or a dance or musical with ethnic costumes. Compare with other members of the group what the experience meant to all of you.

4. Identify an additional dimension of diversity, such as physical characteristics, and develop self-examination questions about it.

Name _____ Date_____

 **Life-Span Development**

Learning Activities

1. Six stages in life-span development are listed. In the spaces provided, indicate at least two characteristics of a person's development during each stage. Characteristics may pertain to any types of life-span development.

   a. Early childhood:

   b. Childhood:

   c. Adolescence:

   d. Young adulthood:

   e. Middle adulthood:

   f. Later adulthood:

2. Trust vs. mistrust is the first stage of psychosocial development, according to Erik Erikson. Explain why the development of trust is the foundation for later stages of positive psychosocial development.

3. Four types of maturity discussed in this chapter are listed below. Write in the blank to the right of each lettered example the number of the type of maturity. You may identify more than one type of maturity in any example if appropriate. When you do, be able to provide brief oral explanations of your choices.

1. Vocational   3. Social
2. Emotional   4. Intellectual

a. Reacts calmly to disappointment   **a.** _____

b. Associates with people of both sexes   **b.** _____

c. Is responsible to others   **c.** _____

d. Can make independent judgments   **d.** _____

e. Associates with people of differing ages, religions, and occupations   **e.** _____

f. Gains satisfaction from work   **f.** _____

g. Is tolerant   **g.** _____

h. Shows justifiable anger   **h.** _____

i. Seeks meaning to life   **i.** _____

j. Can say, "I was wrong"   **j.** _____

k. Can endure injustice without seeking revenge   **k.** _____

l. Is dependable in obligations and promises   **l.** _____

4. Troy's father died when he was 12 years old, and Troy is the oldest of five children. His father owned a small business, which his mother has been managing. Troy is now a junior in high school, hasn't been an honor student, but hopes to receive a scholarship to a vocational-technical college in his state.

You may assume any additional information about his situation that you wish. Identify what you would consider two trials and two triumphs in his life during his adolescent years.

Trials

a.

b.

Triumphs

a.

b.

5. A transport truck from Florida filled with crates of citrus fruit overturned on its way to a northern destination. Crates of fruit were strewn on the roadside. Some crates were broken and the fruit spilled. Define Stage 1 and Stage 4 of moral development, according to Kohlberg, and give an example of how people coming on the scene might react at each of these stages.

a. Definition of Stage 1:

Reactions of people coming on the scene:

b. Definition of Stage 4:

Reactions of people coming on the scene:

....

6. Following are descriptions of behavior of three people. Determine whether you would consider their behavior mature, immature, or understandable. Understandable should be interpreted as not mature, but to be expected for the person's age and probable experience. Circle your choice and explain your decision.

   a. Carla, age six, pushes her friend off the playground swing because it is "my turn."

   mature   immature   understandable

   Reason for decision:

   b. Andrew, age 15, turns off the television program that his sister wanted to watch because he has to do homework. Her homework is finished.

   mature   immature   understandable

   Reason for decision:

   c. Bruce turns down two free tickets to a sports event because he promised to take his daughter skating.

   mature   immature   understandable

   Reason for decision:

7. Describe what you would consider a mature and an immature reaction to the situations described. There can be a number of both mature and immature ways of reacting to a situation, of course.

a. Brenda and Myles have been married for six months. After their marriage, Myles wanted to rent a furnished apartment until they could save some money for the kind of furniture they wanted. Brenda, however, was firm in her belief that they should get all their furniture immediately and make monthly payments, and they did. Now, after six months, Myles is working fewer hours, so their income is lower; their car needs repair; their insurance payments are due; and they can't see how they can make their furniture payments for the next few months.

BRENDA

Mature reaction:

Immature reaction:

MYLES

Mature reaction:

Immature reaction:

b. Hank's supervisor informs him that he will have to keep his work area clean and will have to return all tools to their proper place before he leaves every day.

HANK

Mature reaction:

Immature reaction:

c. Sully was assigned a person of a different (objectionable, in his opinion) race as a work partner. The person assigned as Sully's partner acted friendly and seemed eager that they work together as a team.

SULLY

Mature reaction:

Immature reaction:

....

8. Select one of the characteristics of social maturity from the chapter. Explain how you think you can become more socially mature in this respect. Give a specific example.

Characteristic of social maturity:

How I can become more mature in this respect:

Enrichment Activities

1. A 17-year-old boy feels that his parents consider him immature. He would like to become more mature, if they are correct. How might he do this? Role-play the situation with another person.

2. List all the characteristics of maturity mentioned in the chapter. Give an example of each. Are there any characteristics that you would add to the list?

3. Visit a grade school classroom with the teacher's permission. Observe examples of mental (cognitive, according to Piaget) and psychosocial development and any other type of maturity discussed in the chapter. You may want to check your conclusions with the teacher of the observed class. Report your experience to your class or instructor.

4. Find additional information about a stage of life-span development using two different Internet search engines. Determine how the information could be useful to you or another person who is experiencing this stage of development.

 **Goal Achievement**

Learning Activities

1. The chapter begins with a discussion of success. First, write your own definition of success (without the use of a dictionary). Then obtain a definition of success from another source. This can be another person's definition or one from a reference. Compare the definitions and explain how and why yours differs.

   a. My definition of success:

   b. Definition from another source:

   c. Source of second definition:

   d. How and why my definition differs:

Name _____ Date_____

2. Questions related to goal achievement are listed in the following. Indicate the importance of each of these concepts to you by circling the appropriate number on the right. Write a brief explanation of why you consider any one of them "very important." Use the following rating scale: 1 = very important; 2 = important; 3 = not important.

a. Money—what does it mean?   1 2 3

b. How important is work?   1 2 3

c. How important are relationships with others?   1 2 3

d. How important is freedom?   1 2 3

Why I consider _____ very important:

....

3. In the following description of Melanie and her career goal, identify four factors that you believe have contributed to her progress thus far.

It was Melanie's ambition to have her own furniture store. She frequently made remarks to her family and friends such as, "When I have my furniture store . . . ." While she was attending the local community college, she took numerous courses in both business and marketing, and she took an additional course in word processing in the evening. She also worked as a salesperson in a furniture store on weekends and two evenings a week. She had hoped to get an internship as an assistant buyer in the store, but the buyer could not supervise an intern at that time. She was disappointed, but after she contacted several other furniture stores, a manager told her to check back in about two months. When that time came, she went to see the manager again and was assigned an internship. She continued to work at this store after she graduated because she wanted more experience. She was also able to work more hours so that she could add to her savings.

Melanie plans to get a few more years of experience, take some additional evening classes, and then either open her own independent store or seek a franchise for a nationally known furniture line. She is more enthusiastic than ever about having her own store and is planning to use part of her next vacation to visit a furniture merchandise mart.

Factors that I believe haveqa contributed to Melanie's progress thus far toward achieving her career goal:

a.

b.

c.

d.

....

4. Three types of mistakes were identified in the chapter. Briefly define each type and give what you believe to be an example of each. Also describe a mistake you have made, identify the type you believe it to be, and explain what you did about it.

Type of Mistake   Definition   Example

a. Careless

b. Reasonable

c. Innocent

A mistake I made:

Type of mistake it was:

What I did about it:

....

5. Common causes of failure are listed below. Determine the two causes most likely to interfere with your achieving your goals. Suggest how each can be minimized or eliminated.

Trying to get something for nothing:

Poor money management:

Outdated ideas and useless habits:

Unfavorable personality characteristics:

Fear:

Not profiting from setbacks:

....

6. Describe three types of learning by which you can continue to add to your career competency after you complete your education and begin working full-time. Indicate where you can continue each type of learning.

Type of Learning   **Where Learning Can Be Continued**

a.

b.

c.

7. Identify three reasons for procrastination and suggest how each of these reasons can be counteracted with constructive behavior:

   a. Reason for procrastination:

   Constructive behavior to counteract it:

   b. Reason for procrastination:

   Constructive behavior to counteract it:

   c. Reason for procrastination:

   Constructive behavior to counteract it:

8. Studies of leaders reveal common characteristics, as listed below. Describe a person whom you consider to be an effective leader and identify the leadership characteristics you believe he or she has. If the person has additional leadership characteristics, mention them. Indicate what you consider this person's leadership style to be by circling one of the descriptive terms.

   Common leadership characteristics:

   Personal effectiveness

   Organization

   Ability to communicate

   Energy and enthusiasm

   Courage and integrity

Fairness

Appreciation

Interest in company goals

Additional characteristics:

I believe this person's leadership style to be:

Authoritarian   Democratic   Laissez-faire

Enrichment Activities

1. Collect at least six different quotations relating to goal achievement. You may obtain these from posters, books of quotations, persons, or any other source. Indicate which quotation you like the best and explain why.

2. Talk to two different people who, in your opinion, have been successful in achieving goals. Ask them to explain how they determined what they wanted and why they have been successful. Note any similarities between the two. Be able to give an explanation of any differences.

3. Read an article or biography of a person you consider successful or research information about the person on the Internet. Identify characteristics you believe helped that person achieve his or her goal. Also note experiences that the person considered disappointments or setbacks. How did the person overcome or learn from the setbacks?